The 2000s in America

The 2000s in America

Volume 3

Radiohead—Zuckerberg, Mark

Editor
Craig Belanger
University of Advancing Technology

SALEM PRESS
A Division of EBSCO Publishing
Ipswich, Massachusetts

GREY HOUSE PUBLISHING

Cover photos (clockwise from top left) : World Trade Center, New York City on September 11, 2001 (Getty Images); Barack Obama (left) and George W. Bush (©Gerald Herbert/AP/Corbis); Apple iPhone (©Adriana Williams/Corbis); Michael Phelps with his gold medal for the 400 meter individual medley at the Athens 2004 Summer Olympic Games (Getty Images).

Title page photo: The World Trade Center memorial Tribute in Light, viewed from New York City's Union Square. (Courtesy Christopher Schoenbohm)

The 2000s in America, 2013, published by Grey House Publishing, Inc., Amenia, NY, under exclusive license from EBSCO Publishing, Inc.

∞ The paper used in these volumes conforms to the American National Standard for Permanence of Paper for Printed Library Materials, Z39.48 1992 (R1997).

Library of Congress Cataloging-in-Publication Data

The 2000s in America / editor, Craig Belanger, University of Advanced Technology.
    volumes cm
 Includes bibliographical references and index.
  ISBN 978-1-4298-3883-2 (set) -- ISBN 978-1-4298-3884-9 (volume 1) -- ISBN 978-1-4298-3885-6 (volume 2) --
ISBN 978-1-4298-3899-3 (volume 3) 1. United States--Civilization--1970---Encyclopedias. 2. United States--Civilization--21st century--Encyclopedias. 3. United States--History--1969---Encyclopedias. 4. Two thousands (Decade)--Encyclopedias.
I. Belanger, Craig. II. Title: Two thousands in America.
 E169.12.A178 2013
 973.93--dc23
                                                 2012045422

■ Contents

■ Complete List of Contents

Volume 1

Volume 2

Volume 3

The 2000s
in America

R

■ Radiohead

Definition: British rock band founded in Abingdon, United Kingdom, in 1985

In the wake of two commercially successful, critically acclaimed albums in the 1990s, Radiohead would veer from their guitar rock roots and enter into an exploratory musical realm fusing their elaborate rock melodies with genres ranging from electronica to jazz and drum and bass.

Few musical performing artists entered the 2000s surrounded with as much expectation from fans and critics alike as Great Britain's Radiohead. Lead by the operatic vocal styling of their enigmatic front man Thom Yorke, the group's guitar-laden, orchestral songwriting had made them one of the most critically acclaimed rock acts of the 1990s with their 1995 record *The Bends.* By the year 2000, the band's 1997 release *OK Computer* was already being heralded as one of the most inventive and conceptually engaging rock albums of all time.

The band's follow-up album *Kid A* was released on October 2, 2000. The compilation represented an eccentric departure from the alternative rock sound of Radiohead's earlier catalogue. *Kid A* was composed primarily with effects-modified, keyboard-oriented melodies paired largely electronic percussion. While critics and fans alike debated the merits of the band's departure from its rock roots, the discussion was held amidst widespread acclaim.

Radiohead would continue their experimentation into the realm of electronica with their 2001 album *Amnesiac,* which would be nominated for a Grammy for best alternative album. The band's 2003 release *Hail to the Thief* was recorded in a scant two weeks in Hollywood, California. The record was composed of several songs left over from the group's *Kid A* and *Amnesiac* periods. *Hail to the Thief* was the fifth straight Radiohead record to be Grammy-nominated for the year's best alternative

Thom Yorke and Jonny Greenwood of Radiohead. (Courtesy Dave Bignell)

album. It represented continued experimentation with unusual harmonies and percussion.

Radiohead's final release of the decade, 2007's *In Rainbows,* would defy previously held conceptions of the music industry's sales model while acting as an even more extreme sonic departure from the band's rock music legacy. The band initially self-released the record as a digital download in October of 2007, instructing buyers to set their own purchase price. The event forced both music consumers and executives to reconsider the long established label–artist relationship in the emerging marketplace of digital downloads, one that lacked the physical production and distribution costs of conventional physical copies. *In Rainbows* would win two Grammy Awards, including best alternative music album.

Impact

As demonstrated by their catalogue of work in the 2000s, few contemporary recording artists have as ferociously defended and summarily salvaged their artistic integrity like Radiohead. With commercial success already achieved, Radiohead utilized the 2000s to push the boundaries of their creative expression with little regard to the expectation or concerns of both their fiercely loyal fan base and record label executives. Radiohead's career arc is demonstrative of a new recording industry that emerged throughout the decade, one where artistic financial and creative independence outgrew the influence of major media companies who had monopolized the business for decades.

Further Reading

Randall, Mac. *Exit Music: The Radiohead Story.* London: Omnibus, 2003. Print.

Tate, Joseph, ed. *The Music and Art of Radiohead.* London: Ashgate, 2005. Print.

John Pritchard

■ Ray, Rachael

Identification: American celebrity chef and television personality

Born: August 25, 1968; Glens Falls, New York

Although Rachael Ray never attended culinary school or took any cooking classes, her televised cooking show was an immediate hit on the Food Network. Thanks to the show's success, Ray has written numerous best-selling cookbooks and launched many other successful charity and for-profit ventures.

Rachael Ray started her culinary career by giving cooking lessons in a gourmet grocery story in Albany, New York. After a local television station began airing the lessons, Ray landed a segment on the *Today* show in 2001, which caught the attention of executives at the Food Network. That same year, she became the host of the network's newest show, *30 Minute Meals.* It was an instant hit, and Ray's popularity among viewers led to her hosting several other programs for the network, including *$40 a Day, Inside Dish, Rachael's Vacations,* and *Tasty Travels.* She also began writing companion cookbooks based on the *30 Minute Meals* theme.

In 2005, Ray released the food and lifestyle magazine, *Every Day with Rachael Ray.* She served as its editor in chief and contributed recipes, information about food and cooking, and entertaining tips. The magazine also included celebrity interviews and articles about places to dine across the country. That same year, Ray married John Cusimano, a lawyer and musician. In 2007, she started the nonprofit organization Yum-o! to provide information about healthy eating to children and adults and to help feed hungry families and fund opportunities for cooking education. Ray also added talk-show host to her ever-expanding résumé with the launch of her nationally syndicated show, *Rachael Ray.* The show attracted a loyal fan base and became one of the top-rated talk shows on television.

Ray earned several awards and recognitions for her work. Her original Food Network show, *30 Minute Meals,* earned her a Daytime Emmy in 2006, and she was named one of the Best Leaders of 2006 by *Businessweek. Television Week* also named her the Syndication Personality of the Year in 2007. She won two additional Daytime Emmys for the *Rachael Ray* show in 2008 and 2009. In 2008, Ray developed a line of dog food products called Nutrish, with all proceeds from the sales donated to Rachael's Rescue, Ray's charity for at-risk animals.

Impact

Rachel Ray's can-do approach to cooking and her charismatic personality have won her a legion of devoted fans and have influenced millions in the way they prepare meals. By the end of the decade, her multimedia empire—which included food-related television shows, a talk show, and books and a magazine targeted at busy families—made her the highest-earning cook on television.

Further Reading

Abrams, Dennis. *Rachael Ray: Food Entrepreneur.* New York: Chelsea, 2009. Print.

Johnston, Lori. "Rachael Ray: The Non-Chef Celebrity Chef." *WebMD.* WebMD LLC. 2012. Web. 9 July 2012.

Nowell, Lauren. "Rachael's Bio." *Rachael Ray Show.* KWP Studios, Inc. 3012. Web. 9 July 2012.

Angela Harmon

■ Reality television

Definition: Reality television presents allegedly unscripted situations featuring nonactors to create a genre of television programming that can be humorous, serious, and competitive.

Although reality television programming started in 1948 with the prank show Candid Camera, *the genre did not become wildly popular in the United States until the 2000s. Groundbreaking competition shows such as* Survivor *and* American Idol *eclipsed scripted shows in the ratings and helped usher in dozens of other reality shows in a variety of formats. The concept of a reality show is that it is not scripted, but many critics find this to be misleading, as most reality shows are staged.*

Success of Reality Competition Shows

Reality television shows were popular in the United States before the 2000s. Shows such as *COPS* and *The Real World* were successful, but not until the competition format was introduced did reality programming start to see large increases in ratings and begin to beat scripted shows in prime-time slots. In Europe, reality competitions had been popular for some time when producers decided to adapt them for an American audience. Two of the first reality competition shows, *Survivor* and *Big Brother*, both debuted in the United States in 2000 and became instant successes.

Survivor, based on the Swedish show *Expedition Robinson*, premiered in May 2000. *Big Brother*, based on the show of the same name from the Netherlands, premiered in July 2000. Both shows feature nonactors competing for a cash prize. In *Survivor*, contestants compete in challenges in a variety of exotic locations, and in *Big Brother*, contestants are isolated in a house under constant surveillance. People are voted off (or in the case of *Big Brother*, "evicted") the show each week until only one person remains.

American Idol, the most successful reality competition show in US history premiered in June 2002. It was a spin-off of the British show *Pop Idol*, created by artist manager Simon Fuller. The show is a singing competition in which the viewers get to vote for the contestant they want to win. The winner receives a one million dollar recording contract. The show features a panel of three judges (four for the 2013 season) who offer criticism to the contestants. The original three judges were Simon Cowell, singer Paula Abdul, and musician Randy Jackson. The show has helped launch the careers of several successful artists, including the season-one winner Kelly Clarkson.

Beginning in 2004, *American Idol* became one of the most watched shows on American television, with ratings frequently topping 30 million. Despite its popularity, the show has received much negative criticism. Many critics state that the show purposely humiliates some people. Professional musicians have also negatively criticized the show. *American Idol* influenced several television producers to create their own singing competitions including *The Voice* and *Rock Star*, although none of them has been able to match the success of *American Idol*.

Dating reality competitions have also seen great success. These shows commonly feature a male or female suitor and several contestants competing for him or her. Contestants are eliminated each episode until only one person remains. Popular shows in this category include *The Bachelor*, *The Bachelorette*, and *Temptation Island*.

Another type of reality competition is one in which contestants are competing for a job. These shows commonly feature judges who eliminate contestants based on how well they perform a task related to the job for which they are competing. One of the first job-related reality competitions was *America's Next Top Model*, which premiered in May 2003. Hosted by model Tyra Banks, the show features women competing for a modeling contract.

Celebrity Reality Shows

Documentary-style reality shows about celebrities also became popular in the 2000s. One of the first such shows was *The Osbournes*, which premiered on MTV in March 2002 and lasted four seasons. The show followed around heavy metal music pioneer Ozzy Osbourne and his family, giving the audience a look at their humorous domestic life. The show became known for its heavy use of profanity (that was censored on US television) and for documenting wife Sharon's battle with cancer. The show was a big success and at the time had the highest ratings in MTV history.

In December 2003, the FOX network premiered *The Simple Life*, starring wealthy socialites Paris Hilton and Nicole Richie. The comedic show depicted the two girls as they attempted to work blue-collar jobs on a farm and in a fast-food restaurant. The show lasted five seasons and spawned several international remakes. It also helped Hilton and Richie gain international recognition.

After *The Simple Life* ended in 2007, another reality show depicting socialites premiered in December of that year. *Keeping Up with the Kardashians* follows the wealthy Kardashian/Jenner family, focusing on daughters Kim, Khloé, and Kourtney. The show made Kim Kardashian an international star, and she became one of the highest-paid reality-television stars in the United States.

Occupation Reality Shows

Another popular type of reality show is one in which a professional is filmed doing his or her job. These shows typically depict someone who has a unique or dangerous job. Popular shows in this category include *American Chopper*, *Dog the Bounty Hunter*, and *Miami Ink*. The longest-running reality show in this category is *COPS*, which first premiered in 1989.

Television channels aimed at educating audiences even started to produce original occupation reality shows. For example, the History Channel has produced two successful occupation reality shows: *Ice Road Truckers*, which premiered in July 2007, and *Pawn Stars*, which premiered in July 2009.

Makeover Shows

Several reality shows center on making over a person's style or physical health. These shows are oftentimes meant to be inspirational and educational, specifically educating viewers about physical fitness, diet, and style. One of the first shows to reach success with this format was *Queer Eye*, in which a group of homosexual men gave a heterosexual man a style and diet makeover. The show was a huge success for the Bravo network and led to merchandise like soundtracks and books. The gay community embraced the show, and the five hosts became cultural icons. The show did receive negative criticism however, from people who argued the show made generalizations about gay men being more stylish and knowledgeable than heterosexual men about culture, food, and design.

Queer Eye (whose original title was *Queer Eye for the Straight Guy*) spawned several spin-off reality shows, including *Queer Eye for the Straight Girl* and international versions such as Australia's *Aussie Queer Eye for the Straight Guy*.

The Biggest Loser is a popular reality makeover show that was a crossover with the competition subgenre. The show premiered in July 2004 and has since spawned more than twenty international adaptations. In the show, overweight contestants compete to see who can lose the highest percentage of weight for a cash prize. Contestants are split up into teams of two and compete in several physically exerting tasks.

The show has met with harsh criticism by many health professionals, who state that diet and fitness regimens the contestants partake in on the show are dangerous. Former contestants have come forth explaining how they would starve and dehydrate themselves in order to lose weight during the competition.

Weight-loss reality shows also crossed over with celebrity reality shows, as in *Celebrity Fit Club*. Based on the British show of the same name, *Celebrity Fit Club* premiered in January 2005 and ran for five seasons. The show featured eight overweight celebrities who were split into teams of four. The team who lost the most weight won.

Jersey Shore

Rounding out the decade was one of the most popular reality television shows of all time. *Jersey Shore* premiered in December 2009 and quickly set ratings records for MTV. The show featured eight housemates of Italian American backgrounds and documented their summers at Seaside Heights, New Jersey. The success of the show made the cast members into instant celebrities and earned them millions of dollars in endorsement money. Well-known cast members of the show include Nicole "Snookie" Polizzi and Michael "The Situation" Sorrentino.

The show came under heavy criticism for its use of the slang words "Guido" and "Guidette," which are seen by many as an ethnic slur toward Italian Americans. The Italian American service league UNICO International requested that MTV cancel the show before it even aired. New Jersey governor Chris Christie also criticized the show, stating that it portrayed the state in a negative light.

Criticism

Since their rise in popularity, reality television shows have come under scrutiny and been criticized for many reasons. Possibly the biggest criticism is that reality shows do not represent reality or, at least, that they present a reality altered for heightened drama.

Critics explain how many of these shows use living situations that the average person will never experience. *The Real World,* for example, presents seven people living rent-free in a large house completely fabricated by the show's producers. Former cast member Irene McGee came forward after she left the show to explain how the producers control everything down to what the cast is allowed to drink. Producers design all of the scenarios and tasks on reality competition shows, which creates unrealistic environments.

One of the cultural criticisms is that reality television gains viewers by humiliating people and that this reflects meanness in our society and the desire to see others fail. The cruelty occasionally displayed by *American Idol* judges is mentioned frequently when it comes to this kind of criticism. Some argue, though, that the contestants know exactly what they are getting into and therefore know they may not be portrayed in a positive light.

Many critics worry about the effect reality television has on teenagers. Several reality programs depict young people drinking, using foul language, and having casual sexual relations. Since these shows are incredibly popular with teenagers, critics believe they can influence teens in how they think they should act and look. They explain that anyone on television is perceived as a celebrity; therefore they are idolized by teenagers.

Impact

For better or worse, there is no denying the impact reality television had on popular culture in the 2000s. It completely changed the way producers approached new content, and since reality shows are cheaper to produce, an incredible amount of them were created. Many were canceled during their first season. Television networks such as TLC and A&E that had previously been known for their educational content were forced to produce reality programs to keep up with ratings. Several reality shows made national celebrities out of their cast members, especially for the winners of *American Idol.* At the end of the decade, reality television continued to dominate ratings.

Further Reading

David, Anna, ed. *Reality Matters: Nineteen Writers Come Clean about the Shows We Can't Stop Watching.* New York: It Books, 2010. Print. Presents several essays analyzing the appeal of reality shows and the impact they have on society.

DeVolld, Troy. *Reality TV: An Insider's Guide to TV's Hottest Market.* Studio City: Weise, 2011. Print. Written by a seasoned reality television producer. Looks at how to develop your own reality show.

Escoffery, David S., ed. *How Real Is Reality TV? Essays on Representation and Truth.* Jefferson, NC: McFarland, 2008. Print. Presents essays from different scholars on the idea of representation in reality shows.

Murray, Susan, and Laurie Oullette, eds. *Reality TV: Remaking Television Culture.* New York: New York UP, 2008. Print. Presents eight critical essays examining the different cultural, economic, and visual aspects of reality shows.

Pozner, Jennifer L. *Reality Bites Back: The Troubling Truth about Guilty Pleasure TV.* Berkeley: Seal, 2010. Print. Looks at the portrayal of women on reality shows and how such effects young viewers.

Patrick G. Cooper

■ Religion and spirituality in the United States

Definition: Religion is a set of philosophical and cultural principles concerned with an individual's belief in, and worship of, a higher power, often consisting of one or more gods. Religion also refers to an individual's allegiance to, or membership in, a social group united by shared spiritual beliefs. The term spirituality refers to beliefs regarding the existence of nonphysical forces, entities, or realities, within or beyond the observable universe.

In many cases, religious background influences an individual's political views, and religious organizations can exert influence over the political culture of a geographic region or nation state. For example, religious institutions play a role in the ongoing public debate over the legality and morality of abortion in the United States. Throughout history, the evolution of law in the United States, and in other countries around the world, has been informed by religious morals and ethics. In addition, religion and spirituality are major global industries, accounting for billions in annual public and private spending and donations.

Changing Demographics

According to data from polling and population research organizations, like the US Census Bureau, the Pew Center, and the Gallup Organization, religious demographics in the United States are changing. The United States has been a majority Christian nation since the founding of the country, and remains primarily Christian in terms of organized religious affiliation. Protestants have traditionally represented the largest denomination of American Christians. However, population estimates indicate that an increasing number of Americans are changing their religious affiliations. In 2010, the Pew Center estimated that more than 44 percent of American adults change religions or religious denominations at some point in their lives.

Shifts in religious affiliation relate to an overall increase in the number of religious options available to Americans. Increases in the number of Evangelical Christians, for example, have reduced the number of adherents in other sects of Christianity, including Catholicism and mainline Protestantism. In addition, the United States has seen an increase in the number of Americans practicing "private spirituality," and an increase in the number that identifies as belonging to a religious group, but do not actively participate in religious activities, or raise their children to follow a particular religious tradition.

Christians

In 2012, the Pew Forum for Religious and Public Life estimated that more than 78 percent of the US adult population identify themselves as Christian. The US Census Bureau's estimates indicate that the nation's adult population increased by 21 million from 2001 to 2009, 66 percent of which identified themselves as Christian, indicating a steady decrease in the number of Christian adherents.

The Pew Forum on Religious and Public Life estimated among Christian faiths, Catholicism saw the largest decrease in membership from the 1990 to 2010. Nearly 31 percent of Americans polled were raised in the Catholic faith, and approximately 46 percent of foreign-born Americans identified as Catholic. However, the number of Americans self-identifying as Catholic fell to 24 percent of the population by 2010. These statistics show an increasing trend in individuals leaving Catholicism for other religions, or becoming nonaffiliated.

More than 51 percent of the US population identified themselves as Protestant, making Protestantism the most populous religion in the country. Nonetheless, the number of Protestants fell significantly during the 2000s, from approximately 54 percent of the adult population in 2000 to 51 percent in 2010. This decrease in Protestant affiliation was a continuation of a trend reflected in population studies since the 1950s, at which time Protestants accounted for more than 68 percent of the population.

An increasing number of Christians joined the Evangelical or Born Again denomination of Christianity. The Evangelical population of the United States represented approximately 22 percent of the population as a whole, and a significant number of individuals in the faith migrated to Evangelism from other religions. The percentage of American adults identifying as Evangelical increased by approximately 2 percent between 1990 and 2000. According to the US Census Bureau, this increase continued in the 2000s, with a more than 3 percent increase between 2001 and 2008.

Muslims

During the 2000s, Islam grew in the United States, and around the world. The Pew Center estimated that there were approximately 2.6 million Muslims living in the United States in 2010. In a detailed study of Islam in America conducted in 2007, researchers found that 35 percent of American Muslims were foreign born, and 21 percent had converted to Islam from another religion. Immigration accounted for more than 65 percent of the American Islamic population as a whole. Bangladesh and Pakistan were the leading countries for Islamic immigration to the United States in 2010, a trend that was expected to continue in coming decades.

In the decade following the terrorist attacks of September 11, 2001, Muslims in America faced an increase in prejudice and discrimination throughout the United States. A 2007 Pew Center study found that more than 25 percent of Muslims reported discrimination of one form or another, while more than 50 percent reported that it was difficult to be Muslim in the country after the September 11 attacks.

Pew research also indicates that the Islamic population is growing at a faster rate than most other religious groups in the United States. By the year 2030, there are expected to be more than 6.2 million

Muslims in the United States, at which time the Muslim population will be similar in number to the US Jewish population. High growth rates among Muslim Americans are due to higher than average fertility and birth rates.

Jews

According to US Census Bureau statistics, Jewish Americans constituted 1.7 percent of the US population in 2010. However, some organizations have indicated that Census Bureau data on the Jewish population might be flawed, due to insufficient sampling efforts. The North American Jewish Data Bank released a study in 2010 indicating that there were 6.5 million American Jews, constituting more than 2.1 percent of the population.

A number of separate population estimates showed that the American Jewish population was in a state of decline compared to number of Christians and Muslims in America. The National Jewish Population Survey of 2003 indicated that the Jewish population of the United States had been in decline since 1990, due in part to reduced immigration, lower than average birth rates, and a declining level of conversion. Studies also indicated that a declining number of Jewish Americans were raising their children to follow the Jewish faith, leading to increased numbers of Jewish persons leaving the faith in each successive generation.

Unaffiliated Americans

One of the most significant religious trends of the period between 1990 and 2010 was the increase in the number of Americans who claimed no religious affiliation. Between 1990 and 2001, the number of adults with no affiliation increased from 8 percent to more than 14 percent. In 2012, the Pew Center estimated that 16.1 percent of the US adult population was not affiliated with any religion, including those who identified themselves as atheists and agnostics. The Pew Center also estimated that more than 25 percent of American adults between 18 and 29 were not affiliated to any religion, indicating that the trend is likely to increase markedly in the future.

Among the religiously unaffiliated population in the United States, approximately 25 percent described themselves as nonreligious, atheist, or agnostic. Approximately 6.3 percent of the unaffiliated population said that religion was not important

in their lives, and 5.8 percent described themselves as "religious," but not affiliated with any particular religious school or group. The Gallup Organization found that American affiliation with organized religion has been decreasing since 1958, when it was estimated that only 5 percent of American adults were not members of an organized religion.

The Gallup Organization also found that an increasing number of Americans no longer believed that religion had relevance in the modern world. For instance, the percentage of Americans who believe that religion can "solve major problems," decreased from 80 percent in 1958 to 58 percent in 2010. In 2010, more than 28 percent of the population reported that religion is "old fashioned" and "out of date," whereas only 7 percent of the population held similar beliefs in 1958.

Spirituality in America

Approximately 92 percent of Americans reported that they believe in a god or gods of some kind. The majority (60 percent) claimed belief in a "personal, knowable god," while 25 percent of Americans believed that god is best represented as an "impersonal force." In 2010, polls measured the highest number of Americans in history reporting this shift in belief, towards a belief in god as a nonpersonal entity or force.

The designation "spiritual but not religious" (SBNR) is sometimes used to describe the percentage of the population that holds spiritual views, but does not describe themselves as religious. During the 2000s, many Americans ascribed to non-organized "new age" spiritual systems, and a variety of other spiritualities not classified as organized religion. In 2010, estimates of the SBNR population varied widely between sources, and not all surveys provided SBNR as a choice when judging religious participation. Estimates indicated that SBNR Americans constituted between 5 and 12 percent of the population as a whole.

Even among Americans affiliated with the major religions, there was a net shift toward a more open interpretation of religious dogma. According to Pew Center research, more than 58 percent of Americans relied on "common sense" to define their sense of right and wrong, rather than a religious authority. More than 70 percent of Americans also reported feeling that more than one religion or ideology could lead to eternal life.

Impact

During the decade, religious affiliation played a role in debates surrounding political and social issues. More than 30 percent of social conservatives in the United States described themselves as religious, whereas only 20 percent of social liberals described themselves similarly. On social/political issues like same-sex marriage and abortion rights, religious distinctions played a major role in determining American attitudes.

Increases in the number of SBNR, atheist, and generally unaffiliated Americans may play an increasing role in determining American attitudes about key social issues in coming years. Pew Center data indicated that more than 70 percent of the unaffiliated population supported same-sex marriage in 2011, as compared to 34 percent of the Protestant and 52 percent of the Catholic populations.

Even as religious membership declined slightly in the United States, spirituality as an industry grew, largely through the development of the spiritual/self-help market. According to a 2009 report in *Forbes*, Americans spent more than $11 billion annually on self-help programs. While most of this spending was for body-improvement programs, a significant number of self-help books and other material focused on spiritual development.

According to statistics compiled by the World Bank, Americans spent more than $200 billion each year on religious and social welfare activities, which remains one of the largest facets of the overall American annual budget. University of Tampa sociology professor Ryan Cragun theorizes that spending on religion may have been far greater than known estimates, because the United States allows religious organizations to secure "tax exempt status." According to Cragun's estimates, tax-exemption for religious organizations accounted for a net spending of more than $71 billion annually.

Further Reading

Ecklund, Elaine Howard. *Science Vs. Religion: What Scientists Really Think*, New York: Oxford UP, 2010. Print. Introduction to the conflicts and confluence between science and religion both historically and in the twenty-first century written for the general audience. Includes discussions about the relationship between education, scientific literacy and religious affiliation.

Kosmin, Barry A. and Ariela Keysar. *Religion in a Free Market*, Ithaca: Paramount. Print. Detailed introduction to religious trends in the United States, as measured in 2005. Contains discussions about the significance of religious affiliation trends in the United States.

Newport, Frank, "In U.S., Increasing Number Have No Religious Identity," *Gallup Politics*. Gallup Inc., 2010. Web. 23 July 2012. Results of statistic analysis indicating percentage of Americans with regard to religious identity and affiliation with major religions.

"Population: Religion." *The 2012 Statistical Abstract: PDF Version*. Washington, DC: US Census Bureau, 2012.PDF file. Statistics regarding religious affiliation and related attitudes about religion and spirituality among the US adult population. Contains information about shifts in religious affiliation between 2001 and 2008.

"U.S. Religious Landscape Survey." *Pew Forum on Religion & Public Life*. Pew Forum on Religion and Public Life, 2010. Web. July 23, 2012. Detailed series of reports focusing on religious affiliation, attitudes and trends in the US adult population. Contains statistics regarding changes in religious affiliation in the twenty-first century.

Saad, Lydia, "U.S. Confidence in Religion at a Low Point." *Gallup Politics*. Gallup Inc., 2012. Web. 23 July 2012. Discussion of statistics regarding American faith in religion and belief that religion is helpful to modern culture.

Micah Issitt

■ Retirement income system

Definition: The various government-sponsored, employer-sponsored, and private retirement savings programs that have enabled US workers to retire from full-time employment in their senior years, typically starting around age sixty-five

The retirement income system of the United States faced great challenges in the 2000s, due in large part to two economic recessions. The first recession, which occurred in 2001, was relatively mild, but the latter one, which began in late 2007, caused great harm to the incomes of millions of Americans, who had considerable sums invested in the stock market through defined-contribution retirement plans. As millions lost their jobs during the latter recession, which has come to be known as the Great Recession, the Social Security retirement system, funded primarily by dedicated payroll taxes, also saw its revenues fall.

Between 2000 and 2009, the retirement income system in the United States found itself entering a moment of crisis. Social Security, which typically constitutes the largest portion of an individual's retirement income, was reaching a point of insolvency. Pensions, also known as defined-benefit retirement plans, were fast disappearing from employers' benefits packages. Defined-contribution plans like 401(k)s, which are tied to the stock market, were demonstrating in the economic downturns that they could not always provide true financial security for many US workers. By 2009, the two economic recessions of the decade—coupled with the impending retirement of the baby boom generation (typically defined as Americans born between the years 1946 and 1964)—suggested to many observers that the retirement income system was overburdened, inefficient, and unable to provide the kind of retirement security most Americans had come to expect throughout most of the twentieth century.

Social Security

Social Security was established to grant pension benefits to elderly and unemployed Americans who had suffered greatly during the Great Depression of the 1930s. The Social Security Act of 1935 was extended many times in subsequent decades to include benefits for the disabled and to provide health care to senior citizens under the Medicare provisions signed into law in 1965. Both Medicare and Social Security are supported by dedicated payroll taxes paid by both employers and employees. These tax revenues are then placed into one of several Social Security trust funds, which are used to pay beneficiaries of the program. Whatever money is left over after paying out benefits is then invested in US Treasury securities, the debt-financing tools of the US federal government. Social Security recipients receive a monthly stipend that has been calculated for each individual based on salary and length of participation in the program (via payroll taxes).

In the decades since Social Security's establishment, the benefits paid out to recipients have needed to be periodically adjusted upward against inflation. Social Security's tax revenues have also periodically had to be increased in order to pay promised benefits to all the workers eligible for the program. (In 2012, 94 percent of all US workers were eligible for the program, and nine out of ten senior citizens received income from Social Security.) Prior to the economic crisis of the 2000s, the last time the program

faced serious budget shortfalls was in 1983, when President Ronald Reagan and Democratic leaders in Congress made changes to the program that shored up its finances for roughly another half century. In the 2000s, however, Republican and Democratic leaders could not find a consensus on how to fix Social Security, despite the fact that the program's problems were apparent. In 2001, during the first recession of the decade, the Social Security Board of Trustees announced that the trust fund would face funding shortfalls by 2038. Social Security's prospects did not improve during the decade's weak economic recovery: in 2005, the board announced that Social Security contributions would peak by 2008 and decline thereafter before beginning to pay out more in benefits than it received in payroll taxes by 2018.

The Great Recession, which began in late 2007, was even more damaging to Social Security's finances. Unemployment was far more widespread, and underemployment—defined as the part of the population working part time but would rather work full time—became an acute problem for the US economy. With fewer people working or working full time, less money was going into Social Security, making the problems facing the program that much worse. In 2012, President Barack Obama's administration reported that Social Security's trust fund would run out by 2033, three years sooner than reported just a year earlier; Medicare's hospital fund was estimated to run out in 2024; and Social Security's disability insurance was estimated to run out in 2016. Without the trust funds, tax revenues—coming through the Social Security payroll tax—could only pay for just 75 percent of promised benefits.

Pensions

A longtime part of a US worker's employee benefits package has been the defined-benefit retirement plan, better known as a pension. Like Social Security, it provides a monthly payment for life to retirees but is administered and distributed by an individual's employer, not the US government. Unlike Social Security, most pension checks are not adjusted to rise with inflation. Employer-sponsored pensions go back to 1875, when the American Express Company began administering one for its retirees. In the early part of the twentieth century, many US employers, encouraged by the tax incentives such retirement plans brought them, began offering pensions to their workers. By 1960, nearly 30 percent of the working population—about twenty-three million people—had some kind of private pension through their employers. In 1983, 62 percent of US workers had a pension plan through their companies.

In the early 1980s, employers began moving away from providing pensions, due in part to the fact that many had not been fully funded in the first place, but also because the US government had made it more desirable from a tax perspective for companies to offer employees a defined-contribution plan like a 401(k) instead. In the 2000s, fewer companies offered traditional pensions, and those that did were trying to phase them out. Five notable major US companies (General Motors, American Airlines, AT&T, Verizon, and General Electric) reduced or eliminated their traditional pensions altogether.

In 2006, the Pension Protection Act was passed. The law closed loopholes in earlier laws that had allowed corporations to underfund their pension programs; it also permitted employers to enroll their workers automatically in defined-contribution plans, while at the same time granting those workers even more control over their retirement investments.

IRAs, 401(k)s, and 403(b)s

As of 2007, 63 percent of employees in the United States had some kind of defined-contribution plan, such as a 401(k) or, in the case of nonprofits, a 403(b). These programs, named for their sections in the tax code, are similar to individual retirement accounts (IRAs), which allow workers to place a portion of their pre-tax income into retirement accounts made up of stocks, bonds, and other such investments. Many US companies, though not all—and fewer during the 2000s—offer their employees matching contributions, up to a certain percentage, to make the plans more appealing. Unlike traditional pensions, a worker may receive a lump sum of money, instead of a monthly stipend, upon retirement. The distribution amount depends entirely on how wisely individuals have invested and/or if they have retired at a point in the economic cycle when their investments are doing well.

In the 2000s, the weaknesses of defined-contribution plans became apparent to many Americans who had retired or were on the cusp of retirement. Few US workers were as skilled as professional retirement planners (who manage pensions, for example) in choosing the right investments. Following the collapse of the stock market in 2008, IRAs that invested heavily in stocks saw their values decrease considerably. This decrease in value affected a large swath of the US population: roughly 60 percent of households were headed by someone who was nearing retirement age and had money in some kind of defined-contribution plan. Moreover, personal savings was at an all-time low because of declining home prices, stagnant salaries, rising costs of health care and education, and widespread unemployment. Less than a quarter of households headed by individuals aged sixty to sixty-two had what they needed in defined-contribution accounts in order to maintain their current standard of living in retirement.

Impact

Many economists believe that the economy recessions the nation faced in the 2000s emphasized the enormous problems of the retirement income system in the United States—problems that, left unattended, would only grow worse in the coming decade as millions of baby boomers began to retire. Even if Social Security's finances were repaired in relatively short order, the program typically provides for only 40 percent of a retiree's pre-retirement income. The rest has tended to come from an individual's own money, whether through a pension, a defined-contribution plan like a 401(k), or personal savings built up over a lifetime. Retirement plan managers generally agree that individuals need about 85 percent of their pre-retirement income in retirement. Unfortunately, only half of US households can expect to receive money from a pension upon retirement, and 401(k)-type plans have not provided the security of an expected monthly stipend when a stock market downturn, like the ones endured in the 2000s, devalue retirement accounts.

Just as great a threat facing the retirement income system, observers say, is the US debt crisis, in which the federal government has been borrowing enormous sums of money from other nations in order to finance its current and future obligations. Left unchecked, the US government would not be able to borrow money at the same low interest rates it previously enjoyed. If this were to occur, the government would not only be unable to pay retirement and health care benefits for Social Security and Medicare, but it would also be less likely to pay future retirees the promised benefits they expect to receive by paying their payroll taxes for these programs.

Further Reading

Costa, Dora L. *The Evolution of Retirement: An American Economic History, 1880–1990.* Chicago: U of Chicago P, 1998. Print. Provides a complete overview of how the US retirement system developed into its modern form.

Jason, Julie. *The AARP Retirement Survival Guide: How to Make Smart Financial Decisions in Good Times and Bad.* New York: Sterling, 2009. Print. Written by a personal money manager. Provides insight into the ways individuals can create their own "personal pensions" and get the most out of the retirement income system in the United States.

Landis, Andy. *Social Security: The Inside Story: An Expert Explains Your Rights and Benefits.* Menlo Park: Crisp Learning, 2011. Print. Written by a former representative of the Social Security Administration. Uses clear language to describe to readers how to maximize the benefits they are entitled to as workers who have paid into the Social Security system.

Schieber, Sylvester J. *The Predictable Surprise: The Unraveling of the US Retirement System.* New York: Oxford UP, 2012. Print. Presents a detailed overview of the problems facing the US retirement system, a history of how the nation reached this point, and a blueprint for a way to provide a more secure retirement for every American.

Weisman, Steve. *The Truth about Protecting Your IRAs and 401(k)s.* Upper Saddle River: FT, 2009. Print. Details the best ways for investors to maximize earnings from their defined-contribution plans, while protecting their savings from unnecessary tax burdens.

Christopher Mari

■ Rhode Island nightclub fire

The Event: A fire resulting from a pyrotechnic display that left one hundred nightclub patrons dead and almost two hundred others injured
Date: February 20, 2003
Place: West Warwick, Rhode Island

On the night of February 20, 2003, a fire broke out at a Rhode Island nightclub during a performance by the band Great White. A small pyrotechnic display caused the walls of the club to catch fire. The incident resulted in many deaths and injuries.

The Station nightclub in West Warwick, Rhode Island, was the scene of one of the deadliest nightclub fires in history. One hundred people were killed and almost two hundred more were injured. The fire was triggered by a pyrotechnic display used in a show featuring the band Great White.

The pyrotechnic devices, known as gerbs, were set off about eleven o'clock, just seconds into Great White's set. Once the gerbs were ignited, the sparks they generated came in contact with nearby walls onto which a two-and-a-half-inch layer of polyurethane had been installed by club owners Michael and Jeffrey Derderian to make the building soundproof. The sparks caused the walls to ignite, and the ensuing fire quickly tore through the rest of the structure.

At the time the fire broke out, more than three hundred patrons were inside. The majority of these patrons headed toward the main entrance. This entrance had only a three-foot-wide clearance, causing a severe bottleneck and trapping many inside.

Daniel Biechele, Great White's tour manager and the man who set off the gerbs, was charged with involuntary manslaughter, as were the Derderians. Biechele and Michael Derderian were sentenced to four-year prison terms. Jeffrey Derderian was placed on probation and performed community service.

Impact

Charitable organizations, including the Station Family Fund, were established to help survivors and the families of victims. To prevent another such tragedy, the National Institute of Standards and Technology (NIST) urged enforcement of existing safety codes. Additionally, the Massachusetts Fire Safety Act became law in 2004. The act requires sprinkler systems at clubs and bars; those owners who do not comply with this and other safety regulations will face criminal charges.

Further Reading

Farragher, Thomas. "Deception, Missteps Sparked a Tragedy." *Boston Globe* 8 June 2003: A1. Print.

"Final NIST Rhode Island Nightclub Fire Report Urges Strict Adherence to and Strengthening of Current Model Safety Codes." *National Institute of Standards and Technology* (*NIST*). US Department of Commerce, 29 June 2005. Web. 7 Sept. 2012.

Grosshandler, William, et al. *Report of the Technical Investigation of the Station Nightclub Fire.* Vol. 1.

National Institute of Standards and Technology, 30 June 2005. Web. 7 Sept. 2012.

Jack Lasky

■ Rice, Condoleezza

Identification: US secretary of state, 2005–9
Born: November 14, 1954; Birmingham, Alabama

Condoleezza Rice worked her way through the ranks of the United States government to serve as Secretary of State in the administration of President George W. Bush through 2009. Enrolling in college at the young age of fifteen, she immersed herself first in the world of academia, where she would return later in her career. While serving as the first African American female secretary of state, she was a critical member of President Bush's cabinet and a leading international political figure.

Condoleezza Rice was born on November 14, 1954, in Birmingham, Alabama, and grew up in an era of government sanctioned racial segregation and widespread racial prejudice. She graduated cum laude and Phi Beta Kappa from the University of Denver in 1974, with a bachelor's degree in political science. She received her master's degree in political science from the University of Notre Dame in 1975, and she earned her PhD in political science from the Graduate School of International Studies at the University of Denver in 1981. Her academic specialties included international security policy, the politics of East-Central Europe and the former Soviet Union, and the comparative study of military institutions. While at Stanford University, Rice became a senior fellow of the Institute for International Studies, a fellow of the Hoover Institution, and a member of the Center for International Security and Arms Control.

In 1993, Rice became the Stanford University's provost—the school's head academic and budget officer. She was the youngest person and the first African American to hold the post. As provost, she was responsible for the school's $1.5 billion annual budget, as well as its 14,000 students and 1,400 faculty members. During the time of German reunification and the end of the Soviet Union (1989–91), Rice served as the National Security Council's director of Soviet and East European Affairs under the administration of US President George H. W. Bush.

Condoleezza Rice. (Courtesy World Affairs Council of Philadelphia)

She also acted as special assistant to the president for national security affairs.

During the 2000 presidential campaign, Rice acted as head foreign policy advisor to George W. Bush. Later that year, President-elect Bush appointed Rice as his National Security Advisor. As such, she was directly involved in the administration's response to issues of defense, national security, and foreign policy. Rice's tenure as National Security Advisor was not without controversy. When Bush made the controversial decision to challenge the affirmative action admissions policy at the University of Michigan, Rice was cited as agreeing with the administration's stance.

In 2003, Rice was at the center of a controversy surrounding President Bush's claim that Iraq had attempted to purchase uranium from Niger for use in its alleged nuclear weapons program. Many analysts and officials have since claimed that evidence of this uranium deal, which was used by

Bush to justify the 2003 US invasion of Iraq, was based on intelligence that was completely fabricated. Bush cited the uranium deal in his January 2003 State of the Union Address. Although Rice initially denied any knowledge of the inclusion of faulty intelligence in Bush's address, she eventually claimed some measure of responsibility for the error.

In May of 2004, Rice testified before the 9/11 Commission, a national committee investigating the terrorist attacks of September 11, 2001. Rice defended the actions of the US government during the time leading up to the attacks. She claimed the government did its best to defend the nation's interests and had no way of knowing that terrorists would attack on that day in the manner that they did. After one term of service, Secretary of State Colin Powell resigned from his position on November 15, 2004. President Bush nominated Condoleezza Rice to replace Powell in his administration. Rice accepted the nomination and met before the US Senate Committee on Foreign Relations, who voted in favor of forwarding the nomination to the Senate. On January 26, 2005, the Senate approved her nomination with a vote of 85–13, the largest number against any secretary of state nominee in history. Those senators opposing Rice's nomination stated that they were concerned about the United States' involvement in the war in Iraq.

Much of Rice's tenure as Secretary of State was steeped in the Bush administration's policies of fighting the growth of global terrorism. She often spoke of the policy of "transformational diplomacy," or efforts on the part of the United States to help build well-governed states in problem areas. Rice remained secretary of state until the end of George W. Bush's presidency in January of 2009. In March 2009, she was named the Thomas and Barbara Stephenson Senior Fellow on Public Policy at the Hoover Institution. In addition, she serves as a political science professor at Stanford University. Rice belongs to many organizations and has served on a number of councils during her professional career. She is a member of the boards of directors for the Charles Schwab Corporation, the Chevron Corporation, the University of Notre Dame, the William and Flora Hewlett Foundation, and the International Advisory Council of J.P. Morgan, and has formerly served on the boards of several other corporations.

She is also a fellow of the American Academy of Arts and Sciences. In 2010, Rice was awarded the Thomas D. White National Defense Award.

Impact

As secretary of state, Condoleezza Rice played a significant role in the foreign policy of the United States during the Bush Administration. Rice was influential in promoting democracy in nations that supported terrorism, such as Iraq and other totalitarian countries in the Middle East. She was also the first African American women to hold the title of secretary of state. By overcoming gender and racial boundaries, she has helped pave the way for African Americans and women who wish to attain high-ranking positions in the US government.

Further Reading

Bumiller, Elisabeth. *Condoleezza Rice: An American Life: A Biography.* New York: Random, 2009. Print.

Mabry, Marcus. *Condoleezza Rice and Her Path to Power.* Gordonsville: Modern, 2007. Print.

Rice, Condoleezza. *Condoleezza Rice: A Memoir of My Extraordinary, Ordinary Family and Me.* New York: Delacorte, 2010. Print.

Ryan, Bernard Jr. *Condoleezza Rice: Secretary of State.* New York: Ferguson, 2003. Print.

Lori Cavanaugh

■ *Road, The*

Identification: Pulitzer Prize-winning novel from author Cormac McCarthy about a father and son traversing the dangers of what is left of civilization in a post-apocalyptic world
Author: Cormac McCarthy (b. 1933)
Date: Published on September 26, 2006

Cormac McCarthy's The Road *was one of the most critically acclaimed novels of the decade. Released during a time when environmental protection was highly debated in United State politics and policy, the novel depicted a landscape laid barren by a cause never fully explained.* The Road *won several book awards, including the Pulitzer Prize for Fiction in 2007.*

The Road follows an unnamed father and his son as they travel through a dangerous, decimated landscape in hopes of finding food and shelter from the oncoming winter—the time and location where the story takes place is not specified. There is no more vegetation or animals and the ground is covered in ash. They are armed with a revolver that contains only two rounds, and the father has instructs his son to use the gun on himself rather than be captured by cannibals that are roaming the land. The pair encounter various dangers along their journey while also facing starvation. The son is not aware of the fact that his father is seriously ill.

McCarthy has explained that he was first inspired to write *The Road* while visiting El Paso, Texas, with his son John Francis McCarthy in 2003. He thought about what the landscape would look like in the future and imagined an apocalyptic world. He continued to develop these ideas until he wrote the book a few years later. The relationship between the father and his son is a central theme in the book, and McCarthy dedicated the book to his son. Throughout the story, the father gives the son hope for survival despite impending doom. The mother, who was pregnant at the time of the apocalyptic event, committed suicide. Other themes explored by McCarthy in the novel include memory, community, and ideological conflict. He uses sparse, economical prose in the book that some critics compared to poetry.

Impact

The Road gained national attention when it was chosen by television host Oprah Winfrey as a selection in her book club. The reclusive McCarthy delivered his first television interview on Winfrey's show. The book won the prestigious James Tait Black Memorial Prize in fiction and was a finalist for the National Book Critics Circle Award in 2006 for fiction. It won the 2007 Pulitzer Prize for Fiction and was embraced by many environmentalists for its portrayal of the earth's physical deterioration. In 2009, the book was adapted into a film directed by John Hillcoat and starring Viggo Mortensen .

Further Reading

McCarthy, Cormac. *The Road.* New York: Knopf: 2006. Print.

Halcomb, Mark. "End of the Line: After Decades of Stalking Armageddon's Perimeters, Cormac McCarthy Steps over the Border." *Village Voice* 29 Aug. 2006. Web. 26 July 2012.

Patrick G. Cooper

■ Roberts, John

Identification: Chief justice of the United States since 2005
Born: January 27, 1955; Buffalo, New York

At the age of fifty, John Roberts became the youngest man ever to serve as chief justice of the United States Supreme Court on September 29, 2005. Nominated by President George W. Bush, Roberts was confirmed by one of the narrowest margins in the history of the Supreme Court, with an approval vote of seventy-eight to twenty-two. The saga of Roberts's nomination and confirmation reflects an intensifying battle of political and social positions in the United States that is increasingly played out in the nation's highest court.

From 1979 to 1980, John Glover Roberts Jr. clerked for Second Circuit Court of Appeals Judge Henry Friendly. He was then hired as a clerk for Supreme Court Chief Justice William Rehnquist (then an associate justice on the Court). A year later, in 1981, he was hired as special assistant to US Attorney General William French Smith. In 1982, he became associate counsel to President Ronald Reagan under White House Counsel Fred Fielding.

In 2000 George W. Bush, the son of former President George H. W. Bush, began his first term in office. With an approach to policy and staffing very similar to that of his father, Bush recalled to the White House a number of those who had worked for or with the first Bush administration. In a flurry of judicial nominations, Bush nominated Roberts to the Court of Appeals a second time. However, the country had become too thoroughly divided in its politics, with a greater emphasis on judicial nominees, to allow for an easy approval process. Thirty of Bush's judicial nominees, including Roberts, failed to get confirmation by the Senate.

In January 2003, Bush again nominated Roberts to the Court of Appeals, this time to replace a retiring judge. Roberts's nomination got through the Judiciary Committee with a vote of sixteen to three, and won unanimous approval in the Republican-controlled Senate. Roberts began serving on the Court of Appeals on June 3, 2003.

Roberts remained on the Court of Appeals for only three years. On July 1, 2005, Supreme Court Associate Justice Sandra Day O'Connor announced that she was resigning her position on the Court

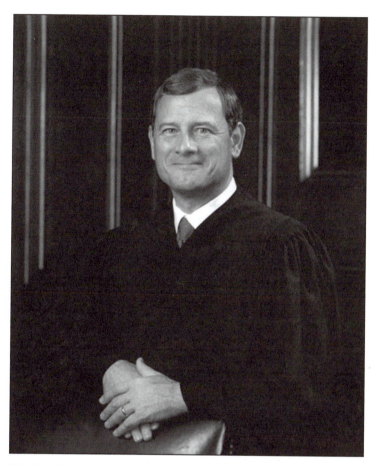

John G. Roberts, Jr. (Collection of the Supreme Court of the United States/ Photograph by Steve Petteway)

effective as soon as her successor could be nominated and confirmed. O'Connor's resignation stirred up the bitter divisions between Republicans and Democrats that have become a familiar part of the judicial nominations process. As a moderate judge whose vote was often the decisive factor in a court otherwise divided between conservative and liberal judicial positions, O'Connor was crucial to the balance of power. Both sides felt that there was a tremendous amount at stake in filling O'Connor's seat.

When Bush nominated Roberts to fill O'Connor's seat on July 19, 2005, a storm of controversy broke out. Since Roberts spent most of his career as an attorney before the appellate courts, there is very little public record of his own views on the nation's most debated issues. However, most have interpreted his active Catholicism and remarks on the Sup-

reme Court abortion decision *Roe v. Wade* to suggest that he would overturn that case if given the opportunity.

Decided in 1973, *Roe v. Wade* has prohibited states from banning first-term abortions for more than thirty years. O'Connor's decision in *Planned Parenthood v. Casey* had opened the door for more state regulation of early stage pregnancies, but had reaffirmed a woman's right to first trimester abortion under the Fourteenth Amendment. The longstanding alliance between the Republican Party and antiabortion groups on the one hand, and between the Democratic Party and advocates for the reproductive rights of women on the other meant that Roberts's ambiguous position on *Roe v. Wade* was central to discussions of his fitness for the Supreme Court.

Of equal concern was how Roberts's appointment to the Supreme Court would affect the existing balances of power between Congress, the executive branch, the judiciary, and the states. The Commerce Clause of the Constitution, for instance, authorizes Congress to make laws with regard to any issues that affect interstate commerce, or business that moves across state borders. In the contemporary United States, this clause authorizes federal legislation of everything from environmental protection to highways and phone services to criminal racketeering.

Roberts's dissent in the case of *Rancho Viejo, LLC v. Norton* (2004) while he was on the Court of Appeals indicated that he believes the Commerce Clause should be interpreted more narrowly than it has been. Liberal organizations point to the Rancho Viejo dissent, along with Roberts's affiliation with strongly conservative groups like the National Legal Center for the Public Interest and the Republican National Lawyers' Association, to argue that Roberts will attempt to radically limit the powers of Congress over a myriad of interstate issues.

On September 3, 2005, with Roberts's confirmation hearings looming, Chief Justice William Rehnquist died suddenly. President Bush quickly withdrew Roberts's nomination for associate justice and nominated him for chief justice on September 6,

2005. Roberts's nomination was approved before the Senate Judiciary Committee on September 22 in a thirteen-to-five vote. He was confirmed by the full Senate on September 29, 2005, in a vote of seventy-eight to twenty-two. Roberts was sworn in as the seventeenth chief justice of the Supreme Court that day.

Roberts lives with his wife and fellow lawyer, Jane Sullivan Roberts, and his two young children, Josephine and Jack.

Impact

John Roberts is the current chief justice of the United States Supreme Court and was appointed by George W. Bush in 2005. At age fifty, he is the youngest member of the Supreme Court and the third youngest person to become chief justice. As chief justice of the Supreme Court, Roberts has overseen numerous cases, including *Gonzales v. Carhart* (2007), *Georgia v. Randolph* (2006), and, most recently, the *National Federation of Independent Business v. Sebelius* (2012), which upheld the Patient Protection and Affordable Care Act.

Further Reading

Banks, Christopher B and John C. Blakeman. *The U.S. Supreme Court and New Federalism: From the Rehnquist to the Roberts Court.* Lanham: Rowman, 2012. Print.

Stevens, John Paul. *Five Chiefs: A Supreme Court Memoir.* New York: Brown, 2011. Print.

Toobin, Jeffrey. *The Oath: The Obama White House and the Supreme Court.* New York: Random, 2012. Print.

Amy Witherbee

■ Rock music

Definition: A genre of music that evolved from rock-and-roll music of the 1950s and grew to encompass a wide variety of musical styles and subgenres.

Rock music in North America entered the 2000s in the wake of a particularly memorable and exciting decade when traditional subgenres and underground styles, notably grunge and punk, ascended to mainstream cultural and commercial success. The proliferation of inexpensive rock instruments and recording technology would give rise to a generation of amateur musicians who embraced a do-it-yourself approach to songwriting and recording that would result in a global embrace of American indie rock throughout the decade.

The Move Away from Grunge

The influential grunge bands of the 1990s were successfully marketed and popularly perceived as unrefined, particularly in contrast to the stereotypically rock-star, ballad-centric "hair-bands" that preceded them in the 1980s. Nevertheless, the nationally known rock acts of the 1990s remained extremely profitable internationally and were capable of selling enormous amounts of records for the major labels that employed them.

While American rock groups such as Soundgarden, Pearl Jam, Alice in Chains, Nirvana, and Stone Temple Pilots embodied the grunge aesthetic in sound and charisma, they were nevertheless comprised of virtuoso musicians working in professional studios with all the pitfalls of fame and fortune, including the best in contemporary sound gear, engineering technology, and big-budget producers.

By the early 2000s, much of the aggression of the grunge movement had faded in the minds of rock fans and critics alike. Few if any of the grunge bands who so rapidly ascended to prominence in the 1990s seemed capable of recapturing the commercial and cultural appeal of their debut albums. Pearl Jam, for example, would receive widespread critical acclaim for its 1993 sophomore effort *Vs.*, and although they continued to record albums throughout the 2000s, they would never again achieve the lofty heights of their landmark 1991 debut *Ten.* By the 2000s, other grunge successes of the 1990s, such as Alice in Chains and Stone Temple Pilots, succumbed to the substance abuse and in-fighting common among musical acts across all genres and time periods.

Post-Grunge Rock Music

With the commercial success of grunge music fading almost as quickly as it had arrived, rock music found itself at a crossroads. While musicians like the California-based stadium rock band Tool and alternative-country artists such as Wilco and Ryan Adams would reign over their respective niche rock genres, neither would crack the mainstream consciousness in the way Nirvana and other grunge acts had during the 1990s. If any singular band can be designated as the bridge between 1990s grunge and the indie rock sound that would eventually flourish in the 2000s, it would be the California-based band Weezer, whose most acclaimed releases would achieve widespread commercial success with their grunge-esque power through an aesthetic that

Inductees into the Rock and Roll Hall of Fame, 2000-2009

2000

Hal Blaine

Eric Clapton

Nat "King" Cole

King Curtis

Clive Davis

Earth, Wind & Fire

Billie Holiday

James Jamerson

Lovin' Spoonful

The Moonglows

Scotty Moore

Earl Palmer

Bonnie Raitt

James Taylor

2001

Aerosmith

Chris Blackwell

Solomon Burke

James Burton

The Flamingos

Michael Jackson

Johnnie Johnson

Queen

Paul Simon

Steely Dan

Ritchie Valens

2002

Chet Atkins

Isaac Hayes

Brenda Lee

Gene Pitney

Ramones

Jim Stewart

Talking Heads

Tom Petty and the Heartbreakers

2003

AC/DC

Benny Benjamin

The Clash

Elvis Costello & the Attractions

Floyd Cramer

Steve Douglas

Mo Ostin

The Police

Righteous Brothers

2004

Jackson Browne

The Dells

George Harrison

Prince

Bob Seger

Traffic

Jann S. Wenner

ZZ Top

2005

Frank Barsalona

Buddy Guy

The O'Jays

The Pretenders

Percy Sledge

Seymour Stein

U2

2006

Herb Alpert and Jerry Moss

Black Sabbath

Blondie

Miles Davis

Lynyrd Skynyrd

Sex Pistols

2007

Grandmaster Flash & the Furious Five

R.E.M

The Ronettes

Patti Smith

Van Halen

2008

Leonard Cohen

The Dave Clark Five

Kenny Gamble and Leon Huff

Little Walter

Madonna

John Mellencamp

The Ventures

2009

Jeff Black

Bill Black

D.J. Fontana

Wanda Jackson

Little Anthony and the Imperials

Metallica

Spooner Oldham

Run-D.M.C.

Bobby Womack

Source: The Rock Hall of Fame

Wilco in concert at the Paradiso in Amsterdam. (Courtesy Guus Krol)

was comprised of still catchier, listener-friendly pop overtures.

The grunge movement was swiftly becoming a faded memory upon the 2003 major label debut of the Detroit-based rock group The White Stripes. *Elephant* would go on to become one of the decade's most highly acclaimed albums and would propel the band to superstar status. Tracks like "Seven Nation Army" and "The Hardest Button to Button" would captivate audiences with aggressive percussion and distorted guitars, but the composition of the band itself would differ greatly from their grunge predecessors: The White Stripes were comprised of a single guitarist and single drummer, in stark contrast to the traditional trio, quartet, and quintet rock ensembles that had been staples of rock genres for decades.

The emergence of The White Stripes would also mark a slow decline for traditional rock music that had been a staple of FM radio and concert arenas for decades. The group's popularity rose from its no-frills arrangements, sing-a-long choruses, and their embodiment of the quintessential blues aesthetic that had powered the birth of American rock music in the mid-twentieth century. Their music allowed rock fans a refreshing contrast to the ornately arranged, classically influenced rock music that had become a staple of the genre. The success of The White Stripes would plant the seed for numerous American artists who would follow throughout the decade, notably The Strokes and The Black Keys.

The Demise of FM Rock

Drastic but swift changes would occur to the music industry throughout the 2000s that would form an entirely new landscape for rock music. The debut of the Apple iPod in 2001 resulted in an industry-wide shift towards digital music files that would transform music as a commercial entity. The proliferation of digital music files would not only allow music consumers to personalize their listening experience and would also allow for on-demand music choices. As a result, rock music fans were no longer beholden to playlists dictated by commercially owned, brick-and-mortar rock radio stations.

While quintessential American rock artists and groups such as Bruce Springsteen, Aerosmith, and Tom Petty as well as newly established titans like Green Day, Beck, Foo Fighters, and Pixies would navigate this new terrain with relative ease buoyed by the tremendous success of their past catalogues, emerging American rock artists would struggle to achieve notoriety in a genre that became increasingly diversified in terms of musical style, composition, and arrangement.

For the rock music world of the 2000s, a succession of FM radio hits and grueling tour schedules was no longer the only path to critical or commercial success. Similarly, since rock continued to steer toward an intimate, individualized experience, much of the pretentiousness and aggression typical of the genre began to yield to bands who were interested in creating a more provocative emotional experience for their audience. This new niche of sentimental rock gave rise to an entirely new rock genre, "emo," but it was also embraced by traditional-rock artists such as the Canadian group Arcade Fire; the American alternative/indie rock bands Bright Eyes, Bon Iver, Death Cab for Cutie, and The National; as well as an emerging group of singer-songwriters such as Sufjan Stevens, Rufus Wainwright, and Cat Power.

Rock music of the 2000s also contained a diverse group of experimental artists and groups who melded a variety of music styles into their sound. Bands such as TV on the radio achieved widespread success for their meld of rock, soul, and electronic music ("electronica"). Other artists would continue to explore such rock subgenres as noise rock, industrial shoegaze, and dream pop, and groups such as

Sonic Youth and Nine Inch Nails as well as Blonde Redhead, Yeah Yeah Yeahs, and The Killers would achieve great acclaim during the decade.

Impact

Much of the rock music of the 2000s offered a retrospective appreciation of the sounds rooted in the 1950s origins of the genre, while simultaneously shunning the trappings of enhanced production in the effort to achieve a more intimate sound. Rock music endured a profound transformation in the 2000s from that of a communal and public experience shared on platforms such as FM radio to that of an individualized and personalized experience in which consumers could easily and immediately choose their own listening experience. What resulted was a new opportunity for artists to achieve notoriety and critical acclaim from grassroots audiences rather than through the limited avenues previously established by the commercial rock establishment.

Further Reading

Boilen, Bob. "The Decade's 50 Most Important Recordings." *NPR Music*. NPR, 16 Nov. 2009. Web. 13 Nov. 2012. An alphabetical list of the fifty most impactful songs as determined by National Public Radio's contributors and listeners.

"The Decade in News." *Pitchfork*. Pitchfork Media Inc., 21 Sept. 2009. Web. 13 Nov. 2012. Provides a discussion on the trends and improvements in music reporting during the 2000s as they relate to the technological advances of the decade.

"The 50 Best Albums of the Decade (2000–2009)." *Paste*. Paste Media Group, 2 Nov. 2009. Web. 13 Nov. 2012. The fifty best albums of the 2000s are listed and discussed. Background information on album cover art, artist, and select songs is provided.

Morford, Mark. "All Hail the Death of Radio/Clear Channel Suffers and Rock Radio is Gasping its Last and, More Importantly, Does Anyone Care?" *San Francisco Chronicle*. Hearst Communications, Inc., 2 Mar. 2005. Web. 13 Nov. 2012. Recounts the decline in quality and listenership of FM radio during the 1990s and 2000s and the subsequent rise of on-demand music and music information.

Stilo, Rocco. "The History of Rock Music: 2000–." *Scaruffi*. Piero Scaruffi, 2010. Web. 13 Nov. 2012.

Provides an analysis of the transformation of rock music during the 2000s as it relates to the social, political, and technological events of the decade.

John Pritchard

■ Romney, Mitt

Identification: American politician and presidential candidate
Born: March 12, 1947; Detroit, Michigan

As governor of Massachusetts from 2003 to 2007, Mitt Romney proposed far-reaching reforms for the state's government and established near-universal health care coverage in the state. He became widely known for his management of the 2002 Winter Olympics and gained national attention after becoming a candidate for the 2008 Republican Party presidential nomination.

Willard Mitt Romney was born on March 12, 1947, in Detroit, Michigan, the son of Lenore Romney, who ran for the Michigan senate in 1970, and the George Romney, former Michigan governor and one-time presidential candidate. Before Romney entered Brigham Young University, where he received his bachelor of arts degree in 1971, he attended Stanford University for his freshman year and spent the following summer in France on a mission for the Church of Jesus Christ of Latter-day Saints.

In 1975, Romney earned a master's degree in business administration from Harvard Business School and was named a Baker Scholar. The same year, he received his law degree from Harvard Law School. From 1978 to 1984, Romney was a vice president of Bain & Company, a management-consulting firm based in Boston. In 1984, he started Bain Capital, a venture capital firm that founded, acquired, or invested money in hundreds of companies.

In 1994, Romney was the Massachusetts Republican nominee for US Senate, running against the formidable Democrat Ted Kennedy. Even though he lost, Romney took 41 percent of the vote and gained valuable experience in Massachusetts politics.

Romney ran for governor of Massachusetts in 2002 on issues including proposals for holding the line on taxes and spending, improving education, mandating English immersion for all foreign-language students, and attracting jobs and economic development to

Mitt Romney. (Courtesy Gage Skidmore)

Massachusetts. He was in favor of low taxes and funding the Clean Elections law (although not with taxpayer dollars), and he supported the death penalty. In November 2002, Romney was elected governor of Massachusetts. His top priorities, as expressed during his campaign, were education, economic growth, streamlining government, and improving the quality of life in Massachusetts.

Upon taking office in January 2003, he faced a much larger deficit than anticipated. His plan to remedy the state's finances represented the most sweeping change to state government in a generation and involved proposals to restructure and streamline several areas of state government. Romney opted not to seek reelection as governor in 2006. In February of 2007, he officially announced his candidacy for the 2008 Republican Party nomination for president.

Romney critics and rivals lambasted him for having employed illegal immigrants to do landscaping work at his home. In addition, Romney's repeated claims that his father participated in civil rights era marches with Martin Luther King, Jr. were discovered to be unfounded. However, Romney placed second in the 2008 Republican caucus in Iowa, finishing with 25 percent of the vote.

Romney published a book entitled *No Apology: The Case for American Greatness* (2010). He was the Republican Party candidate for president in 2012, losing a close popular vote to incumbent Barack Obama.

Impact

In addition to being a successful businessman, Romney was the seventieth governor of Massachusetts and a candidate for US president in 2008 and 2012. As governor of Massachusetts, Romney implemented a number of reforms, including near-universal health care. He is also noted for his role as president and CEO of the Salt Lake Organizing Committee for the Olympic and Paralympic Winter Games of 2002 and adding a surplus of $100 million to the organization's budget.

Further Reading

Kranish, Michael, and Scott Helman. *The Real Romney*. New York: Harper, 2012. Print.

Romney, Mitt. *No Apology: The Case for American Greatness*. New York: St. Martin's, 2010. Print.

Scott, Ronald B. *Mitt Romney: An Inside Look at the Man and His Politics*. Guilford: Lyons, 2012. Print.

Wendy Evans

■ *Roper v. Simmons*

The Case: US Supreme Court ruling on constitutionality of capital punishment for minors
Date: Decided on March 1, 2005

Deferring to international standards, national trends, and the psychological limitations of juveniles, the Supreme Court ruled that imposing capital punishment on minors was "cruel and unusual" and thus unconstitutional. Addressing its patchwork of cases that assessed minors and the death penalty, the court created a more comprehensive stance to reflect, in the words of Justice Anthony Kennedy, its "evolving standards of decency."

In 1993, seventeen-year-old Christopher Simmons was accused of murdering forty-six-year-old Shirley Crook. Initially given the death penalty, his sentence was commuted to life in prison after he claimed a lack of effective council. The state of Missouri appealed this ruling, and the case rose to the US Supreme Court.

Prior to hearing *Roper v. Simmons*, the Supreme Court had issued mixed rulings on capital punishment. In 1988, the court ruled in *Thompson v. Oklahoma* against issuing the death penalty to offenders under sixteen. Later, in *Stanford v. Kentucky* (1989), the court allowed capital punishment for those aged sixteen and older. That same year, the court upheld capital punishment for the mentally handicapped in *Penry v. Lynaugh*. Leading up to *Roper v. Simmons*, the court heard *Atkins v. Virginia* (2002), which overruled Penry on the basis of cruel and unusual punishment.

Supporting Simmons, the American Psychological Association (APA) and the Coalition for Juvenile Justice (CJJ) filed amicus briefs. The APA questioned the sufficient development of adolescents, citing that brain development in the area of decision making continued into young adulthood. The APA contended that as minors were not fully developed, their threat to society was undeterminable. Joining them, the CJJ referenced development issues and emphasized the trend of wrongful imprisonment and sentencing for minors, which was often based on coercion and faulty confessions. Both groups claimed that imposing capital punishment on minors robbed them of basic rights.

Under a close decision of five to four, the Supreme Court ruled in favor of Simmons. Justice Anthony Kennedy delivered the majority opinion, citing the Eighth and Fourteenth Amendments and linking the Atkins case to assertions of limited development in minors. The ruling overturned *Stanford v. Kentucky*.

Impact

Utilizing an inclusive view of cruel and unusual punishment, the *Roper v. Simmons* decision inspired greater leniency in cases involving juvenile offenders. This stance influenced the court's decision in *Graham v. Florida* (2010), which prohibited life in prison without parole for minors convicted of all crimes excluding murder.

In addition, the *Roper v. Simmons* ruling questioned the court's deliberation process. While the decision was made on constitutional grounds, it also considered international views and state trends regarding capital punishment. Critics argued against the use of such views—external to law—to decide the case and create these "evolving standards of decency." The use of such external sources called into question what bound the court to US law and the Constitution itself.

Further Reading

Garland, David, Randall McGowen, and Michael Meranze, eds. *America's Death Penalty: Between Past and Present*. New York: NYU P, 2011. Print.

Tydings, Joseph D., et al. "Brief of the Coalition for Juvenile Justice as Amicus Curiae in Support of Respondent." *Coalition for Juvenile Justice*. Coalition for Juvenile Justice, 19 July 2004. Web. 12 Oct. 2012.

Lucia Pizzo

■ Rove, Karl

Identification: American political consultant
Born: December 25, 1950; Denver, Colorado

Karl Rove was called "the brain" of the George W. Bush administration. His work as a political consultant for the Republican Party began during his college days, and both his connection to the powerful Bush family and his talent for securing election and public opinion wins for politicians have placed him in the spotlight of national politics in the United States.

Karl Rove was born on December 25, 1950, in Denver, Colorado. In 1969, he began studying political science at the University of Utah, but he abandoned the liberal campus atmosphere of the day to pursue his role as chairman of the College Republicans National Committee. He traveled across the western states, enlisting and coaching young Republican hopefuls. While fulfilling his duties as chairman, Rove met and became friends with George H. W. Bush. While working for Bush, Rove developed many political connections. After the campaign, he started his own business as a political consultant specializing in direct-mail marketing. Among his early clients were Texas senator Phil Gramm and governor Bill Clements, as well as several other right-wing political figures.

Rove also worked closely with George W. Bush beginning with his successful presidential bid in 2000. As lead advisor to the president, he handled matters in the Office of Strategic Initiatives, the Office of Political Affairs, and the Office of Public Liaison. He was credited with steering Bush in the carefully conservative and brutally competitive manner that enabled the Republican Party to obtain majority control in Congress. Considered a strategic genius in the world of politics, Rove held great influence over the behavior and statements of the Bush presidential administration, earning the dubious titles of "Bush's brain" and "Bush's puppet master."

Former US ambassador Joseph C. Wilson claimed in August of 2003 that Rove was responsible for the leak to the news media of his wife Valerie Plame's identity as a member of the Central Intelligence Agency. Wilson said his wife's name was leaked as punishment for him writing a *New York Times* editorial that was highly critical of the

Karl Rove (left) makes a point while George Mitchell looks on. (©iStockphoto.com/Justin Sullivan)

Bush administration's rationale for invading Iraq and toppling the government of Saddam Hussein. Although Rove was never charged in the case, Vice Presidential Chief of Staff Lewis "Scooter" Libby was convicted by a jury for perjury charges related to the affair. Many critics felt that Libby was made a scapegoat in order to deflect legal action against Rove.

Although many consider Rove a political mastermind, his integrity has often been questioned. Frequently accused of "dirty politics," he has admitted only to being extremely competitive. It has been rumored that he trained college Republicans in deliberately unethical politics and publicized false stories about opposing candidates.

The extent to which Rove controlled the decisions made by President Bush was a cause for controversy. Issues of particular concern in this department, in addition to the invasion of Iraq, included the debate over stem-cell research and the firing of several US attorneys. While his reputation remains controversial, Rove has certainly established a place in history as a man with unquestionable political skill and ambition.

Impact

Rove is known for his political campaigns that have aided numerous Republicans in winning elections, including George H. W. Bush, Phil Gramm, and William Clements. Most notably, however, was his victory with George W. Bush in both the Texas gubernatorial race and the presidential races of 2000 and 2004. After the success of the election, Rove was appointed senior advisor and the Deputy Chief of Staff to the president. During the 2012 election cycle, Rove served as a Republican political strategist and fundraiser via his donor groups, Crossroads GPS and American Crossroads, which channeled hundreds of millions of dollars to Republican congressional candidates and the campaign of presidential challenger Mitt Romney. Romney and all but two of the congressional candidates Rove supported lost their election bids, however, and it remains to be seen whether he will continue to have the same degree of influence in the Republican Party going forward.

Further Reading

Israel, Bill. *A Nation Seized: How Karl Rove and the Political Right Stole Reality, Beginning with the News.* Spokane: Marquette, 2010. Print.

Moore, James, and Wayne Slater. *The Architect: Karl Rove and the Dream of Absolute Power.* New York: Random, 2006. Print.

Rove, Karl. *Courage and Consequence.* New York: Simon, 2010. Print.

Lori Cavanaugh

■ Rowley, Coleen

Identification: Former FBI agent and whistle-blower
Born: 1954; New Hampton, Iowa

Former special agent Coleen Rowley triggered a massive reorganization of the Federal Bureau of Investigation (FBI) when a thirteen-page memo she had written was leaked to the press. The memo detailed her department's inaction in the weeks leading up to the terrorist attacks of September 11, 2001. Rowley's testimony was significant during the investigation of the events surrounding the attacks.

In 2001, FBI agent Coleen Rowley received information about a suspected terrorist named Zacarias Moussaoui who had enrolled in a local flight school to learn to fly a commercial airplane. Rowley's team took the information to their superiors, and the suspect was arrested on August 15 on immigration charges. Rowley requested a warrant to search the man's laptop computer, but her request was denied. On September 11, 2001, four passenger airplanes were hijacked in the United States as part of an organized terrorist attack that killed more than three thousand people.

Rowley believed more could have been done to prevent the attacks, which were later linked to Moussaoui. She wrote a memo in May 2002 to FBI Director Robert Mueller detailing her concerns. The memo was quickly leaked to the press, and Rowley was identified as the whistle-blower in one of the most controversial investigations in the history of the United States. The information contained in the memo prompted an inquiry into the FBI. Rowley testified at a Senate hearing two weeks later, accusing the agency of mishandling the investigation. She also indicated that issues within the organization, particularly poor coordination and communication between agents and FBI headquarters, contributed to the failure. Her testimony spurred a widespread restructuring of the FBI.

Rowley remained with the FBI for two more years. She led an unsuccessful campaign against the war in Iraq in 2003 while working for the legal division of the agency, after which she returned to her post as special agent before retiring in 2004. That year she wrote a chapter for the book *Patriotism, Democracy, and Common Sense*, a collection of essays critiquing American government policies.

Rowley was recommended by Minnesota legislators to serve on the Privacy and Civil Liberties Oversight Board in 2005. She did not receive the appointment, however. The following year, she ran for US Congress in Minnesota's Second Congressional District, but lost the election.

Impact

Rowley's commitment to truth and her dedication to her duties helped shed light on a flawed federal organization. Though she was criticized within the FBI, her courage was not without reward. She was named one of *Time* magazine's Persons of the Year in 2002. She works as a public speaker, speaking about ethical decision-making and civil liberties. She also writes a blog for the *Huffington Post.*

Further Reading

Huffington Post. "Coleen Rowley." *Huffington Post.* TheHuffingtonPost.com, n.d. Web. 12 July 2012.

PBS. "Coleen Rowley." *PBS Now.* PBS, 4 March 2005. Web. 12 July 2012.

Ripley, Amanda, and Maggie Sieger. "Coleen Rowley: The Special Agent." *Time.* Time, 30 Dec. 2002. Web. 12 July 2012.

Rowley, Coleen. "Coleen Rowley's Memo to FBI Director Robert Mueller." *Newsmax.com.* Newsmax.com, 21 May 2002. Web. 12 July 2012.

Cait Caffrey

■ Rumsfeld, Donald

Identification: US secretary of defense, 2001–6
Born: July 9, 1932; Evanston, Illinois

Donald Rumsfeld was no stranger to Washington, DC, or to the Pentagon, when he accepted the position of secretary of defense under President George W. Bush in 2000. Rumsfeld also served as defense secretary in the Gerald Ford administration and advised several other Republican presidents on matters of defense.

Donald Henry Rumsfeld was born in Chicago, Illinois, on July 9, 1932. A skilled high school wrestler, he continued to wrestle at Princeton University, where he earned a bachelor's degree in 1954. During his stint in the US Navy, he served as a pilot and a flight instructor and earned the all-Navy wrestling title.

Rumsfeld's years in the private sector served to further his political career. As chief executive officer of pharmaceutical company G. D. Searle and Company and electronics firm General Instrument, he amassed a considerable personal fortune and developed close ties with many corporate conservatives, who had influence in the realms of both business and politics. Rumsfeld also served as chairman of the RAND Corporation military think tank.

After George W. Bush assumed the presidency in 2001, he nominated Rumsfeld as secretary of defense, twenty-five years after he first held that post. During Bush's campaign, he employed many of the same tactics that Rumsfeld had suggested to Dole in 1998, and he adopted Rumsfeld's conservative views on national defense and military policy.

Returning to the Pentagon, Rumsfeld made it clear that his agenda had changed since 1975, and he fought to increase military funding, update equipment, and employ new defense technology such as unmanned planes and quick-deploy forces. He continued his efforts to persuade the president and Congress of the need for a missile defense program.

George W. Bush looks on as Donald Rumsfeld addresses the nation from the Oval Office. (Department of Defense/Photograph by James Bowman, U.S. Air Force)

Rumsfeld's plans to redefine the mission of the US military were temporarily sidetracked in September 2001, when terrorists launched a series of attacks against the United States. He was in his office on September 11, when Flight 77 crashed into the Pentagon, but he escaped unharmed. In the aftermath of the attacks, Rumsfeld refocused the military to concentrate on the invasion of Afghanistan and, in 2003, the invasion of Iraq.

As the US occupation of Iraq wore on, it became apparent that the regime of Iraqi dictator Saddam Hussein did not possess weapons of mass destruction. The Bush administration, and Rumsfeld in particular, came under increasing criticism because Hussein's possession of such weapons was said to be the main impetus for the US invasion. Rumsfeld was also criticized for the administration's inability to stem the spread of civil war in Iraq and for not being better able to prevent lethal attacks on US troops on the part of various insurgent groups.

President Bush continued to voice his support for Rumsfeld despite the growing number of complaints regarding his job as defense secretary, including those from former military leaders and members of the Republican Party. Nonetheless, Bush announced Rumsfeld's resignation the day after Democratic Party leaders regained control of both houses of Congress following the nationwide elections of November 7, 2006. The return of the Democratic majority in Congress was largely viewed as a public repudiation of the Bush administration's handling of the Iraq war. Robert Gates was appointed Rumsfeld's successor in December of 2006.

Impact

In addition to his successful career in the private sector, Rumsfeld had a significant political career, serving in many high-ranking positions, including the secretary of defense and the White House Chief of Staff. Rumsfeld is credited with modernizing the military—transforming it to meet twenty-first-century standards—and playing a major role in military actions after the September 11 terrorist attacks. Although lawsuits were filed against Rumsfeld in 2005 for his alleged involvement in abusive interrogation techniques used on suspected terrorists held at US detention centers overseas including Abu Ghraib, Iraq, and Guantánamo Bay, Cuba, a judge in the case ruled that he could not be held personally responsible.

Further Reading

Cockburn, Andrew. *Rumsfeld: His Rise, Fall, and Catastrophic Legacy.* New York: Scribner, 2007. Print.

Graham, Bradley. *By His Own Rules: The Ambitions, Successes, and Ultimate Failures of Donald Rumsfeld.* New York: Perseus, 2009. Print.

Scarborough, Rowan. *Rumsfeld's War: The Untold Story of America's Anti-Terrorist Commander.* Washington, DC: Regnery, 2004. Print.

Jennifer Monroe

S

■ Saddam Hussein capture

Definition: Search and eventual capture of the fugitive Iraqi dictator in wake of the US-led invasion of that country, which ousted him from power in 2003

While the US-led forces that invaded Iraq in the spring of 2003 faced few formidable military obstacles from the Iraqi army on their march to Baghdad, the main focus of the campaign, capturing and/or killing Iraqi dictator Saddam Hussein, remained unfinished for months after the war began.

In early 2003, the US government launched Operation Iraqi Freedom against the regime of Saddam Hussein, the dictatorial president of Iraq. In a radio address delivered on March 22, 2003, President George W. Bush clarified the purpose of the mission: to remove the weapons of mass destruction allegedly in Hussein's possession, to end Hussein's alleged support of al-Qaeda, and to remove Hussein from power and thereby liberate the Iraqi people. The initial air raids that destroyed crucial parts of Iraqi army logistics at the outset of the war also targeted Saddam Hussein and his sons and top lieutenants, Qusay and Uday Hussein. While these initial strikes were reported to have nearly struck the Iraqi president and several of his top aides on several occasions, these reports were ultimately proved to be unfounded.

Hussein remained a constant presence on Iraqi television in the hours leading up to the invasion, expressing confidence in his forces, most notably his elite Republican Guard. Upon the arrival of US forces in Baghdad, extensive searches of the former dictator's elaborate array of properties in and around Bagdad by invasion forces yielded few clues regarding his whereabouts. Hussein's continued elusion of coalition forces in the weeks following the invasion would become major problem for US generals who believed that his continued perseverance led to the possibility, however scant, of an eventual return to political or military power, which was potentially reducing support for US forces in the eyes of Iraqis who still feared the reach of Hussein's power. Coalition leaders also believed that Hussein's continued evasion was significantly contributing to the guerilla-style uprising encountered by invasion forces throughout the country, particularly in cities like Tikrit, which had been traditionally loyal to Hussein's regime.

In July 2003, a six-hour firefight between combatants and US Special Forces in the northern Iraqi city of Mosul resulted in the death of both of Saddam Hussein's fugitive sons. Two $15-million dollar rewards were given to anonymous sources in exchange for the information that lead to their whereabouts. The administration of President George W. Bush remained equally anxious to capture and or kill Hussein, particularly because, in the weeks following the invasion, the massive stockpiles of chemical and biological weapons that had been used to justify the invasion had yet to be found.

Fugitive Status

Hussein would evade authorities for several more months after the death of his sons. In interrogations following his arrest, Hussein would describe to the US Federal Bureau of Investigation how he eluded capture by traveling in borrowed vehicles and without the protective detail of aides that were constantly by his side during his time in power. US and Iraqi opposition forces were often under the belief that Hussein utilized decoys of himself during his escape and during his time in power, but Hussein himself refuted this assertion.

It is believed that Hussein spent his time as a fugitive in as many as thirty rudimentary hiding places throughout Iraq, many that comprised little more than a single room and rudimentary kitchen. According to a report in the *New York Times* following Hussein's arrest and detention, US military authorities claimed that Hussein's numerous hideouts may have been accessed by small boats via the Tigris River.

Capture

Nearly three months after the fall of Bagdad, following the interrogations of Hussein's extended family members and those with tribal connections to the former regime by US-led occupation forces, coalition intelligence began to center in on the dictator's location. On December 13, 2003, a contingent of US soldiers found Hussein on a remote farm outside of the city of Tikrit. The former dictator was found in a crude underground bunker armed with a pistol and surrounded by meager supplies. He did not resist, nor were any members of the US military injured in his capture. DNA tests conducted by US forces confirmed his identity. Hussein's disheveled physical appearance at the time of his capture came as a profound shock to the Iraqi people who for decades had seen him as a decorated military leader.

Hussein would spend over a year in the custody of US forces before he was allowed to face trial for crimes against humanity, which was conducted by the new Iraqi government in June 2005. The interrogation of Saddam Hussein shed light on numerous questions still held by both the US military and the American people. The former dictator stated that he was no longer in possession of weapons of mass destruction or the capability to produce such weapons prior to the invasion, and that the stockpile destroyed by US weapons inspectors prior to the US invasion had in fact been the last of his army's supply. Hussein also denied any affiliation, contact, or cooperation with al-Qaeda terrorist forces or their leader, Osama Bin Laden, whom he considered to be a religious fanatic. Hussein also remained unapologetic about the numerous atrocities he committed throughout his time in power. According to George Piro, the FBI's lead interrogator, Hussein deemed his 1988 use of chemical weapons against Kurdish Iraqis in the northern part of Iraq as "necessary." Hussein also made known his desire to eventually rebuild his chemical weapons program had the US invasion never occurred.

Saddam Hussein was found guilty of crimes against humanity at Iraq's High Tribunal on November 5, 2006. Though his preference was to die by firing squad, Hussein was sentenced to execution by hanging. While the majority of Iraqis rejoiced in the news of his death sentence, those who remained loyal to Hussein felt the verdict was the result of pressure by US military forces.

Impact

While the capture of Saddam Hussein was crucial to maintain the already tenuous domestic and international support for the US-led invasion of Iraq, it served for generations of Iraqis as a moment of transcendence for their country. While the United States and allied global coalition forces ultimately failed to find any of the massive stockpiles of weapons of mass destruction that had been the precursor for war, the second major reason for the invasion, ousting Hussein and liberating the Iraqi people from his tyrannical regime would be one of the Iraq War's few lasting successes.

Further Reading

Bennett, Brian. "Dispatch: Inside the Hunt for Saddam." *Time*. Time Inc., 28 July 2003. Web. 11 Nov. 2012. Offers an account of the ongoing effort to track down and capture Saddam Hussein.

Borger, Julian, and Gary Younge. "Dead: The Sons of Saddam." *Guardian*. Guardian News and Media Ltd., 23 July 2003. Web. 12 Nov. 2012. Announces the deaths of Qusay and Uday Hussein.

CBS News. "Interrogator Shares Saddam's Confessions." *60 Minutes*. CBS Interactive Inc., 11 Feb. 2009. Web. 11 Nov. 2012. Discusses the interrogation of Hussein by FBI agent George Piro during the former dictator's confinement.

MacFarquhar, Neil. "Saddam Hussein, Defiant Dictator who Ruled Iraq with Violence and Fear, Dies." *New York Times*. New York Times Co., 30 Dec. 2006. Web. 12 Nov. 2012. Describes the life, regime, and execution of the deposed Iraqi president.

Sachs, Susan and Kirk Semple. "Ex-Leader, Found Hiding in Hole, Is Detained Without a Fight." *New York Times*. New York Times Co., 14 Dec. 2003. Web. 12 Nov. 2012. Offers an account of the mission that led to the capture of Saddam Hussein.

John Pritchard

■ Same-sex marriage

Definition: Political and cultural debate throughout the 2000s amid repeated legislative victories surrounding the civic recognition of marriage between homosexual couples

The recognition of civil unions between homosexual couples by the Vermont state legislature in 2000 helped to spark a

decade-long cultural and political debate on the issue of same-sex marriage in the United States, which would draw interest throughout the world. The decision was also the first in numerous legislative actions across several states in favor of same-sex marriage. Canada would become the first country in the world to legalize same-sex marriage nation-wide in 2005. Same-sex marriage would become legally recognized in Mexico City, the capital city of Mexico, in 2009.

Early Landmark Legislation

In the spring of 2000, the Vermont State Supreme Court, with the support of Democratic Governor Howard Dean, ruled that same-sex couples were privy to the same benefits, tax entitlements, and other rights of marriage granted to heterosexual couples. The ruling made Vermont the first of the United States to grant full equal rights to gays and lesbians. Later that year, civil unions would be made legal in Vermont.

Vermont's landmark legislation would be echoed in neighboring Massachusetts in November 2003, when the supreme court in that state issued a four-to-three decision decreeing that homosexual couples had a constitutional right to marry. The court decreed that any attempt by the state to deny homosexuals the protections and benefits bestowed by civil marriage would be in violation of the Massachusetts Constitution, which, according the court, was meant to protect the equality of all its citizens.

The legislation passed in Massachusetts sparked nationwide political controversy and international intrigue surrounding the issue of same-sex marriage. Following the state's decision, President George W. Bush condemned the Massachusetts high court for acting in violation of his belief that marriage was a sacred institution between one man and one woman. Bush also pledged to work with leaders in Congress to embark on legislation defending the "sanctity" of marriage. Civil and gay rights groups, meanwhile, applauded the ruling as a victory for fairness and liberty.

When the Massachusetts state legislature failed to construct any legislative opposition against the state supreme court's decision by May of 2004, same-sex marriage became legal in the state.

Opposition against Equal Marriage

While proponents of same-sex marriage hoped that the legislation in Massachusetts would spark a nation-wide trend of support of marriage rights, it instead gave rise to a significant and vocal opposition nation-wide. Over three thousand gay and lesbian couples would seek marriage licenses in San Francisco, California, in the spring of 2004, in the hopes that that state would follow Massachusetts's lead toward legislative establishment. But in March of 2004, the California Supreme Court ordered a halt on the issuance of marriage licenses to homosexual couples while the state awaited the result of a proposed amendment to the US constitution banning same-sex marriage across the country.

In lockstep with his vocal opposition to the 2003 Massachusetts legislation, President Bush announced his support for a constitutional amendment banning same-sex marriage in February of 2004. In a speech in support of the proposed amendment, President Bush said, "Marriage cannot be severed from its natural roots without weakening the good influence of society."

Despite the support of the president, the proposed constitutional amendment banning same-sex marriage in the United States was blocked by the US Senate in July of 2004, when the measure received only forty-eight of the sixty votes needed for approval.

While the amendment was similarly rejected by the US House of Representatives later that year, opposition to same-sex marriage continued to prosper at the state legislative level. In November of 2004, eleven states—Arkansas, Georgia, Kentucky, Michigan, Mississippi, Montana, North Dakota, Ohio, Oklahoma, Oregon, and Utah—passed state amendments to their respective state constitutions outlining the definition of marriage as a union between a man and a woman only, thereby banning same-sex marriage. By 2005, eight other states would pass similar measures.

Many state legislatures bypassed popular Republican opposition to same-sex marriage by opting to pass laws legalizing civil unions, which ensure same-sex couples the same rights to workplace benefits as married heterosexual couples. Civil unions were legalized in Connecticut in 2005, while New Jersey followed suit in 2006.

Same-Sex Marriage in the 2008 Election Cycle

Marriage equality would remain a centrifugal issue in the 2008 national election cycle and a major point of opposition between the Republican presidential nominee Senator John McCain and his Democratic opponent Senator Barack Obama. Senator McCain publically announced his support for divisive 2008 state ballot initiatives in California, Arizona, and Florida that would bar same-sex marriage in those states. Senator Obama would stop short at voicing full support for marriage equality or plans to enact relevant legislation supporting it at the federal level. Obama would, however, deem attempts to ban same-sex marriage in state constitutions as "divisive and discriminatory."

Democrats nationwide declared similar stances for fear that banning same-sex marriage could potentially jeopardize the tax, health care, and inheritance rights made available to same-sex couples in states that had legalized or that were on the path to legalizing civil unions. Despite their opposition, the same-sex marriage bans were eventually enacted by voters in all three states that featured it as a ballot question in 2008.

Impact

By the end of 2009, same-sex marriage would be legal in five states: Vermont, Massachusetts, Connecticut, New Hampshire, and Iowa, as well as in the District of Columbia. While the issue of same-sex marriage would continue to be deliberated at the state legislative level in the United States, the Canadian federal government passed a bill legalizing same-sex marriage across all of Canada in 2005. By decade's end, the issue of marriage equality in the United States would be strictly divided across the lines of Democrats and Republicans.

While opponents of same-sex marriage continued to cite the historical value of "traditional" marriage across the spectrum of established religions, both homosexual and heterosexual advocates of same-sex marriage continued to view opposing legislation as a direct attempt to quash the ever-increasing civil liberties and societal acceptance earned by homosexuals in North American culture.

Further Reading

Belluck, Pam. "Same-Sex Marriage: The Overview; Marriage by Gays Gains Victory in Massachusetts." *New York Times.* New York Times Co., 19 Nov. 2003. Web. 26 Nov. 2012. Discusses reactions to the Massachusetts November 2003 court ruling and what that ruling might mean for the future regarding the legalization or banning of same-sex marriage.

"Bush Calls for Ban on Same-Sex Marriages." *CNN.* Cable News Network, 25 Feb. 2004. Web. 26 Nov. 2012. Discusses President George W. Bush's proposed constitutional amendment to ban same-sex marriage nationally.

Healy, Patrick. "Hopefuls Differ as They Reject Gay Marriage." *New York Times.* New York Times Co., 31 Oct. 2008. Web. 26 Nov. 2012. Reports on Obama and McCain's differing stances on same-sex marriage during the 2008 presidential race.

Krauss, Clifford. "Gay Marriage Is Extended Nationwide in Canada." *New York Times.* New York Times Co., 29 June 2005. Web. 26 Nov. 2012. Reports on Canada's 2005 ruling that made same-sex marriage legal for Canadian couples nationwide.

Pierceson, Jason, Adriana Piatti-Crocker, and Shawn Schulenberg. *Same-Sex Marriage in the Americas: Policy Innovation for Same-Sex Relationships.* Lanham: Lexington, 2010. Print. Discusses the increasing number of political policies regarding same-sex relationships in the Americas, including the various political, religious, legal, and cultural factors that have helped or prohibited the recognition of rights for same-sex couples.

Rauch, Jonathan. *Gay Marriage: Why It Is Good for Gays, Good for Straights, and Good for America.* New York: Holt, 2004. Print. Discusses the debate over same-sex marriage as it stood by the time of the book's publication. Argues that banning homosexuals from marrying would harm the institution of marriage, whereas legalizing same-sex marriage would benefit American communities at large.

Stevenson, Mark. "Mexico City Enacts Region's 1st Gay Marriage Law." *Boston Globe.* New York Times Co, 29 Dec. 2009. Web. 26 Nov. 2012. Reports on Mexico City's legalization of same-sex marriage in 2009.

John Pritchard

■ Sarbanes-Oxley Act of 2002

The Law: Federal legislation designed to increase levels of corporate responsibility and combat corporate and accounting fraud through increased corporate financial disclosure requirements
Date: July 30, 2002
Also known as: Sarbanes-Oxley; Sarbox; SOX

In the early 2000s, increasing and severe instances of corporate accounting and financial fraud were perpetrated by some of the United States' largest, most profitable corporations. Such scandals resulted in significant financial loss to their investors and a decrease in investor confidence. Implementing new and additional corporate reporting responsibilities, criminal penalties, and a new regulatory agency, the Sarbanes-Oxley Act of 2002 sought to create and enhance the financial reporting requirements for corporations, their key employees, and the accounting firms that audit and certify the accuracy of corporate financial information, and thereby restore corporate accountability and a level of confidence in consumers' investments.

In the early 2000s, the confidence of the American public in their financial investments had been shaken by several instances of corporate fraud perpetrated by some of the country's largest and most profitable publicly traded corporations. Between 2000 and 2002, companies such as Enron, WorldCom, and Tyco had engaged in acts of fraud primarily related to the reporting and accuracy of financial information they disclosed to their stockholders, who had relied on the accuracy of such information when making investment decisions. The case of Enron, which came to a head in late 2001 and early 2002, is representative of these acts of fraud. Through irregular accounting techniques, Enron hid certain debts or corporate losses in so-called special purpose entities, which resulted in those important losses not being included in Enron's financial statements released to the public. Accordingly, Enron's stock was highly overvalued. When the accounting practices came to light, Enron's stock plunged, and the millions of Enron shareholders were left with a stock that was only worth pennies per share. The widespread nature of these fraudulent activities resulted in decreased confidence in the securities market.

Foundation of the Act

As a result of these scandals, Congress convened hearings that resulted in the framework for what eventually became the act. The hearings, at which several financial experts testified, underscored numerous areas of concern in the financial reporting and accounting field. Specifically, the hearings and testimony revealed that auditors—the supposedly independent entities charged with accurately reporting financial information for companies—were often not independent, leading to conflicts of interest; that the United States Securities and Exchange Commission (SEC), the federal agency charged with enforcing securities and finance laws, was not adequately funded; that financial disclosure provisions

were inadequate; and that corporate governance procedures were insufficient.

In response to these findings, Democratic senator Paul Sarbanes and Republican representative Michael Oxley each submitted a version of what would eventually become the act in both Houses of Congress. Sarbanes's version of the act passed in the Senate 97–0; Oxley's version passed in the House of Representatives 334–90. After a committee was formed to reconcile the differences in the respective bills, the act was approved by both the Senate and the House, in a nearly unanimous combined vote of 423–3. Shortly thereafter, President George W. Bush signed the act into law. At the signing ceremony, Bush stated, "No more easy money for corporate criminals. Just hard time." He added that the act was "the most far-reaching reforms of American business practices since the time of Franklin Delano Roosevelt."

Specific Provisions of the Act

The act consists of eleven titles, or subdivisions. The first title of the act created the Public Company Accounting Oversight Board, a nongovernment entity with whom public accounting firms must register. The board established new quality control standards with respect to the auditing process, and it has the power to inspect public accountants, commence investigations, and sanction offending accountants for violation of standards.

The second title concerns auditor independence and prohibits specific activities, such as engaging in management functions for the company being audited. To avoid the possibility of collusion, the second title also states that an accounting firm may not audit a corporation for more than five consecutive years. Title 3 established an audit committee for every publicly traded company, whose members—primarily members of a corporation's board of directors—are held responsible for the selection and compensation of independent auditors and are ultimately responsible for the auditors' work. Finally, a separate provision of this title requires a corporation's principal officers to certify the integrity of the financial reports. The goal of title 3 is to prevent a corporation or its members from suggesting that it is unaware of fraudulent activities or false information contained in an audit.

Title 4 is one of the more important titles of the act. It requires companies to disclose so-called off-balance-sheet transactions—which were used by companies such as Enron to hide or disguise certain debts held—as well as stock transactions of certain members of the corporation. The title also prohibits personal loans to corporate executives from the corporation itself. Title 5 addresses conflicts of interest with securities analysts and was designed to restore investors' confidence in securities analysts. Among other provisions, the title prevents bankers or investment brokers from retaliating against a security analyst following a perceived negative research report that could have an adverse impact on the business.

The sixth title addresses the SEC's authority to regulate the provisions of the act. In particular, the SEC has the authority to censure individuals who have violated a securities law, and federal courts have the power to prevent the issuance of a penny stock, which is a low-value stock that is particularly susceptible to those seeking to commit securities fraud. Title 7 primarily concerns research and reporting by the Government Accounting Office (GAO) and the SEC addressing investment banks and agencies that issue credit ratings. That title also required research and reporting on past instances of alleged securities and investment fraud in the years 1998 to 2001.

Title 8, another important provision of the act, concerns criminal liability for those who engage in corporate or accounting fraud. Specifically, that title establishes a prison term of up to twenty years for anyone who knowingly alters or destroys a document pertaining to investigations or bankruptcy proceedings, requires retention of corporate audit records for a minimum of five years with prison terms for violators, and provides legal protection for "whistle-blowers"—employees who report potentially illegal business activities of their employer. The ninth title increases the criminal penalties for those who attempt or conspire to commit white-collar crime to align with the penalties for those who actually complete such crimes. Title 10 states the Senate's opinion that chief executive officers should sign their companies' federal tax returns. Finally, title 11, among other provisions, gives the SEC the ability to freeze the funds of a corporation suspected of having committed securities fraud.

Impact

The perceived success or failure of the act has been widely debated by scholars, economists, and politicians. On the one hand, it is important to note that the act has had significant financial costs for companies in terms of compliance with the new provisions. Congressman Ron Paul cited in 2005 that the act had cost companies an average of five million dollars in compliance expenses the previous year and claimed it "had increased costs associated with being a publicly held company by 130 percent." While many viewed the compliance measures as important and necessary in the wake of scandals such as Enron, others believed that the increased compliance costs made doing business as a publicly owned company in the United States too costly, as costs ultimately were passed onto consumers and quelled both private investment and job creation. Moreover, critics note the diminishing number of initial public offerings—the first sale of shares of a stock in a company going public—following the implementation of the act. Opponents of the act also contend that the Lehman Brothers accounting scandal, in which that company altered quarterly loss figures to make such losses seem less severe than they actually were, is evidence that the act is not always successful in preventing corporate accounting fraud.

Conversely, many praised the act as a necessary government reaction to the widespread corporate scandals of the early 2000s. In a July 25, 2012, opinion piece for the *New York Times*, attorney Michael W. Peregrine stated that the act "has increased the accountability expectations we have of directors and officers, and their legal and accounting advisors as well." Accordingly, some of its success is not readily apparent; rather, the benefits of the act may be seen in the reduction in the number or severity of instances of corporate accounting fraud. Additionally, other countries—competitors of the United States with respect to the private sale of goods and services—have implemented provisions of the act in their own regulatory schemes, suggesting that the act and its goals are noteworthy. Finally, many view the act as being primarily responsible for the restoration of investor confidence in publicly traded companies.

Further Reading

Anand, Sanjay, and Jayne Wilson. *The Sarbanes-Oxley Act: An Introduction*. Zaltbommel: Van Haren, 2008. Print. Soxbok Ser. A comprehensive guide to the act that covers all provisions and provides information from legal, finance, and accounting perspectives.

Bainbridge, Stephen M. *The Complete Guide to Sarbanes-Oxley: Understanding how Sarbanes-Oxley Affects Your Business.* Avon: Adams, 2007. Print. A well-written and comprehensive guide to compliance with the act, providing practical advice and information geared toward business owners and professionals.

Butler, Henry N., and Larry E. Ribstein. *The Sarbanes-Oxley Debacle: What We've Learned; How to Fix It.* Washington, DC: AEI, 2006. Print. Details the business effects of the act, arguing that the act constrains corporations, is detrimental to investors, and could result in excessive litigation.

Lander, Guy. *What is Sarbanes-Oxley?* Madison: Mc-Graw, 2004. Print. A primer on the act directed to employees and officers of corporations, but written a manner that is easily understood by students and professionals alike.

Andrew E. Walter, JD

■ Satellite radio

Definition: Satellite radio is a broadcasting medium that uses satellites to broadcast a radio signal concurrently across an entire country. Unlike terrestrial radio, which is free for the public, satellite radio requires a paid subscription and proprietary equipment or software. Unlike terrestrial radio, satellite radio is not subject to Federal Communications Commission (FCC) content regulations.

Satellite radio was conceived as an alternative to traditional AM and FM stations. It addressed several issues consumers had with existing radio stations, notably the small broadcast area of most stations, the presence of commercials, and the limited variety of programming.

In the 1990s, satellite companies, looking for additional applications of their technology, convinced the FCC to set aside a portion of the 2.3 GHz S band (a section of the spectrum previously reserved for radar, NASA communications, and wireless network signals) for a digital audio radio service. In 1997, two licenses were awarded to XM Satellite Radio and CD Radio (later renamed Sirius Satellite Radio).

Launch and Initial Reaction
In September 2001, XM launched its service in two markets, San Diego and Dallas. After a promising initial response, it made the service available nationwide in November. In February 2002, Sirius launched in four states, followed by a nationwide rollout completed in July. Both companies offered a wider variety of programming than what was typically available on terrestrial radio, including stations focused solely on electronic music, comedy, and reggae. The services were successful; XM gained over thirty thousand subscribers within the first eight weeks of operation.

While subscriptions continued to increase, both companies realized that in order to gain more listeners they had to enter the space in which most Americans listened to terrestrial radio: their cars. XM announced a partnership with General Motors in early 2002. By the start of the next year, XM receivers came standard in vehicles from Volkswagen, Toyota, and Honda. Sirius followed suit, placing their receivers in vehicles made by BMW, Dodge, and Ford.

Sensing yet another potential market, both companies entered negotiations for broadcast sports rights. In December 2003, Sirius announced that they had made a $220 million deal to be the exclusive satellite radio broadcaster for the National Football League (NFL) through 2010. XM responded by entering negotiations with Major League Baseball (MLB). In 2004, they announced a $650 million eleven-year broadcast contract.

Censorship Refugees
In 2004, radio broadcaster WNEW dropped talk show hosts Gregg "Opie" Hughes and Anthony Cumia after they hosted a controversial segment that provoked protests from the Catholic League. Shortly afterward, the *Opie and Anthony* show moved to XM. Since the FCC had no control over the aired content on satellite radio, the hosts felt they would be able to say or do what they wanted without fear of repercussions.

The year 2005 saw a significant censorship crackdown on radio and television following singer Janet Jackson's brief moment of accidental exposure during the Super Bowl XXXVIII halftime show. This prompted "shock jock" Howard Stern to announce that he disliked being on a medium that was subject to government censorship. In 2006, he moved his radio show to Sirius. The company awarded Stern with a $100 million operating budget, as well as stock bonuses. In exchange, a large number of subscribers joined Sirius to listen to Stern's show.

While satellite radio content is not susceptible to FCC regulation, hosts are still required to comply with certain decency regulations. Following an *Opie and Anthony* segment in which a character from the show made offensive comments about then secretary of state Condoleezza Rice and First Lady Laura Bush, XM suspended the radio hosts for thirty days. Fans of the show were outraged, and many canceled their subscriptions in protest of the suspension.

Merger

Despite successful placement in vehicles and increased subscriptions, and a large line-up of celebrity-hosted shows and sports programming, by 2007 both Sirius and XM faced bankruptcy due to mounting corporate debt. On February 19, the two companies announced plans to merge, citing that exclusive content rights were harmful to both companies, since they forced users to choose one or the other. Additionally, the merger allowed the companies to reduce staff and budget in redundant areas. Content previously exclusive to each network (such as MLB and NFL games) became accessible to all subscribers for an additional monthly fee.

Previous FCC rulings stipulated that such a merger would violate licensing and monopoly regulations. However, the companies protested the ruling. In June 2007, the FCC announced that it would review the potential merger and provide a verdict within six months, but no decision was made by the deadline. To demonstrate support for the merger, the companies held shareholder votes. Shareholders approved the proposed merger by a wide margin. In July 2008, the FCC finally approved the merger, on the conditions that the companies keep as many channels from both providers as possible and that subscriber rates not be increased for three years. On July 29, the companies merged under the name SiriusXM. Nonetheless, the new company still experienced financial difficulties. In February 2009, it was announced that SiriusXM had hired financial advisers in preparation for a potential bankruptcy filing. Media mogul John Malone rescued the company by providing $500 million in exchange for 40 percent ownership.

Impact

SiriusXM continues to broadcast. Since the merger, it has dropped some radio channels from its lineup, but it continues to offer a broader variety of programming than terrestrial radio. Some content is available to subscribers on demand. Though the merger freed up a satellite radio license, no company has applied for it, and SiriusXM remains the sole satellite radio company in America. In response to satellite radio's nationwide availability and genre offerings, terrestrial broadcasters ClearChannel and CBS have created mobile phone applications and streaming websites, making a wide selection of their stations available to smartphone users and radio listeners nationwide.

Further Reading

Edwards, Bob. *A Voice in the Box: My Life in Radio.* Lexington: UP of Kentucky, 2011. Print. A biographical account of a radio personality who moved from terrestrial to satellite radio.

Keith, Michael C. *The Radio Station: Broadcast, Satellite and Internet.* Burlington: Focal, 2010. Print. An overview of satellite and terrestrial radio stations and the effects of government regulations on them.

Lin, Carolyn A. "Satellite Radio Adoption Demand." *Journal of Broadcasting & Electronic Media* 54.2 (2010): 265–81. Print. An analysis of consumer reaction to satellite radio.

Sadler, Roger L. *Electronic Media Law.* Thousand Oaks: Sage, 2005. Print. An explanation of court rulings and laws on electronic media, including satellite radio.

Sidak, J. Gregory, and Hal J. Singer. "Evaluating Market Power with Two-Sided Demand and Preemptive Offers to Dissipate Monopoly Rent." *Journal of Competition Law and Economics* 4.3 (2008): 697–751. Print. An evaluation of the repercussions and effects of the SiriusXM satellite radio merger.

Leland Spencer

■ *Saw* franchise

Definition: The *Saw* franchise is a series of seven horror movies that began in 2004 and ended in 2010

The Saw *films and their accompanying video games and comic books make up one of the most financially successful horror franchises of all time. Despite receiving mainly negative reviews from critics, the* Saw *films remained lucrative at the box office. From 2004 to 2010, a* Saw *film was released in theaters every October on the Friday before Halloween.*

Created by Australian filmmakers James Wan and Leigh Whannell, the series of *Saw* films were extremely graphic in their depiction of physical and psychological torture. To help get the first *Saw* film financed, Wan and Whannell shot a short film in 2003 to show production companies. They took their short film, which featured the iconic "Billy" puppet seen in the films, to Lions Gate Entertainment who gave Wan and Whannell $1.2 million to create their feature film. The first *Saw* film was released in October 2004 and grossed over $100 million worldwide. Only one of the seven *Saw* films, *Saw VI* (2009), made less than $100 million. This installment only grossed $68.2 million, which was still a financial success against its $11 million dollar budget.

The primary focus of the *Saw* series is the fictional Jigsaw Killer, whose real name is John Kramer (portrayed by Tobin Bell). The Jigsaw Killer abducts people and then sets them up in deadly traps that he feels reflect their personal flaws. The only way out of the traps is to undergo severe physical or psychological pain. In the films, Kramer is a former civil engineer who is suffering from an inoperable brain tumor. He survived a suicide attempt, which gave him a renewed appreciation of life. The motive for his actions is to force people into respecting their own lives through his elaborate torture traps. When people fail these tests, he cuts a puzzle piece out of their flesh, inspiring his nickname, the Jigsaw Killer. Though he dies in *Saw III* (2006), Kramer still appears in the subsequent films, mainly through flashbacks.

Other actors that appeared in the *Saw* films included Danny Glover, Shawnee Smith, and Donnie Wahlberg. Wahlberg played the recurring character of police detective Eric Matthews in three of the *Saw* films.

Impact

Each of the seven *Saw* films received predominantly negative reviews from critics, but were applauded by fans of the horror genre. The character of John Kramer was especially liked by fans, with many seeing him as one of the most terrifying and complex villains in contemporary horror cinema. The films popularized the horror subgenre known as "torture porn," a term disliked by the filmmakers but one that would attract a large mainstream audience. The financially lucrative *Saw* films brought graphic depictions of torture and violence to a mainstream audience once a year, for seven years in a row.

Further Reading

Briefel, Aviva, and Sam J. Miller, eds. *Horror after 9/11: World of Fear, Cinema of Terror.* Austin: U of Texas P, 2011. Print.

Derry, Charles. *Dark Dreams 2.0: A Psychological History of the Modern Horror Film from the 1950s to the 21st Century.* Jefferson: McFarland, 2009. Print.

Patrick G. Cooper

■ School violence

Definition: Acts of violence that occur on school grounds; this includes emotional and physical bullying, cyberbullying, fighting, rape, and homicide

Since the April 1999 shootings at Columbine High School in Jefferson County, Colorado, in which twelve students and one teacher were killed before the two gunmen committed suicide, national attention has been given to the subjects of violence and bullying in US schools. Concern grew during the 2000s as reported incidents of school violence grew at an alarming rate. Bullying also became a major issue as more students reported being harassed at school and on social-media websites. Raising awareness about potentially violent behavior and intervention became strong focus points of school violence studies.

From 2000 to 2009, there were more than two hundred school-associated violent deaths. This tally factors in shootings, stabbings, fights, and suicides performed on school grounds. The highest percentage of deaths during the decade occurred from gunshot wounds. Violent deaths in schools during the decade included not just students, but also teachers and parents. The Centers for Disease Control and Prevention (CDC) performed research on school violence throughout the decade. They found that a large percentage of school-associated violent deaths occurred during transitionary times of the school day such as lunch and in-between periods. Their research also showed that rates of violent deaths were higher for males, secondary school students, and students in central cities.

Perhaps most alarming are their findings that nearly 50 percent of perpetrators of homicides in schools had provided some kind of warning sign before the event, such as a note or an online message. This fact has left many people concerned that teachers and school authorities are not taking warning signs seriously enough to prevent violent deaths in schools. The yearly report "Indicators of School Crime and Safety" published by the Institute of Education Sciences stated that during the 2008–9 school year there were thirty-eight in-school violent deaths.

Virginia Tech Massacre

The worst school shooting in US history occurred during the 2000s. The incident occurred on April 16, 2007, at the Virginia Polytechnic Institute and State University in Blacksburg, Virginia. A twenty-three-year-old undergraduate student named Seung-Hui Cho shot and killed thirty-two people and injured an additional seventeen others before committing suicide. The shootings took place at two areas on campus with several hours in between each incident. This time lapse in between the shootings caused many to criticize the school and police for not warning students of potential danger. It was later revealed that Cho had a long history of depression and mental illness.

The incident caused international debates over US gun laws, the responsibility of the college administration, and the treatment of the mentally ill in the United States. The college administrators received a great amount of criticism for not taking certain actions that may have reduced the number of casualties. Media outlets also received criticism for airing portions of Cho's filmed manifesto. Virginia Governor Tim Kaine created a panel to investigate the various aspects of the tragedy. The panel concluded that the school and police did not sufficiently notify students of the situation after the first shootings that killed two people. In the end, however, the panel stated that the massacre was nobody's fault but Cho's.

The tragedy did prompt President George W. Bush to sign into law the first federal gun control measure in over a decade. This measure strengthened existing federal restrictions on handgun purchases by offering federal grants of up to $1.3 billion to states in order to improve the tracking of individuals who have a recorded mental illness, which makes them ineligible to buy a gun. Many agreed that if this federal measure had been in effect prior to April 2007 the tragedy would have never taken place.

Northern Illinois University Shooting

The second-deadliest school shooting of the 2000s occurred on February 14, 2008, at Northern Illinois University (NIU) in DeKalb, Illinois. That afternoon, twenty-seven-year-old graduate student Steven Kazmierczak entered a lecture hall that held approximately 120 students. He fired at them and the instructor with a shotgun and several pistols. He shot a total of twenty-one people, killing five, before shooting himself.

Kazmierczak had been treated for mental illness while in high school, but campus police and peers at NIU described him as a good student. His girlfriend, Jessica Baty, stated that during their two-year relationship she had never seen him exhibit any kind of violent behavior. However, leading up to the shooting, Kazmierczak stopped taking his prescribed antidepressant medications. Afterward, police took possession of several parcels he had sent Jennifer. Some of the contents included ammunition and a book on serial killers.

Bullying

As early as 2001 studies were finding that bullying in US schools was becoming an increasingly serious problem. A survey that year funded by the National Institute of Child Health and Human Development found that almost 16 percent out of the 15,686 school children surveyed were victims of bullying at the hands of their classmates. Some 10 percent of these children claimed they had been bullied but had not bullied others. Another 13 percent of students claimed to never have been bullied themselves, but confessed to bullying other students. Researchers have defined bullying as any act purposely meant to inflict bodily or emotional harm. These acts include teasing, hitting, and shoving.

With the rise of social media and more students carrying cellular phones, a new form of bullying arose that became known as "cyberbullying." Cyberbullying involves the use of computers, social media, cellphones, and other electronics to cause emotional harm. Cyberbullies use these outlets to humiliate, threaten, and denigrate fellow students. Reports of cyberbullying by students gradually increased over the decade. According to the 2009 report of the

"Indicators of School Crime and Safety," 6 percent of students ages twelve to eighteen reported being cyberbullied.

Profiling Research

Due to the extreme number of violent school incidents in the 2000s, research on school violence increased a great deal during the decade. Several studies were conducted involving the risk factors for perpetrating violence and how best to intervene before a violent act can occur. A lot of this research involved how to profile potential perpetrators. Many government organizations including the CDC conducted detailed research on the subject of profiling.

Materials published by the CDC list specific risk factors to look for in profiling potential perpetrators of school violence. These factors include poor academic performance, poor behavioral control, and high emotional distress. However, the US Secret Service conducted studies through which they found that there is no easy way to profile a potential perpetrator. They claim that any profile would fit numerous students, making the profile counterproductive. The Federal Bureau of Investigation (FBI) has also stressed the importance of assessing critical threats in schools.

The FBI has presented a list warning signs to help prevent school violence. They identified four critical areas to look into: family dynamics, school dynamics, social dynamics, and characteristics/personality. This includes determining whether the student comes from a neglectful or an abusive home. The FBI notes that many of the more publicized school shootings occur in middle-class neighborhoods and some people contend that uninvolved or neglectful parents in these neighborhoods should be held partly responsible for school violence.

One important warning sign stressed by the FBI is the casual disclosure of negative feelings by a student. Such a sign could include descriptions of negative fantasies or intentions, whether in letters, videos, or drawings. A study by the American Medical Association found that nearly 50 percent of perpetrators of school homicides presented a warning sign of some sort.

Preventative Measures

As awareness of school violence increased throughout the 2000s, so did the strategies and programs to help prevent these incidents. Besides the installation of metal detectors at school entrances and hiring security guards at some schools, there have been several studies on the various factors that could possibly lead to incidents of school violence and steps to prevent violent incidents before they happen.

The US Secret Service developed a threat-assessment system that involves a collaborative effort between law enforcement and educators. This system features six principles, including the use of multiples sources of information such as students and teachers, knowledge of the student's environment, and the use of warning signs as guidelines, never absolutes.

School resource officer (SRO) programs expanded throughout the 2000s in reaction to the increase in school violence. These programs assign law-enforcement officers to elementary, middle, and high schools to help prevent harmful incidents and to promote a healthy relationship between students, educators, and law enforcement. SRO programs also offer counseling to students, educators, and parents. An aim of the SRO programs is to establish a safety plan with the school and officers to respond to threat assessments and emergency situations.

One popular preventative measure during the 2000s was the implementation of zero-tolerance policies. Under these policies, students, parents, and staff are punished for any infraction of a school rule regardless of the circumstances. This includes the possession of drugs, weapons, and any other item illegal on school grounds. Under zero-tolerance rules, these infractions can lead to immediate suspension or even expulsion. The policies have come under criticism by those who believe they lead to flagrant punishments. Critics also argue that the policies could lead to a decline in students and educators reporting illegal behavior. In 2006, the American Bar Association (ABA) found discrimination in zero-tolerance policies through a study that found that minority students are more likely to be punished than white students. Studies from the ABA as well as the American Psychological Association concluded that there is no evidence that zero-tolerance policies effectively prevent incidents of school violence.

Impact

The rise in school violence in the United States during the 2000s led to several debates on the both the community and federal level. Tragedies have led to the modification of gun laws and the reexamination of the treatment of those who suffer from mental illness. Prevention of these fatal and nonfatal acts of school violence became the subject of several studies from both government and nongovernment entities. While no absolutes were found in how to prevent an incident of school violence, the amount of awareness raised on the subject has been important to building collaborative efforts to improve school safety.

Further Reading

Fast, Jonathan. *Ceremonial Violence: Understanding Columbine and Other School Rampage Shootings.* New York: Overlook, 2009. Print. This book examines thirteen school shootings and examines the connections between the perpetrators from a psychological standpoint.

Newman, Katherine S., et al. *Rampage: The Social Roots of School Shootings.* New York: Basic, 2005. Print. This book looks at several school shootings in the United States and examines the communities in which they occurred.

Roy, Lucinda. *No Right to Remain Silent: The Tragedy at Virginia Tech.* New York: Three Rivers, 2009. Print. The former chair of the English Department at Virginia Tech wrote this book about the shooter, Cho, and her attempts to counsel him.

Thomas, R. Murray. *Violence in America's Schools: Understanding, Prevention, and Responses.* Westport: Praeger, 2009. Print. This book uses case studies to examine the problem of violence of schools and also discusses consequences and treatment of the problem.

Patrick G. Cooper

■ Schwarzenegger, Arnold

Identification: Austrian-born American actor and politician
Born: July 30, 1947; Thal, Austria

Arnold Schwarzenegger made his mark as an actor as the star of a string of popular action films. The former bodybuilder is arguably one of the most famous people in the world. In 2003, he was elected governor of California and subsequently reelected in 2006.

Arnold Schwarzenegger's first two films of the 2000s did not fare well at the box office. *The 6th Day* (2000), a science-fiction thriller about a man who is unwill

Arnold Schwarzenegger. (Courtesy Lon R. Fong)

ingly cloned, was not well received. Audiences were similarly reserved about *Collateral Damage* (2002), about a man seeking revenge after losing his wife and child to a terrorist attack. Although the film finished production before the terrorist attacks of September 11, 2001, its release was delayed in order to avoid offending audiences with images of explosions and violence. Nevertheless, the film was neither commercially nor critically successful.

In 2003, Schwarzenegger reprised his role as cyborg John Connor in *Terminator 3: Rise of the Machines.* Connor is on the run from a female cyborg assassin in the film, set several years after the previous Terminator film. While the movie received positive reviews, it did poorly at American box offices.

In 2003, during a guest appearance on *The Jay Leno Show,* Schwarzenegger announced his candidacy in the California gubernatorial recall election. Although his announcement surprised many, Schwarzenegger successfully leveraged his movie star status and several prominent endorsements to win the recall election. In homage to his previous career as an action film star, Governor Schwarzenegger began being referred to in the media as the Governator.

During his tenure as governor, Schwarzenegger helped to pass important legislation aimed at balancing California's budget. He was also a passionate supporter of stem cell research and the fight against global warming. He went against his fellow Republicans in 2006, when he allocated $150 million in funding to stem cell research. Schwarzenegger was reelected that same year.

Despite Schwarzenegger's efforts as governor, California's budget deficit continued to grow. He attempted to increase taxes to cover the gap, but most of his proposals were denied. Schwarzenegger's popularity as governor began to wane as his second term came to an end. Following the end of his tenure as governor, Schwarzenegger returned to acting.

Impact

With one of the most recognizable faces in the world, Arnold Schwarzenegger is one of the most successful actors in the entertainment industry. In addition to his foray into state politics, he is a successful businessman. Schwarzenegger is a founder of the international restaurant chain, Planet Hollywood.

Further Reading

"Arnold Schwarzenegger." *New York Times.* New York Times, 18 May 2011. Web. 8 Oct. 2012.

"Arnold Schwarzenegger: Biography." *Schwarzenegger.com.* Arnold Schwarzenegger, 2012. Web. 8 Oct. 2012.

Cait Caffrey

■ Science and technology

Definition: Science is a branch of human learning that seeks to define, explore, and understand the properties and processes of the physical universe. Technology can be defined as the application of scientific knowledge for practical purposes.

Major scientific discoveries and the technological innovations that emerge from applied science help to define historic periods. For instance, the 2000s have been grouped by some historians into what is sometimes called the digital age, which can be partially defined by the advent of the Internet and the shift toward digital information storage and transfer. The scientific and technological developments achieved each year have a transformative effect that radiates through society, often touching every level of human existence.

Space Exploration

One of the major areas of scientific development during the 2000s came in the field of space explora-

tion. In 2005, astrophysicists discovered Eris, an astronomical body with a mass larger than that of Pluto, which was long considered the ninth planet of the solar system. Rather than designating Eris as the tenth planet, astrophysicists created a new, more specific definition of what constitutes a planet, which led to Pluto being redefined as a dwarf planet. The decision to "demote" Pluto initiated a global debate and redefined the solar system as having eight planets and two dwarf planets, rather than the traditional nine planets taught in schools for decades.

In addition, explorations of Mars intensified in the 2000s with the landing of the Mars Exploration Rover (MER) in 2004. The MER landing produced the first quality images of the Martian surface, which circulated through the scientific and mainstream communities. In late 2008, scientists announced that they had definitively discovered frozen water, or ice, beneath the Martian surface. This discovery could play a major role in future efforts to colonize Mars, constituting a resource that could prove invaluable to colonization efforts.

Another major development in the 2000s was the beginning of space tourism in 2001, with American engineer and multimillionaire Denis Tito becoming the first man to privately fund a voyage into space. Over the remainder of the decade, there were six additional privately funded voyages into space. Prices for space tourism increased over the decade from $20 million to over $40 million for a single passenger. By 2010, a number of companies were in the process of developing spacecraft or programs aimed at space tourism, and a few companies had released information on their intention to develop facilities, such as hotels, for space tourists.

In the 1990s, astrophysicists first reported strong scientific evidence for the existence of planets orbiting other stars in the Milky Way Galaxy; in 2000, astronomers made the first conclusive measurements of an exoplanet, or extrasolar planet, in the universe. By 2010, more than four hundred exoplanets had been identified in the galaxy using NASA's Hubble Space Telescope and the Kepler Space Telescope launched in 2009. The first images of exoplanets were obtained by NASA scientists in 2008, making global headline news. Infrared images from the Keck Observatory showed three planets orbiting the star designated HR 8799, approximately 150 light years from Earth.

Astronauts Andrew Feustel (left) and John Grunsfeld work to upgrade the Hubble Space Telescope. (NASA/Getty Images News/Getty Images)

Genomics, Genetic Research, and Human Origins

The Human Genome Project, a multidisciplinary scientific investigation aimed at discovering the structure of the human genetic code, produced the first, rough version of the human genome in 2000, followed three years later by a more exact and complete version of the genome. The genome project and the study of genomics are among the most important developments of the late twentieth and early twenty-first centuries, opening the door to a broad spectrum of scientific developments in medicine and genetic engineering. In 2005, scientists launched a related project, known as the Genographic Project, which aims to link the human genome to historic patterns of migration and development in an effort to create a genomic history of the human species.

As scientists began to use genomics to investigate human origins, anthropological discoveries also helped to bring scientists closer to understanding the history of the species. In 2009, scientists discovered the first remains of a new species, *Ardipithecus ramidus*, nicknamed "Ardi," which is the oldest ancestor of the human species yet discovered. The 4.4 million-year-old remains indicate that the species walked upright but also climbed trees frequently and had a varied diet. Anthropologists further speculated that Ardi may represent the period in history when males and females first began living in pairs rather than in breeding groups.

Also during the 2000s, physicians reported the first successful use of gene therapy to treat disease, and gene therapy research remained a major avenue of medical investigation throughout the decade. While gene alteration produced a large number of potential practical benefits, scientists also demonstrated the ability to alter genes in novel ways, such as creating mice and fish that glow when exposed to ultraviolet light.

In the early 2000s, scientists were conducting genetic research into gene therapy using embryonic stem cells, which are undifferentiated cells taken from embryos at an early stage of development. The use of embryonic stem cells was controversial because many felt that the derivation of the cells constituted a moral crime akin to murder. Many of these objections came via the portion of the population opposed to abortion. In 2007, scientists demonstrated the ability to derive stem cells from adult cell sources, thereby avoiding the controversy over the use of embryonic stem cells. By 2009, scientists were using adult stem cells for a variety of projects, including the development of new gene therapy and gene replacement procedures believed to have the potential to address a variety of inherited diseases and genetic disorders.

Communication and Social Networking

Personal communication and connectivity increased rapidly during the 2000s, driven by widespread use of cellular phone technology. Text messaging was introduced to the United States by AT&T in the year 2000 and was soon offered by competing cellular service providers. During the course of the decade, text communication evolved from a specialized feature on some phones to become one of the most basic forms of general communication, on par with voice communication and e-mail.

Another notable development in cellular technology that occurred in the 2000s was the popularization and spread of smartphone technology. Smartphones combine technology for personal computers with cellular phone features. By the middle of the 2000s, smartphones had become a major facet of the cell phone market. Major innovations in the smartphone market include the introduction of the Blackberry family of devices in 1999 and the debut of Apple's iPhone in 2007. By 2010, most cell phone manufacturers were integrating certain smartphone features, such as e-mail and web access into most of the commercially available cell phones.

The use of Internet and cellular technology greatly increased during the 2000s, both among American users and throughout the world. According to the International Telecommunications Union, the percentage of individuals using cellular phones worldwide increased from 15 to 77 percent of the global population between 2001 and 2010.

Another innovation of the decade was the advent and spread of social networking websites on the Internet. The first site to gain widespread use was Friendster, which debuted in 2003. Myspace, which

also debuted in 2003, was the most visited social networking site in the world until 2008, when it was eclipsed in rank by Facebook, a social networking site that originated in 2004 and was initially aimed at Ivy League college students. By the end of the decade, Facebook was one of the most often visited Internet sites in the world and the most popular social networking site. In 2006, a new trend in social networking, sometimes known as "microblogging," was initiated with the advent of Twitter, a site that allows users to communicate to groups of other users using short, instant messages broadcast over the Internet.

The advent and spread of social networking fundamentally changed the way that people around the world communicate and stay connected. While social media initially appealed to younger persons, eventually people of all ages began using social networking as an alternative and supplement to e-mail and telephone communication. By the end of the decade, social media had become an important part of global marketing, allowing businesses and entrepreneurs to utilize social networks for advertisement and promotion.

Internet Technologies and File Sharing

While the advent and spread of the Internet was one of the technological developments that defined the 1990s, the 2000s saw the development of broadband Internet technology and wireless Internet for private use. These two innovations greatly improved both Internet speed for many users and access to the Internet around the world. The United States Census Bureau figures published in 2010 indicated that the proportion of American homes with Internet access increased from 42 to more than 70 percent during the decade. According to the International Telecommunications Union, the percentage of households utilizing the Internet worldwide grew from just over 8 percent to more than 29 percent from 2001 to 2010.

Also notable during the 2000s was the controversy over Internet file sharing. The website Napster, which emerged in 1999, allowed users to upload and share music files via the Internet. Napster was forced to close in 2001, due to legal actions on the part of music publishers. Nevertheless, the site became the forerunner for a file sharing phenomenon that continued throughout the decade. In addition to music, file sharing sites allowed users to share videos and a variety of other digital products, thereby stimulating a major legal battle between representatives of the music and film industries and websites hosting file sharing services.

As judicial authorities across the United States ruled that sharing copyrighted material was illegal and forced the closure of certain peer-to-peer file sharing sites, new methods of sharing files were created, including torrents, which allow participants to share pieces of files rather than complete files, thereby spreading the guilt of sharing across users and preventing any single user from being guilty of sharing a complete, copyrighted file. Though torrents make use of a loophole in the laws, music and film industry representatives have continued their efforts to shut down torrent sharing sites in addition to direct file sharing sites.

Studies on the economic impact of file sharing have been largely inconclusive. For instance, North Carolina State University researcher Robert G. Hammond released a study in 2012 indicating that file sharing may actually stimulate record sales for well-known and established artists, though Hammond's research also indicated that emerging artists will suffer from reduced sales due to peer-to-peer sharing.

Also during the 2000s, the global market for entertainment rapidly shifted toward the sale of digital movies, music, and even digital-format books. Apple introduced its iPod family of digital music players in 2001, followed by a variety of competing products from other manufacturers. During the course of the decade, digital music sales grew from 5 percent to more than 50 percent of the market for music around the world. In 2007, Internet retailer Amazon released the Kindle, a device for storing and reading digital books. By 2010, the digital book market in the United States was approaching sales of traditional book formats and, in 2011, Amazon Marketplace announced that sales of digital books through its website had eclipsed sales of traditional books for the first time in US book market history.

Climate Change and Automotive Evolution

While environmental concern about global warming and climate change began in the 1970s and intensified in the 1980s and 1990s, it was not until the 2000s that climate change entered the global consciousness as the premier environmental issue of the modern world. The Intergovernmental Panel on Climate Change (IPCC), established in 1988, was one of the key players in the ongoing climate change debate, helping to fund and publish a variety of scientific studies pertaining to climate change around the world. In 2007, the IPCC shared the Nobel Prize with former vice president Al Gore for helping to inform the world about the potential dangers of climate change.

As mainstream acceptance of climate change intensified during the 2000s, so too did arguments stating that climate change had been overestimated or misrepresented by the media and the IPCC in an effort to gain support for environmental initiatives. A number of corporations in the United States, including prominent corporations involved in oil production, were later linked to funding information aimed at contradicting the prevailing view of climate change promoted by the IPCC and other scientific bodies. Some of the evidence against the IPCC stance on climate change came from scientists with opposing views on the sources and development of climate change patterns.

The climate change debate helped to fuel international concern about the pollution produced by the burning of fossil fuels. These factors played a role in the development of the hybrid automobile market, which produces vehicles that use a combination of electricity and fossil fuels and therefore consumes less fuel than traditional vehicles. Interest in hybrid vehicles, though criticized by some in the environmental communities as a relatively minor step toward addressing automotive pollution, grew during the decade after Toyota introduced the Toyota Prius to worldwide markets in 2000, constituting the first commercially available hybrid car on the general market.

Impact

Many of the key scientific and technological developments of the 2000s represent fundamental alterations in the scientific understanding of the universe and similarly profound changes to human society. The rapid spread and growing dominance of the Internet as an avenue of education, commerce, and communication has had massive impacts on human culture around the world, as has the growth of cellular phone technology and social media. The shift toward digital transmission and storage of information is a development as significant to human culture as the advent of television or radio communication in previous generations, and the 2000s saw these technologies reaching a much broader audience around the world.

The 2000s also saw scientists, physicians, and engineers make major strides in the development of medical technology due to the advent and development of genetic therapy and genetic engineering. Many scientists and physicians believe that genetic manipulation could potentially constitute a new era of medical treatment and may represent the key to developing cures and treatments for a wide variety of genetic and inherited disorders.

The climate change debate is another of the central issues that has defined scientific discourse throughout the first decade of the twenty-first century, and it continues to exert a major influence over political and technological developments around the world. In addition to stimulating hybrid automobile technology, the potential environmental threats of climate change have helped to initiate increased interest in alternative energy. Many scientists and engineers have speculated that alternative energy research will remain a major avenue for technological and commercial development in the coming decades.

Further Reading

Aigrain, Philippe. *Sharing: Culture and the Economy in the Internet Age.* Amsterdam: Amsterdam UP, 2012. Print. Discusses file sharing, peer-to-peer networks, and issues surrounding the legality of file sharing Web services. Includes some basic analysis of the economic effects of file sharing.

Bolin, Bert. *A History of the Science and Politics of Climate Change.* New York: Cambridge UP, 2008. Print. Covers the emergence of climate change research and the history of Earth sciences and climate change sciences into the first half of the 2000s. Provides historical and sociological analyses of climate change studies.

Ceruzzi, Paul E. *Computing: A Concise History.* Cambridge: MITP, 2012. Print. Covers notable developments in the history of computing, including the advent and development of the Internet as well as microcomputing and the developments leading to smartphone technology and other modern tools.

"Found It! Ice on Mars." *NASA Science.* NASA, 28 May 2002. Web. 26 Nov. 2012. Discusses the discovery of ice on Mars and subsequent theories regarding the potential for life on Mars in the past and for future colonization. Also contains links to a variety of other articles regarding Mars discoveries.

Le Grice, Keiron. *Discovering Eris: The Symbolism and Significance of a New Planetary Archetype.* Edinburgh: Floris, 2012. Print. Discusses a variety of issues surrounding the discovery of Eris and the redesignation of planets and dwarf planets. Also discusses a variety of other scientific issues of the 2000s.

Smith, Moyra. *Investigating the Human Genome: Insights into Human Variation and Disease Susceptibility.* Upper Saddle River: Pearson, 2011. Print. Discusses the discoveries and breakthroughs surrounding human genome research as well as the potential for future development in genomics, gene therapy, and genetics research.

Micah Issitt

■ Second Life

Definition: Online virtual world where players can interact with each other through avatars

In the summer of 2003, the virtual world of Second Life was introduced to the public. Second Life allowed users to escape from the real world and construct their own alternate universe online. The program became a means of socialization and commerce, as users could buy, sell, and trade goods and services they created within the online universe.

The idea for Second Life grew from an online video game created by Linden Labs founder Philip Rosedale and his team. Rosedale had an idea to create an online world where users could create their own avatars and build their own virtual environments. Rosedale was also interested in giving users the ability to be entrepreneurial within their online universe.

Funding was initially difficult to find. Many potential investors did not understand Rosedale's idea. As a result, Linden Labs suffered. The company eventually found an investor who provided enough backing to keep it afloat. The funds helped Linden Labs develop what would become Second Life, which was officially offered to consumers in June of 2003.

Second Life was not an immediate success. Linden Labs came very close to shutting down before the company came up with a unique design that enticed investors. Linden Labs decided to give full creative rights to their users, or Residents, as they were called.

This meant that anything a Resident created on Second Life was his or her intellectual property. Rosedale and his team also decided to give value to the virtual property that could be bought and sold within the online world. Residents would conduct business using the Linden dollar as currency. This cyber currency could then be exchanged for real US dollars.

By 2006, Second Life users could participate in a virtual free-market economy in which people could buy and sell virtual products but also promote real-world products. Internationally known companies including Nike, American Apparel, and Reebok created shops within the virtual community to sell both simulated and real-life products. Second Life became a marketing essential for many businesses.

Impact

Second Life continued to permeate the online virtual world throughout the 2000s. Residents used the space as a forum for gatherings such as business meetings and class reunions. Second Life even received a technology and engineering Emmy Award in 2008. Its virtual economy had grown so much by 2009 that some users were grossing more than $250,000 annually from virtual land and currency holdings.

Further Reading

Au, Wagner James. *The Making of Second Life: Notes from the New World.* New York: Harper, 2008. Print.

Rosedale, Philip. "How I Did It: Philip Rosedale, CEO, Linden Lab." *Inc.* Mansueto Ventures, 1 Feb. 2007. Web. 6 Dec. 2012.

Siklos, Richard. "A Virtual World but Real Money." *New York Times.* New York Times Co., 19 Oct. 2006. Web. 6 Dec. 2012.

Cait Caffrey

■ Sedaris, David

Identification: American autobiographical essayist and humorist

Born: December 26, 1956; Johnson City, New York

A master of the satirical essay, writer David Sedaris has been compared to Mark Twain, James Thurber, and Dorothy Parker. His books have been translated into over two dozen languages and sold millions of copies worldwide.

Prior to the publication of *Me Talk Pretty One Day* in 2000, David Sedaris had already established himself as a well-known memoirist and satirist with his works *Naked* (1997) and *Holidays on Ice* (1997). Several stories in *Me Talk Pretty* were published previously in the *New Yorker, Esquire,* and *GQ,* and some were read by Sedaris on NPR's *This American Life.* The best-selling book presents Sedaris's comical reflections on his upbringing in North Carolina, and his insights and opinions of French culture after moving to Normandy. In 2001, *Time* magazine named Sedaris the Humorist of the Year. In addition, Sedaris was awarded the 2001 Thurber Prize for American Humor.

In 2004, Sedaris published *Dress Your Family in Corduroy and Denim,* another collection of autobiographical essays. In addition to continued explorations of France and his family, Sedaris writes about his father's reaction to his homosexuality and about his relationship with his partner. *When You Are Engulfed in Flames,* published in 2008, further explores the themes familiar to Sedaris's readers, presented in his trademark wry and earnest style.

Some critics have faulted Sedaris for exaggerating many autobiographical events and have questioned whether is work is "nonfiction" in the truest sense of the word. Sedaris has responded by asserting that certain techniques of storytelling are required in works of satire.

In 2004, David Sedaris: Live at Carnegie Hall (2003) was awarded a Grammy Award for best comedy album. In 2005, he edited a collection of short stories entitled *Children Playing before a Statue of Hercules.* Sedaris published a collection of short stories entitled *Squirrel Seeks Chipmunk: A Modest Bestiary* in 2011. The book explores dark humor and the nuances of relationships via anthropomorphism, or the literary technique of imbuing animals with human qualities.

Impact

David Sedaris has been credited with reviving the art of satire and for providing reading audiences with welcome comic relief from the seriousness and cynicism of contemporary writing. His essays are read widely in creative nonfiction, memoir, and gay literature courses, and have inspired countless writers. As an openly gay American, Sedaris has lent his voice and talent toward changing prejudicial attitudes about homosexuality, and has inspired other gay authors to discuss their sexual identities publicly.

Further Reading

Sedaris, David. "All You Have to Do Is Live: David Sedaris on Writing, Reading and Gay Marriage." Interview by Susanna Schrobsdorff. *Newsweek*. Newsweek/Daily Beast, 30 May 2008. Web. 8 Oct. 2012.

—. "David Sedaris." Interview by Allison Block. *Booklist* 1–15 June 2008: 114. Print.

—. Interview by Terry Gross. *Writers Speak: Fresh Air with Terry Gross*. HighBridge, 2004. CD.

Sally Driscoll

■ Self-publishing

Definition: Book printing and promotion process utilized by authors to publish their work independent of the traditional commercial publishing industry

The publishing industry was one of several major media sectors to undergo a significant transformation in the 2000s. Rapid advances in print technology made it possible for small printing houses to print books of a quality similar to that of major publishing firms. Additionally, the rise of Internet-based promotional tools also made book marketing easier for authors who lacked the large budgets and marketing campaigns of major book publishing houses.

Genesis

The concept of authors printing, promoting, and selling their own books has existed as long as publishing itself. Self-publishing has been utilized for centuries by hobbyists as well as fringe, niche, and insurrectionary authors whose works were considered unfit, too controversial, or untraditional for mainstream publishers and their readers.

In the 2000s, authors across all genres began to utilize self-publishing as a primary method with which to usurp the exclusory world of major publishing companies. Many writers had become increasingly frustrated with the limited amount of publishing options presented to them, as well as with repeated rejections of their work by established publishing firms due to reasons such as inexperience, controversial content, editorial guidelines, creative differences, or a perceived lack of potential popularity and profitability.

Benefits

The proliferation of self-published books was largely spurred by fiction authors fed up with repeated rejections from major publishing companies eager for titles with widespread commercial viability. Many authors felt shut out by the traditional editorial models at large publishing houses that frowned on works many in the industry considered imitative, unconventional, and incapable of mass commercial appeal. Writers wanted to bypass these editorial and commercial standards. Self-publishing in the 2000s also provided an easily accessible venue for publication for independent and first-time authors more interested in sharing their work than in financial gain.

Many authors also opted to utilize the self-publishing model in the 2000s as a means to maintain the intellectual and artistic rights to their work without being beholden by lengthy contracts to major publishing companies. Such contracts customarily placed time constraints on book release windows and author output.

In the 2000s self-publishing gave authors full control over the marketing and promotional aspects of their work. Unfettered from traditional annals of promotion, authors could tailor their marketing campaigns to target audiences with which they were intimately familiar. This proved to be particularly effective for authors working in niche fiction genres. Many self-published authors were able to cultivate new audiences through such niche marketing methods.

One of the biggest advantages of self-publishing for unknown authors in the 2000s was the newfound credibility that can be fostered by having a published work. A reader is more likely to pick up a book by an established author—one whose books have received a number of positive reviews—than someone who has not yet published. As with the traditional publishing market, the more positive reviews a book receives, the more popular it becomes, and the more copies it sells. One way for self-published authors to help this process along is by selling the book at a much cheaper price than a traditional publisher would offer. A reader will be more likely to try a new author if he or she does not have to invest much in that author. Some authors of best-selling self-published books have even been picked up by traditional publishing houses, which further increased their popularity.

Drawbacks

The decade's self-publishing renaissance was not without drawbacks. Authors choosing this method of publication are responsible for the numerous preliminary costs associated with book publication, including proofreading, fact and reference checking, and press and image coordination. While technological advances throughout the 2000s made such processes more accessible than they had previously been, they remained costly. Self-promotion on a large scale proved to be expensive and time consuming as well, especially without the experience of a publishing house's marketing team to rely upon.

Online and traditional brick-and-mortar booksellers also remained skeptical of abandoning the long established distribution avenues set in place by major publishers, often leaving self-published authors off their shelves and websites. In addition, booksellers and even many readers were wary about the quality of self-published books. The lack of a traditional, professional publisher to fact check, edit, and format a book could lead to inaccuracies, as well as typos and other errors that would make the work difficult to read.

The ambivalence of major booksellers toward self-published authors in the 2000s was further propelled by an increase in the proliferation of biased reviews. Many self-published authors in the 2000s were found to have paid reviewers to create positive reviews of their work to generate interest and boost sales. Such incidences caused further rifts between writers and retailers who championed the self-publishing process and the established publishing industry that remained wary of its increased popularity.

Impact

The self-publishing renaissance was one of many sea changes in the publishing world in the 2000s. The proliferation of digital books and disintegration of conventional publishing markets into a multitude of niche realms dictated by individual readers led to a sharp decline in the sale of printed books and to the closure of several independent booksellers and national bookselling chains alike.

While self-publishing became a viable avenue for fledgling authors to establish experience in the publishing world, the stigma attached to books created through this process remained at decade's end.

Further Reading

Denn, Rebekah. "A Cautionary Tale for Self-Published Authors." *Christian Science Monitor.* Christian Science Monitor, 7 Feb. 2011. Web. 10 Oct. 2012. Focuses on best-selling science fiction author Diane Duane. Duane had initially achieved success through traditional publishing; her "experiment" in self-publishing online did not succeed.

Motoko, Rich. "Self-Publishers Flourish as Writers Pay the Tab." *New York Times.* New York Times Co., 27 Jan. 2009. Web. 10 Oct. 2012. A discussion of how self-publishing companies have flourished, particularly by making money off their authors.

Steinberg, Scott. "What the Publishing Industry Doesn't Want You to Know." *Huffington Post Business.* TheHuffingtonPost.com Inc., 15 Aug. 2012. Web. 10 Oct. 2012. Details the various steps an author should take in order to become successful at self-publishing.

Streitfield, David. "The Best Book Reviews Money Can Buy." *New York Times.* New York Times Co., 25 Aug. 2012. Web. 10 Oct. 2012. Discusses the practice of authors paying for positive reviews of their self-published books. Focuses in particular on Todd Rutherford, a marketing specialist who became a paid reviewer.

Trachtenberg, Jeffrey A. "Secret of Self-Publishing: Success." *Wall Street Journal.* Dow Jones & Co., 31 Oct. 2011. Web. 10 Oct. 2012. Provides examples of self-published authors who have achieved success through e-publishing and low sale prices.

John Pritchard

■ September 11, 2001, terrorist attacks

The Event: Four terrorist passenger jet hijackings culminating in suicide attacks via deliberate crash landings
Date: September 11, 2001
Place: New York, New York; Washington, DC; Shanksville, Pennsylvania

The terrorist attacks of September 11, 2001, collectively represent one of the most consequential events of modern American history. In addition to causing over three thousand casualties, the attacks resulted in immediate and far-reaching changes in US defense policy, homeland security, and American civil liberties.

The World Trade Center in New York City, September 11, 2001. (Detective Greg Semendinger/NYC Police Aviation Unit)

On Tuesday, September 11, 2001, between 8:00 and 9:00 a.m. eastern standard time, four passenger airplanes routinely departed from major airports on the East Coast of the United States. American Airlines Flight 11 and United Airlines Flight 175 each took flight from Boston's Logan Airport, while American Airlines Flight 77 departed from Dulles International Airport in Virginia. All three airplanes were destined for Los Angeles, California. United Airlines Flight 93, the last of the four airplanes to take flight, left Newark Liberty International Airport in New Jersey for San Francisco, California.

Shortly after take-off, each of the four airplanes was hijacked by groups of assailants armed with crude, sharp objects that had gone undetected by security systems on the ground. The three flights from Boston were each hijacked by teams of five hijackers, while Flight 93 from Newark was assailed by four hijackers.

During emergency contact with ground controller operators in Boston, a flight attendant on Flight 11 claimed she had been attacked with an unidentifiable lacrimatory, or tear-inducing, agent. The exact weaponry utilized by the hijackers on each airplane would never be known, although experts would later speculate that box cutters or utility knives, in addition to pepper spray or mace, may have been utilized to disable flight personnel and take control of each airplane. It is also thought that at least one of the teams of terrorists claimed to have had explosives on board.

At approximately 8:45 a.m., Flight 11 crashed into the North Tower of the World Trade Center in the lower Manhattan district of New York City. The collision was initially assumed to be a tragic accident by numerous media outlets and witnesses on the ground. The scale of the emergency prompted droves of New York City fire and rescue personnel to the vicinity of the World Trade Center. In a matter of minutes, helicopters and other media personnel and apparatus descended on the scene.

A global television audience had amassed by the time United Airlines Flight 175 crashed into the World Trade Center's South Tower shortly after 9:00 a.m. By then, it was clear to both officials and the general public that the crashes were not accidents, but systematic terrorist strikes.

President George W. Bush was informed of the first airplane striking the World Trade Center moments prior to a public appearance at a Sarasota, Florida, elementary school. When the second airplane struck and the nature of both crashes was understood, the president left Florida immediately.

Bush was en route to Washington, DC, on Air Force One, when the United States military ordered every nonessential aircraft in US airspace to land and grounded all other scheduled flights. Shortly after 9:30 a.m., American Airlines Flight 77 crashed into the Pentagon building in Washington, DC—the headquarters of the United States Department of Defense.

With Washington subsequently deemed unsafe, President Bush and his traveling staff were informed of the developments while in the air. Unaware how many airplanes had been hijacked but aware high profile buildings such as the Pentagon were being targeted, security officials ordered an immediate evacuation of both the US Capitol building and the White House in Washington, DC.

Cockpit voice recordings and cell phone calls later revealed that the passengers on the final hijacked airplane, United Airlines Flight 93, were aware of the morning's other hijackings and World Trade Center attacks in New York City. Cell phone recordings from on board the airplane also revealed that the passengers plotted to regain control of the aircraft. The National Commission on Terrorist Attacks investigation later concluded that the terrorist hijackers, outnumbered and aware that the passengers were about to attempt to regain control of aircraft, deliberately brought the airplane down rather than continue to their intended target.

At just after 10:00 a.m., Flight 93 crashed into a field in Shanksville, Pennsylvania, killing all forty-four people on board. The hijacker's target for Flight 93 was never established, though experts would later assume it was likely a target in Washington, DC. By 10:30 a.m., both World Trade Center towers in New York City had collapsed as a result of fires caused by the impact of each airplane.

Immediate Aftermath

At the Pentagon, 125 people were killed instantly, though the building itself would survive the serious structural damage it endured in the attack. The loss of life and damage to lower Manhattan was catastrophic. Half of the entire New York City Fire Department was deployed to the World Trade Center, soon dubbed "Ground Zero," to look for survivors, though few were found. Over 2,600 people died at the site of the New York attacks, including 421 New York Fire Department, police, and emergency personnel first responders who ventured into and around the buildings after the attack began. The crashes of the four hijacked airplanes killed all 246 people on board.

Flights in and out of United States airspace were grounded until Thursday, September 13, when a small number of military approved airports resumed flights. The nation's entire commercial and passenger air system did not fully resume operation until Friday, September 14, when it did so under previously unseen security measures.

Every major media outlet in world carried extensive coverage of the attacks and their aftermath. Accounts and reactions to the attacks received front page billing in every major newspaper throughout the world. Numerous governments and geopolitical allies of the United States offered formal condolences, while citizens across the world formed makeshift memorials to the victims at American embassies worldwide. Subsequent research on the attacks would reveal that as many as 12 percent of the victims were citizens of countries other than the United States.

American Response

Two weeks after the attacks, the Federal Bureau of Investigation (FBI) was able to utilize debris analysis, passenger lists, and preflight security video footage to link the teams of hijackers to al-Qaeda, a fringe anti-Western terrorist organization comprised of several factions throughout the Middle East. The group would eventually maintain responsibility for the attacks in October of 2001.

NATO was quick to classify the attacks as a symbolic aggression toward all its member nations, though the ambiguity and unknown whereabouts of its designers made the recourse of any immediate military response difficult.

Previous aggressions of this scale against the United States, specifically the 1941 Japanese attack on Pearl Harbor, had been carried out with conventional military methods. However, the al-Qaeda terrorists who carried out the September 11 attacks were unified primarily by a fringe religious fanaticism paired with a collective anti-Western ideology. No single state or geopolitical entity was at fault.

Nonetheless, the public outcry for revenge was severe, and President Bush himself made known that retaliatory action would be taken in due course in numerous public addresses. The Bush administration had in fact formally sought and received congressional approval for military action in response to the September 11 attacks on September 14, 2001.

Tragically, during the weeks following the attacks, incidences of harassment and hate crimes against Muslims, Sikhs, and people of Middle Eastern heritage residing in the United States numbered in the hundreds and even resulted in one death.

Intelligence services in both the United States and Europe learned that the many terrorists affiliated with the al-Qaeda network had received refuge, training, and supplies in Afghanistan, where they reportedly continued to be given state protection by the ruling Taliban government. On October 7, 2001, President Bush addressed the nation to let it be known that the United States and a NATO coalition had begun striking Taliban-held targets within Afghanistan in response to the September 11 attacks.

Commission on Terrorist Attacks and Victim Compensation Fund

In November of 2002, the National Commission on Terrorist Attacks Upon the United States was created at the request of President Bush to investigate and explicate the September 11 attacks and provide advice to government agencies on preventing similar attacks in the future. The bipartisan commission was comprised of members of Congress from both the House and the Senate. The commission released its final report in August 2004, after two years of research.

The Commission on Terrorist Attacks concluded that bureaucratic and logistical lapses in both the Central Intelligence Agency (CIA) and Federal Bureau of Investigation (FBI) led to the suspension, neglect, and evasion of information regarding al-Qaeda's plot to commit a major attack using airplanes. Their final report also stated that, had suspicions of an al-Qaeda attack been adequately vetted, they may have potentially been thwarted.

The subsequent creation of the Department of Homeland Security was one of numerous administrative actions taken by the federal government in response to the September 11 attacks, which itself resulted in the greatest reorganization of federal staff in history. The newly created cabinet agency absorbed the United States Immigration and Naturalization Service, Border Patrol, the Animal and Plant Health Inspection Service, and the Immigration and Customs Enforcement agency.

In 2001, Congress allotted seven billion dollars to create the September 11th Victim Compensation Fund (VCF), in order to provide monetary reparation to those who suffered injuries in the attacks and to the families of those killed. Victims and their families were given financial compensation in exchange for forfeiting their right to appeal the amount awarded by the funds administration, as well as their right to sue the airline companies whose airplanes were hijacked. The average payment for claims made by the VCF ranged from $400,000 to $2,000,000.

Recovery and Environmental Effects

The section of the Pentagon building damaged in the September 11 attacks was fully repaired and functional by August 2002. Incidentally, the portion of the Pentagon destroyed by Flight 77 was undergoing renovation at the time to bolster the building's ability to withstand bomb attacks, which helped to minimize the damage.

The fires at the site of the attack on the World Trade Center burned until December of 2001. It took a year and five months of around-the-clock debris removal before the cleanup and recovery effort officially ended. It also took over six months to clear dust and debris from streets and buildings around Ground Zero.

Many workers who took place in the cleanup at Ground Zero suffered long-term negative health effects. It is estimated that between 40,000 and 90,000 workers and volunteers spent time on the cleanup project. In December of 2010, Congress enacted $4.3 billion to create the James Zadroga 9/11 Health and Compensation Act, which in turn established the World Trade Center Health Program. The program was created to assist in the medical cost of those affected by the attacks, particularly first responders, rescue personnel, and construction crews who were affected by the fumes, dust, and smoke during the cleanup operation.

Impact

The most significant outcome of the September 11 attacks, second only to the horrific loss of life, was the logistical failure of the United States government and its related intelligence infrastructure to effectively protect innocent civilian life. The unconventional methods with which the September 11 attacks were executed led both politicians and scholars to question the future effectiveness of conventional military strategy against anti-American forces that could not be traced to a single enemy state.

Security measures enacted in the wake of the attacks resulted in legislation that allowed for a never-before-seen potential for government intrusion into the lives of American citizens. New security measures also permanently changed procedures for commercial air travel all over the world, as demonstrated by legislature such as the Patriot Act.

Enacted by President Bush in October 2001, in direct response to the September 11 attacks, the Patriot Act lifted numerous restrictions placed on federal law enforcement agencies in their ability to covertly acquire intelligence. The act allowed new leeway in the federal government's ability to acquire information through telephone wiretaps, access to individual and corporate financial records, and the detainment and deportation of immigrants suspected of criminal or terrorist-related activities.

The September 11 attacks immersed the United States into new era of international relations, in which the conventional rules of diplomacy and military engagement no longer exclusively applied. The attacks also forced both American citizens and their political leadership to grapple with a new understanding that, despite the nation's vast network of intelligence, security apparatus, and modern military capabilities, the United States could no longer maintain the long-standing assumption that a foreign terrorist-style attack on its mainland was a logistical improbability.

Further Reading

Barry, Ellen. "Lost in the Dust of 9/11." *Los Angeles Times*. Los Angeles Times, 14 Oct. 2006. Web. 12 Oct. 2012. Discusses how dust from the World Trade Center debris damaged the health of those involved with its cleanup.

Brunn, Stanley D., ed. *11 September and Its Aftermath: The Geopolitics of Terror*. Portland: Cass, 2004. Print. Essays from a variety of perspectives on the impact of the September 11 attacks on foreign policies and international relations.

"Extract: 'We Have Some Planes.'" *BBC News*. British Broadcasting Company, 23 July 2004. Web. 12 Oct. 2012. Report on the Commission on Terrorist Attack's explanation of each September 11, 2001, hijacking, complete with transcripts of communications between ground control, flight personnel, and hijackers.

Letschert, Rianne, Ines Staiger, and Antony Pemberton, eds. *Assisting Victims of Terrorism: Towards a European Standard of Justice*. London: Springer, 2009. E-Book. Analyzes the psychological, social, and legal needs of terrorist victims.

National Commission on Terrorist Attacks. *The 9/11 Commission Report: Final Report of the National Commission on Terrorist Attacks Upon the United States*. New York: Norton, 2004. Print. Compiled results of official investigations made into the September 11 attacks. Also discusses the need for revised efforts to prevent future attacks and revised measures of response.

Wright, Lawrence. *The Looming Tower: Al Qaeda and the Road to 9/11*. New York: Knopf, 2006. Print. Examines the history of events that led to the September 11 attacks, from terrorist planning to Western intelligence failures. The book's narrative lens focuses specifically on the leaders of al-Qaeda—Osama bin Laden and Ayman al-Zawahiri—FBI counterterrorism chief John O'Neill, and Saudi intelligence leader Prince Turki al-Faisal.

John Pritchard

■ *Shrek* film series

Definition: Animated children's film series
Executive Producer: Jeffrey Katzenberg (b. 1950)
Date: Released on May 18, 2001; May 19, 2004; May 18, 2007; May 21, 2010

Based on the children's book by William Steig, the Shrek *film franchise follows the many adventures of a gruff yet kindhearted ogre named Shrek. The popular series spawned several sequels and spinoffs and was one of the highest-grossing film franchises of the decade.*

Filmmaker Steven Spielberg purchased the rights to William Steig's book *Shrek!* in1991. Chris Farley was to star as the ogre, but he died during production of the first movie in the series, *Shrek*. Comedian Mike Myers took his place, giving the character his signature Scottish brogue. Cameron Diaz voiced Princess Fiona, while Eddie Murphy voiced Donkey. Production of the first film was completed in 2001.

Shrek, a reclusive ogre in the Kingdom of Far, Far Away, unwillingly embarks on an adventure because of an unjust mandate against magical beings. Along the way, he meets Donkey and the beautiful Princess Fiona, and he discovers the importance of love and friendship. *Shrek* made more than $40 million in its opening weekend and grossed almost $268 million domestically. The film also won an Academy Award for best animated feature.

After the success of the first film, the original cast returned for *Shrek 2*, released in 2004. In the second installment, Shrek competes with a handsome prince for the love of Princess Fiona. The film made more than $100 million in its opening weekend and grossed nearly $437 million domestically and more than $919 million worldwide. *Shrek 2* won four People's Choice Awards and earned an Academy Award nomination for best animated feature.

Following *Shrek 2*'s success, two more Shrek films, with all the main actors attached, were announced. In *Shrek the Third* (2007), Shrek's marriage to Princess Fiona puts him in line for the throne after the king's death. Despite mixed reviews, audiences responded favorably and the film out-grossed *Shrek 2*'s opening weekend, generating more than $121 million. The film earned an impressive $800 million overall. The fourth feature-length film in the franchise, *Shrek Forever After*, opened on May 21, 2010.

Impact

Shrek was the first film to receive an animated feature Oscar, an award that has given new meaning and heft to animated entertainment. The series went on to become the highest-grossing animated movie franchise in history. Its popularity continued to attract moviegoers, and several movie spinoffs were produced, as well as animated television specials. The *Shrek* story was developed as a Broadway musical in 2008, earning eight Tony Award nominations.

Further Reading

"Box Office / Business for *Shrek.*" *IMDb.* IMDb.com, n.d. Web. 7 Dec. 2012.
"Box Office / Business for *Shrek the Third.*" *IMDb.* IMDb.com, n.d. Web. 7 Dec. 2012.
"The Highest Grossing Movie Franchises of All Time." *CNBC.* CNBC LLC, n.d. Web. 7 Dec. 2012.
"*Shrek 2* Awards." *IMDb.* IMDb.com, n.d. Web. 7 Dec. 2012.

Cait Caffrey

■ *The Sims*

Definition: A series of simulation video games developed by Maxis that focus on creating and controlling the lives of virtual people called Sims
Date: Released in 2000

The Sims pioneered and popularized the life-simulation genre of video games. The game broke sales records in 2002, surpassing Myst *as the highest-selling game of all time. As one of the first video games to develop an open-ended and nonlinear model of gameplay,* The Sims *attracted audiences outside of the standard gaming populace, becoming especially popular with female gamers.*

The Sims franchise includes *The Sims* (2000), *The Sims 2* (2004), and *The Sims 3* (2009), as well as a number of associated expansion packs and ports (a recreated version of the game for other platforms). Several spin-off titles were also released, such as *The Sims Online*, a massively multiplayer online game, and *The Sims Stories*, a version of the game developed specifically for lower-end systems such as laptops.

Game designer Will Wright built a prototype of the game in 1993, working with programmer Jamie Doornbos to develop a behavioral engine that would drive the Sims' actions and determine how Sims would interact with their environment based on eight "needs," such as hunger and hygiene. Wright's coworkers at Maxis were initially skeptical of releasing a game with no clear objectives and no scripted plotline, but when Electronic Arts bought out Maxis in 1997, they cited *The Sims* concept as one of the primary reasons for the acquisition.

When *The Sims* was released in February 2000, it exceeded all sales expectations, becoming the best-selling game for four out of five years following its release. Electronic Arts then began producing expansion packs for the game, adding new items and elements based on fan feedback. By 2004, *The Sims* and its seven expansion packs had sold more than 41 million copies, and *The Sims* was one of the most expanded games on the market. With *The Sims 2* and *The Sims 3*, the game's developers introduced 3D graphics, an aspiration system with reward points, increased options to customize content, and other improvements. *The Sims 3* broke sales records in 2009, selling more than 1.4 million units in its first week.

Impact

In the twelve years following its release, *The Sims* games sold more than 125 million units worldwide and have been translated into sixty different languages, making the series one of the best-selling video games of all time. In addition to record-breaking sales, the open-ended gameplay of *The Sims* has attracted fans outside of the traditional gaming community.

With nearly 60 percent of Sims users being women, the game's user-generated narrative structure expanded the typical demographic for video games.

Further Reading

Daily News Staff. "Women Really Click with The Sims." *Daily News.* NYDailyNews.com, 16 Apr. 2008. Web. 29 July 2012.

Kosak, Dave. "Will Wright Speaks Simlish." *GameSpy.* GameSpy.com, 27 Feb. 2005. Web. 11 July 2012.

Reid-Walsh, Jacqueline. *"The Sims." Girl Culture: An Encyclopedia.* Ed. Claudia Mitchell and Jacqueline Reid-Walsh. Westport: Greenwood, 2008. Print.

Andrew Maul

■ Slang and slogans

Definition: Informal words or phrases generally associated with spoken language and short phrases used for advertising or marketing purposes

The slang of the 2000s developed out of some of the most important cultural innovations of the decade, including the shift toward digital communication. Similarly, the decade's political and advertising slogans represented overarching consumer trends of the period, including the rapid spread of computer and Internet technology

Some of the most recognizable slang terms of the 2000s began developing during the previous decade, specifically from the Internet slang that emerged from e-mail and instant messaging technology. Abbreviations developed to facilitate communication via the Internet entered the popular lexicon in the 1990s but became more widely known in the 2000s. By the middle of the decade, phrases such as "LOL," or "laughing out loud," and "OMG," or "oh my God," were used in conversation and included in slang dictionaries.

A variety of other informal slang terms were popularized during the 2000s, many for their comedic value or because they were used in popular films or songs. For instance, the term "bromance" referred to an emotional friendship between men, while "peeps" referred to a person's friends, or "people." Other popular terms during the decade were "tight," used to describe something enjoyable and high quality, and "meh," an interjection that indicated a feeling of indifference toward a certain topic or object.

Political slogans of the 2000s reflected the major social changes that occurred during the decade. The administration of George W. Bush produced the catchphrases "Compassionate Conservatism" and "No Child Left Behind." In contrast, the 2008 presidential campaign of Barack Obama campaign introduced the slogans "Change" and "Yes We Can," representing the administration's progressive focus.

Advertising slogans of the period notably included a variety of slogans created by car manufacturers in an effort to reinvigorate the US automotive industry. Slogans such as "Ford. Drive One" were part of this larger effort to create a new image for the US automobile market. Technology companies were also prominent advertisers during the 2000s, and many of their slogans, such as Apple's "Think Different" and AT&T's "Your World. Delivered," became widely recognized.

Impact

The rapidity with which new linguistic innovations were transmitted in the twenty-first century fundamentally changed the nature of slang, enabling it to transition to mainstream language at a faster rate. Much of the popular slang of the 2000s, particularly the many terms originally based in online communication, continued to be widely used in the following decade, even among individuals who may have been unfamiliar with the slang's origins. Political and advertising slogans changed frequently in response to new campaigns and products. However, the broader trends of the 2000s, such as the ongoing attempt to emphasize the reliability and affordability of American-made cars, continue to shape the slogans of the next decade.

Further Reading

Coleman, Julie. *The Life of Slang.* New York: Oxford UP, 2012. Print.

Roberts, Robert North, and Scott John Hammond. *Presidential Campaigns, Slogans, Issues and Platforms.* Santa Barbara: ABC-CLIO, 2012. Print.

Sivulka, Juliann. *Soap, Sex, and Cigarettes: A Cultural History of American Advertising.* Boston: Wadsworth, 2012. Print.

Micah Issitt

■ *Slumdog Millionaire*

Identification: Film about an eighteen-year-old orphan in India who has the chance to change his life by competing on a popular television game show
Director: Danny Boyle (1956–)
Date: Released on November 12, 2008

Slumdog Millionaire *was one of the most popular movies of 2008. The film made more than $100 million at the box office and won several major awards. Although the movie was received well by critics and audiences, it did cause some controversy.*

Slumdog Millionaire was directed by Danny Boyle, known for the films *Trainspotting* (1996) and *28 Days Later* (2003). The screenplay, written by Simon Beaufoy, was an adaptation of Vikas Swarup's 2005 novel *Q&A*. The movie tells the story of Jamal (played as an adult by Dev Patel), an eighteen-year-old orphan who works as a tea servant in India. His life takes a dramatic turn when he becomes a contestant on *Who Wants to Be a Millionaire?* Jamal is one question away from winning when he is taken into police custody. Suspecting the teenager of cheating, the police interrogate him to try to find out how an uneducated young man from the slums could know the quiz answers. The movie flashes back to Jamal's childhood, during which he lost his mother in a riot. Jamal tells the story of how he and his older brother, Salim (played as an adult by Madhur Mittal), struggled to survive. During their journey, Jamal fell in love with the orphaned Latika (played as an adult by Freida Pinto) and learned the answers to the questions that would one day change his life.

Slumdog Millionaire was one of the most critically-acclaimed movies of the year. It won four Golden Globe Awards and seven British Academy of Film and Television Arts (BAFTA) Awards. The movie also won several Academy Awards, including the awards for best picture and best director.

Impact

Slumdog Millionaire was not without its share of controversy. Some Indians, including Bollywood star Amitabh Bachchan, criticized the film for its portrayal of India as an impoverished nation. Others argued that the film does not address the true cause of poverty in India—discrimination against the country's poorest citizens. Despite this, some believed the success of *Slumdog Millionaire* would help bridge the gap between Indian and American cultures.

Further Reading

Dargis, Manohla. "*Slumdog Millionaire* (2008): Orphan's Lifeline Out of Hell Could be a Game Show in Mumbai." *New York Times.* New York Times Co., 11 Nov. 2008. Web. 4 Sept. 2012.
Giridharadas, Anand. "The 'Slumdog' Effect: Afflict the Comfortable." *New York Times.* New York Times Co., 26 Feb. 2009. Web. 4 Sept. 2012.
Varma, Meena. "India's Elephant in the Room." *Guardian* [London]. Guardian News and Media, 11 Feb. 2009. Web. 4 Sept. 2012.

Rebecca Sparling

■ Smith, Will

Identification: American actor; film producer; rap artist
Born: September 25, 1968; Philadelphia, Pennsylvania

During the 2000s Smith solidified his place as a serious actor. Although he still appeared in comedies, he focused more on dramatic roles and was recognized by the film industry with several prestigious awards and nominations. Smith did not abandon his music, however, and he continued to release albums while acting and producing for film and television.

American actor and rapper Will Smith was mostly known for his comedic work before 2000. He began the decade, however, with the dramatic role of a mystical caddy in *The Legend of Bagger Vance* (2000). He followed this with the biopic *Ali* (2001), in which he portrayed famed boxer Muhammad Ali. This role earned him several notable awards and nominations in 2002, including Oscar and Golden Globe nominations. Smith's personal life was also growing with the addition in 2000 of his third child and second with wife and fellow actor Jada Pinkett-Smith: daughter Willow Camille Reign.

Smith reprised his popular film roles for the sequels *Men in Black II* (2002) and *Bad Boys II* (2003). He also returned to television, this time teaming with his wife to create, write, and produce the sitcom *All of Us*. Smith then starred in *I, Robot* (2004), which was produced by his company Overbrook Entertainment. He revisited his comedy roots for his next few

Will Smith. (©iStockphoto.com/Pascal Le Segretain)

Although Smith spent most of the decade acting and producing, he pursued writing and musical projects as well. He authored the children's book *Just the Two of Us* (2001), which shared the title and lyrics of his hit song from the 1997 solo album, *Big Willie Style.* He recorded the album *Born to Reign* in 2002. In 2003 he ended his relationship with Columbia Records in 2003 and signed with Interscope Records the following year. In 2006, he released the album *Lost and Found*, which included the theme song from *Hitch.*

Impact

Smith's career grew on and off the big screen during the 2000s. The former funnyman evolved while he took on and succeeded in more serious roles and responsibilities. He gained enormous popularity and recognition throughout the decade to become a respected actor and producer. In addition to developing his skills as a performer, Smith used his increased leverage in the entertainment industry to develop and produce more films.

Further Reading

Doeden, Matt. *Will Smith: Box Office Superstar.* Minneapolis: Lerner, 2010. Print.

Iannucci, Lisa. *Will Smith: A Biography.* Santa Barbara: Greenwood, 2010. Print.

Angela Harmon

■ Soccer

Definition: The world's most popular sport, played between two teams of eleven players who, apart from the goalkeepers, cannot touch the ball with their hands or arms

Beloved across much of the world for centuries, soccer did not find solid footing as a major participatory or spectator sport in the United States and Canada until the 1990s. The sport benefited significantly from an expansion of scholastic participation following the 1994 FIFA World Cup, which was hosted by the United States.

Soccer in the United States

The popularity of soccer in the United States was significantly bolstered by the performance of the US women's national soccer team in the 1999 Fédération Internationale de Football Association (FIFA)

movies, providing the voice for Oscar, the animated star of *Shark Tale* (2004), and starring in the romantic comedy *Hitch* (2005). and he produced and starred with his son Jaden in drama The Pursuit of Happyness, in which he played a single father struggling to provide a life for himself and his son. In 2007 Smith produced and starred in the film adaptation of Richard Matheson's novel *I Am Legend*, and the following year he starred in the superhero comedy *Hancock*. Also in 2008, Smith joined The Pursuit of Happyness director Gabriele Muccino as the producer and star of the drama Seven Pounds. He also coproduced the films *Lakeview Terrace* (2008) and *The Secret Life of Bees* (2008).

Landon Donovan, in the #10 jersey, makes a play for the ball in the first half of the 2004 Sierra Mist Major League Soccer All-Star game. (U.S. Army/Photograph by Sergeant Lorie Jewell)

World Cup. Nearly one hundred thousand spectators were in attendance at the Rose Bowl, a stadium long known for its historical connections to collegiate American football, to witness the United States play China in the event's final championship matchup. The Americans' thrilling victory following a penalty-kick shootout made members of the US women's team instant celebrities. Their success was subsequently credited with having a profound effect on the growth of the game in the United States.

At the 2002 men's FIFA World Cup in Korea and Japan, the US men's national team, bolstered by a shocking upset against international powerhouse Portugal, advanced to the quarterfinals. Despite their eventual elimination, the performance marked the best placement by a US men's team in the World Cup since 1930.

The consecutive successes and growing popularity of the US national teams led to a resurgence of interest in Major League Soccer (MLS), the highest-level professional league in the United States and Canada. Founded in 1993, the fledgling league had been on the brink of extinction by the early 2000s, even having to close down two of its member clubs in 2001.

Soccer in Canada

The steady growth of television ratings and attendance figures for Major League Soccer was crucial to the league's decision by the mid-2000s to expand into major Canadian markets. The city of Toronto was awarded a franchise in 2007; Vancouver was awarded one in 2009. Also in 2009, the Ontario-based Canadian Soccer League (CSL) was granted conditional approval by the Canadian Soccer Association to become the country's national professional soccer league. The first CSL team from outside Ontario, Montreal Impact Academy, was founded in 2010.

The Canadian men's national team started the decade strong, winning the Confederation of North, Central American and Caribbean Association Football (CONCACAF) Gold Cup championship in 2000. Their continental success did not carry over to success in international play, however, as the Canadian men failed to qualify for the FIFA World Cup throughout the decade, extended a streak of absence from World Cup play that began following its first-round elimination in 1986.

The Canadian women's national team had a tremendously successful decade in the 2000s. In addition to qualifying for every FIFA Women's World Cup held in the 2000s, the Canadian women finished in fourth place in 2003, when the event was hosted by the United States. It was the highest-ever finish of any Canadian national soccer team in World Cup play.

Soccer in Mexico

International soccer in Mexico was dominated by the play of their men's national team. While Mexico's women's team failed to qualify for FIFA World Cup play in the 2000s, the men's team reached the second round, known as the round of sixteen, in both 2002 and 2006, continuing their reign as the most successful North American entry in World Cup tournaments.

The Mexican professional soccer league, Liga MX, continued to be North America's most widely televised and popular professional soccer league throughout the 2000s. The eighteen-team league agreed to broadcast rights that would air Liga MX competitions throughout the United States and Canada.

British Soccer in North America

The 2000s were marked by a huge surge in popularity of Great Britain's professional soccer league, the Premier League, known internationally as the English Premier League (EPL), throughout North America. Widely hailed by soccer analysts and players as one of the world's three most talented domestic leagues (along with Spain's La Liga and Italy's Serie A), the EPL aired more games in North America in the 2000s than in any previous decade, thanks to advances in broadcast technology and live Internet streaming.

The prominence of British soccer was also bolstered by the widespread scheduling of exhibition games between MLS and EPL clubs. Major League Soccer also pitted its team of league all-stars against prominent British clubs throughout the decade.

Impact

In the 1990s, sports sociologists and marketing analysts alike lamented the poor growth of soccer in North America, particularly the United States, with experts wondering if the sport would ever gain a significant foothold there in terms of popularity. Yet by the mid-2000s, soccer had achieved levels of popularity previously unseen throughout the continent. Bolstered by continued exposure to high-quality international play and elite European leagues, soccer's prominence among the major North American sports leagues grew steadily throughout the decade. Alienation of some fans in the wake of incidents of labor strife in major American sports leagues such as the National Hockey League and National Basketball Association in the 2000s may have also incrementally boosted soccer's prestige among North American audiences, particularly those in the United States.

Further Reading

Desbordes, Michel, and Simon Chadwick. *Marketing and Football: An International Perspective.* Burlington: Butterworth, 2007. Print.

Freedman, Jonah. "The Throw-In: Did Eliminating Tampa, Miami Save MLS?" *MLS Soccer.* MLS, 5 Jan. 2012. Web. 7 Dec. 2012.

Markovits, Andrei S., and Steven L. Hellerman. *Offside: Soccer and American Exceptionalism.* Princeton: Princeton UP, 2001. Print

"US Soccer Timeline." *US Soccer.* US Soccer, n.d. Web. 7 Dec. 2012.

John Pritchard

■ Social media

Definition: Internet-based applications and websites that promote the sharing of user-generated content, communication, and participation on a large scale

Social media took the Internet by storm during the 2000s. By 2010, it accounted for 22 percent of all time spent online in the United States. A large variety of user-generated applications makes up what is considered social media. These applications include blogs, social networks such as Facebook, and audio podcasts. Throughout the decade, social media gradually became used for marketing and as an alternative news source. It had a significant impact on the 2008 US presidential election. Although the aim of social media is to make it easier for individuals to communicate and engage in conversations, many argue that it has led to a reduction in human interaction.

The idea of social media began in the mid-to-late 1990s, when Internet users were first given the ability to make their own websites through servers such as Geocities. Blogging and social networks also began around the time. Sixdegrees.com, launched in 1997, was one of the first websites that allowed users to create a profile and add lists of friends. It was not until 2002 and the launch of Friendster that the concept of a social network become highly popular. Within three months of its launch, Friendster had gained three million users. Other popular social media applications launched around this time include the social networks MySpace and LinkedIn, the music service iTunes, and the image-hosting website Flickr.

Social media is classified in several ways. Any application that allows users to create a profile and build a friend list is considered a social network. The most popular example of this is Facebook, which was launched in 2004 and gained close to 600 million users by the end of the decade. Blogs allow users to generate a variety of content for publication on the Internet. Several websites are devoted to hosting users' blogs; one of the most popular of these servers is WordPress. Forums are another classification that allows users to voice their opinion on a range of topics. Video and audio podcasts allow users to record themselves discussing different topics. Internet users can then download or stream these recordings. Collaborative websites known as "wikis," which allow users to generate informational content on a variety of topics, also became very popular; the most famous of these is Wikipedia.

Multiplayer online games are also a prevalent type of social media. These games, such as the popular World of Warcraft, allow users to communicate with other players while participating in a virtual world. Other popular examples of these games are The Sims and Second Life, which allowed users to create avatars and interact with other users. Other more general varieties include e-mails, instant messaging, and video sharing. Many of these varieties have been aggregated with social networks.

The rise in smartphone technology allowed individuals to access an array of social media applications while mobile. Geographic tagging applications allowed users to "tag" themselves at specific locations such as restaurants and stores and post these tags on social media websites like Facebook and Foursquare.

MySpace and Facebook

The most popular social media and networking tool in the world is Facebook. The website was launched on February 4, 2004, by computer programmer and Harvard sophomore Mark Zuckerberg. When the website was first created, it was exclusively for students of Harvard University and others with college-based e-mail addresses. It was opened to everyone on September 26, 2006, and quickly gained hundreds of millions of users. Although the website requires users to be at least thirteen years old, it has been reported that several million users are under age thirteen.

Facebook allows users to build a personal profile that includes pictures and cultural interests, to exchange messages, and to share thoughts, pictures, and videos. The website drew heavy comparisons with MySpace, an earlier social networking website. The owners of Facebook argue that their website allows more customization and requires users to give their true identity, which MySpace does not.

MySpace was launched in August 2003 and quickly became one of the most visited websites in the United States. It was surpassed by Facebook in 2008 but still enjoyed several million unique users by 2009. Near the end of the decade, the website catered heavily to musicians and was revamped to make it easy for users to upload and share music from established and upcoming artists.

Twitter

The social networking and microblogging website Twitter rose to immense popularity in the 2000s. It allows users to create a small profile, follow other users, and post brief messages restricted to 140 characters long. These messages are known as "tweets." The application was launched in July 2006 by web developer Jack Dorsey, and gained hundreds of millions of users around the globe by the end of the decade, with hundreds of millions of tweets being sent every day from computers and several mobile devices.

The application is significant for the way it allows people to organize quickly. For example, Twitter was used to rally individuals for political protests around the world, as in the 2009 election protests in Iran. Politicians utilized it as a way to garner support and interact with voters. US president Barack Obama used it heavily during his 2008 campaign. He encouraged voters to ask him questions via Twitter and Facebook throughout the campaign.

It has also been used to report breaking news, although many critics argue that Twitter users rarely perform fact checking before sending out news tweets. Twitter has also been frequently used in police investigations, education, and public relations.

Twitter further encouraged interaction and online conversations through the use of hashtags. A hashtag, represented by the pound symbol before a word or group of words, allows users to search for and view every tweet with that specific hashtag attached. The most popular current hashtags are known as "trending topics."

Social Media Marketing

Since social media is accessible through a broad range of applications, it has become a heavily used tool in marketing. Companies can manufacture advertisements that social media users can easily share at no cost to the company, making it an inexpensive alternative to traditional marketing.

Social networking sites such as Facebook allow companies to join them and create a profile for marketing purposes. On Facebook, users can "like" the page of companies to get updates and offers from them, as well as communicate with them. This approach was especially successful for small businesses that used Facebook to promote their brand through special events and offers.

Brands utilized Twitter to market and interact on a more individual level. When users "follow" brands online, short messages posted by the brand appear on the main Twitter feed page. Many times these messages included links that a user could click on to learn more about offers and specific products. This too was a very inexpensive method of online marketing.

Foursquare is another social media application frequently used by businesses in online marketing. This application allows users to "check-in" at the location of a store, restaurant, or other business. Their check-in is then posted on the Foursquare website as well as on other applications such as Facebook. Businesses encouraged return customers by offering incentives for checking in many times.

The video-sharing website YouTube was another popular place for advertisers. Marketing on YouTube was personalized through various language-detection programs that analyzed users' individual interests and marketed to them accordingly. Advertisers were able to attach specific advertisements to relevant videos being searched, making it easy for them to reach a target audience. An increasingly popular method of no- or low-cost advertising on YouTube was through "viral videos." These videos, which were oftentimes humorous and culturally relevant, were created with the goal of having users spread them organically across the web.

Other popular social media applications that were heavily used in marketing were blogs where advertisements could be posted, business-profile websites such as Yelp, and the business-networking website LinkedIn.

Privacy Concerns

One of the biggest debates concerning social media in the 2000s was over privacy and protection of user information. Those concerned with these issues argued that social networking sites such as Facebook and Twitter do not take the proper steps to protect the information users share with each other. Debates looked at ownership of the content on social networking websites. Users generate it onto these websites, but corporations own the websites.

In November 2007, Facebook came under heavy negative criticism for implementing Beacon, a system that allowed partner websites to send information concerning the actions of Facebook users on their own websites. This information included items purchased at online retailers and games users played online. Beacon aroused concerns over privacy of information and users' lack of control over how their information was used. Facebook spokespersons argued that it allowed users to further share their interests with friends and help refer them to online retailers. Beacon was discontinued in September 2009.

There were also concerns over federal and local authorities using Facebook to acquire personal information in the investigation of crimes. Facebook's privacy policy states that they may turn over any information they believe may be related to an illegal or criminal activity, but many argued that personal information was harvested even when authorities lacked reasonable suspicion. This raised further questions about what online information falls under the US Electronic Communications Privacy Act (ECPA) of 1986, which regulates what electronic messages and information can be legally seized or intercepted by authorities. Critics argue that the bill is very loose in its language and out-dated with respect to contemporary information sharing.

Data mining to extract user information was another serious concern for social network users. They worried that companies and individuals were freely allowed to harvest information and use it for various purposes. In 2005, as part of a project on Facebook privacy, two students from the Massachusetts institute of Technology (MIT) demonstrated the possibility of simple data mining on Facebook. They used an automated script to download the Facebook profiles of over seventy thousand users.

Facebook has since developed higher security methods for their users, including customizable security, but privacy concerns nevertheless continued to grow into the next decade.

Impact

During the 2000s, social media changed everything from politics to public relations. While it helped people connect and share their ideas, it also came under heavy negative criticism and skepticism. Critics argued that it only created the illusion of connection and in reality decreased the need for actual human interaction. Others stated that it led to an increase in cyberbullying, in which people are harassed on social networks. Many employers banned social media at work due to concerns that it decreased productivity. The ultimate concern into the following decade, however, was one of privacy and the misuse of personal information. Users found many positive aspects, though. Many reconnected with old friends and continued to keep in touch. Musicians such as Justin Bieber first saw success on social networks before getting a record contract. For better or worse, social media continued to increase in popularity into the next decade.

Further Reading

Kirkpatrick, David. *The Facebook Effect: The Inside Story of the Company That Is Connecting the World.* Simon, 2011. Print. Looks at the origins of Facebook, its creators, and its affect on communication throughout the world.

Lovink, Geert. *Networks without a Cause: A Critique of Social Media.* Cambridge: Polity, 2011. Print. Explores the negative consequences social media has on the lives of its users and the obsession with online self-image.

Morozov, Evgeny. *The Net Delusion: The Dark Side of Internet Freedom.* New York: Public Affairs, 2011. Print. Examines how social media and networking have affected democracies and totalitarian nations around the world.

Qualman, Erik. *Socialnomics: How Social Media Transforms the Way We Live and Do Business.* Hoboken: Wiley, 2010. Print. Looks at social media from a business and marketing standpoint.

Shirky, Clay. *Here Comes Everybody: The Power of Organizing without Organizations.* New York: Penguin, 2009. Print. Examines the effect of the Internet and social media on contemporary group dynamics.

Patrick G. Cooper

■ *The Sopranos*

Identification: Highly acclaimed television drama focused on the fictional DiMeo crime family based in New Jersey and their boss, Tony Soprano

Executive Producer: Chase, David (b. 1945)

Date: January 10, 1999–June 10, 2007

The Sopranos aired for eight seasons on Home Box Office (HBO) and was one of the most critically acclaimed television series of the 2000s. Many critics have pointed to the show's influence in ushering in a revolution in television storytelling that saw a more complex approach to writing, characters, and storylines.

Veteran television producer David Chase created *The Sopranos*, which he originally conceived as a feature film. Chase drew inspiration for the show from his own life, specifically his upbringing in New Jersey and his relationship with his mother. He explained that he had been fascinated with mobster movies and television shows since he was a child, and he wanted to develop a story that delved into the interpersonal relationships and family dynamics of members of the Mafia.

Much of *The Sopranos* was shot on location in several cities in New Jersey including Kearny, Lodi, and Elizabeth, and starred a cast of actors who were mainly Italian-American. For the lead role of Tony Soprano, actor James Gandolfini, an Italian-American from New Jersey, was chosen. For his portrayal of Tony, Gandolfini won several acting awards, including the Emmy Award for outstanding lead actor

The cast of The Sopranos (left to right) Robert Iler, Edie Falco, James Gandolfini and Jamie-Lynn Sigler. (Dimitrios Kambouris/ WireImage for St. Jude Children's Research Hospital/ Getty Images)

in a drama series three times. For her portrayal of Tony's wife Carmela, actress Edie Falco won four Emmys. *The Sopranos* was nominated for an Emmy for outstanding drama series every year it aired, winning it in 2004 and 2007. It was the first show on a cable network to win this award.

The show focused on the inner workings and politics of the DiMeo crime organization as well as the Soprano family dynamics. While he was respected as a crime figure, Tony's family, who were not completely aware of the extent of his criminal life, oftentimes perceived him as a less-than-perfect husband and parent. His troubled relationship with his mother Livia (Nancy Marchand) was an essential plot point and cause of conflict. Tony's relationship with his therapist, Dr. Jennifer Melfi (Lorraine Bracco), whom he began seeing due to his panic attacks, was also a major element of the show. The show explored several themes such as masculinity, how a younger generation tries to fix the mistakes of their elders and how wealth can lead to emotional emptiness.

Impact

The Sopranos is often cited as the most important and groundbreaking television show of its day and the best show of the decade. Its depth and complex characters raised the bar for television dramas. The series was frequently commended for its novelistic approach to its characters and plots, which were presented in arcs that lasted several seasons.

Further Reading

Greene, Richard, and Peter Vernezze, eds. *The Sopranos and Philosophy: I Kill Therefore I Am.* Chicago: Carus, 2004. Print.

Lavery, David. *Reading The Sopranos: Hit TV from HBO.* London: Taurus, 2006. Print.

Yacowar, Maurice. *The Sopranos on the Couch: The Ultimate Guide.* London: Continuum, 2007. Print.

Patrick G. Cooper

■ Sotomayor, Sonia

Identification: American supreme court justice
Born: June 25, 1954; New York, New York

The first Hispanic justice to serve on the United States Supreme Court, Sonia Sotomayor was sworn in on August 8, 2009. Prior to her appointment as associate justice, Sotomayor worked as an attorney and circuit judge.

Sonia Sotomayor was born and raised in the Bronx, a borough of New York City. After graduating from Cardinal Spellman High School as valedictorian, Sotomayor attended Princeton University. She graduated summa cum laude in 1976 with a bachelor's degree in history. She went on to enroll in Yale Law School, where she served as editor of the *Yale Law Journal* and managing editor of *Yale Studies in World Public Order* (now titled the *Yale Journal of International Law*).

Sotomayor began her career as an attorney following her graduation from Yale in 1979. She worked for Robert Morgenthau, the district attorney of Manhattan, and in 1984 began working at a private law firm in New York, Pavia and Harcourt, where she switched from criminal to civil law. Three years later, she was appointed to the State of New York Mortgage Agency, a group that helped low-income people attain mortgages and insurance, by New York governor Mario Cuomo. From 1988 until 1992, Sotomayor served on the New York City Campaign Finance Board, to which she was appointed by the city's mayor, Ed Koch.

Judge

In 1991, President George H. W. Bush nominated Sotomayor for a US District Court judgeship in Manhattan. She was appointed in 1992, becoming the first Hispanic federal judge in the state of New York. In 1997, President Bill Clinton nominated So

Sonia Sotomayor. (Collection of the Supreme Court of the United States/Photograph by Steve Petteway)

tomayor for a judgeship with the United States Court of Appeals for the Second Circuit. After her nomination, Republicans alleged she was too liberal and that she was being groomed for the US Supreme Court. Despite these objections, Sotomayor was confirmed as circuit judge in October 1998 in a Senate vote of 67 to 29 after a year-long confirmation process.

During her eleven-year tenure as a circuit judge, Sotomayor wrote over 380 majority opinions. Five of her opinions were later reviewed by the Supreme Court. Of the five, three were overturned, including her ruling in *Correctional Services Corporation v. Malesko*, in which Sotomayor determined that an inmate who had sustained injuries at a halfway house could sue the private contractor he deemed responsible. Also overturned was *Entergy Corp. v. Riverkeeper Inc.*, in which Sotomayor found that cost-benefit analyses could not be used by the Environmental Protection Agency (EPA) to determine the best methods through which power plants could draw cooling water. Of the five reviewed, two were upheld: *Empire Healthchoice Assurance, Inc. v. McVeigh* and *Knight v. Commissioner.*

Supreme Court Justice

In April 2009, members of the press discovered that Supreme Court Justice David Souter was planning to retire in the summer of that year. By May of 2009, it was widely speculated that President Barack Obama would nominate Sotomayor to replace him. Obama nominated Sotomayor to the Supreme Court on May 26, 2009.

In light of the Supreme Court nomination, Sotomayor faced criticism for her number of Supreme Court reversals, which increased in the summer of 2009 when her decision as part of a panel of judges in *Ricci v. DeStefano* went before the US Supreme Court. In this case, a group of white firefighters from New Haven, Connecticut, alleged racial discrimination as a result of the city's decision not to use test scores as a basis for promotions, which had been the primary intention behind the test. No African American firefighters had scored well enough on the test to qualify for a promotion, and only two Hispanic firefighters' test scores had qualified them; the city therefore disregarded the test results in an attempt to avoid a lawsuit alleging that the test itself was discriminatory. Sotomayor and the other judges on the panel upheld the ruling of the original court, which had ruled in favor of the city. However, the US Supreme Court overturned the panel's decision.

Sotomayor's confirmation hearings before the Senate Judiciary Committee began in July 2009. On August 6, 2009, her nomination was confirmed in a vote of 68 to 31. She was sworn in two days later, becoming the third female justice in the history of the court. She also became the first Hispanic judge in the court's history, and her appointment marked the first time that six out of the nine Supreme Court justices were Roman Catholics.

Impact

During her tenure as associate justice, Sotomayor was involved in a number of significant court cases, including *Citizens United v. Federal Election Commission*, *Berghuis v. Thompkins*, and *Arizona v. United States.* She received numerous awards and honors as well as honorary law degrees from Princeton and New York University and has been inducted into the prestigious American Philosophical Society.

Further Reading

Amador, Margarita. *Sonia Sotomayor: An Introduction to the Prospective Court Justice.* Seattle: Amador, 2009. Print.

Felix, Antonia. *Sonia Sotomayor: The True American Dream.* New York: Penguin, 2010. Print.

Green, Meg. *Sonia Sotomayor.* Santa Barbara: ABC-CLIO, 2012. Print.

McElroy, Lisa Tucker. *Sonia Sotomayor: First Hispanic US Supreme Court Justice.* Minneapolis: Lerner, 2010. Print.

Shichtman, Sandra H. *Sonya Sotomayor: Supreme Court Justice.* Greensboro: Reynolds, 2010. Print.

Terris, Daniel, Cesare Roman, and Leigh Swigart. *The International Judge: An Introduction to the Men and Women Who Decide the World's Cases.* Waltham: Brandeis, 2007. Print.

Elizabeth Adams

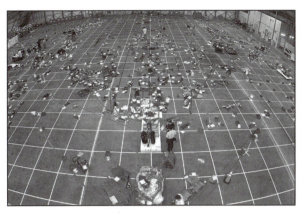

Kennedy Space Center grid used to position pieces of Columbia's *debris as the* Columbia *Reconstruction Project Team investigates the accident.* (NASA)

■ Space shuttle *Columbia* disaster

The Event: The space shuttle *Columbia* exploded and disintegrated over Texas and Louisiana while re-entering Earth's atmosphere

Date: February 1, 2003

Place: Texas and Louisiana

When the space shuttle Columbia *was returning from its twenty-eighth flight to space, it began to break apart as it traveled through Earth's atmosphere. In a matter of minutes, the shuttle had completely disintegrated in midair, killing all seven crew members. An investigation later determined that the disaster was caused by damage that occurred during the shuttle's launch.*

At approximately 9 a.m. on February 1, 2003, observers of the space shuttle *Columbia*'s reentry into Earth's atmosphere witnessed a disaster that devastated the United States and its space program. *Columbia* was returning from a sixteen-day scientific mission and was scheduled to arrive at the Kennedy Space Center in Florida at 9:16 a.m. The National Aeronautics and Space Administration (NASA) lost communication with the shuttle's crew a few minutes before its scheduled landing. Witnesses reported hearing two loud bangs and seeing debris fall from the sky shortly after.

The shuttle's disintegration was caused by a problem that transpired during takeoff. When *Columbia* was launched, a piece of foam detached from the shuttle's external tank and damaged the thermal protection system on the left wing. The damage allowed extreme heat to build up in the insulation of the wing during reentry, and the wing's aluminum began to melt. This melting deteriorated the structure of the wing, and the shuttle eventually lost control. The wing began to break apart, followed by the remainder of the shuttle. All seven crew members, including the first Israeli citizen to travel in space, perished.

There had been trouble with the shuttle's foam panels in the past. Prior to the disaster, there were seven other instances in which a piece of foam had been lost during flight, causing minor damage to *Columbia*. These instances were considered unavoidable but not a safety threat, and the launches continued. This fact stirred much debate about measures that could have been taken to prevent the disaster from happening.

Impact

The NASA space shuttle program was suspended after the loss of *Columbia*, and construction on the International Space Station was halted as a result. In January 2004, President George W. Bush announced his vision for space exploration, which included the development of a new space vehicle. A plan for this vehicle was devised and later became the *Orion* spacecraft. The suspension of the space shuttle program was eventually lifted in 2005 with the launch of *Discovery*.

Further Reading

Columbia *Crew Survival Investigation Report.* Houston: Natl. Aeronautics and Space Administration, 2008. PDF file.

"Space Shuttle *Columbia* Disintegrates, Crew Lost."
National Geographic News. National Geographic Society, 1 Feb. 2003. Web. 7 Sept. 2012.

"Timeline: America's Space Program." *NPR.* National Public Radio, 2012. Web. 7 Sept. 2012.

Cait Caffrey

■ Space tourism

Definition: Commercial space travel meant for recreation

Space tourism, a notion once found only in the plots of science fiction books and movies, became increasingly possible with the rapid advances in space travel during the late twentieth century. At the dawn of the new millennium, the first space tourist was launched into orbit. Interest in commercial space travel grew and flights into space were available to those who could afford the high cost.

In 2001, American businessman Dennis Tito paid $20 million to travel into space to visit the International Space Station. The National Aeronautics and Space Administration (NASA) had many concerns about Tito's trip, but eventually international space officials and the private space travel firm Space Adventures reached an agreement. On April 28, 2001, Tito became the first space tourist. Space Adventures subsequently launched several other paying individuals into space.

Space tourism is classified as either orbital or suborbital. Orbital space flights such as Tito's trip travel high enough into space to achieve orbit around the Earth. Suborbital space flight does not travel as far, but simply ascends into space and then returns to Earth. Suborbital flight has been deemed the most marketable venture for the space tourism industry. Many suborbital flight projects were in the works by the end of the 1990s. In 2004, Virgin Mobile founder Richard Branson's commercial space company, Virgin Galactic, began developing plans for suborbital passenger flights that reached sixty-two miles above Earth at a price of $200,000 per ticket.

Several wealthy entrepreneurs, recognizing the potential for orbital space travel, set about financing their own space tourism projects. Space X, a private space travel firm founded by entrepreneur Elon Musk, sought to revolutionize space travel by developing its own rockets, with an overall goal of transporting people to other planets. Plans for hotels in space were also being formulated. Robert Bigelow, founder of the hotel chain Budget Suites of America, began developing inflatable space habitats in early 2000. The first prototype, known as Genesis I, was launched in July of 2006. More advanced prototypes meant to accommodate humans followed.

Impact

Surveys have suggested that while the majority of the population would like to participate in space travel, the cost has limited participation to the wealthiest of people. Developers have expected the prices to fall as technology continues to advance. With that in mind, some companies have extended their tourism plans beyond Earth's boundaries, starting with trips that would orbit the moon.

Further Reading

McKinley, Jesse. "Space Tourism Is Here! Wealthy Adventurers Wanted." *New York Times.* New York Times Co., 7 Sep. 2012. Web. 5 Dec. 2012.

Thompson, Mark. "Bigelow's Inflatable Space Stations." *SEN.* Sen TV, 27 Aug. 2012. Web. 5 Dec. 2012.

Wall, Mike. "First Space Tourist: How a US Millionaire Bought a Ticket to Orbit." *Space.com.* TechMediaNetwork.com, 27 Apr. 2011. Web. 5 Dec. 2012.

Cait Caffrey

■ Spears, Britney

Identification: American singer, actress
Born: December 2, 1981; Kentwood, Louisiana

Spears is one of the most successful singers in the world. Her first three albums debuted at number one on the Billboard pop music charts and produced several hit songs. In the late 2000s, her career was temporarily disrupted by personal and health issues.

In early 2000, Britney Spears was one of the most popular entertainers in the world. She marked professional and personal milestones that year, releasing her second album, *Oops! I Did It Again*, which sold more than a million copies in the first week following its debut, and revealing her relationship with singer Justin Timberlake. In 2001, she released her third album, *Britney*, which also debuted at number one.

Spears's romance with Timberlake had ended in 2001, and the performer began working to change

Britney Spears. (©iStockphoto.com/Sion Touhig)

her innocent image. After a racy cover spread in *W* magazine in 2003, she gained more media attention after kissing singer Madonna at the MTV Video Music Awards. Also in 2003, Spears released her fourth album, *In the Zone*, which produced the single "Toxic." The song earned the star her first Grammy Award. Spears generated national headlines in 2004 with her fifty-five hour marriage to her friend Jason Alexander, whom she wed in Las Vegas. By the end of 2004, Spears had married again, this time to dancer Kevin Federline. In 2005, Spears gave birth to the couple's son, Sean Preston. She surprised fans in 2006 when she appeared on the cover of *Harper's Bazaar* pregnant with the couple's second child, Jayden James, who was born a few months later.

The following year marked the beginning of trouble for Spears. She and Federline divorced, and he was awarded custody of their children following a long dispute that involved allegations of drug abuse.

Spears then checked into rehab after several incidents of widely reported erratic behavior, which included shaving her head. Although Spears's performance at the 2007 MTV Video Music Awards show was widely criticized, her fifth album, *Blackout* (2007), was a critical and commercial success. However, in 2008, Spears was hospitalized for another breakdown.

Later in 2008, Spears made a guest appearance on the television show *How I Met Your Mother* and returned to the MTV Video Music Awards, where she received three awards. At the close of the year, she released her new album, *Circus* (2008), and toured to promote the album throughout 2009.

Impact

During the 2000s, Spears transformed from a teenage pop princess to a successful, if sometimes troubled, musician. During several difficult years, critics predicted that her career was over, and many wondered whether or not she would survive the challenges of fame and her issues with substance abuse. However, Spears persevered and remained one of decade's most popular entertainers .

Further Reading

Dennis, Steve. *Britney: Inside the Dream: The Biography.* London: Harper, 2009. Print.

Heard, Christopher. *Britney Spears: Little Girl Lost.* Montreal: Transit, 2010. Print.

People. "Britney Spears Biography." *People.* Time Inc., n. d. Web. 12 July 2012.

Angela Harmon

■ Spielberg, Steven

Identification: American director and producer
Born: December 18, 1946; Cincinnati, Ohio

As a director and producer, Steven Spielberg created some of the most memorable, entertaining, and financially successful films in Hollywood history. Characterized by staggering technical ingenuity, sentimental story lines, and uplifting endings, Spielberg's films delighted global audiences during the 2000s.

Steven Spielberg began his career as a filmmaker while still in high school, writing and directing the science-fiction feature *Firelight* in 1964. He gained

Steven Spielberg. (©iStockphoto.com/Jason Merritt)

critical attention for his work on the made-for-television film *Duel* (1971) and achieved commercial success with the release of *Jaws* (1975). Over the course of his career, Spielberg directed, wrote, and produced films in a wide variety of genres, ranging from science fiction to action-adventure to historical drama. In 1994, he joined friends and fellow media executives David Geffen and Jeffery Katzenberg to form DreamWorks, a film studio and production company.

In the first decade of the twenty-first century, Spielberg's influence continued to grow and spread into new forms of popular entertainment. He directed several Academy Award–nominated films during the period, including *A.I. Artificial Intelligence* (2001), which he also cowrote; *Catch Me If You Can* (2002); and *Munich* (2005). He also lent his name and skills as producer to a number of projects, including the Academy Award–winning war drama *Letters from Iwo Jima* (2006). He served as executive

producer for *Transformers* (2007) and *Transformers: Revenge of the Fallen* (2009), the first two installments in a blockbuster franchise, as well as *The Lovely Bones* (2009), an adaptation of the bestselling novel of the same name. Spielberg's projects typically feature strong narratives with clearly defined central characters and obvious conflicts. His projects display core themes and characteristics such as fondness for children and their sense of wonder, fascination with the single mother as caregiver, the search for the good father, remarkably staged action sequences, and highly accomplished and innovative special effects. Known as a technical wizard since the beginning of his career, Spielberg has broadened his interests to include issues of social and historical concern while still connecting to diverse audiences worldwide.

Impact

Named by *Time* magazine as one of the hundred most important people of the twentieth century and labeled the most influential person of his generation by *Life* magazine, Spielberg is one of the most financially successful directors in Hollywood history. He continued to make groundbreaking, critically lauded, and commercially successful films into the second decade of the twenty-first century, and by 2012, several films he directed or produced remained among the top fifty box-office hits of all time.

Further Reading

Buckland, Warren. *Directed by Steven Spielberg: Poetics of the Contemporary Hollywood Blockbuster.* New York: Continuum, 2006. Print.

Friedman, Lester D. *Citizen Spielberg.* Urbana: U of Illinois P, 2006. Print.

Kowalski, Dean A., ed. *Steven Spielberg and Philosophy.* Lexington: U of Kentucky P, 2008. Print.

Carolyn Anderson, PhD

■ Stem cell research

Definition: Medical research involving the use of stem cells, which have the ability to renew and differentiate into other cells

While adult stem cells had been researched for decades, stem cell research drew significant attention in the late 1990s when a biologist isolated the first embryonic stem cells. Un-

like adult stem cells, these were able to divide into any type of human cell. Scientists faced hurdles, however, when the United States placed limits on embryonic stem cell research during the 2000s.

Adult, or somatic, stem cells are found throughout tissues and organs of the body. They are able to divide and regenerate a range of cell types, though this ability is limited to a cell's tissue or organ of origin. Embryonic stem cells are typically obtained from embryos created for in vitro fertilization procedures. The embryos that are not needed for uterine implantation are often offered for research with the consent of the donor. These embryonic cells differ from adult stem cells in that they can differentiate into any type of cell, produce a greater number of cells, and are easier to grow. Scientists quickly found that embryonic stem cells held tremendous potential for medical research and gathered support for this work. They were met with opposition from abortion opponents and other groups, who argued that embryos were human life and should be treated as such.

In 2001, President George W. Bush announced his decision to allow embryonic stem cell research on cell lines already in existence. He decided to allow the research because the destruction of an embryo had already taken place, but he banned funding on future cell lines. Proponents of stem cell research were happy that the president would allow the research but unhappy with the limits on cell lines. They knew that they would need new cell lines to keep up with research. Opponents wanted a full ban. Over the next few years, researchers discovered that there were fewer existing cell lines than originally thought and found that many of them were unusable. They worried that other countries would take the lead in stem cell research and regenerative medicine.

A Push for Reform
By 2004, the stem cell debate had heated up again and many scientists and health care officials wanted to reform the 2001 policy. Members of Congress sent letters to the president requesting that he reform his strict policy, and the Stem Cell Research Enhancement Act of 2004 was introduced. The act sought more support for stem cell research, but it did not pass the House of Representatives. Stem cell research became a main issue of the 2004 presidential election

when Democratic presidential candidate Senator John Kerry supported increased funding for research. The Bush administration would not budge on the issue, defaulting to the 2001 policy.

The following year, the Stem Cell Research Enhancement Act was reintroduced, but this time, it passed the House and then went to the Senate for consideration. In 2006, the Senate announced the creation of two additional bills on the issue. One of the bills supported stem cell research without the destruction of human embryos; the other prohibited creating embryos exclusively for research. The Senate passed all three bills in July 2008, but only two of the bills, including the Stem Cell Research Enhancement Act, made it through the House. Bush passed the other bill and vetoed the Stem Cell Research Enhancement Act.

In 2007, the House and the Senate again passed the Stem Cell Research Enhancement Act but with some provisions. The House and Senate also passed another bill regarding the way stem cells were derived, but again the president vetoed them.

A Victory for Stem Cell Research
During the 2008 presidential campaign, Democratic candidate Barack Obama pledged to reform the Stem Cell Research Enhancement Act. The bill was reintroduced in February 2009, along with the Stem Cell Research Improvement Act, and both were sent to committee. On March 9, 2009, President Obama kept his promise, overturning the Bush policy through an executive order. This paved the way for additional human embryonic stem cell lines and allotted funding for this research. The order allowed the National Institutes of Health (NIH) to establish ethical guidelines for the use, creation, and research of all stem cells. The NIH published these guidelines in July 2009.

Impact
Stem cell research is vital to identifying how stem cells can be used to treat diseases and other medical conditions. Stem cells could be used to generate cells and tissues to treat conditions and to replace damaged tissues and organs. For example, scientists hope to generate healthy heart muscles for those with heart disease and to help those with type 1 diabetes create their own insulin-producing cells. Utilizing stem cells to grow organs and tissues could help alleviate the great, unmet need for organ donors. Stem

cells can also be used to test potential new drugs. In addition to heart disease and diabetes, some of the diseases and conditions that scientists hope to treat with stem cells include Alzheimer's disease, burns, cancer, osteoarthritis, Parkinson's disease, rheumatoid arthritis, spinal cord injuries, and stroke.

Further Reading

"AAAS Policy Brief: Stem Cell Research." *American Association for the Advancement of Science.* American Assn. for the Advancement of Science, 12 Aug. 2011. Web. 18 Dec. 2012. Explains the US policy regarding stem cell research.

Kelly, Evelyn B. *Stem Cells.* Westport: Greenwood, 2007. Print. Explains what stem cell research is and outlines the basic ethical debates surrounding the topic.

Scadden, David T. "Current Human Clinical Applications Using Adult Stem Cells." *International Society for Stem Cell Research.* International Soc. for Stem Cell Research, 14 Aug. 2006. Web. 18 Dec. 2012. Outlines how adult stem cells are used to treat medical conditions.

Stem Cell Information. Natl. Institutes of Health, 7 Sept. 2011. Web. 18 Dec. 2012. Includes an FAQ section, lists research topics in the field, and provides information on federal policies and litigation relating to stem cell research.

"What Are Stem Cells?" *Medical News Today.* MediLexicon International, n.d. Web. 26 Nov. 2012. Examines stem cells and what they do.

Angela Harmon

Prominent Players Listed in the Mitchell Report.

Position Players	Career Batting Avg. (as of 2012)
Bonds, Barry	.298
Canseco, José	.266
Dykstra, Lenny	.285
Giambi, Jason	.281
Justice, David	.279
Knoblauch, Chuck	.289
Lo Duca, Paul	.286
Roberts, Brian	.280
Sheffield, Gary	.292
Tejada, Miguel	.285
Vaughn, Mo	.293
Williams, Matt	.268
Pitchers	**Career Earned Run Avg. (as of 2012)**
Brown, Kevin	3.28
Clemens, Roger	3.12
Gagné, Éric	3.47
Neagle, Denny	4.24
Pettitte, Andy	3.85
Rocker, John	3.42
Stanton, Mike	3.92

■ Steroids in baseball

Definition: Many of Major League Baseball's biggest stars were accused of using steroids during the 2000s

In 2003, Major League Baseball implemented a policy to test players for performance-enhancing drugs such as steroids. Following a raid on a laboratory believed to be supplying illegal steroids to players, a number of the league's biggest stars were accused of taking steroids. Throughout the decade, federal investigations and a league-wide review of steroid use in baseball implicated nearly ninety players. The fallout from the use of steroids in baseball sullied the league's reputation and threatened the legacies of some of baseball's most revered players.

At the end of the 1990s and the beginning of the 2000s, some of Major League Baseball's (MLB) biggest stars—Mark McGwire, Barry Bonds, and Sammy Sosa—were celebrated for surpassing the single-season home-run record. However, at the start of the 2000s, it was revealed that the league, which banned the use of performance-enhancing drugs (PEDs) but did not have a testing program in place, had a PED-use problem that likely included these superstars. The "steroid era" of baseball had a major impact on the sport and its fans during the 2000s.

The BALCO Raid

In 2003, federal investigators raided the Bay Area Laboratory Co-Operative (BALCO) in Burlingame,

California, on suspicion that the company was supplying undetectable steroids and other PEDs to professional athletes. Following the raid, a grand jury convened to investigate BALCO. Among the BALCO figures under scrutiny was Greg Anderson, who was a trainer for San Francisco Giants player Bonds, one of the players subpoenaed to testify about his connections to BALCO. Another player, Jason Giambi, admitted to using BALCO-supplied PEDs, while Bonds admitted that Anderson gave him a balm and a cream that he did not realize were steroids.

The BALCO raid and investigation sent shock waves through the league, and Commissioner Bud Selig called upon the players union to work with him to rid baseball of PEDs. However, this mandate, along with many teams' reactions to the BALCO revelations, seemed to analysts somewhat hypocritical; many people close to the league indicated that seemingly everyone involved in baseball either knew or should have known that allegations of PED use were not only attached to some of the biggest names in baseball but also that use was rampant throughout the league.

The Mitchell Report

In order to better understand the breadth of steroid use in baseball, MLB officials turned to former senator George Mitchell. In 2006, Mitchell was asked to investigate steroid use among players since the beginning of the 2000s (although he was given license to look back further in some cases). Mitchell's panel interviewed hundreds of people associated with Major League Baseball, such as general managers, coaches, and trainers (although, with a few exceptions, players refused to cooperate with his inquiry).

Mitchell's final report was damning for the entire league. The panel took to task both the commissioner's office and the players union for failing at least to acknowledge the use of PEDs if not creating an environment in which such behavior was acceptable. The report also named nearly ninety players who, the panel was told, used steroids. Among them were Bonds, former Cy Young Award–winning pitcher Eric Gagné, 2002 Most Valuable Player Miguel Tejada, and pitching superstar Roger Clemens.

The Mitchell report was considered an eye-opener for professional sports in general. However, it was not without controversy. Players in particular argued that the report was based on hearsay rather than on facts. Players and their agents and attorneys argued that

since the players themselves did not cooperate, the others were not in positions to make such accusations. To be sure, when Mitchell reached out to the players and the players union, the athletes flatly refused, citing their concern that any information uncovered about the players would somehow make it to the public eye. With Mitchell's panel unable to guarantee confidentiality, the information provided in the report was derived from apparent witnesses, not the players themselves.

Federal Investigations

As the revelations about BALCO and of the Mitchell Report came to light, players named in either of the proceedings were quick to defend themselves. One player in particular, Bonds, was targeted not only by the grand jury and the Mitchell Report but also in another federal investigation. Bonds had told the BALCO grand jury that he was unknowingly given steroids by his trainer. Others involved in the Mitchell Report and the BALCO grand jury investigation refuted Bonds's claim, stating that Bonds knew exactly what he was using and, in fact, had used other steroids repeatedly throughout the latter part of his career.

The contradictory stories surrounding Bonds led to a formal federal investigation, determined to assess whether Bonds perjured himself before that grand jury. Anderson refused to cooperate with the Bonds investigation and was subsequently jailed for a lengthy term. Meanwhile, another of Bonds's associates, Steve Hoskins (a longtime friend and business partner) told the grand jury that Bonds complained to him of soreness from his frequent steroid injections. Hoskins also secretly recorded Anderson in 2003; in the recording, Anderson states that he injected Bonds on a number of occasions. This "evidence," according to Bond's defense, was sullied by the fact that Hoskins and Bonds had had a falling out after Bonds reported to federal agents that Hoskins had stolen from their business venture.

Meanwhile, Clemens was also targeted, although in this case, it was Congress that accused the baseball star of perjury. Clemens, who testified at a congressional committee in 2007 with other baseball stars named in the Mitchell Report, told the committee that he never knowingly took steroids or any other PEDs. Congress turned over the case to the Justice Department, believing that evidence (such as Brian McNamee's claims in the Mitchell Report that he had personally injected Clemens) indicated that Clemens lied to the legislative committee. Clemens maintained his innocence throughout the affair, as investigators and detractors continued to accuse him of drug use. By the end of the 2000s, the Clemens case remained unresolved, while Clemens retired from professional baseball to deal with the ongoing case. (He was acquitted on all charges in 2012.)

The Bonds and Clemens cases provided illustrations of the zeal with which investigators and others wished to hold athletes responsible for their alleged use of PEDs. Many, including supporters of these and other players, argued that the Bonds and Clemens cases amounted to a witch hunt, with prosecutors fighting with unnecessary vigor to make an example of these players. Even when hard evidence was difficult to obtain, these individuals claimed, prosecutors continued to push, stretching the cases out for years.

Drug Testing

The revelation that PED use was widespread in baseball (and the fact that Major League Baseball had clearly failed to address the issue) damaged the league's reputation. Baseball needed to repair the disastrous public image this issue created for the sport by making some sort of statement that seemed genuinely apologetic—a difficult undertaking, considering the prevailing perception that baseball could have policed itself years prior. League officials also had to look to the future by installing a new steroid testing policy, one that would result in serious punishments for those caught using PEDs. This task for the league was seemingly as daunting as the task of repairing its image; in fact, the two seemed to go hand in hand.

After the BALCO case and the Mitchell Report came to bear, the players union and league officials began discusses a new testing policy that was mutually agreeable to both parties and which would show a league-wide desire to curb steroid use in the sport. The final policy, agreed upon in 2005, involved random testing of players (even during the off-season), with lengthy suspensions for those caught using steroids for the first time. These punishments would also be made public, a point that Commissioner Bud Selig argued would further deter steroid use.

In the minds of many onlookers and analysts, parts of the testing policy seemed strict, but overall the policy did not go far enough to prevent further steroid use in baseball. For example, the tests looked for

steroids but not human growth hormone or amphetamines. Furthermore, the policy did not seem to account for the ever-evolving nature of the PED industry—BALCO and other steroid-producing laboratories were consistently working to develop new, undetectable, and more effective steroids for professional athletes. Some experts argued that the policy had too many loopholes and lacked any external oversight to truly make a difference. Meanwhile, as the end of the decade approached, several superstars, many of whom were considered likely Baseball Hall of Fame inductees, were linked to PED use. These players included Manny Ramirez, who was suspended for fifty games in 2009 for testing positive for human chorionic gonadotropin (a testosterone-increasing hormone), and Alex Rodriguez, who admitted in 2009 that he had used steroids for three seasons at the beginning of the decade.

Impact

The raid of the BALCO facility and the subsequent federal investigation made public what many people within Major League Baseball apparently knew for years: steroid use was rampant, particularly during the 1990s. The Mitchell Report that followed went even farther, humiliating not only the players but also the league, which it suggested ignored the drug use of its players. Only a few years earlier, both fans and the league celebrated the record-setting accomplishments of such players as McGwire, Sosa, and Bonds, but by the early 2000s, these players were thrust into the spotlight as representatives of the steroid era.

The revelation of steroid use in baseball had strong implications for all professional sports. Each professional sport (baseball included) in the United States was called upon to ensure that it had strict testing standards governing steroids, human growth hormone, and other PEDs. Major League Baseball implemented such a program that resulted in several high-profile suspensions. Meanwhile, the accomplishments of Clemens, Bonds, and McGwire were marred. Clemens and Bonds remained under federal investigation at the end of the 2000s, ensuring that the steroid issue in baseball would continue into the next decade.

Further Reading

Comarow, Avery, and Lisa Stein. "Baseball's Iffy Steroid Test." *US News and World Report* 136.8 (2004). Features an interview with a steroids expert, who expresses his views on the developing 2005 testing policy implemented by Major League Baseball.

Fainaru-Wada, Mark, and Lance Williams. *Game of Shadows: Barry Bonds, BALCO, and the Steroids Scandal That Rocked Professional Sports.* New York: Gotham, 2007. One of the first in-depth accounts of the steroid scandal in professional baseball.

Radomski, Kirk. *Bases Loaded: The Inside Story of the Steroid Era in Baseball by the Central Figure in the Mitchell Report.* New York: Hudson, 2009. Radomski describes his career and how he supplied players with steroids, human growth hormone, and other PEDs during the 1990s.

Schmotzer, Brian, Patrick D. Kilgo, and Jeff Switchenko. "'The Natural'? The Effects of Steroids on Offensive Performance in Baseball." *Chance* 22.2 (2009): 21–32. Discusses the steroid scandal, shedding light on why baseball players used PEDs throughout the 1990s.

Verducci, Tom. "Reason to Believe." *Sports Illustrated* 102.8 (2005): 39–45. Discusses the 2005 baseball season, the first full season following the steroid scandal. Reviews the new testing policy put forth after the scandal broke.

Michael Auerbach

Jon Stewart. (Department of Defense/Photograph by Air Force Technical Sergeant Adam M. Stump)

■ Stewart, Jon

Identification: American television personality
Born: November 28, 1962; New York, New York

A comedian turned commentator, Jon Stewart offered biting political satire and skepticism about the news media during the 2000s as host of Comedy Central's Daily Show with Jon Stewart. *Despite his program's comedic nature, Stewart became an influential figure in American political media, particularly among younger viewers.*

Jon Stewart, born Jonathan Stuart Leibowitz, made his comedy debut at the Bitter End in New York's Greenwich Village in 1987 and worked as a stand-up comic, actor, and television writer and host throughout the 1990s. Stewart's major opportunity came in 1998, when he was asked to take over *The Daily Show* on Comedy Central, replacing host Craig Kilborn. Stewart, whose name was incorporated into the show's title in 1999, took the show in a new direction, making it a platform for his critiques on the current state of politics and bias in the news media.

Viewership of *The Daily Show* increased tremendously during Stewart's tenure. Stewart effectively used "satire and humor to critique media and politics with a revealing and unabashed honesty, calling attention to hypocrisy in politics and the media and warning viewers of the dangers of taking everything they saw on television at face value. The show garnered a particularly large share of the viewing audience in the thirty-and-under demographic, sparking an interest in political issues in the United States and abroad among those viewers.

As Stewart's fake news" show began to be taken more seriously, Stewart interviewed powerful figures in the realm of politics and the news media, including presidential candidates and prominent television news journalists. Stewart's humorous yet intelligent and incisive coverage of such major political events as the 2000 and 2004 presidential elections attracted many young people whom much of American media had previously considered apathetic about political issues. In recognition of its election coverage, *The Daily Show* received the prestigious Peabody Award for electronic media in 2000 and 2004. Stewart's mock textbook *America (The Book): A Citizen's Guide to Democracy Inaction*, cowritten with the *Daily Show* writing staff and published just prior to the 2004 election, became a best seller. Stewart continued to cover politics and major events in the United States and elsewhere through the latter half of the decade, hosting *The Daily Show* and making guest appearances on more traditional news programs on other networks.

Impact

Over the course of his professional career, Stewart evolved from a relatively obscure stand-up comedian into an influential political satirist and media critic. He remained host of *The Daily Show* into the next decade, continuing to call public attention to news events and covering political events such as the 2012 presidential election.

Further Reading

Baym, Geoffrey. *From Cronkite to Colbert: The Evolution of Broadcast News.* Boulder: Paradigm, 2010. Print.

Cassino, Dan, and Yasemin Besen-Cassino. *Consuming Politics: Jon Stewart, Branding, and the Youth Vote in America.* Madison: Fairleigh Dickinson UP, 2009. Print.

Hamm, Theodore. *The New Blue Media: How Michael Moore, MoveOn.Org, Jon Stewart, and Company Are Transforming Progressive Politics.* New York: New, 2008. Print.

Brad C. Southard

■ Stewart, Martha

Identification: American entrepreneur and television personality
Born: August 3, 1941; Jersey City, New Jersey

Martha Stewart's many how-to books, website, and television shows teach cooking, homemaking, gardening, and decorating skills. Stewart also founded Martha Stewart Living Omnimedia, a successful publishing and merchandising company. After being convicted on charges of insider trading in 2004 and serving time in prison in the mid-2000s, she rebuilt her media empire.

Martha Stewart. (Courtesy David Shankbone)

At the height of Martha Stewart's highly successful career, America's first self-made woman billionaire suddenly faced charges of insider trading. In December 2001, she sold 3,926 shares of her stock in ImClone, which had produced an anticancer drug that was not going to receive approval from the US Food and Drug Administration (FDA). While it appeared that Stewart was acting on illegal insider information, she claimed that her stockbroker had a standing order to sell her shares whenever the stock fell beneath a certain level.

In 2003, the Justice Department and the Securities Exchange Commission (SEC) questioned Stewart about her sale of ImClone stock. On June 4, 2003, she was indicted for misleading the investigators. A federal grand jury also charged her with securities fraud, obstruction of justice, and conspiracy. That same day, Stewart resigned as CEO and chair of Martha Stewart Living Omnimedia.

On February 27, 2004, US district judge Marian Cedarbaum decided that the securities fraud charge was "unfounded" and should be dropped. Stewart's case soon went to trial in New York City; on March 5, she was found guilty of conspiracy, obstruction of justice, and two counts of false statements. On March 8, the CBS television network stopped airing *Martha Stewart Living*. Seven days later, Stewart resigned from the board of Omnimedia.

Stewart faced twenty years in prison; however, on July 17, Judge Cedarbaum decided on a lighter sentenced of five months in jail, five months of house arrest, and a fine of thirty thousand dollars. Stewart and her lawyers decided to appeal, but she told the public that she would serve her jail time as soon as possible.

On October 8, 2004, Stewart entered Alderson Federal Prison Camp, a low-security facility in West Virginia. Stewart was released on March 4, 2005, at which time she flew home to Bedford, New York, where she was placed under house arrest. After Stewart's house arrest ended on August 31, 2005, she remained on probation until March 2007.

After her release from prison, Stewart began to rebuild her career. She rejoined her magazine and began hosting a new television show, called *Martha*. She also starred in the reality game show *The Apprentice: Martha Stewart*, which was cancelled after its first season.

In 2005, she published *The Martha Rules*, which gives readers advice about starting and running a business. She was also featured on her own satellite radio program and produced several new how-to videos. In 2010, Stewart's longtime friend and associate Mariana Pasternak published a book entitled *The Best of Friends: Martha and Me*.

Impact

Martha Stewart is known for her business success, having created an empire that spreads across media, publishing, merchandising, and online commerce. In addition to writing best-selling books, she has created *Martha Stewart Living*, a successful magazine, and an internationally broadcasted talk show. She has received numerous awards, and in 2011, she was inducted into the New Jersey Hall of Fame.

Further Reading

Byron, Christopher. *Martha Inc.: The Incredible Story of Martha Stewart Living Omnimedia*. New York: Wiley, 2002. Print.

Stewart, Martha. *The Martha Rules: 10 Essentials for Achieving Success as You Start, Build, or Manage a Business*. New York: Random, 2005. Print.

Stoynoff, Natasha. *Being Martha: The Inside Story of Martha Stewart and Her Amazing Life*. Hoboken: Lloyd, 2006. Print.

Ellen Moser

■ Subprime mortgage crisis

Definition: The central economic crisis of the 2000s, in which banks and other lending institutions granted home mortgages to borrowers who could not afford to pay them, leading to a price collapse in the US housing market and the worst global economic downturn since the Great Depression of the 1930s

Through much of the 2000s, US home prices were spurred on to ever-greater heights by historic low interest rates and relaxed lending standards. In late 2007, the booming US housing market collapsed as a result of the subprime mortgage crisis. As the crisis spread, banks and other lenders found themselves holding large amounts of bad debt, which in turn led to plunging property prices, tightening credit, and a near-collapse of the financial system. By decade's end, the United States was facing the most punishing economic conditions since the Great Depression.

In decades past, banks and other lending institutions were very strict about whom they gave mortgages because they financed such loans through the deposits made by their customers. This changed in 1999, when the US Congress, with the support of the Clinton administration, repealed the Glass-Steagall Act of 1933. This law was enacted in the aftermath of the Great Depression, an economic downturn that had put a full quarter of the US workforce out of work. Glass-Steagall separated the business actions of investment banks from those of regular commercial banks in an effort to control the sort of rampant speculation that had spawned the Depression. The act also established the Federal Deposit Insurance Corporation (FDIC), a government body that guarantees bank deposits up to a certain value. With the end of Glass-Steagall, banks were allowed to take more risks in order to produce greater returns for their investors.

Lead-up to Crisis

One way that banks sought to make greater profits was to sell the mortgages they issued to the bond markets. When the dot-com bubble burst in 2000, leading to the decade's first economic recession in 2001, investors sought to find a new area to place their money. One investment seen as potentially very lucrative was the bond market, where banks were beginning to sell mortgage-backed securities—considered a safe investment because borrowers tended to pay their mortgages regularly for the life of their loans. Investors seeking to earn high interest rates could not place their money in US Treasury securities or municipal bonds, as the US Federal Reserve had dropped interest rates to 1 percent in June 2003 and kept them low in order spur the sluggish economy. High-yield mortgage-backed securities seemed a far better return on investment, especially in light of the fact that credit-rating agencies such as Fitch, Moody's, and Standard & Poor's (S&P) had claimed such securities were as safe as US Treasuries, the debt-financing instrument of the federal government.

Mortgage-backed securities, however, were not as safe as US Treasury securities and became less safe as more of them were sold to the bond market. As banks sold more and more such mortgage securities to the bond market, they were less careful about whom they were issuing mortgages. Fund managers in turn did little research on the mortgage securities they were buying, instead relying on the assurances of the credit-rating agencies. Moreover, such securities had no oversight and were not regulated by any independent financial institution or government body.

Subprime Market Expands

From 2002 to 2007, banks and other lending institutions invested heavily in the mortgage-bond market, an area that had been previously been controlled by the Federal National Mortgage Association (better known as Fannie Mae) and the Federal Home Loan Mortgage Corporation (better known as Freddie Mac). These two government-sponsored enterprises (which are also publicly traded companies) were established to pool mortgage securities and expand opportunities for mortgage lending and new home purchases. Fannie Mae and Freddie Mac often helped grant loans to so-called subprime borrowers—people with poor credit histories and/or low incomes who

might have difficulty paying their mortgages regularly. In the 2000s, private institutions wanted to lend to these borrowers as well. By 2006, Fannie and Freddie no longer dominated the market: banks and other private lending institutions had granted approximately 84 percent of subprime mortgages issued that year.

Banks earned a fee for each mortgage-backed security they sold to fund managers. By 2007, the mortgage-bond market was estimated to be worth $6 trillion, the largest chunk of the US bond market, then worth upward of $27 trillion. In fact, mortgage bonds were more valuable than US Treasury bonds during this period. The urge for ever-higher profits spurred banks and Wall Street investment houses to become even more creative, by bundling subprime mortgages, reselling them after holding them for short periods of time, and ignoring traditional lending standards, such as evaluating a potential borrower's credit rating and income. Banks also moved away from traditional twenty- and thirty-year fixed rate mortgages and toward exotic mortgages. These included interest-only loans; adjustable rate mortgages (ARMs), in which low initial rates spiked after a fixed period; and negative amortization loans, in which a borrower's debt actually increased month after month. These subprime mortgages came to dominate the bond market; by 2005, 20 percent of mortgages granted in the United States were subprime.

Collapse and Fallout

The drive for short-term profits spawned an unstable housing market. Beginning in 2007 and continuing through the end of the decade, banks started repossessing homes across the country as countless subprime mortgages reset to higher interest rates. A flood of borrowers had found themselves unable to continue repaying those mortgages. As repossessions increased, home prices across the country collapsed, leading to the first national reversal in home prices since the Great Depression. In January 2008, economists reported that the country had seen the largest single-year drop in new single-family home sales in twenty-seven years. In addition to affecting home sales and housing prices, the subprime mortgage crisis devastated the home-building industry, which had contributed as much as 6.3 percent of US gross domestic product in 2005. Moreover, the overall US economy—and the global economy—plunged into the worst economic downturn in decades, a downturn that came to be known as the Great Recession.

Many large and extremely powerful financial institutions that had invested heavily in mortgage-backed securities found themselves on the point of collapse. Although little noticed at the time, HSBC Bank announced in February 2007 that it would see larger-than-expected losses due to defaults on subprime mortgages. In April of the same year, one of the largest subprime mortgage lenders in the United States, New Century Financial, filed for bankruptcy. As the crisis spread, the US Federal Reserve began cutting interest rates. It would not only cut rates ten times between mid August 2007 and late October 2008, but it also began to loan money directly to both commercial banks and Wall Street investment houses. It even accepted now-toxic mortgage-backed securities as collateral, all in an effort to keep the financial system functioning.

In March 2008, at the prompting of the Federal Reserve, J. P. Morgan Chase bought out the Wall Street investment bank Bear Sterns. In September of the same year, another huge Wall Street firm, Lehman Brothers, filed for bankruptcy protection, which sparked a worldwide panic in the financial markets. By month's end, Bank of America had acquired the Wall Street brokerage house Merrill Lynch; Wachovia Bank collapsed and was bought out by Wells Fargo the following month; and Washington Mutual became the largest bank failure in US history. Other banks around the world also faced collapse.

Also in September 2008, at the direction of the administration of President George W. Bush, the US Treasury bailed out Fannie Mae and Freddie Mac, which put the US government in charge of over $5 trillion in home mortgages. In order to save the private financial sector, the Bush administration asked Congress to pass the Troubled Asset Relief Program (TARP), which it did in October 2008. TARP used $700 billion to buy assets and equity from financial institutions to keep the country's financial institutions stable and hold off a possible economic depression.

Impact

The subprime mortgage crisis led directly to the financial crisis that followed, in which credit tightened significantly and businesses and individuals could no longer get loans as easily. As a result, businesses that were unable to get new lines of credit sought to save money by making their organizations more efficient,

which led to massive layoffs across the country. From December 2007 to June 2009, approximately 7.9 million jobs were lost, a decrease of 6.1 percent in the overall US workforce. Moreover, the subprime mortgage crisis had an enormous impact on the global economy, hitting the nations of Greece, Spain, Ireland, Italy, and Portugal particularly hard. Although the United States emerged from the recession in mid-2009, the national economy remained sluggish in the anemic recovery that followed. Hiring was weak and unemployment high through the end of the decade.

While interest rates remained at historic lows, many consumers were unwilling or unable to borrow money at the same levels they had through much of the 2000s. This was due in part to the fact that many consumers had spent far more than they earned in this period and were seeking to put themselves on a more secure financial footing. Others had been so severely hurt by stagnant wages, depreciated retirement accounts, and falling home prices in the fallout from the subprime mortgage crisis and the Great Recession that they simply could not borrow any more. Still others had been bankrupted by all that had transpired. Many economists believed it would take several years for the overall US economy to return to the levels of prosperity it had enjoyed at the end of the twentieth century.

Further Reading

Lewis, Michael. *The Big Short: Inside the Doomsday Machine.* New York: Norton, 2010. Describes how individuals working for the bond and real estate derivative markets helped to create the subprime mortgage crisis.

Morgenson, Gretchen, and Joshua Rosner. *Reckless Endangerment: How Outsized Ambition, Greed, and Corruption Led to Economic Armageddon.* New York: Holt, 2011. Examines how government regulators were negligent in their oversight of the subprime mortgage market and helped to create a climate in which the drive toward short-term financial gain helped wreck the global economy.

Muolo, Paul, and Mathew Padilla. *Chain of Blame: How Wall Street Caused the Mortgage and Credit Crisis.* Hoboken: Wiley, 2008. Seeks to untangle the subprime mortgage crisis by providing a narrative of how everyone from first-time homeowners to global banks became embroiled in the crisis.

The Subprime Solution: How Today's Global Financial Crisis Happened and What to Do about It. Princeton: Princeton UP, 2008. Examines the subprime mortgage crisis and offers a number of solutions, including more economic engineering, to prevent another such devastating economic bubble. Written by a Yale economist who had predicted the dot-com bubble before it burst in the early 2000s.

Financial Shock: A 360° Look at the Subprime Mortgage Implosion, and How to Avoid the Next Financial Crisis. Harlow: Financial Times Prentice, 2008. Provides a detailed analysis of the subprime mortgage crisis and offers suggestions on ways out of the current financial crisis. Written by the political advisor and economist who cofounded Moody's Economy.com.

Christopher Mari

■ Super Bowl XXXVIII halftime show controversy

The Event: A "wardrobe malfunction" during the Super Bowl XXXVIII halftime performance featuring Janet Jackson and Justin Timberlake
Date: February 1, 2004
Place: Houston, Texas

The New England Patriots beat the Carolina Panthers in Super Bowl XXXVIII; however, the game itself was not as widely discussed as the halftime show. Singer Janet Jackson experienced a "wardrobe malfunction" during her performance with Justin Timberlake that exposed her breast, angering viewers and eliciting a lawsuit from the Federal Communications Commission (FCC).

On February 1, 2004, CBS broadcast Super Bowl XXXVIII, in which the New England Patriots defeated the Carolina Panthers in a three-point win. The Patriots' win was overshadowed, however, by the halftime show. The performance, which was produced by MTV, featured singers Janet Jackson and Justin Timberlake. The duo performed a medley of songs that included Jackson's "Rhythm Nation" and Timberland's "Rock Your Body." Timberlake ripped off a piece of Jackson's costume, exposing her right breast. Jackson quickly covered up as cameras cut away. The incident was not mentioned on the air, but more than 140 million viewers had already seen the incident. Following the halftime show, the singers claimed that only Jackson's bra was supposed to be revealed. CBS and MTV officials, who had attended

the rehearsals leading up to the show, said they were unaware of this part of the performance. Jackson later disclosed that she and Timberlake had added the "costume reveal" during their final rehearsal but never intended to expose her breast.

MTV and CBS immediately issued apologies, acknowledging they had no prior knowledge of the costume reveal part of the performance. Timberlake also offered an apology, reiterating that the wardrobe malfunction was not intentional. On February 2, Jackson apologized for the incident, also claiming it was an accident. The same day, FCC chairman Michael Powell announced an investigation into the matter. He said the FCC believed the stunt was planned to promote Jackson's new single, "Just a Little While," which was released the same day as her apology.

Impact
The FCC filed a lawsuit against CBS for the incident and fined the network $550,000. The lawsuit eventually made its way through the appeals courts, but the FCC lost when the US Supreme Court refused to hear the case. Because of the incident, the FCC changed its indecency regulations. The incident also increased public support for the Broadcast Decency Enforcement Act of 2005, which allowed the FCC to pursue harsher penalties against television stations for violating indecency regulations. In the months that followed, CBS and a number of other networks edited or removed any potentially offensive scenes from television shows in order to avoid charges of indecency. In addition, the National Football League banned MTV from future involvement in Super Bowl halftime performances.

Further Reading
Flint, Joe. "Supreme Court Rejects FCC Fine over 2004 'Wardrobe Malfunction.'" *Los Angeles Times.* Los Angeles Times, 30 June 2012. Web. 9 Aug. 2012.
Hilden, Julie. "Jackson 'Nipplegate' Illustrates the Danger of Chilling Free Speech." *CNN.* Cable News Network, 20 Feb. 2004. Web. 9 Aug. 2012.
Mihoces, Gary. "NFL, FCC Upset by Halftime Show; CBS Apologizes." *USA Today.* Gannett, 2 Feb. 2004. Web. 9 Aug. 2012.
Ogunnaike, Lola. "Capitalizing on Jackson Tempest." *New York Times.* New York Times, 4 Feb. 2012. Web. 9 Aug. 2012.

Angela Harmon

■ *Super Size Me*

Identification: A documentary film focused on the fast-food industry and its effects on consumers
Director: Morgan Spurlock (1970–)
Date: Released in 2004

The rising obesity rate became a major concern in the United States during the early 2000s. The issue piqued Morgan Spurlock's interest, and he began looking for potential causes. Believing that the fast-food industry was largely to blame for the growing epidemic, Spurlock initiated an experiment during which he ate nothing but McDonald's fast food for thirty days. He recorded his experience on film for his debut documentary, Super Size Me.

The documentary *Super Size Me* (2004) challenged viewers to take a closer look at the fast-food industry. However, Spurlock challenged himself first by sacrificing his own health and well-being to undertake a thirty-day diet consisting of nothing but McDonald's fast food. Spurlock set up a number of guidelines for the experiment—he had to eat at McDonald's three times each day and he had to try everything on the menu at least once. Additionally, if a clerk asked if he wanted to "super size" his meal, Spurlock had to say yes.

The documentary focused on Spurlock's rapid physical and mental decline while on the diet. A series of documented visits to the doctor showed that Spurlock was swiftly gaining weight and that the fast-food diet was damaging his liver. During the course of the experiment, Spurlock gained nearly twenty pounds, suffered from mood swings and lethargy, and saw his cholesterol levels soar. In addition to his examination of the physical effects of fast-food consumption, Spurlock also analyzed the effects of the industry's marketing techniques on consumers, which often targeted children.

In his film, Spurlock presents an array of statistics supporting his case against fast food, but some considered his investigation flawed due to the improbability that someone would eat fast food for every meal. Despite this, Spurlock questions why, given all the evidence pointing to its detriments, American consumers continue to patronize fast-food restaurants. Spurlock's overall message to viewers is that it is their responsibility to educate themselves about the potential health risks of fast-food consumption and not succumb to the industry's marketing strategies.

Impact

Spurlock's film drew attention to the potential hazards of the fast-food industry while also stressing the larger issue of obesity. His attempt to connect the fast-food industry to the rising obesity epidemic interested moviegoers and critics. *Super Size Me* won a Grand Jury Prize at the 2004 Sundance Film Festival and received an Academy Award nomination in 2005. Several weeks after Spurlock's film was released, McDonald's removed the "super size" option from its menu. The chain also reworked its menu to include healthier options, such as more salads and wraps. As for Spurlock, it took fourteen months to lose the weight he had gained during thirty days of filmmaking.

Further Reading

NBC News. "McDonald's Phasing Out Supersize Fries, Drinks." *NBC News.* NBCNews.com, 3 Mar. 2004. Web. 2 Aug. 2012.
Schlosser, Eric. *Fast Food Nation.* New York: Houghton, 2001. Print.
Spurlock, Morgan. *Don't Eat This Book: Fast Food and the Supersizing of America.* New York: Putnam, 2005. Print.
Cait Caffrey

■ Superhero films

Definition: A genre of films, generally based on pre-existing comic book properties, that features the stories of superpowered or supernatural beings.

In the 2000s, superhero films shifted in tone from the light, campy features of the 1990s to ones that favored gritty realism and generally reflected the political and social climate of the decade.

In the summer of 2000, 20th Century Fox released the film *X-Men*. Directed by Bryan Singer, it set the tone for superhero films to come over the past decade. Unlike previous superhero films, which often favored popular actors and emphasized comedy and violence over drama, *X-Men* featured a diverse cast that included noted stage actors Ian McKellen and Patrick Stewart.

In 2002, Sony Pictures Entertainment released the film *Spider-Man*. Though its tone was relatively comedic, the film, set in New York City, unintentionally echoed the terrorist attacks of September 11, 2001, and their aftermath. The film's depiction of New

Yorkers banding together during a crisis particularly struck a chord with moviegoers.

Following the poor reception of the campy 1997 film *Batman & Robin*, Warner Brothers rebooted the franchise with a more serious tone. In 2005 the studio released *Batman Begins*, starring Christian Bale in the titular role and directed by Christopher Nolan. The film retold Batman's origin story, loosely basing the plot on more modern Batman comics, such as *Batman: The Long Halloween* (1996), than the Batman films of the 1990s. The film was a success and led to the 2008 sequel *The Dark Knight*.

The Dark Knight is notable for its use of political allegory, touching on subjects such as extraordinary rendition, citizen surveillance, and other tactics that had been utilized by the US government following the passing of the Patriot Act in 2001. The film *Iron Man* (2008), starring Robert Downey Jr., takes a similar approach; in the film, the head of a weapons manufacturing company is forced to come to terms with the worldwide effects of the materials his company has produced.

While most superhero films released in the 2000s were based on preexisting comic books or graphic novels, there were a few films that featured original superheroes. Examples include the films *Unbreakable* (2000) and *Hancock* (2008), which explore unusual representations of the superhero more intimately.

Impact

Since the 2000s, superhero films have continued to increase in popularity. Films such as *Iron Man 2* (2010) and *The Avengers* (2012) have been commercially successful, consistently challenging box office records. Films such as *X-Men: First Class* (2011) and *The Dark Knight Rises* (2012) have continued the strain of superhero films that examine the superhero from a political context. Finally, a number of filmmakers—inspired by their big budget counterparts—have made smaller-scale, more personal superhero films.

Further Reading

Berninger, Mark, Jochen Ecke, and Gideon Haberkorn, eds. *Comics as a Nexus of Cultures: Essays on the Interplay of Media, Disciplines and International Perspectives.* Jefferson, NC: McFarland, 2010. Print.

Di Paolo, Marc. *War, Politics and Superheroes: Ethics and Propaganda in Comics and Film.* Jefferson, NC: McFarland, 2011. Print.

Leland Spencer

■ Supreme Court decisions

The United States Supreme Court releases dozens of decisions each year on matters of civil and criminal law, corporate law, and the regulation of the legal profession. Interestingly, many of the court's decisions are unanimous or near unanimous and do not garner much press outside of the legal profession. Each year, however, the court releases decisions on highly contested cases of great interest not only to attorneys, but also to the public in general. The first decade of the 2000s saw several such landmark decisions.

Bush v. Gore

The Case: US Supreme Court ruling that effectively decided the result of the 2000 presidential election between George W. Bush and Al Gore

Date: Decided on December 12, 2000

The US Supreme Court held that the method that the state of Florida sought to use to recount ballots violated the equal protection clause of the Fourteenth Amendment, and, therefore, that Florida's previous certification of Bush as the winner of that state's electoral votes stood. As a result, Bush received 271 electoral votes and won the presidency.

The 2000 presidential election was one of the closest and most contested elections in US history. Republican George W. Bush, governor of Texas and son of former president George H. W. Bush, was facing Democratic candidate and then vice president Al Gore. Under the US election laws, the results of the presidential election are decided by the Electoral College, whereby the candidate who wins the popular vote in most states is allocated all of that state's electoral votes. Electoral votes are based on population and are equal to the number of delegates each state and the District of Columbia send to Congress. For instance, California has fifty-five electoral votes, whereas Wyoming has only three, as does the District of Columbia. As a result, even though each voter votes for a candidate, the individual state legislatures award the electoral votes to the candidate who has won the popular vote of that state. In Maine and Nebraska, the only two states that do not follow the winner-take-all elector allocation model, each congressional district votes for an elector and two electors are chosen by a statewide popular vote. At least 270 votes out of 538 total votes are required for a candidate to have a majority of the Electoral College and win the election.

Following the November 7, 2000, presidential voting, Bush was revealed to have won the state of Florida by only 1,748 votes, which, because the margin of victory was less than 0.5 percent of the total votes cast, resulted in an automatic recount pursuant to a state statute. The recount—conducted by a machine—resulted in Bush's lead diminishing to only a few hundred votes. Thereafter, Gore requested a hand recount of the ballots in four counties. After the Florida secretary of state determined that none of the four counties were entitled to an extension of time to count the ballots, the secretary of state certified Bush as the winner.

Subsequently, the Florida Supreme Court ordered a statewide hand recount, and the US Supreme Court stayed that decision. Following oral arguments before the US Supreme Court, a majority of the court determined that the Florida Supreme Court's decision calling for the statewide recount violated the equal protection clause of the US Constitution because the counties had different standards for conducting recounts. The US Supreme Court therefore stopped the proposed recount. Although Gore could have petitioned the Florida Supreme Court for further proceedings, he conceded the election to Bush.

Impact

Undoubtedly, *Bush v. Gore* was a landmark Supreme Court ruling. Although the court did not declare Bush the winner, it is generally recognized that the decision effectively decided the outcome of the election. Some have criticized the case for violating the separation of powers, because they believe the court unnecessarily intruded into legislative branch and election affairs and because many of the justices voted in favor of the party that represented their own political viewpoints.

Lawrence v. Texas

The Case: US Supreme Court ruling that declared unconstitutional a Texas state law prohibiting sodomy, thereby ruling that same-sex sexual activity was legal in the United States

Date: Decided on June 26, 2003

Overruling a 1986 decision specifically concluding that there was no right to participate in homosexual

sodomy, the US Supreme Court held, in a 6–3 decision, that a Texas law that classified homosexual sodomy as a criminal offense violated the due process guarantees of the US Constitution. This thereby legalized the right of consenting homosexual adults to engage in private and intimate sexual conduct.

In 1986, in a 5–4 opinion, the US Supreme Court decided in *Bowers v. Hardwick* that there was no right in the Constitution to engage in homosexual sodomy. The court cited the general proposition that any "right" to participate in sexual activity was related to propagation and that the general moral opposition to homosexual conduct was sufficient to defeat the claim of any specific constitutional right to participate legally in such behavior. Seventeen years later, the court considered the identical question in *Lawrence*.

Following a domestic dispute, the plaintiff, John Lawrence, was arrested in his apartment. Two of the responding police officers claimed that they witnessed Lawrence and another man participating in sexual acts, and both men were charged with a violation of Texas's antisodomy law. After filing a motion to quash the charge on the ground that it violated the equal protection and privacy rights of both the United States and Texas constitutions, which motion was denied, Lawrence pleaded no contest to the charge. Thereafter, a panel of the Texas Fourteenth Court of Appeals concluded that the state law violated the 1972 Equal Rights Amendment of the Texas Constitution and ordered judgment of acquittal. Subsequently, the appeals court granted the state's motion for a rehearing and, following argument before that entire court, affirmed the judgment of conviction.

The US Supreme Court reversed the appeals court's decision, overruling *Bowers* and concluding that the Texas law violated the due process protections of the US Constitution because the intimate conduct engaged in was worthy of constitutional protection and that there was no legitimate rationale for the state law. Justice Anthony Kennedy, writing for the majority, famously stated, "*Bowers* was not correct when it was decided, and it is not correct today."

Impact

Following *Lawrence*, homosexual conduct became legal in every state and territory in the United States. Undoubtedly, the recognition by the US Supreme Court of a constitutional right to engage in same-sex sexual activity has paved the way for subsequent numerous state supreme court decisions and state laws recognizing same-sex marriage or civil unions.

Hamdi v. Rumsfeld

The Case: US Supreme Court ruling that a US citizen who, following the September 11, 2001, terrorist attacks, was detained indefinitely as an "enemy combatant," had the right to challenge his detention to an impartial magistrate

Date: Decided on June 28, 2004

Although no single opinion commanded a majority of the court, eight of nine justices agreed that the executive branch of the federal government could not indefinitely detain a US citizen who was suspected as a terrorist and classified as an enemy combatant. Thus, the court established that even those citizens strongly suspected of committing acts of terror are entitled to basic due process rights.

Yaser Esam Hamdi was born in the United States and was consequently a US citizen. He moved to Saudi Arabia as a child and was arrested in Afghanistan in November 2001, shortly after the September 11 terrorist attacks. The US government suspected Hamdi of being a member of the Taliban and fighting against the United States. Following his capture, Hamdi was detained approximately three years, first at Guantánamo Bay, Cuba, and later at military prisons in the United States. He was never charged with specific crimes and was not allowed access to an attorney.

The George W. Bush administration claimed that Hamdi could be held indefinitely as an "illegal enemy combatant," that such a course of action was authorized by certain laws passed after the September 11 terrorist attacks, and that Hamdi's indefinite detention was therefore constitutional. After Hamdi's father filed a habeas corpus petition on Hamdi's behalf, the trial court ordered the government to turn over certain documents in connection with the case. The government appealed that order, and the United States Court of Appeals for the Fourth Circuit concluded that it lacked jurisdiction hear a case involving Hamdi as a result of the broad powers of the president during a time of war and the separation of powers doctrine. The US Supreme Court reversed the Fourth Circuit's decision and concluded that Hamdi was entitled certain due process provisions enjoyed by all citizens, including to notice of the charges against him and an opportunity to have counsel.

Impact

The *Hamdi* decision underscored that all US citizens have certain due process rights and that there are limits on executive powers—even during times of war. This case also is somewhat similar to the subsequent decision in *Hamdan v. Rumsfeld*, which concluded that military commissions established to try Guantánamo Bay detainees breached the Geneva Convention and the Uniform Code of Military Justice.

Roper v. Simmons

The Case: US Supreme Court ruling that it violates the Eighth Amendment prohibition against cruel and unusual punishment to execute a person for a crime committed when the person was under eighteen years of age

Date: Decided on March 1, 2005

A majority of the US Supreme Court held, under the "evolving standards of decency test" and after considering similar laws in foreign jurisdictions, that it was unconstitutional to impose the death penalty on individuals who had committed crimes when they were juveniles, citing, among other information, scientific data indicating that juveniles lacked maturity and a full understanding of their actions.

In 1993, seventeen-year-old Christopher Simmons committed a murder for which he was convicted and sentenced to death. On appeal of the conviction to the Missouri Supreme Court, that court overturned the death sentence, concluding that Simmons's execution would constitute cruel and unusual punishment. The Missouri Supreme Court commuted the sentence to life without the possibility of parole, and the State of Missouri appealed the case to the US Supreme Court.

The Supreme Court rejected the state's challenge. In 2002, the court had ruled that it was unconstitutional to execute convicts with intellectual disabilities under the "evolving standards of decency" test, and the court's holding in *Roper* flowed from the result in that 2002 case. In deliberating

Roper, justices considered laws in other countries (among them, the fact that only seven other countries in the world, including Iran and Saudi Arabia, had executed juvenile defendants); the mental capabilities of juveniles; and the decreasing number of states that were imposing capital punishment on juvenile offenders. The court subsequently determined that Simmons's execution would have constituted cruel and unusual punishment and therefore that such a law allowing juvenile offenders to be executed was unconstitutional.

Impact

The ruling in *Roper* invalidated any state law that permitted execution of individuals who committed capital crimes as juveniles and, accordingly, had an immediate and substantial effect on criminal law and jurisprudence across the country. Also interesting in this decision was the majority's reliance on social science studies and laws from other countries, as reliance on such external information is somewhat controversial.

District of Columbia v. Heller

The Case: US Supreme Court ruling that the Second Amendment right to bear arms applies to individuals in federal enclaves, thus establishing the "individual right to bear arms"

Date: Decided on June 26, 2008

A majority of the Supreme Court held that an individual may lawfully possess a firearm (unconnected to militia or military service), that the drafters of the Constitution envisioned an individual right, and that a handgun ban and trigger-lock law in the District of Columbia, a federal enclave, therefore violated the Second Amendment.

Heller was brought before the court as a test case— a case in which plaintiffs are carefully selected to challenge a particular law. In this case, a District of Columbia law prevented most district residents from owning handguns and required those who owned firearms, such as rifles, to keep those weapons disassembled or with a trigger-lock mechanism, thus limiting the weapons' applicability during the event of a home invasion or similar crime. The district court dismissed the lawsuit, and the US Court of Appeals for the District of Columbia Circuit overturned the trial court's dismissal.

In one of the most controversial opinions of recent years, the US Supreme Court concluded that the district's handgun ban and trigger-lock requirement infringed on Second Amendment rights. In so concluding, the court tied the Second Amendment to self-defense and noted that the right is individual in nature—as opposed to a right to possess a firearm for military use.

Impact

Heller was a highly politicized case. In fact, the ruling likely has more political than legal ramifications. Only a couple years after *Heller*, the Supreme Court ruled in *McDonald v. Chicago* that the Second Amendment applies to the individual states, not just the federal enclaves such as the District of Columbia. The majority in *McDonald* relied on *Heller* in its decision.

Further Reading

Carpenter, Dale. *Flagrant Conduct: The Story of* Lawrence v. Texas. New York: Norton, 2012. Print.

Greenhouse, Linda. "The Supreme Court: Detainees; Access to Courts." *New York Times.* New York Times, 29 June 2004. Web. 3 Dec. 2012.

Lane, Charles. "54 Supreme Court Abolishes Juvenile Executions." *Washington Post.* Washington Post, 2 Mar. 2005. Web. 3 Dec. 2012.

—. "Justices Back Detainee Access to U.S. Courts: President's Powers are Limited." *Washington Post.* Washington Post, 29 June 2004. Web. 3 Dec. 2012.

Liptak, Adam. "Few Ripples from Supreme Court Ruling on Guns." *New York Times.* New York Times, 16 Mar. 2009. Web. 3 Dec. 2012.

Mears, Bill. "High Court Strikes Down Gun Ban." *CNN.* Cable News Network, 26 June 2008. Web. 3 Dec. 2012.

Richards, David A. J. *The Sodomy Cases:* Bowers v. Hardwick *and* Lawrence v. Texas. Lawrence: UP of Kansas, 2009. Print.

Stout, David. "Supreme Court Bars Death Penalty for Juvenile Killers." *New York Times.* New York Times, 1 Mar. 2005. Web. 3 Dec. 2012.

Toobin, Jeffrey. *Too Close to Call: The Thirty-Six Day Battle to Decide the 2000 Election.* New York: Random, 2002. Print.

Zelden, Charles L. Bush v. Gore: *Exposing the Hidden Crisis in American Democracy.* Lawrence: UP of Kansas, 2010. Print.

Andrew E. Walter, JD

■ *Survivor*

Identification: A competitive reality television show in which a group of people are left to survive in the wilderness
Creator: Charlie Parsons (1958–)
Date: Premiered in 2000

In 2000, Survivor *introduced television viewers to a new type of reality programming. The show features participants living in a remote location without access to any luxuries. As they attempt to withstand the elements, they must also compete against their cast mates for a grand prize. The show was popular with viewers and critics, earning an Emmy Award for Outstanding Non-Fiction Program (Special Class) in 2001.*

Charlie Parsons, a British television producer best known for his affiliation with the former Planet 24 television production company, developed the idea for *Survivor* several years before it appeared in the United States. The reality competition first aired in the United States on CBS in May 2000. Parsons and Mark Burnett, a British television producer, became executive producers of the show.

Although each season of *Survivor* features a different remote location and new participants, the rules of the competition remain the same. Sixteen to twenty contestants live and compete in the wilderness for about thirty days. Besides the contestants, only the host, Jeff Probst, and camera crew are on location. The contestants start with a few tools and some food. They survive by using only what is available to them on the island. Contestants are not allowed any modern conveniences, such as electricity, cell phones, or computers. In the beginning, the group is split into two "tribes" that compete in challenges to win small prizes, such as food or phone access. The winner of the challenges receives immunity from being voted off the island by the other contestants that week. The losing team votes a member of their team off the show. As the show progresses, the two groups merge into one, and individuals compete against one another in the challenges. At the end, the previously voted-off contestants return as members of a council. The council votes off one of the two final participants, and the last remaining contestant receives a $1 million prize. The formula proved popular, and *Survivor* had aired twenty-five seasons by the fall of 2012.

Impact

In the early 2000s, reality television mainly focused on programs about individual people's daily lives, such as MTV's *The Real World.* The arrival of *Survivor,* however, changed the format of the genre, and an abundance of competitive reality television shows soon followed. Viewers began passing over scripted television series in favor of new reality competitions for singing, dating, and weight loss, such as *American Idol, The Bachelor,* and *The Biggest Loser.*

Further Reading

Conlan, Tara. "Parsons Follows His Nose to Support Talent." *Guardian.* Guardian News and Media Ltd., 14 Apr. 2007. Web. 2 Aug. 2012.
Hatch, Richard. *101 Survival Secrets: How to Make $1,000,000, Lose 100 Pounds, and Just Plain Live Happily.* New York: Lyons, 2000. Print.
Poniewozik, James. "Reality TV at 10: How It's Changed Television—and Us." *Time.* Time Inc., 22 Feb. 2010. Web. 2 Aug. 2012.

Angela Harmon

■ Sustainable food movement

Definition: A movement that seeks to replace shipped and processed foods with locally grown and minimally processed options; also known as the local food movement

The sustainable, or local, food movement garnered much attention in the 2000s. The purpose of the self-proclaimed "locavores," or followers of the local food movement, is to eat food that is fresh, unprocessed, and locally grown. These foods are typically produced in home gardens or found at farmers markets and specialty food stores. Drawbacks, such as availability and expense, are some of the hurdles to eating local.

Throughout the 2000s, Americans became increasingly aware of what they were eating as well as the sources of these foods. This awareness was driven in part by factors such as growing obesity rates and numerous books and documentaries about the food industry. Author Eric Schlosser gave readers the story behind the fast-food industry in his 2001 book *Fast Food Nation.* In 2006, Michael Pollan published the book *The Omnivore's Dilemma,* which

Joel Salatin conducts a workshop on sustainable agriculture at Polyface Farm in Virginia. (Courtesy Kirstin Corris)

looked at the way Americans eat and introduced many to the concept of sustainable, or local, eating. The two authors teamed up as narrators for the 2008 documentary *Food, Inc.*, in which filmmaker Robert Kenner explored the use of genetically modified seeds, the impact of chemical fertilizers, and the abuse of animals and workers within the US corporate farming industry. These, along with books and films on similar topics, were a wake-up call to many Americans to think about the foods they were choosing.

"Local food" can mean different things, but the description typically applies to food that is grown, made, or produced within one hundred miles of one's home. It can also mean food that is grown, made, or produced in one's state. To some, local food is environmentally and socially sustainable,

meaning it is produced in a way that does not harm the planet, people, or profits—a combination of factors known as the "triple bottom line." In other words, farmers produce food using humane and environmentally friendly ways, treat their employees fairly, and sell food at honest prices.

As interest in local foods grew, these products became easier to find. Consumers could find local products at farmers markets, specialty stores, and even chain stores such as Wal-Mart and Whole Foods. They also participated in community-supported agriculture (CSA) programs, in which consumers purchase shares of the harvest from one or more farmers. Each consumer then receives a weekly box of locally grown foods that typically include produce and other products, such as eggs or meat, from the farmer or group of farmers.

Rise of Local Food Movement

The popularity of the local food movement became evident in many ways. The number of small farms increased by over eighteen thousand from 2002 to 2007, according to the 2007 Census of Agriculture from the US Department of Agriculture (USDA). The number of farmers' markets and CSAs increased dramatically in just a few decades. In 2006, the USDA reported that more than forty-six hundred farmers' markets were in operation throughout the United States. By the end of the decade, this number increased to almost six thousand. In 1986, only two CSAs could be found in the country. This number jumped well into the thousands during the 2000s.

Numerous restaurants boasting only local ingredients began popping up all over the country, joining the ranks of Chez Panisse in Berkeley, California, which had been serving up local, organic foods for decades. School districts also joined the movement. By 2008, more than twelve hundred school districts had partnered with local farms to feed fresh and local foods to schoolchildren. Some colleges, prisons, and detention centers followed suit. Even the White House supported the movement. After President Barack Obama took office in 2009, First Lady Michelle Obama created a garden at the White House and focused her efforts on combating childhood obesity. After the First Lady began her initiative, Secretary of Agriculture Tom Vilsack created a garden of his own outside his Washington office. Soon after, the Department of Agriculture introduced the Know Your Farmer, Know Your Food program.

Barriers to Eating Local

The major obstacles to eating local were the availability of local foods and the expense. With more retailers carrying local options and the abundance of farmers markets, finding local foods became somewhat easier in many areas. The price of local foods, however, was not dropping, which made it difficult for many Americans who simply could not afford the added expense of shopping local.

During the downturn of the economy between 2007 and 2008, many families struggled just to buy food. The USDA reported that more than fifty million Americans were food insecure, which means they might and sometimes do run out of food before they could afford more. Low-income families typically allot most of their food budgets to highly caloric and processed foods because they are less expensive than healthier options such as produce. Also, many poor neighborhoods lack well-stocked supermarkets that contain fresh foods.

Impact

Proponents of the sustainable food movement believe buying and eating local food is good for the environment and for business and is healthier and fresher, as foods may contain fewer chemicals and preservatives. Local food requires less energy consumption since the products do not have to be shipped very far. Buying and eating local may also strengthen a community's economy, since keeping more money local can in turn help create new local jobs.

Further Reading

Black, Jane. "The Economics of Local Food." *All We Can Eat.* Washington Post, 8 Sept. 2009. Web. 6 Dec. 2012. Describes how buying local food stimulates the local economy.

Gogoi, Pallavi. "The Rise of the 'Locavore.'" *Bloomberg Businessweek.* Bloomberg, 20 May 2008. Web. 6 Dec. 2012. Discusses the rise of the local food movement.

Hahn Niman, Nicolette. "America's Good Food Fight." *Los Angeles Times.* Los Angeles Times, 9 Jan. 2011. Web. 6 Dec. 2012. Provides an overview of the debate between sustainable food and corporate farming.

"Local & Regional Food Systems." *Grace Communications Foundation.* Grace Communications Foundation. Web. 6 Dec. 2012. Explains local food, the mainstream food distribution network, and food safety and health concerns, among other related topics.

Martin, Andrew. "Is a Food Revolution Now in Season?" *New York Times.* New York Times Co., 21 Mar. 2009. Web. 6 Dec. 2012. Details the impact of the local food movement.

Miller, Lisa. "Divided We Eat." *Newsweek.* Newsweek/Daily Beast Co., 22 Nov. 2010. Web. 6 Dec. 2012. An in-depth look at the relationship between food choices and socioeconomic class.

Walsh, Bryan. "Foodies Can Eclipse (and Save) the Green Movement." *Time.* Time Inc., 15 Feb. 2011. Web. 6 Dec. 2012. Talks about the local food movement within the context of environmentalism.

Angela Harmon

T

■ Tea Party movement

Definition: The grassroots political movement of the decade, which grew out of its supporters' fears that the US government's record spending is leading to the nation's economic and political decline. Tea Party activists support curbs in government spending, the elimination of deficit spending, lower taxes, and a strict legal interpretation of the US Constitution. They oppose the financial regulations put in place after the 2008 recession, cap-and-trade proposals to control carbon emissions, and the Patient Protection and Affordable Care Act (PPACA), the major health care reform law passed in 2010.

During the 2000s, the United States endured two economic recessions. The first occurred in 2001; the second, which has since come to be known as the Great Recession, began in late 2007. Although both recessions seriously damaged the US economy and helped drag the nation further into debt, the second was so severe that it required the US government to take some extraordinary measures. These measures included propping up major banks, bailing out the automobile industry, and creating an economic stimulus package worth an estimated $787 billion at the time of its approval. While many economists and politicians believe these efforts, enacted during the administrations of President George W. Bush and President Barack Obama, helped to stave off an economic depression, many average Americans came to fear that the federal government was spending far more than it could ever pay back. Out of these fears, the Tea Party movement—named after the 1773 Boston Tea Party protest against British taxation prior to the American Revolution—was born. The movement called for, among other things, reductions in government spending and taxation.

Various groups have embraced the Tea Party moniker since at least the 1990s, when a group of antitax demonstrators protested against US taxation each April 15—the day income taxes are due to the government. The inspiration for the modern Tea Party movement, however, is credited to Rick Santelli, a CNBC reporter. During a live report from the floor of the Chicago Mercantile Exchange on February 19, 2009, Santelli complained about a government proposal, supported by the Obama administration, which would allow homeowners to refinance their mortgages in the wake of the subprime mortgage crisis instead of having them face foreclosure. Speaking against the backdrop of the US government's bailout of the banking institutions that had helped bring about a global recession through reckless lending practices, Santelli argued that the government was continuing to reward bad behavior by promising to also help people who had taken out huge mortgages they could not ultimately afford.

Santelli's "rant," as it has been widely called, was not only cheered on the trading floor but later garnered wide circulation on the Internet. Santelli also advocated for the formation of a "tea party" for securities traders to dump their mortgage-backed derivatives into the Chicago River. Almost overnight, Tea Party organizations formed through websites such as ChicagoTeaParty.com and reTeaParty.com, as well as the social media website Facebook. Thousands of Americans, concerned about the country's future and the government's spending habits, flocked to these sites.

A Movement Forms

On April 15, 2009, the Tea Party movement earned its first national recognition when organizers staged income tax day protests that drew between 250,000 and 500,000 people in over two hundred US cities. Invigorated by the response, the movement's loose association of local groups organized a series of protests across the country to demonstrate against President Obama's proposal to overhaul the nation's health care system. Most Tea Party supporters believed that the president's plan, which would require every US citizen to own health insurance, was both a government overreach and an unnecessary financial burden on citizens in a time of economic uncertainty.

People's Protest rally on Capitol Hill against the "Obamacentric" healthcare bill, organized by Tea Party activists. (Courtesy Asterio Tecson)

Throughout July and August, Tea Party activists and other demonstrators forcefully expressed their opposition to the health care proposal at town hall meetings held by US lawmakers across the country. Many of the town hall meetings were boisterous and tumultuous and received a great deal of press. Depending on one's political perspective, the Tea Party activists' actions were either an example of true democracy at work, in which concerned citizens voiced their complaints to their elected representatives, or a frenzied pushback against two branches of government then controlled by Democrats. In March 2010, for example, a number of Tea Party activists were heard yelling racial and antigay insults at Democratic lawmakers who were on their way to the final vote on the

Obama health care law, which ultimately was approved by Congress and upheld by the US Supreme Court. The majority of Tea Party supporters condemned this conduct.

On September 12, 2009, upward of seventy thousand Tea Party supporters traveled to Washington, DC, to march on the US Capitol. This Taxpayer March on Washington was organized to protest the political direction of the country. While some observers felt that the Tea Party was being led by hysterical radicals who feared anything that President Obama and Democratic lawmakers were attempting to do, others felt that the movement was truly populist in nature and could likely impact the upcoming 2010 midterm congressional elections.

Influence on Elections

The first real success the Tea Party experienced in elective politics came in January 2010, when the Tea Party–backed Republican candidate Scott Brown won a special election to fill the US Senate seat vacated upon the death of Senator Edward Kennedy, a longtime liberal voice in the Democratic Party. Yet Tea Party activists were not satisfied with this singular victory. During the primary season before the 2010 midterm elections, Tea Party supporters sought to have their candidates win Republican Party nominations across the country, often against longtime incumbents. Some Tea Party candidates who beat out established Republican figures during the 2010 primaries included Charles Perry over the incumbent Delwin Jones; Rand Paul over Trey Grayson; Mike Lee over Senator Bob Bennett; and Anna C. Little over Diane Gooch. In July 2010, US Representative Michele Bachman, a Republican from Minnesota, established the House Tea Party Caucus, which counted forty-nine Republicans in the House of Representatives among its members just a month later. Following the formation of the caucus, Bachman raised $10 million through her political action committee (PAC) and used the money to help fund the campaigns of Tea Party–backed candidates like Sharon Angle, Christine O'Donnell, Rand Paul, and Marco Rubio. Although not all of these candidates won in the general election, Representative Bachman's influence helped establish her as a key Tea Party figure.

Following the 2010 midterm elections, the Republican Party took back control of the US House of Representatives, gaining sixty-three seats, and made significant inroads in the US Senate, gaining six seats. Fully 129 candidates for the House and nine candidates for the Senate had received the grassroots movement's significant support. Tea Party activists hoped their chosen candidates, who were generally more fiscally conservative than either Democrats or many incumbent Republicans, would roll back some of the spending initiatives of the previous Congress and repeal the new health care law. Four out of ten voters polled following the 2010 midterm elections expressed support for the movement's objectives.

The Tea Party was less influential in the run-up to the 2012 presidential election. After former Alaskan governor Sarah Palin, a Tea Party favorite since the movement held its first national convention in February 2010, announced that she would not seek the Republican nomination for president, a number of Republican candidates, including Michele Bachman, tried to assume the Tea Party mantle. Also looking to represent the Tea Party's views during the Republican primary season were businessman Herman Cain and Governor Rick Perry of Texas, both of whom ultimately dropped out of the presidential race.

After Mitt Romney, a former governor of Massachusetts widely acknowledged to be a moderate, secured the Republican nomination for president, he named Representative Paul Ryan of Wisconsin as his vice presidential running mate on the 2012 ticket. Although an established congressman with a voting record that included supporting the bailouts of the auto and banking industries, Ryan was seen as a Tea Party favorite. This was due in large part to his fiscally conservative budget plan that would change, among other proposals, the nature of entitlement programs like Medicare to make them more cost-effective for the federal government and senior citizens.

Impact

Whether the Tea Party would remain a significant force in American politics was yet to be seen by the end of the 2000s. Many of the movement's core beliefs—balancing the budget, reducing the national debt, reforming the tax code by lowering rates, and strictly adhering to the exact wording of the US Constitution—have had widespread support among both conservative-minded citizens and many Republicans. Indeed, a number of Tea Party ideas, including repealing the new health care law, have become the main focus of many Republican leaders in Congress. Some of the movement's other beliefs, including the idea that government should not give anything to citizens that citizens cannot get for themselves, seem to be contradictory to broadly popular programs like Social Security, which grants pension benefits to seniors and the disabled, and Medicare, which provides seniors with health insurance after age sixty-five.

It also remained to be seen at the end of the decade if the movement would expand beyond its current group of supporters. According to a New York Times/CBS poll conducted in April 2010, the Tea Party is not nearly as fringe or as extremist as it has sometimes appeared. While only 18 percent of those surveyed identified themselves as supporters of the movement, the majority of those supporters tended to be older than forty-five, white, male, married, and members of the Republican Party—all fairly mainstream attributes.

They were, however, somewhat more conservative, typically wealthier, and better educated than average Americans. They also believed that the Obama administration favored helping the poor and minorities over the middle class or wealthy Americans.

Further Reading

DiMaggio, Anthony R. *The Rise of the Tea Party: Political Discontent and Corporate Media in the Age of Obama.* New York: Monthly Rev. Press, 2011. Print. Examines the influence of corporate media on the public's perception of the Tea Party movement.

Formisano, Ronald P. *The Tea Party: A Brief History.* Baltimore: Johns Hopkins UP, 2012. Print. Presents the evolution of the Tea Party movement through its members' frustrations with the current political culture and discusses whether the movement has real staying power.

Lepore, Jill. *The Whites of their Eyes: The Tea Party's Revolution and the Battle over American History.* Princeton: Princeton UP, 2010. Print. Takes a wry and critical look at the Tea Party and suggests that its supporters believe in mythical tales of America's founding and of the US Constitution.

Paul, Rand. *The Tea Party Goes to Washington.* New York: Center Street, 2011. Print. Staunchly advocates for the Tea Party principles of limited government and a balanced budget and argues that the movement is neither extreme nor a passing fad.

Skocpol, Theda, and Vanessa Williamson. *The Tea Party and the Remaking of Republican Conservatism.* New York: Oxford UP, 2012. Print. In addition to providing a historical overview, the authors interviewed various members of the grassroots movement to present a nuanced and balanced portrait of the Tea Party.

Zernike, Kate. *Boiling Mad: Inside Tea Party America.* New York: Times Books, 2010. Print. Gives a brief chronicle of the Tea Party movement and how its influence has impacted both the policies of the modern Republican Party and the Obama administration.

Christopher Mari

■ Television

Definition: The 2000s saw a change in television programming trends as well as advances in digital cable services and home television set technology

Throughout the decade, there were several significant developments in television technology as well as a shift in the type of programming that was popular. Advances in digital cable led to a nationwide transition in the United States in which television stations ended their broadcasts of analog signals. The introduction of digital video recorders (DVR) gave users the ability to digitally record shows, expanding the viewing experience. The popularity of episodic television programs led to some groundbreaking series that brought new depth to characters and storytelling. Reality television programs also saw immense popularity in the 2000s.

Television Set Technology

Television set technology advanced greatly in the 2000s. For decades television sets used cathode ray tube (CRT) display technology to produce images. To house the CRT technology, television sets were designed to be thick with lots of space behind the screen. This also made television sets very heavy. The development of liquid-crystal display (LCD) and plasma display technology revolutionized television sets. With these display technologies, television sets could be manufactured that were much thinner and lighter than CRT sets. They also allowed for larger screens to be more easily manufactured.

By 2007, LCD televisions were outselling both CRT sets and plasma televisions, making them the most popular and widely sold sets on the market. In the large-screen format category, LCD televisions outsold both plasma televisions and rear-projection televisions. LCD and plasma televisions also utilized developing high-definition (HD) technology, which advanced greatly in the 2000s. HD television debuted in the late 1990s, but did not become popular with broadcast channels until the 2000s. HD technology creates a clearer image with brighter colors and sharper details.

Digital Television

Analog television broadcasts were ordered by US federal law and the Federal Communications Commission (FCC) to cease on June 12, 2009. As part of the law, digital broadcasts have to meet Advanced Television Systems Committee (ATSC) standards. These standards dictate digital transmission criteria including consistency and accessibility. To help consumers with the transition from analog to digital the US government offered consumers a coupon towards

Actor and camera operator at work on a real time broadcast. (©iStockphoto.com/EdStock)

a digital converter box, which converts digital signals for analog television sets.

Digital cable provides a better picture and sound quality, while also freeing up parts of the broadcast spectrum for public safety communications such as those from police and fire departments. Broadcasting in digital allows stations to offer several channels of programming instantaneously. Known as multicasting, this type of broadcasting gives viewers more program options and provides a more interactive viewing experience.

Digital broadcasting helped improve interactive program guides (IPG) in the United States. These guides allow viewers to browse through the different channels on a grid or listing on their televisions and jump right to the program they wish to watch. Viewers can also select a program on the IPG to record on their digital video recorder (DVR). High-end digital receivers commonly come with a built-in IPG and DVR. These DVR systems can record several hours of programming, allowing the user to view them at their leisure and fast-forward, pause, or rewind as they wish.

Television On Demand

Another aspect of television technology that improved and became popular in the 2000s was television on demand (TVD). These services allow a user to watch programs that have already aired without having to use a DVR to record them. Cable companies use TVD to provide a variety of services and

viewing options, including films, music, shows, and sporting events. Some cable companies provide a subscription service, in which a viewer can schedule a show to be recorded every time it airs.

While many broadcast channels offer their programs for free, there are some programs viewers have to pay for. TVD is an improvement over traditional pay-per-view services in which the viewer had to call their cable company to request the program they wished to watch. With TVD, users can select the program via their IPG menu. Different cable providers like Comcast and Bright House offer different TVD choices, such as films and concerts. The fees for TVD also differ for each cable provider.

TVD also changed the way networks schedule programs in the 2000s. Networks had to consider that viewers could now watch a program whenever they liked because of TVD, which particularly affected daytime television shows such as game shows and soap operas. Networks constantly had to change their approach to programming because of TVD, online resources, portable electronics such as iPods, and other electronic advances in the 2000s.

Reality Television

Reality television programs such as *COPS* and *The Real World* were very popular before the 2000s, but it was not until this decade that reality programs found massive success and became some of the most popular shows on television. In particular, reality competition and talent shows became increasingly popular throughout the decade. By the end of the decade basic cable networks were putting more reality programs in prime-time spots than scripted shows. In addition to being popular, reality shows are cheaper to produce and require a smaller production crew than traditional shows.

Reality competition shows portray nonactors in extraordinary situations. The first one to find huge success in the United States was *Survivor*, which premiered in May 2000. The show starred contestants in exotic locations competing for a cash prize and became an instant success. In July 2000 the reality competition show *Big Brother* premiered. This competition features nonactors who all live in a house together under constant surveillance.

Popular 2000s Sitcoms

Program	Airdates	Network
King of the Hill	1997-2009	FOX
Sex and the City	1998-2004	HBO
That 70's Show	1998-2006	FOX
The King of Queens	1998-2007	CBS
Family Guy	1999-2002, 2005-present	FOX
Malcolm in the Middle	2000-2006	FOX
Yes, Dear	2000-2006	CBS
Curb Your Enthusiasm	2000-present	HBO
My Wife and Kids	2001-2005	ABC
The Bernie Mac Show	2001-2006	FOX
Reba	2001-2007	The WB/The CW
According to Jim	2001-2009	ABC
Scrubs	2001-2010	NBC/ABC
George Lopez	2002-2007	ABC
Monk	2002-2009	USA
Arrested Development	2003-2006	FOX
Reno 911!	2003-2009	Comedy Central
Two-and-a-Half Men	2003-present	CBS
Entourage	2004-2011	HBO
Everybody Hates Chris	2005-2009	UPN/The CW
How I Met Your Mother	2005-present	CBS
The Office	2005-present	NBC
It's Always Sunny in Philadelphia	2005-present	FX
Weeds	2005-present	Showtime
My Boys	2006-2010	TBS
The New Adventures of Old Christine	2006-2010	CBS
30 Rock	2006-present	NBC
The Big Bang Theory	2007-present	CBS
Rules of Engagement	2007-present	CBS
Modern Family	2009-present	ABC

The most popular American reality show of the 2000s was *American Idol*, which premiered in June 2002. The show is a talent competition in which contestants from across the United States compete and are voted off by viewers and a panel of three celebrity judges. The show was adapted from the British show *Pop Idol*. By 2004 ratings for *American Idol* were frequently over 30 million and millions of viewers were calling in to vote for their favorite contestant each week. The show did receive negative criticism, however, for what some critics saw as the exploitation of some of the less talented contestants.

Other popular reality shows included *The Bachelor*, in which female contestants competed to get engaged to a suitor; *America's Next Top Model*, in which female contestants competed for a modeling contract; and *The Biggest Loser*, in which obese contestants won by losing the most weight.

Episodic Dramas

The 2000s brought about what many critics and viewers saw as a renaissance in episodic dramas. These shows, which delivered story arcs across entire seasons and series, brought more depth to their characters, plots, and themes. These shows propelled writers and directors into the spotlight alongside actors and broadened what a television drama was capable of.

The show cited as being the most groundbreaking of these dramas was *The Sopranos*, which aired on Home Box Office (HBO) from January 1999 to June 2007. This series, created by David Chase, examined the relationships and dynamics within a New Jersey mafia organization. The show revolved around the character of Tony Soprano, played by actor James Gandolfini, and looked at how his mafia lifestyle impacted his family. The show won several awards and is considered by many critics to be the greatest television series of the 2000s.

Another groundbreaking episodic show of the 2000s was *24*. The show was an action drama that aired from November 2001 to May 2010. Each episode of the show

First Gay and Lesbian TV Network is Launched in Canada

In September of 2001, Canada's PrideVision TV, the world's first LGBTQ television network to broadcast around the clock, began broadcasting to subscribers on digital cable. The impact of PrideVision TV was felt in both the media and political landscapes in Canada and internationally. Many expected the network to falter early, citing its high price tag for digital subscribers and perceived limited audience. The launch of the network also received significant mainstream media attention, culminating in a widely publicized lawsuit against Canada's major cable company, Shaw Communications. During the free preview period for PrideVision, Shaw implemented a roadblock that forced viewers to incur a one-cent charge and "approve" their access to the network at every program change. Shaw attempted to defend itself with the claim that they were protecting the sensitivities of their subscribers, but the Canadian Radio-television and Telecommunications Commission (CRTC) ultimately ruled in favor of PrideVision. The network continued programming as PrideVision until March of 2005, when it was renamed OUTtv.

depicted the fictional events that took place in a single hour; each twenty-four-hour season represented one action-packed day in the life of fictional US Counter Terrorist Unit special agent Jack Bauer, played by actor Kiefer Sutherland. Each season featured Bauer thwarting a different terrorist threat. The show was remarkable for its real-time presentation and for being the first American show to address national concerns following the terrorist attacks of September 11, 2001.

Other notable episodic dramas of the decade include *The Wire*, which revolved around the drug trade in Baltimore, Maryland; *Breaking Bad*, about a high school teacher who decides to become an illegal drug manufacturer after he is diagnosed with cancer; and *Mad Men*, a series set in the 1960s which follows several professionals in the advertising industry.

Impact

Television in the 2000s progressed in nearly every aspect, from technology to the programming. Developments in digital broadcasting and HD television revolutionized the way viewers could pick and choose what shows they watched and when they watched them. Networks had to alter their scheduling in order to adapt to digital formats. Television sets became lighter, larger, and thinner thanks to plasma and LCD technology. Groundbreaking episodic dramas showed new dimensions in televisions characters and storylines and raised the bar for shows in the next decade.

Further Reading

Chambers, Jennifer. "Trashing the Tube: Digital Conversion May Spark Glut of Toxic Waste." *Detroit News*. Detroit News, 23 Jan. 2009. Web. 12 Nov. 2012. Addresses the concerns of toxic waste created by old televisions being thrown away as LCD and plasma television sets grew in popularity.

Guerrero, Peter F., and Lennard G. Kruger. *Digital Television: An Overview*. Hauppauge: Nova, 2002. Print. Details the development of DTV technology and the regulations of the Federal Communications Commission.

Hart, Jeffrey A. *Technology, Television, and Competition: The Politics of Digital TV*. Cambridge: Cambridge UP, 2004. Print. Looks at the politics of creating DTV standards in the United States, Japan, and Europe.

Lotz, Amanda D., ed. *Beyond Prime Time: Television Programming in the Post-Network Era*. New York: Routledge, 2009. Print. Television scholars and critics address how television networks have had to adapt in the digital age.

Murray, Susan, and Laurie Ouellette, eds. *Reality TV: Remaking Television Culture*. New York: NYU P, 2008. Print. Presents several essays concerned with the social, cultural, and economic aspects of reality television.

Patrick G. Cooper

■ Terri Schiavo case

Definition: A US court case in which the husband and parents of Terri Schiavo argued about whether to keep her on life support

The Terri Schiavo case captivated America in the mid-2000s. The high-profile case for Schiavo's life sparked heated

debates about living wills, euthanasia, and end-of-life issues. Schiavo had suffered from cardiac arrest in 1990 and had been in a vegetative state for several years when her husband petitioned to have her removed from life support, sparking a grueling five-year court battle with her parents.

Terri Schiavo had been in a vegetative state for eight years when her husband, Michael, petitioned to have her feeding tube removed in 1998. She had made no living will, and as a result, the state had designated her husband as her legal guardian. Schiavo's parents, Robert and Mary Schindler, were against this petition and took Michael Schiavo to court in early 2000. The court heard a great deal of testimony about Terri's feelings on the subject of artificially prolonged life and ruled in favor of Michael Schiavo, ordering his wife's feeding tube removed on April 24, 2001.

A myriad of appeals, petitions, and civil suits by the Schindlers followed as they attempted to keep their daughter on life support. The Schindlers wanted Michael Schiavo to divorce their daughter, thereby forfeiting his guardianship and his inheritance of $700,000 in trust that Terri had received from a malpractice suit. Her husband insisted that his wife would not want to go on living a wholly dependent life and refused to relinquish his guardianship.

The Schindlers filed a civil suit against Michael Schiavo on charges of perjury. Schiavo's tube, which had been removed two days earlier, was reinserted while the case was reviewed. An evidentiary hearing was called in October 2002, and five neurologists examined Schiavo to determine her cognitive abilities. The court did not find sufficient evidence of mental cognition and affirmed the initial diagnosis that Terri was in a persistent vegetative state.

The feeding tube was once again removed in October 2003. A few days later, Florida governor Jeb Bush ordered the tube to be reinserted after the state legislature passed a special law known as Terri's Law, which granted the governor the right to intervene in the case. This law was eventually deemed unconstitutional, and Schiavo's feeding tube was removed for a final time on March 18, 2005. Despite the involvement of President George W. Bush, the Supreme Court repeatedly declined to intervene in the case. Schiavo died on March 31, 2005.

Impact
Terri Schiavo's death incited massive public debate and crusading. As a result, issues such as end-of-life decisions, living wills, and euthanasia were illuminated and widely discussed. The case also encouraged debates about government intervention in cases such as Schiavo's. It remains one of the most deliberated cases in American history.

Further Reading
Copeland, Larry, and Laura Parker. "Terri Schiavo's Case Doesn't End with Her Passing." *USA Today,* USA Today, 31 Mar. 2005. Web. 14 Dec. 2012.
Fuhrman, Mark. *Silent Witness: The Untold Story of Terri Schiavo's Death.* New York: Morrow, 2005. Print.
Nohlgren, Stephen. "Schiavo Tapes: Snippets, Then Not Much." *St. Petersburg Times.* Tampa Bay Times, 10 Nov. 2003. Web. 14 Dec. 2012.

Cait Caffrey

■ Terrorist attacks

Definition: A number of significant acts of international terrorism took place during the 2000s, generating a major global response

Throughout the 2000s, virtually every corner of the globe was impacted by acts of international terrorism. In many of these incidents, terrorists, who attacked civilian as well as military targets, killed thousands of people using a wide range of methods. Most prominent of these terrorism groups was al-Qaeda, which was responsible for the deaths of nearly three thousand people in the attacks of September 11, 2001, as well as hundreds of people around the world in separate attacks. Other groups who staged terrorist attacks during the 2000s included the ETA, Hezbollah, Chechen rebel groups, Hamas, LeT, Tamil Tigers, al-Shabaab, and the IRA.

The 2000s marked a major period for terrorist incidents. Attacks were significantly larger in scale—both in their complexity and destructiveness—than attacks of the past. Terrorists utilized modern technology, enormous organizational capabilities, and considerable financial resources to launch attacks around the world, including several against the United States and its allies. Terrorist attacks took the lives of several thousand people during the decade. These incidents prompted a global backlash, as the international community shared intelligence and

The Pentagon in flames moments after a hijacked jetliner crashed into building at approximately 9:30 on September 11, 2001. (Department of Defense/Corporal Jason Ingersoll, United State Marine Corps)

resources to collectively combat terrorist groups on every continent.

Al-Qaeda and the LeT

Arguably the most notorious terrorist organization to launch attacks during the 2000s, al-Qaeda distinguished itself from other groups because of its global presence. Al-Qaeda is a decentralized network that has connections in virtually every part of the world. Established by Saudi exile Osama bin Laden, al-Qaeda is also known for its grandiose methods, frequently involving multiple bombs or attacks on a single target area in order to inflict the maximum amount of damage and chaos. For the attacks of September 11, 2001, al-Qaeda took over four airliners, successfully destroying the World Trade Center in New York City and severely damaging the Pentagon building in Washington, DC. The attacks caused the deaths of nearly three thousand people and threw the US economy and the American population alike into turmoil.

Al-Qaeda was also responsible for attacks against civilian and military targets all over the world before and after the September 11 attacks. In 2000, the group successfully launched a suicide bomb attack against the USS *Cole*, an American warship, killing seventeen people and injuring nearly forty others.

In 2008, the Pakistani terrorist group known as LeT (Lashkar-e-Taiba) launched an assault on a luxury hotel in Mumbai, India, killing 166 people. It was soon learned that al-Qaeda was behind the attack, funding LeT and training the attackers. Intelligence reports after the Mumbai attack suggested that, thanks to al-Qaeda's assistance, LeT had grown from a local terrorist group to a worldwide terrorist organization that posed a direct threat to Europe and the United States in addition to the South Asian theater.

Europe

North America experienced few foreign-based terrorist attacks (successful or otherwise) compared to Europe during the decade. London, for example, was bombed by al-Qaeda on July 7, 2005. The terrorist group attacked the city's public transportation system, killing fifty-six people and injuring seven hundred others. The United Kingdom also dealt with attacks by the Irish Republican Army (IRA). In many ways, the IRA—which had been active for generations and showed signs that it would continue to operate well beyond the 2000s—was a far cry from the global and seemingly wanton destruction of al-Qaeda, as its efforts were focused on British rule and influence in Northern Ireland. Even so, the IRA was capable of raising enormous amounts of international money and supplies to support its cause. The IRA experienced major changes during the 2000s, splintering into several groups, the most prominent of which were the Continuity IRA and the Real IRA. The IRA was also affected by the September 11 attacks: although their cause was considerably different from al-Qaeda, and the scale of their attacks, which continued throughout the 2000s, was smaller and more localized, the IRA was placed on the same list of international terrorist organizations as al-Qaeda. As a result, its monetary support networks became at risk, since few people wanted to be caught supporting any form of international terrorism.

Another European terrorist group captured greater international attention during this period. The Euskadi Ta Askatasuna (ETA)—Basque Homeland and Liberty—has spent nearly a century fighting to separate the Basque regions of Spain from the rest of the country. The ETA was responsible for a large number of car bombs, assassinations, and other attacks during the 2000s. In 2001, the European Union stood alongside the Spanish government and labeled the ETA a terrorist organization. With the exception of a few short-lived cease-fires, the ETA retained this reputation by killing politicians and police throughout 2000s. In 2004, ten bombs were detonated simultaneously aboard commuter trains during rush hour in Madrid, killing nearly two hundred people and injuring hundreds of others. Although the act was later determined to have been committed by al-Qaeda, immediate blame was placed on the ETA. This misdirected blame underscored the international community's psychological linking of the ETA, a local terrorist organization, to global terrorism.

In the breakaway region of Chechnya, rebels have fought with the Russians since the 1990s, with the government of the latter insisting that there would be no negotiations due to the Chechens' involvement in terrorism. Chechen terrorists were responsible for a number of large-scale attacks on civilians during the 2000s, including taking hundreds of theater patrons hostage in Moscow in 2002, an attack which cost the lives of 130 people, and a brutal assault on a school in Beslan, Russia, in 2004. The United States offered its support to the Russian government by identifying several Chechen rebel groups as terrorists. However, the United States also criticized the heavy-handed tactics of Russian troops in Chechnya during that region's attempts to break away from Russia. In the minds of many Chechens (and other observers), the acts of Chechen terrorists were in fact responses to equally brutal Russian actions in Chechnya.

The Middle East

For decades, the Middle East has provided some of the world's most high-profile forms of terrorism. Groups like pro-Palestine Hamas, which in 2007 took over governance of the Gaza Strip but continued to carry out terrorist campaigns against Israel; the Palestine Liberation Front; and Syrian-backed Hezbollah continued their efforts throughout the 2000s, despite the increased international scrutiny they received following the September 11 attacks.

Keeping these groups motivated was the continued efforts of Israel to secure its borders with Lebanon and expand its settlements in disputed territories. Also fueling their actions was the United States, which after the September 11 attacks funneled money into the region for governments like Saudi Arabia to use to combat terrorism. The latter of these issues has been seen by some as misguided policy that failed to effectively target the roots of terrorism. The recipients of the money used the funds for military actions against the terrorists in their midst, emboldening these terrorists to continue their respective attacks. Iraq, for example, saw its dictator, Saddam Hussein, ousted by US military force in 2003 and replaced with a West-friendly government. Those loyal to Saddam Hussein continued to use terrorist methods, such as improvised explosive devices (IEDs), suicide bombings, and kidnappings to counter the US presence there.

South and Central Asia

Following the September 11 attacks, attentions turned to Afghanistan, where Osama bin Laden and his al-Qaeda leadership team were hiding. The United States forcibly removed the Taliban government and from there, engaged al-Qaeda. The Taliban was exiled but became a terrorist threat. Backed by al-Qaeda, the Taliban were responsible for a number of roadside IED and suicide bomb attacks in the cities and elsewhere in Afghanistan.

Meanwhile, Pakistan and India continued their border dispute over the Kashmir and Jammu regions. This issue prompted the many different terrorist organizations in Pakistan, including the aforementioned LeT, to launch a campaign of attacks in India. These attacks were usually committed by radical Muslim Indian nationals who were trained by LeT and other groups. Al-Qaeda's presence in the dispute was not known, but its assistance to LeT helped Pakistan's Islamic terrorist groups to keep up their efforts in India.

In Sri Lanka, still another terrorist organization continued its activity during the 2000s. There, the minority ethnic Tamils sought independence from the Sinhala majority. Aiding in their cause were the Liberation Tigers of Tamil Eelam (the "Tamil Tigers" or LTTE), which has led the world in terms of the number of suicide terrorist attacks. In 2007, an international peace accord was signed between the Sinhala government and the Tamil rebels, but the Tamil Tigers quickly broke that cease-fire by killing twenty-two sailors at a naval base and detonating a bomb in a crowded marketplace in the capital of Colombo. During the 2000s, it became clear that the Tamil Tigers were not just a local insurgency, but rather an international terror group with support coming from Tamils around the world, including in the United States, Canada, South Africa, Australia, and Western Europe.

Africa

Since the 1990s, war, poverty, and famine have nearly left Somalia in chaos, with the capitol city of Mogadishu in a state of virtual lawlessness. These lawless years have fostered international terrorism; for example, the 2002 attack on Mombasa, Kenya, was organized and launched from Somalia. In 2006, the Islamic Courts Union (ICU) threatened the newly-installed transitional government to surrender or face attack. The attacks came from ICU's military wing, al-Shabaab. With Ethiopia's help, the transitional government defeated the ICU, but al-Shabaab became a terrorist insurgency. Constituted of militant Muslim extremists, al-Shabaab quickly claimed

to be aligned with al-Qaeda and began recruiting members from other countries to join their growing numbers. From 2006 through 2009, al-Shabaab was responsible for thirteen suicide attacks, targeting not only transitional government officials but Ethiopians and any other foreign troops, such as those of the African Union.

Impact

A large number of terrorist attacks during the 2000s were well-organized, well-financed, and highly brutal. Acts of terrorism occurred on every continent, some of which were regional in nature, while others were committed across borders (and oceans). The attacks committed by al-Qaeda were among the most high-profile incidents, underscoring the global terrorist network's organization and penchant for destruction and chaos. Al-Qaeda's support of and influence on many other groups, as well as the actions of groups that acted alone in their respective acts, demonstrated that terrorism remained a global threat during the 2000s.

Further Reading

Cunningham, Christopher P. "Northern Ireland and the 'War on Terror': Political Perceptions." *Irish Political Studies* 24.3 (2009): 285–302. Print. Discusses public perceptions about different terrorist groups. Specifically describes how people connect groups like al-Qaeda to Sinn Fein and the IRA, undercutting the latter's ability to gain favor in the public eye.

Hughes, James. "The Chechnya Conflict: Freedom Fighters or Terrorists?" *Demokratizatsiya* 15.3 (2007): 298–311. Print. Describes how the definition of an act of terrorism can be blurred based on the perspective of those who commit the attack. Discusses the conflict in Chechnya, the terrorist attacks of Chechen groups against civilians in Russia, and the international community's perceptions of such attacks.

Kegley, Charles W. *The New Global Terrorism: Characteristics, Causes, Controls.* Upper Saddle River: Pearson, 2003. Print. Discusses the issues behind the terrorist attacks of the early 2000s, and provides information on how the destructiveness of future terrorist attacks might be prevented.

Lutz, James M., and Brenda J. Lutz. *Global Terrorism.* London: Routledge, 2004. Print. Provides the reader with an overview of the historical and ideological roots of global terrorism as well as the strategies employed by terrorists.

Swami, Praveen. "The Well-Tempered Jihad: The Politics and Practice of Post-2002 Islamist Terrorism in India." *Contemporary South Asia* 16.3 (2008): 303–322. Print. Discusses the activity of terrorist groups in India as part of the Kashmir and Jammu dispute between India and Pakistan.

Michael P. Auerbach, MA

Texting on cellphones. (©iStockphoto.com/EdStock)

■ Texting

Definition: The act of sending typed, electronic messages between devices, especially mobile phones

Throughout the 2000s, texting became one of the predominant ways modern American society communicated. New technology allowed people to send multimedia messages, including pictures and videos, as well as simple typed messages. By the end of the decade, American cellular phone users were sending a combined total of more than 100 billion text messages per month. Despite the many benefits of texting, some individuals became concerned about the potentially damaging effects its prevalence could have on society.

By the start of the twenty-first century, mobile technology was a part of daily life for many Americans. Cell phone users were accustomed to faster connection speeds and more enhanced features. A surge of new devices that offered additional connectivity emerged as the communications industry realized the potential for such a market. First introduced as "short message service" (SMS), text messaging, commonly called texting, grew popular as mobile phone technology improved. By the early 2000s, texting had become a social phenomenon, especially among the younger generation. It further permeated the culture with the advent of social media computer technology, as users were able to send text messages online.

Cell phone providers soon updated their technologies to allow users to send and receive pictures and videos. Many users—most notably teenagers—soon preferred texting over having phone conversations. By 2004, 45 percent of teenagers owned cell phones; by the end of 2009, 75 percent owned these devices. In a survey conducted by the Pew Research Center in the summer of 2009, a third of the teens surveyed reported sending more than one hundred text messages per day; 43 percent of participants sent at least one text message per day while in school. Many questioned the distraction caused by texting, and eventually some schools banned cell phone use in the classroom. Because people tended to divert their attention exclusively to their phones while texting—even while engaged in such activities as driving a car—many became concerned about the activity.

Texting and Driving

By the time texting became widespread, people were already used to talking on the phone while driving. Texting while behind the wheel was a natural progression. As texting normally required people to avert their eyes to their phone, the habit of texting while driving was considered very dangerous. A 2009 study conducted by *Car and Driver* magazine found that the drivers surveyed were more distracted when texting than when driving drunk. This activity was especially common among teenagers. A 2009 Pew Research Center survey found that 26 percent of all American teenagers have texted while driving.

In light of such findings, by 2009 fourteen states had banned texting while driving. Federal legislators vowed to withhold federal highway funds from states that did not make texting while driving illegal.

Many accidents—including fatalities—have been caused by people texting and not paying attention while operating vehicles. For example, in July 2009, a Boston trolley car rear-ended another trolley because the driver was distracted by text messaging; forty-six people were injured in the crash.

Social Impact

Texting inspired debate on a number of issues during the 2000s. Some scholars believed that the abbreviated language used in text messages was damaging to language in general and affected people's ability to spell. Many worried that too much texting would hinder people's ability to hold face-to-face conversations. This concern was mainly directed at adolescents, who at that age are still developing social skills. A 2009 Pew Research Center survey found that texting was the preferred means of communication for teenagers aged twelve to seventeen. However, a separate Pew survey also found that the amount of time teens spent talking with friends face-to-face outside of school increased from 28 percent to 37 percent in 2009.

Impact

During the 2000s, the rise of texting gave the world a broader sense of connectivity than ever before. Though it proved to be beneficial in terms of instant contact, texting was also credited with creating some separation in terms of generational etiquette. While older cell phone users were comfortable with spoken conversations, both face-to-face and by telephone, younger generations, particularly those who grew up with texting technology, began to take a different approach to human interaction. Despite this divide, texting dominated the 2000s. Some estimates counted trillions of text messages being sent each year worldwide, making it one of the most important technological advances in history.

The national effort to outlaw texting while driving resulted in the majority of states passing legislation on the issue. Many states enacted primary enforcement laws prohibiting the activity, which allowed law enforcement officers to cite drivers for texting while driving without any other offenses.

Further Reading

Crace, John. "Gr8 db8r Takes on Linguistic Luddites." *Guardian.* Guardian News and Media, 15 Sept. 2008. Web. 26 Dec. 2012. An interview with author David Crystal, who expressed the belief that text speak is enhancing rather than hindering communication and creativity.

LeBeau, Philip. "Texting and Driving Worse Than Drinking and Driving." *CNBC.* CNBC LLC, 25 June 2009. Web. 26 Dec. 2012. Discusses a report by *Car and Driver* magazine on the dangers of texting while driving.

Lenhart, Amanda. "Teens and Mobile Phones." *Pew Internet and American Life Project.* Pew Research Center, 20 Apr. 2010. PDF. 26 Dec. 2012. This study found that teenagers consider text messaging the centerpiece of their communications strategies with friends.

—. "Teens, Smartphones & Texting." *Pew Internet and American Life Project.* Pew Research Center, 19 Mar. 2012. PDF. 26 Dec. 2012. A report regarding the increasing use of texting by teenagers, as well as the increasing number of teenagers who own smartphones.

Madden, Mary, and Amanda Lenhart. "Teens and Distracted Driving." *Pew Internet and American Life Project.* Pew Research Center, 16 Nov. 2009. PDF. 26 Dec. 2012. This survey finds that many teenagers have texted while driving.

Richtel, Matt. "Senators Seek a Ban on Texting and Driving." *New York Times.* New York Times Co, 29 July 2009. Web. 26 Dec. 2012. Discusses politicians' work toward banning texting while driving.

Santa Cruz, Nicole. "Americans Have Gone Text-Crazy." *Los Angeles Times.* Los Angeles Times, 16 Dec. 2009. Web. 26 Dec. 2012. Reports on how the number of text messages sent increased by 80 percent in 2009.

Cait Caffrey

■ *There Will Be Blood*

Identification: Film set in the early twentieth century about an oil prospector and his son attempting to drill on the land of a religious family in California.
Director: Paul Thomas Anderson (b. 1970)
Date: Released on December 26, 2007

Loosely based on the novel Oil! *(1927) by Upton Sinclair,* There Will Be Blood *explores themes such as greed, religion, and capitalism. A critical success, the film was nominated for eight Academy Awards and won for best actor and best cinematography.*

There Will Be Blood (2007) was director Paul Thomas Anderson's first film since *Punch-Drunk Love* (2002). Anderson wrote the screenplay, loosely based on

Upton Sinclair's 1927 novel *Oil!*, and worked with cinematographer Robert Elswit to portray the bleak oil fields of 1900s California. Elswit won an Academy Award for Cinematography for his work on the film. Anderson wrote the screenplay with actor Daniel-Day Lewis in mind for the leading role of oil prospector Daniel Plainview. Lewis agreed to do the film before the script was even finished. It took two years to get the film financed, and principle photography began in June 2006. The soundtrack for the film was composed by Johnny Greenwood, guitarist from the British rock band Radiohead. The score was nominated for a Grammy Award in 2008.

There Will Be Blood follows the capitalistic ventures of Plainview, an oil prospector, in early twentieth century California. Plainview and his adopted son, H.W. Plainview (played by Dillon Freasier), travel to the fictional town of Little Boston, where they learn of an oil deposit on the farm of the Sunday family. One of the twin brothers of the Sunday family, Eli (played by Paul Dano), questions Plainview's faith in God and wants Daniel to help him fund a church for his congregation, the Church of the Third Revelation. Plainview continues to clash with Eli, as well as with a larger oil company that is hoping to acquire the same land that Plainview has purchased. *There Will Be Blood* follows Plainview's career trajectory as an oilman, and investigates his struggle to balance success in business with spiritual redemption and morality.

Impact

There Will Be Blood was a critical success, and received numerous award nominations. Many critics saw the film commentary on the energy crisis in America that began with an increase in oil prices in 2003. The price increase was attributed to many factors, including a decline in petroleum reserves, the war in Iraq. *There Will Be Blood* won several major awards and was chosen by several critics as the best film of the decade. Over fifteen movie critics, including Manhola Dargis of the *New York Times* and Lisa Schwarzbaum of *Entertainment Weekly*, named the film as the best film of 2007.

Further Reading

Sinclair, Upton. *Oil!* New York: Penguin, 2007. Print.

Thomson, David. *The New Biographical Dictionary of Film: Fifth Edition, Completely Updated and Expanded.* New York: Knopf, 2010. Print.

Patrick G. Cooper

■ Timberlake, Justin

Identification: American singer and actor
Born: January 31, 1981; Memphis, Tennessee

Justin Timberlake was a member of pop group *NSYNC in the early 2000s, but later pursued a successful career as a solo singer and actor, distancing himself from his previously clean-cut image.

In the early 2000s, Justin Timberlake released two albums as part of the boy band *NSYNC. *No Strings Attached*, released in 2000, set sales records after selling two million copies in its first week of release. In 2001, the group released their final album, *Celebrity*. Following the band's breakup, Timberlake put out his first solo album, *Justified* (2002). Featuring production from noted producers the Neptunes and Timbaland, the album won the 2004 Grammy Award for best pop vocal album. The single "Cry Me a River" also won Timberlake a Grammy for best male vocal pop performance.

In February 2004, Timberlake appeared as part of the Superbowl XXXVIII halftime show with singer Janet Jackson. The performance was televised live on CBS. While performing his hit "Rock Your Body," Timberlake pulled off a piece of Jackson's costume, revealing part of her breast. The incident became one of the most widely reported media controversies of 2004. CBS received complaints from a large number of viewers and media critics. The event, which came to be referred to as the Superbowl "wardrobe malfunction," resulted in the Federal Communications Commission fining CBS $550,000.

In 2006, Timberlake released a second solo album, *FutureSex/LoveSounds*. Producers Timbaland, Danja, and Rick Rubin worked with Timberlake on the release, which spawned six successful singles.

During the late 2000s, Timberlake focused on film and television work. He appeared as host on *Saturday Night Live* twice—in 2006 and 2008—and made numerous cameo appearances on the show. His 2008 appearance as host spawned the digital short "Dick in a Box," which won a creative arts Emmy for outstanding original music and lyrics.

Timberlake has appeared in supporting roles in the films *Alpha Dog* (2006), *Southland Tales* (2006), *Black Snake Moan* (2006), *The Love Guru* (2008), and *The Open Road* (2009) and lends his voice to the character of Artie in *Shrek the Third* (2007). Timberlake

Justin Timberlake. (©iStockphoto.com/Alberto E. Rodriguez)

appeared on tracks by artists such as Madonna, TI, 50 Cent, and Duran Duran in the years following the release of *FutureSex/LoveSounds.*

Impact

Timberlake's appearance on the Superbowl halftime show has had significant effects on television and radio censorship. Live events that aired in the following years often have lengthy broadcast delays—sometimes as long as ten minutes—in order to prevent similar controversies. Timberlake has become one of the best-known entertainers in popular culture, renowned not just for his musical talent, but for his work as a dramatic actor and comedic actor.

Further Reading

Hawkins, Stan. "[Un]justified: Gestures of Straight-Talk in Justin Timberlake's Songs." *Oh Boy!: Mascu-*

linities and Popular Music. Ed. Freya Jarman-Ivens. New York: Routledge, 2007. 197–212. Print.
Summers, Kimberly Dillon. *Justin Timberlake: A Biography.* Santa Barbara: Greenwood, 2010. Print.

Leland Spencer

■ Troubled Asset Relief Program (TARP)

Definition: Programs enacted by the United States government to stabilize the country's economy in the wake of the 2008 financial crisis.

The 2008 financial crisis officially began when the Dow Jones Industrial Average peaked in October 2007 due to a historic, yet unheeded, asset bubble, which deflated throughout 2008. The programs under the Troubled Asset Relief Program, or TARP, were enacted to stop the damage caused by the collapse of the credit default swap market. Essentially, banks had given out mortgages to people who could not pay them back. Through the complicated infrastructure of the financial industry, almost every company owned a piece of these mortgages. Thus, a mass default on them precipitated a global crisis.

Three men played important roles in the lead up to TARP in September 2008: Henry Paulson—a former chairman of Goldman Sachs—secretary of the Treasury under President George W. Bush; Ben Bernanke, chairman of the Federal Reserve; and Timothy Geithner, president of the New York Federal Reserve, who would later serve as secretary of the Treasury under President Barack Obama. The rationale for government intervention in the crisis was historical, at least from Bernanke's point of view. Bernanke, an expert on the Great Depression, argued that lawmakers in the 1930s had allowed banks to collapse, which in turn constricted credit and made the depression worse.

Problems had arisen early in 2008, months before the stock market plummeted in September. In March, Paulson and Bernanke oversaw a merger between the failing investment bank Bear Stearns and JPMorgan Chase; to facilitate the deal, the government invested $29 billion in Bear Stearns's troubled assets. In early September, the Treasury pledged $200 billion to rescue the government-backed private mortgage agencies Fannie Mae and Freddie Mac. It was only after the collapse of the investment bank Lehman Brothers—which caused extensive and unprecedented damages—that Congress was jarred to action. The Treasury turned its attention to the American International Group (AIG), an American multinational insurance corporation. The Federal Reserve Bank of New York provided some assistance based on Federal Reserve Act Section 13, which allowed the lending as an "unusual and exigent" circumstance, but the Federal Reserve alone could not tackle the extensive financial problems at AIG; it was clear that the government needed to step in to prevent a larger meltdown.

Enacting TARP

When Paulson and Bernanke originally proposed TARP to Congress, they asked for $700 billion to buy back the troubled assets, or the mortgage-backed securities that had become nearly worthless, at a premium. The idea was that the infusion of capital would boost investor confidence. The plan was rejected by the House of Representatives. Detractors in Congress, both Democrat and Republican, argued that TARP amounted to a "blank check" for Paulson, who would have ultimate authority over the fund. The legislation was slightly altered—including provisions addressing executive compensation and oversight—and passed the Senate as the markets continued their downward spiral. The still largely unpopular bill passed the House days later and then was hastily signed into law by President Bush on October 3, 2008.

TARP was authorized by the Emergency Economic Stabilization Act of 2008 (EESA), which allotted $700 billion to the program to be administered in three installments. The figure that was actually spent was closer to $431 billion at a $32 billion cost to the government, according to the Congressional Budget Office. The third installment was released in February 2009—under the new Obama administration—along with the passage of the American Recovery and Reinvestment Act (ARRA), a stimulus package. ARRA extended TARP funds to the automotive industry and placed other restrictions on the institutions receiving TARP funds.

The Bank Bailout

The bank bailout, initiated to stabilize the banking system, was a five-part bank investment program that totaled $245 billion. The program included the Capital Purchase Program (CPP); the Supervisory

Capital Assessment Program (SCAP); the Capital Assistance Program (CAP); the Community Development Capital Initiative (CDCI); Targeted Investment Program (TIP); and the Asset Guarantee Program (AGP).

The Capital Purchase Program was perhaps the most significant program under TARP. CPP allowed the Treasury to inject troubled financial institutions with capital through the purchase of their preferred stock instead of through the purchase of their so-called toxic assets, as TARP was originally designed to do. Paulson announced this change in November 2008. The US Treasury provided capital to 707 financial institutions in forty-eight states. In the first round of funding, nine of the largest banks each received $25 billion.

The Supervisory Capital Assessment Program (SCAP) and Capital Assistance Program (CAP) program aimed to restart lending by ensuring that banks had adequate capital buffers to withstand losses and meet credit needs. The successful measure bolstered investor confidence. SCAP was a public stress test designed to measure the financial health of the nineteen largest bank holding companies. According to the US Treasury, eighteen of the nineteen institutions were found to have adequate buffers. CAP closed in November 2009 without making any investments.

The Community Development Capital Initiative (CDCI) was created in 2010 to help community development financial institutions (CDFIs) provide financial services to underserved communities. Under CDCI, CDFI banks, thrifts, and credit unions—eighty-four institutions in total—received $570 million in investments from the Treasury.

In December 2008, the Targeted Investment Program gave the Treasury flexibility to provide additional or new funding to financial institutions. Through the program, the Treasury purchased $20 billion of preferred stock from Citigroup and Bank of America. The program ended in December 2009 when the institutions paid back those investments in full.

A joint program of the US Treasury, the Federal Reserve, and the Federal Deposit Insurance Corporation (FDIC), the Asset Guarantee Program (AGP) provided Bank of America and Citigroup with funds to support the value of their assets.

Additional TARP Programs

The Automotive Industry Financing Program (AIFP) was enacted in December 2008. Under this program, the Treasury invested $80 billion to prevent the "uncontrolled liquidation" of General Motors (GM) and Chrysler. A potential collapse of the two industry giants would threaten the collapse of the American automobile industry.

The Term Asset-Backed Securities Loan Facility (TALF) facilitated the extension of credit to consumers and small businesses. TALF was carried out by the Federal Reserve Bank of New York, though Congress passed an act to force the Federal Reserve to reveal where and to whom the money went.

Other programs included the Public Private Investment Program (PPIP), a plan that facilitated a relationship with private investors to purchase toxic assets, and the American International Group (AIG) Investment Program, in which the Treasury provided funding for AIG. TARP's authority officially expired on October 3, 2010.

Oversight

Several organizations were created under EESA to oversee the implementation of TARP, including the Congressional Oversight Panel (COP), the Office of the Special Inspector General for TARP (SIGTARP), and the Financial Stability Oversight Board (FSOB). Along with the Government Accountability Office (GAO), these organizations acted as TARP watchdogs, though with varying degrees of success. Oversight proved to be as complicated—if not more so— than the legislation itself. Conflicting reports, a profound lack of transparency, and an incoherent plan made implementation a public mess. Two leaders of the effort were candid about their frustration: Elizabeth Warren, a Harvard professor, bankruptcy expert, and chairwoman of COP, to whom many executives and lawmakers were openly hostile; and Neil Barofsky, TARP's special inspector general, who wrote a scathing book about the mismanagement of TARP after he stepped down in 2011 (*Bailout: An Inside Account of How Washington Abandoned Main Street While Rescuing Wall Street*, 2012).

Impact

Economists have widely agreed that the bailout was a necessary evil. Without the government's intervention, the results of the financial crisis would have been catastrophic. However, the subsequent behavior of financial executives riled both Democrats and Republicans. The bailout resulted in a backlash from conservative Republicans, who would have let the banks collapse in accordance with their free market ideology; liberal Democrats, who were enraged at the idea of using taxpayer money to rescue overpaid executives from a disaster they themselves had created; and the Tea Party, whose antigovernment members would be elected to Congress in 2010. The bailout also spurred the Occupy Wall Street movement.

Many complained that the bailout favored Wall Street companies. Others pointed to the lack of accountability among the executives who supported the reckless investments that began the crisis. Without an adequate punishment, went the argument, the government was perpetuating the dangerous culture of (too much) risk.

Many hoped that TARP would allow for a major restructuring of Wall Street's operations, but as companies resisted any disclosure of how they were spending bailout money and executives put enormous pressure on government officials to subvert TARP dictates—like the $500,000 cap on executive compensation—it became clear that those changes would not happen under the program. However, the crisis led to the Dodd-Frank Wall Street Reform and Consumer Protection Act. Signed into law by President Obama in 2010, it was widely touted as the most comprehensive financial regulatory reform since the Great Depression. The act led to the establishment of the Consumer Financial Protection Bureau. The brainchild of Elizabeth Warren, the bureau is comparable to the Consumer Protection Agency, though it deals exclusively with financial products.

Further Reading

Gandel, Stephen, and Leo Cendrowicz. "After Three Years and Trillions of Dollars, Our Banks Still Don't Work." *Time* 178.12 (2011): 40–45. *Academic Search Complete*. Web. 26 Dec. 2012. Argues that the bank bailouts during the 2008 to 2009 financial crisis were not successful.

"Initiatives: Financial Stability." *US Department of the Treasury*. United States Department of the Treasury, n.d. Web. 26 Dec. 2012. An extensive collection of reports and up-to-date information on TARP.

Kashkari, Neel. "Troubled Asset Relief Program: Many Challenges Lie Ahead." *Vital Speeches of the Day* 75.2 (2009): 64–68. *Academic Search Complete*. Web. 26 Dec. 2012. Transcript of a speech given to the Brookings Institution by Neel Kashkari, the interim assistant secretary for financial stability, on January 8, 2009. Discusses the Treasury's implementation of TARP and the various challenges associated with its programs.

Lewis, Michael. *The Big Short: Inside the Doomsday Machine.* New York: Norton, 2010. Print. Describes the mortgage credit default swaps that led to the financial crisis.

Perdue, William. "Administering crisis: The Success of Alternative Accountability Mechanisms in the Capital Purchase Program." *Yale Law & Policy Review* 29.1 (2010): 295–336. *Academic Search Complete.* Web. 26 Dec. 2012. Explains the administration of the Capital Purchase Program.

Stewart, James B. "Eight Days: The Battle to Save the American Financial System." *New Yorker.* Condé Nast, 21 Sept. 2009. Web. 26 Dec. 2012. Provides a close look at discussions between the US Treasury, the Federal Reserve, and financial institutions in the wake of the financial crisis.

Molly Hagan

Donald Trump. (Courtesy Gage Skidmore)

■ Trump, Donald

Identification: American entrepreneur and television personality

Born: June 14, 1946; New York, New York

Donald Trump is an American businessman and the president of the Trump Organization, a company that develops hotels, resorts, and other real estate ventures in New York City and elsewhere. Trump also founded Trump Entertainment Resorts, which manages casinos and hotels in Atlantic City.

Donald John Trump was born in New York City on June 14, 1946, to Frederick and Mary MacLeod Trump. He attended school at a military academy and later earned a bachelor's degree from the Wharton School of the University of Pennsylvania. Upon his graduation, Trump joined his father in a shared office in Brooklyn, New York. The elder Trump used his business savvy to grow Trump Organization into an extremely successful business, which the younger Trump took over in 1975.

In 1999, Trump joined the presidential race, challenged by conservative candidate Pat Buchanan for the Reform Party nomination. It was also during this year that he divorced his second wife, Marla Maples.

Working in Trump's favor for the campaign were his vast personal funds and the publicity he received because of his high profile. Trump also maintained that his overseas business experience would be an asset in handling foreign policy.

Trump told prospective voters that he planned to impose a one-time tax on the rich to help relieve the nation of some of its national debt. Trump promised to continue the trade embargo against Cuba in order to exert political influence over the island's Communist government. He also supported the creation of an American missile defense system to thwart what was seen as a potential Russian nuclear threat. Despite garnering a fair amount of support, Trump dropped out of the race on February 14, 2000, citing internal conflict within the Reform Party.

Though his political career never took off, Trump remained a significant figure in real estate. The Trump Corporation controlled hotels, condominiums, apartments, casinos, golf courses, and vacation resorts around the globe. In addition, Trump authored several books, including *Trump: The Art of the Deal* (1987), *Trump: The Art of Survival* (1990), and *Trump: The Art of the Comeback* (1997). He also made cameo appearances on television programs such as *Spin City*, *The Nanny*, and *Suddenly Susan*, as well as in movies such as *Home Alone 2: Lost in New York* (1992), *Celebrity* (1998), and *54* (1998).

In 2004, Trump began a reality television show called, *The Apprentice.* The show consisted of contestants competing for executive positions in one of Trump's many companies. Trump consistently and dramatically used the phrase "You're fired!" when he terminated contestants who did not meet his standards. Trump would eventually copyright the phrase. Also in 2004, the *Trumped!* radio program was launched. The show, which consisted of commentaries on world events and advice on business ventures, debuted as the largest syndicated radio program in history.

Trump published the books *Trump 101: The Way to Success* in 2007 and *Never Give Up: How I Turned My Biggest Challenges into Success* in 2008. In 2009, he began a new business venture known as the Trump Network to sell a variety of weight-loss, vitamin, and health products.

Impact

Trump has had significant success with his business ventures in branding and licensing, entertainment, and real estate. He has also been involved in politics. In 2006, *Forbes* estimates Trump's net worth at approximately $2.6 billion.

Further Reading

Blair, Gwenda. *Donald Trump: Master Apprentice.* New York: Schuster, 2000. Print.

Slater, Robert. *No Such Thing as Over-Exposure: Inside the Life and Celebrity of Donald Trump.* Upper Saddle River: Pearson, 2005. Print.

Trump, Donald. *Trump: The Art of the Deal.* New York: Random, 1987. Print.

Keira Stevenson

■ 24

Identification: Television thriller starring Kiefer Sutherland as an agent of the fictional US antiterrorist agency the Counter Terrorist Unit (CTU)
Executive Producers: Joel Surnow (b. 1955), Robert Cochran
Date: November 6, 2001–May 24, 2010

The serial action drama series 24 *was groundbreaking for its use of real-time storytelling. Although the series was pop-ular and won many awards, it also received negative criticism for its portrayal of federal agents using torture as an interrogation tool and for its allegedly negative portrayal of Muslims.*

Created by executive producers Joel Surnow and Robert Cochran, *24* premiered on November 6, 2001, to great critical acclaim. Surnow wanted to develop a show that took place in one day, in real time. He and Cochran came up with the idea of making it an action thriller series that would use a visible ticking clock to heighten the suspense. Veteran film and television actor Kiefer Sutherland was cast as the show's lead, Jack Bauer, a special agent for the US Counter Terrorist Unit (CTU), based in Los Angeles, California. Throughout the show's eight seasons, Bauer saved the United States from various terrorist acts such as bombings, presidential assassinations, and computer infrastructure breaches. The show was also celebrated for its casting of an African American man (Dennis Haysbert) as the US president.

Each season of *24* presented a new terrorist threat to the United States that Bauer is called upon to prevent. For example, the first season revolved around a Serbian terrorist plot to assassinate President David Palmer (Haysbert), and the second season concerned the threat of a nuclear weapon being set off in Los Angeles. Bauer faced threats not just from terrorists, but also from corrupt politicians and double agents within his own organization. Each season featured subplots, oftentimes featuring Bauer's family members and other agents within CTU.

The series was applauded for its unique approach to storytelling and its production; the show, its actors, and creators won numerous awards, including twenty Emmy Awards, two Golden Globe Awards, and four Screen Actors Guild Awards. Sutherland won several awards for his role. However, the show did receive criticism in the media and even from military officials for Bauer's frequent use of torture as an interrogation tool. This aspect of the show made it a reference point in political discussions, and high-profile commentators such as former US president Bill Clinton and Supreme Court Justice Antonin Scalia remarked upon it. Also of concern to many critics was the show's depiction of Muslim terrorists. In response to this feedback, the show's creators were seen to tone down certain aspects in later seasons.

Impact

Premiering just two months after the terrorist attacks on the World Trade Center in New York City, *24* depicted an aggressive approach to fighting terrorism. This helped make the series politically and socially relevant while also addressing the challenging themes of patriotism and self-sacrifice. Its use of real-time storytelling and compression of time was unique at the time for a television drama.

Further Reading

Cassar, John. *24: Behind the Scenes*. San Rafael: Insight Editions, 2006. Print.

Goldman, Michael. *24: The Ultimate Guide*. DK: New York, 2007. Print.

Wardrop, Murray. "Kiefer Sutherland Character Jack Bauer in *24* Accused of 'Glamorising Torture.'" *Telegraph*. Telegraph Media Group, 28 Nov. 2008. Web. 6 Aug. 2012.

Patrick G. Cooper

■ *Twilight* series

Definition: Young-adult vampire novels by American author Stephenie Meyer, set primarily in the real-life town of Forks, Washington, which have been made into a series of motion pictures

During the 2000s, when social networking websites like MySpace, Facebook, and Twitter exploded across the Internet, Stephenie Meyer's Twilight *series was the first best-selling book series to propel sales and draw legions of fans primarily using social media. The series became a multimedia juggernaut and spawned an eponymous film franchise that became a worldwide phenomenon.*

Stephenie Meyer's *Twilight* series, consisting of the novels *Twilight* (2005), *New Moon* (2006), *Eclipse* (2007), and *Breaking Dawn* (2008), combined fantastical elements of vampire and werewolf mythology with classic old-fashioned romance. The series centers on Bella Swan, an insecure, awkward, and relatively average teenage girl who moves from Phoenix, Arizona, to Forks, Washington, to live with her divorced single father. Shortly after arriving in Forks, she becomes enamored with a mysterious and handsome boy named Edward Cullen. She eventually learns that Edward, despite his youthful appearance, is actually a hundred-plus-year-old telepathic vampire and a member of an equally mysterious coven of vampires who drink animal blood rather than human blood. Despite the obvious complications of a human-vampire relationship, Bella and Edward fall in love. The series focuses on the many consequences Bella and Edward face as a result of their forbidden union, as well as on a love triangle that ensues between Bella, Edward, and Bella's best friend, Jacob Black, a werewolf of the Quileute Indian tribe and rival of the Cullen clan.

Bolstered by savvy social media and online marketing strategies that included the launch of numerous fan appreciation sites, blogs, and discussion groups, the *Twilight* novels became runaway best sellers, selling over one hundred million copies worldwide in more than thirty-five languages and creating a global frenzy. Meanwhile, Meyer, a first-time writer when *Twilight* was published, enjoyed a meteoric rise to literary superstardom.

The phenomenal success of the *Twilight* novels made it inevitable that Hollywood would come calling, leading to the creation of *The Twilight Saga* film series. The series comprises five films—*Twilight* (2008), *New Moon* (2009), *Eclipse* (2010), *Breaking Dawn: Part 1* (2011), and *Breaking Dawn: Part 2* (2012)—based on the four novels. Unsurprisingly, the films enjoyed staggering commercial success, grossing over two billion dollars in worldwide box office receipts. Its two main stars, Kristen Stewart and Robert Pattinson, were catapulted to unprecedented fame, as they embarked on a highly publicized romance of their own.

Impact

Vampires have generally been portrayed in American popular culture as sexually charged creatures with a penchant for blood, violence, and other debauched activities. The *Twilight* series helped transcend the traditional vampire archetypes, while eschewing overt representations of sex in favor of messages of abstinence. These elements broadened the appeal and accessibility of vampires to wider audiences, especially teenage girls. Greater appeal combined with technological advances in social media networks ultimately transformed the *Twilight* series into a multibillion-dollar global brand that included not only books and films, but also clothing, cosmetics, doll, and toy lines, as well as other branded merchandise.

Further Reading

Green, Heather. "The Online Fan World of the Twilight Vampire Books." *Bloomberg Businessweek.* Bloomberg, 30 July 2008. Web. 26 Nov. 2012.

Grossman, Lev. "It's Twilight in America: The Vampire Saga." *Time* 23 Nov. 2009: 52–55. Print.

Miller, Laura. "Touched by a Vampire." *Salon.* Salon Media Group, 30 July 2008. Web. 26 Nov. 2012.

Chris Cullen

■ Twitter

Definition: An online microblogging site where users can find and share information and messages in 140-character increments

Twitter enabled unprecedented real-time communication between people around the world, as well as widespread visibility into that communication.

Twitter is a microblogging service that allows users to respond—in 140 characters or less—to the website's prompt" "What are you doing?" (later changed to "What's happening?"). These updates are called "tweets" and displayed on a user's Twitter profile. Users can follow updates from other users and reply to one another publicly (using an @ sign before the other user's name) or privately through direct messages. It is also possible for users to "retweet" (reshare) another user's commentary and "favorite" select tweets. Members can utilize privacy settings that limit who can see their tweets, but the default setting is public to facilitate discovery and exchange.

Features such as hashtags—which use the # symbol—allow users to follow a discussion on particular subjects and also help them find other like-minded people. Trending topics, added in April 2009, showcase current topics of discussion and popular hashtags. In 2009, Twitter lists enabled users to create public or private lists of users by topic. Twitter has shown value on several fronts, primarily as a content sharing and discovery application. Unlike the social network Facebook, where users generally interact primarily with friends, Twitter is generally open. Any user can follow any other user, unless the user's tweets are protected. This makes the service almost as concerned with the flow of information as the identity of the people exchanging it, and

has led to many beneficial uses such as political activism and citizen journalism.

Origins

In 2006, employees at a podcasting platform called Odeo in San Francisco were asked to come up with new product ideas due to languishing consumer interest in the company's core product. An employee named Jack Dorsey suggested working on a text message–based social status update system, an idea he had formed based on his interest in dispatch routing and experience routing cabs and bike messengers.

Dorsey tackled the idea with Odeo cofounder Noah Glass, a contract developer named Florian Weber, and Christopher "Biz" Stone. Glass is often credited with coming up with the name Twitter (initially styled Twttr). The initial concept was presented to the Odeo team in February 2006. Work on the project continued and Twitter was founded in March 2006 before being launched publicly in July.

In October 2006, Obvious Corporation was formed as a parent company for Twitter and the soon-to-be-dissolved Odeo after Odeo CEO Evan Williams bought back all shares from the company's investors. Williams's decision to regain control of Odeo without telling investors about Twitter was seen as questionable; some thought he should have disclosed more information or invited Odeo investors to invest in Twitter as well. Twitter has also been seen as failing to fully acknowledge the role of some Odeo employees, particularly Noah Glass, in the company's beginnings.

Growth

Initially, Twitter was focused on text messaging; some called the service a "group text chat." Early users, including Odeo employees, generated high cell phone bills by sending high volumes of text messages. The 140-character limit on tweet length was developed in part due to text messaging limitations.

In August 2006, an earthquake in San Francisco—where Twitter and many of its early users were located—was widely discussed on Twitter. This was a preview of how important real-time conversations would be to the service's growth.

Twitter first saw broad exposure at the 2007 South by Southwest Interactive (SXSWi) conference held in Austin, Texas. Many conference attendees started using the service if they had not been doing so already and spread the word to their colleagues and friends. Usage tripled from twenty thousand to sixty thousand daily tweets during SXSWi. Other major events in 2007, including the MTV Music Awards and the Apple Worldwide Developer's Conference, proved popular on Twitter.

The release of the iPhone in July 2007 boosted smartphone usage and enabled users to access Twitter directly from the web, rather than through texts. This increased Twitter's popularity further, particularly among the tech-savvy set. Several iPhone apps were also developed to help users tweet on their phones. Usage grew from four hundred thousand tweets per quarter in 2007 to one hundred million tweets per quarter in 2008. The number of tweets may indicate usage more accurately than number of users because many people sign up for the service but never actually tweet. The vast majority of tweets (some estimates say 75 percent) come from a small percentage of overall users.

In October 2008, Dorsey stepped down and Williams became CEO. Later that fall, Twitter rejected an acquisition offer from Facebook. Twitter reached 1.3 million users by March 2008 and would grow to 6 million users by April 2009. The company's revenue sources were unclear as of 2009, but many anticipated that it would offer some sort of advertising. The company was valued at $1 billion in that year. Investors included Union Square Ventures, Charles River Ventures, Digital Garage, Spark Capital, and Bezos Expeditions.

Twitter acquired several companies, including Summize (search and filter) in July 2008, Values of n (social software design) in November 2008, and Mixer Labs (geolocation) in December 2009. All of these acquisitions could be seen as steps toward consolidating features and keeping users more closely integrated with the Twitter ecosystem. Other external tools were crucial in building interest, such as 2008's TwitPic, a way to tweet pictures.

Twitter was created using the Ruby on Rails web development framework, MySQL database and a FlockDB graph database to connect users. Twitter developers have asserted that the system was built primarily as a content management system, not a messaging system. This led to frequent service outages when the system was overloaded, which was not corrected without major changes to the site's architecture.

Uses and Restrictions

Despite some perception of Twitter as a tool for banal exchanges, the service was integral in supporting political activism and citizen journalism. One of the first and highest-profile instances of Twitter as a news tool took place in November 2008, when local updates about bomb attacks at a hotel in Mumbai, India, were widely shared on the service. Twitter's potential for organizing protests led the Iranian government to block the service during its 2009 presidential elections; to support Iranian users, Twitter kept servers up at that critical time despite planned maintenance.

The service is also widely used during events such as sporting games, television shows, or awards ceremonies; the 2008 Summer Olympic Games in Beijing and 2008 presidential election were two examples of major events widely covered on Twitter. When pop star Michael Jackson died in June 2009, a record 456 tweets per second were sent about his passing, reflecting the growing importance of Twitter for sharing timely information.

Impact

Twitter changed the way that people interact, fostering shorter messages in real time, and enabling discovery across professional and geographic boundaries.

Further Reading

O'Reilly, Tim, and Sarah Milstein. *The Twitter Book.* Sebastopol: O'Reilly, 2011. Print. Overviews Twitter's features and uses with attention to its social and business uses.

Sagolla, Dom. *140 Characters: A Style Guide for the Short Form.* Hoboken: Wiley, 2009. Print. An early Odeo employee discusses the tweet in depth and the use of short-form writing on Twitter.

Schaefer, Mark. *The Tao of Twitter: Changing Your Life and Business 140 Characters at a Time.* New York: McGraw, 2012. Print. Examines Twitter's personal and business applications with a discussions of its philosophical effect on users.

Kerry Skemp, MA

■ 2007 Southern California wildfires

The Event: Two dozen wildfires that burned close to one million acres in one of the mostly densely populated regions of the United States
Date: Beginning October 20, 2007

Severe drought conditions, high temperatures, and high winds fueled wildfires in Southern California that led US president George W. Bush to declare a federal emergency for the region. State and federal agencies were criticized by some local authorities for delaying the release of firefighting aircraft until crews and assignments could be coordinated. The delay occurred even though protocol existed to handle such emergencies.

Santa Ana winds, which are common to Southern California in the fall, worsened conditions for two dozen wildfires, or brush fires, that broke out in the region in late October of 2007, mostly in San Diego and Los Angeles counties but including the counties of Santa Barbara, Ventura, Orange, Riverside, and San Bernardino. The wildfires, which burned both in mountain and residential areas of the suburban foothills, had a variety of direct causes, including arson, downed power lines, and accidental ignition (a child playing with matches).

Emergency teams fighting the fires included those from the California National Guard and US military personnel. Mostly contained within two weeks, the fires burned close to one million acres, destroyed or damaged several thousand homes and other structures, led to the evacuation of hundreds of thousands of persons, and caused several deaths and hundreds of reported injuries. Damage was estimated at $1.8 billion.

Impact

The October 2007 wildfires in Southern California reinvigorated debates in two areas: the ongoing costs and coordination of fire prevention and suppression and the issue of building and zoning codes, especially in residential areas of the foothills. Several emergency agencies are tasked with fighting fires in California; coordinating fire suppression with inadequate resources takes critical time. Southern California authorities and residents affected by the 2007 wildfire criticized the delayed emergency response. Furthermore, experts agree that highly flammable building materials and poor urban planning and zoning continue to worsen the impact of brush fires in a region with weather conditions primed for massive wildfires. Houses themselves, and the often dense brush and other plant life around those houses, fed the approaching flames.

Further Reading

Hawthorne, Christopher. "New Developments Mask Wild Land's Deadly Threat." *Los Angeles Times*. Los Angeles Times, 30 Oct. 2007. Web. 7 Aug. 2012.

Keeley, Jon E., et al. "The 2007 Southern California Wildfires: Lessons in Complexity." *Journal of Forestry* 107.6 (2009): 287–96. Print.

Perry, Tony, H. G. Reza, and Garrett Therolf. "San Diego County Officials Decry State's Bureaucracy." *Los Angeles Times*. Los Angeles Times, 26 Oct. 2007. Web. 7 Aug. 2012.

Desiree Dreeuws, MA

U

■ United States v. Zacarias Moussaoui

The Case: The criminal trial of al-Qaeda member Zacarias Moussaoui, the first individual tried in connection with the terrorist attacks of September 11, 2001

Date: February 6–May 4, 2006

In February 2006, Zacarias Moussaoui went on trial for his alleged involvement in the terrorist attacks of September 11, 2001. After Moussaoui entered a guilty plea, the trial served to determine whether he should face the death penalty or life in prison.

Less than a month before the terrorist attacks of September 11, 2001, US authorities arrested Zacarias Moussaoui for an immigration violation after he overstayed his ninety-day visa. At the time, he had been training at a Minnesota flight school. While in custody, Moussaoui admitted he had ties to al-Qaeda. He initially said he was to have been part of a post–September 11 plot to free incarcerated Egyptian cleric Sheik Omar Abdel-Rahman, though he later recanted.

In December 2001, Moussaoui faced formal indictment on six separate charges, including attempting to commit terrorism transcending national boundaries, aircraft piracy, the use weapons of mass destruction, the murder US government employees, and destruction of US government property. After initially refusing to enter a plea, Moussaoui changed courses abruptly, deciding to enter a guilty plea on all counts. As a result, with his guilt no longer in question, the focal point of the trial became whether his crimes warranted a death sentence or life imprisonment.

Though it appeared at times that Moussaoui was attempting to incite the jury to choose the death penalty with inflammatory comments, the jurors could not come to a unanimous decision. As a result, a life sentence was handed down automatically. The *Washington Post* later reported that for much of the deliberations, only a single member of the jury dissented.

Impact

On May 4, 2006, Moussaoui was formally sentenced to six life terms in prison, without the possibility of parole, by US District Court judge Leonie Brinkema. Several days after being spared the death sentence, Moussaoui claimed he believed he could receive fair treatment from an American jury and attempted to rescind his guilty plea in hope of getting a new trial. His request was denied, and he remained imprisoned.

As the first proceeding of its kind, Moussaoui's trial served as a precedent for other terrorism-related trials that followed. The defendant's requests for testimony from other suspects held in secret locations by the US government let to a discussion of the legal implications of holding individuals suspected of terrorism.

Further Reading

Associated Press. "Moussaoui Formally Sentenced, Still Defiant." *NBCNews.com.* NBCNews.com, 4 May 2006. Web. 11 Oct. 2012.

Mariner, Joanne. "Moussaoui and the Hidden Detainees." *FindLaw.* Thomson Reuters, 10 Nov. 2003. Web. 11 Oct. 2012.

Moussaoui, Abd Samad, and Florence Bouquillat. *Zacarias, My Brother: The Making of a Terrorist.* New York: Seven Stories, 2003. Print.

Jack Lasky

■ US Airways Flight 1549

The Event: After the engines of US Airways Flight 1549 were disabled by a collision with geese, pilot Chesley "Sully" Sullenberger landed the aircraft in the Hudson River.

Date: January 15, 2009

Place: Hudson River, near Weehawken, New Jersey

In early January 2009, US Airways Flight 1549 encountered a flock of Canada geese several minutes after takeoff. Some of the birds struck the engines of the Airbus A320 aircraft, causing significant damage. Without thrust, the airplane was unable to reach an airport, forcing the pilots to perform an emergency landing in the Hudson River. There were no causalities, and the actions of the crew were universally lauded.

On January 15, 2009, US Airways Flight 1549 departed from LaGuardia Airport in New York City heading to Charlotte Douglas International Airport in North Carolina. First Officer Jeffrey B. Skiles was flying the aircraft, with Captain Chesley B. Sullenberger III serving as monitor. The aircraft carried a total of 150 passengers, three cabin crew members, and two pilots.

Shortly after the Airbus A320 became airborne, it flew into a flock of Canada geese. Several of the large birds struck both of the plane's turbofan engines, causing them to lose power. Sullenberger took control, and the crew began following emergency procedures. After several unsuccessful attempts to reignite the engines, the pilots realized they would be unable to reach LaGuardia or the nearby Teterboro Airport. Sullenberger decided to attempt a water landing on the Hudson River.

Using the plane's manual steering mechanism, Sullenberger landed the plane in the water while keeping the vessel intact. The crew evacuated the passengers onto the wings and into inflatable emergency rafts. The proximity of the floating airplane to nearby boat terminals aided the rescue operations. Commercial ferry boats were among the first responders and were able to begin evacuation efforts within minutes of the landing. The National Transportation Safety Board accident report revealed no fault of the crew and found their professionalism to be of the highest standard.

Impact

The actions of Captain Sullenberger and the crew of US Airways Flight 1549 became an example of timely and professional decision making under pressure. The captain and crew received the Guild of Air Pilots and Air Navigators Master's Medal. Captain Sullenberger became a celebrity hero, and was honored at high-profile events such as President Barack Obama's inauguration and the 2009 Super Bowl. He emphasized that experience and

training were the determining factors in the successful outcome of the incident.

Further Reading

Lisberg, Adam. "City to Honor Chesley (Sully) Sullenberger and Crew." *Daily News.* NYDailyNews.com, 7 Feb. 2009. Web. 10 Aug. 2012.

National Transportation Safety Board. *Loss of Thrust in Both Engines After Encountering a Flock of Birds and Subsequent Ditching on the Hudson River US Airways Flight 1549 Airbus A320-214, N106US Weehawken, New Jersey January 15, 2009.* Washington: National Transportation Safety Board, 4 May 2010. PDF file.

Newman, Rick. "How Sullenberger Really Saved US Airways Flight 1549." *U.S.News & World Report.* U.S. News & World Report LP, 3 Feb. 2009. Web. 10 Aug. 2012.

Miroslav Farina

■ US sanctions against Iran

Definition: The coercive economic measures the United States has employed against Iran in order to prevent the Islamic republic from engaging in certain actions, most notably supporting terrorism-related activities and developing nuclear power and long-range missiles

The United States of America and the Islamic Republic of Iran have had an adversarial relationship since 1979, when Shah Mohammad Reza Pahlavi was overthrown and his government replaced by a fundamentalist Islamic regime led by Ayatollah Ruhollah Khomeini. In the decades since, the two nations have tangled over a number of contentious issues, including Iran's nuclear program. The program is in violation of the Nuclear Non-Proliferation Treaty of 1968, which had been signed by the Iranian government. During the 2000s, the administrations of President Bill Clinton (1993–2001), President George W. Bush (2001–9), and President Barack Obama (2009–) sought to impede the program's further development by restricting US corporations from doing business with Iran and by targeting Iran's oil and banking industries with punishing economic sanctions. The US government has also asked the United Nations (UN) to enforce harsh sanctions on Iran and has urged other nations to treat it as a pariah state—a nation acting outside of international law.

In the years between the end of World War II (1939–45) and 1979, the United States and Iran maintained a close relationship, in large part because the shah exported large quantities of Iranian oil to the United States. Yet this large natural oil reserve did not benefit the vast majority of Iranians. The shah used his nation's oil revenues both to enrich his family and close associates and to update and westernize his country. These measures enraged many Iranians, particularly Islamic leaders like Ayatollah Ruhollah Khomeini, who was forced into exile in 1964 following his public condemnations of the shah. In 1978, Shah Reza Pahlavi brutally suppressed public demonstrations and strikes against his regime and imposed martial law in Iran. He did these things while receiving the support of President Jimmy Carter (1977–81), whose administration saw the shah as one of America's key allies in the Middle East. After the shah was forced into exile in January 1979 and the ayatollah returned from his own exile the following month, relations between the United States and the Islamic leaders taking control in Iran quickly deteriorated. In November 1979, Islamic students seized the US Embassy in Tehran and took American hostages. Their demand: the return of the shah, who was receiving cancer treatment in the United States, to Iran. When the United States refused, the militants held fifty-two of the hostages for 444 days, finally releasing them just minutes after the new US president, Ronald Reagan (1981–89), had been sworn into office on January 20, 1981. By the time of the hostages' release, Shah Pahlavi had been dead for about six months.

Since that time, the United States has had no formal relations with Iran, has imported no oil from the country, and, more often than not, has maintained strict sanctions on the Islamic Republic. (During President Reagan's second term, however, in what came to be known as the Iran-Contra Affair, members of his administration illegally sold weapons to Iran, believing that the arms sale would help free US hostages being held by a pro-Iranian group in Lebanon, as well as fund the contras in Nicaragua.) Relations between the two nations eased somewhat following the end of the Iran-Iraq War (1980–88) and the death of the ayatollah in 1989. In 1995, however, the administration of President Bill Clinton again prohibited trade with Iran because of the nation's efforts to acquire nuclear weapons, its support of terrorist groups, and its desire to thwart the peace process between Israelis and Palestinians. Clinton then followed this executive order by signing the Iran and Libya Sanctions Act (ILSA) of 1996, which imposed sanctions on any company doing business with Iran's oil industry. The act has since been renewed, though it has not applied to Libya since 2006. (It later became known as the Iran Sanctions Act, or ISA.)

Sanctions under Bush

On September 11, 2001, terrorists associated with the al-Qaeda network overseen by Osama bin Laden hijacked four commercial jetliners and flew them into the World Trade Center in New York City, the Pentagon outside Washington, DC, and a field in Shanksville, Pennsylvania. The attacks—which killed almost three thousand people, destroyed the Trade Center, and severely crippled the Pentagon—refocused US foreign policy toward the prevention of terrorist acts and against the proliferation of weapons of mass destruction (WMDs).

On September 23, 2001, President George W. Bush signed Executive Order 13224, which sought to block the financial support that terrorists received from organizations or governments that had funded them in the past. Included in this group was the Iranian government. In January 2002, Bush further targeted Iran by describing it, Iraq, and North Korea as an "axis of evil," for trying to acquire WMDs (like long-range missiles) and ignoring international laws and treaties. In September 2003, the International Atomic Energy Agency (IAEA), which is the United Nations' nuclear watchdog group, asked the Iranian government to prove that it was not developing nuclear weapons. As negotiations between the IAEA and Iran went back and forth, the US government sought to continue to impede the Iranian nuclear program's development through harsher sanctions. On June 28, 2005, Bush signed Executive Order 13382 to slow Iran's nuclear program by freezing the assets of entities, groups, and companies helping to develop WMDs for rogue governments. In late October 2007, Bush announced new sanctions on Iran—reported at the time to be the toughest since the United States began imposing them on the Islamic Republic—because he believed that such actions would prevent another war in the Middle East, this time between Israel and Iran. In addition to punishing banks and other Iranian financial institutions, the 2007 sanctions also targeted the Iranian military for the first time, by labeling Iran's Revolutionary Guard Corps as a distributor of WMDs and the Quds Force as a supporter of terrorism.

Sanctions under Obama

In March 2008, the United Nations Security Council, which is the main UN body that enforces international peace, placed additional economic sanctions on Iran, in the hopes of forcing the Iranian government to comply with IAEA requests. In May, the IAEA announced that Iran was still hiding facts about its nuclear program. As sanctions seemed to be having little effect, the international community, most notably the European Union (EU), offered Iran trade incentives to curtail its nuclear program. By September, with incentives having produced no results, the UN Security Council again resolved to demand that Iran stop developing its nuclear program. However, the council did not add new sanctions, as Russia, one of the Security Council's five permanent members with veto power, declared it would not support new sanctions.

In November 2008, Barack Obama, who had offered an unconditional dialogue with Iran, was elected US president. The overture, however, did not produce tangible results. Before long, Ayatollah Ali Khamenei, who had replaced the Ayatollah Khomeini upon his death in 1989, was claiming that President Obama was pursuing a similar path as his presidential predecessors.

In May 2009, the US Department of State reported that Iran had become the "most active state sponsor of terrorism" in the world. In late 2009, the Iranian government began testing long-range missiles capable of hitting Israel or US bases in the Persian Gulf. The government also continued to enrich uranium for its nuclear reactors, despite an IAEA condemnation against such actions in November 2009. In reaction, the Obama administration tried to ratchet up the pressure on Iran through a series of executive orders between 2010 and 2012.

Impact

Time and again in the 2000s, the United States sought to impede Iran's nuclear enrichment program through economic and trade sanctions. During the following decade, the Obama administration continued these efforts through more sanctions. Executive orders imposed sanctions on eight Iranian officials responsible for human rights abuses; increased the penalties established under the Iran Sanctions Act on entities working with Iran; imposed sanctions on individuals associated with the Iranian petrochemical and energy industries; blocked the property of the Iranian government and its financial institutions; blocked the property of individuals associated with human rights abuses and prevented their entry into the United States; and suspended entry into the United States of anyone evading Iranian sanctions, among other actions. Additionally, the National Defense Authorization Act of 2012 contains a section that specifically imposes US sanctions against the Central Bank of Iran, which is the main place where the nation's oil revenue profits are cleared.

The United States has also urged international bodies like the European Union and the United Nations to aid in its efforts against Iran, fearing that a nuclear-powered Iran would be a threat to the Middle East, one of the more politically unstable regions of the world. The US government believes that Iran is a particular threat to Israel, which the Iranian regime considers to be an illegitimate nation. Some international observers have thought that the cumulative effect of the sanctions was beginning to have an impact on the Iranian economy after the 2000s, particularly as more nations have added their own economic sanctions to those imposed by the United States and the United Nations. In July 2012, for example, the European Union instituted a boycott of Iranian oil. With fewer and fewer markets to sell to, the theory behind the boycott is that Iranians will have little choice but to bow to international pressure and stop their uranium enrichment and missile programs. Also in 2012, Canada broke off diplomatic relations with Iran over the latter's nuclear program; the European Union targeted Iranian banks, trade, and gas imports with further sanctions; and the rial, Iran's currency, lost some 80 percent of its value against the US dollar since heavy international sanctions went into effect against the Islamic Republic in 2011. Yet, whether the sanctions imposed on Iran by the United States—as well as the ones imposed by the United Nations and other organizations like the European Union—ends the threat of the Iranian government's nuclear program, has remained to be seen.

Further Reading

Abrahamian, Ervand. *A History of Modern Iran.* Cambridge: Cambridge UP, 2008. Print. Presents a history of Iran during the twentieth century, covering such important events as the discovery of oil in Iran, the fall of the shah, the Iranian Revolution, and the nation's nuclear program.

Fitzpatrick, Mark. *The Iranian Nuclear Crisis: Avoiding Worst-Case Outcomes.* Oxford: Intl. Inst. for Strategic Studies, 2008. Print. The author, a veteran US diplomat who specialized in nuclear non-proliferation, analyzes the status of the Iranian nuclear program in historical context and looks at the ways in which Western efforts at deterrence have succeeded and failed.

Satrapi, Marjane. *The Complete Persepolis.* New York: Pantheon, 2007. Print. This single volume collects Satrapi's critically-acclaimed comic strip memoir detailing her coming-of-age during the Iranian Revolution in Tehran, Iran.

Wagner, Heather Lehr. *The Iranian Revolution.* New York: Chelsea, 2010. Print. Intended for high school students, this volume provides a complete overview of modern Iran, from the lead-up to the Iranian Revolution through modern-day relations between the Islamic Republic and the West.

Wright, Robin B., ed. *The Iran Primer: Power, Politics, and US Policy.* Washington, DC: US Inst. of Peace, 2010. Print. Wright, a respected journalist and foreign policy analyst who had written for a wide variety of publications, collects analyses from some fifty experts to present a detailed yet easy-to-read overview of Iran and its relations with the United States.

Christopher Mari

■ USA PATRIOT Act

The Law: Federal legislation that expanded the power of law enforcement agencies in order to facilitate antiterrorism efforts

Date: Signed on October 26, 2001

Also known as: Patriot Act; Uniting and Strengthening America by Providing Appropriate Tools Required to Intercept and Obstruct Terrorism

Passed into law following the terrorist attacks of September 11, 2001, the USA PATRIOT Act sought to prevent future acts of terrorism against the United States by facilitating information sharing between intelligence and law-enforcement agencies, among other provisions. Many opponents considered the act unconstitutional because it sacrificed personal privacy for the sake of public security.

Initially called the Anti-Terrorism Act of 2001, the Patriot Act was proposed by Attorney General John Ashcroft and the Department of Justice in an effort to remove obstacles to law-enforcement efforts in monitoring and detaining terrorists. While the act updated existing laws, modernizing surveillance techniques to address new technology, it also focused on addressing federal weaknesses that allowed the September 11, 2001, attacks to occur. The Patriot Act enabled information sharing between the Central Intelligence Agency (CIA) and Federal Bureau of Investigation (FBI) in order to address the information disconnect between the two groups. Since the attacks were made using airplanes, the act included provisions to increase airport security. The act also allowed indefinite detention of immigrants suspected of terrorist ties, a provision fraught with controversy. Another intrusive provision of the Patriot Act allowed government officials to search citizens' homes and records secretly. While the federal government maintained that secrecy was vital to the success of these searches, opponents viewed the provision as invasive.

Opponents criticized the Patriot Act for its infringement on civil liberties. Early on, Senator Russ Feingold strongly opposed the act and voted against it. The American Civil Liberties Union (ACLU) and the Electronic Privacy Information Center claimed that the act violated the Fourth Amendment, which protects Americans from unreasonable searches and seizures. The Electronic Frontier Foundation joined in opposition, touting the freedoms guaranteed by the First Amendment.

Most criticized was the act's section 215, which gave the FBI authority over the personal records of US citizens, including medical, financial, telephone, and library records. To obtain records, the FBI would submit a national security letter (NSL), which included a gag order to preemptively eliminate discussing the receipt of the NSL and prohibiting challenge of the NSL in court. The ACLU charged that section 215 and its gag order violated the First Amendment's protection of free speech. They were joined by the American Library Association, which stated strong opposition to this invasion of privacy.

To curb the law's potential abuses, Congress members proposed several amendments. These included Senator Bernie Sanders's Freedom to Read Protection Act and Senators Larry Craig and Dick Durbin's Security and Freedom Ensured Act, though these measures failed to pass.

Impact

Although many provisions of the Patriot Act were set to expire in 2005, both Presidents George W. Bush and Barack Obama renewed several of the act's provisions. Many critics of the Patriot Act contend that, since its enactment, law-enforcement agencies have disproportionately and unfairly targeted law-abiding Muslim Americans for surveillance. As the act lives on, the US government must reconcile protecting American privacy with protecting American lives, particularly as surveillance technology advances. While the law began as a measure to combat terrorism, critics of the act fear that it could be used to transform the US government into an oppressive force.

Further Reading

Finan, Christopher M. *From the Palmer Raids to the Patriot Act.* Boston: Beacon, 2007. Print.

Herman, Susan N. *Taking Liberties: The War on Terror and the Erosion of American Democracy.* New York: Oxford UP, 2011. Print.

Lucia Pizzo

■ Usher

Identification: American singer, actor, and record producer

Born: October 14, 1978; Dallas, Texas

In the early 2000s, well-known singer Usher began pursuing a second career in acting. Following a string of top twenty singles during the 2000s, he was named Billboard *magazine's Top Hot 100 Artist of the Decade.*

Having already established himself as a successful singer, Usher (born Usher Terry Raymond IV), began the millennium as a budding actor. After a few singles from his third album were leaked, he delayed its release and made changes to the album. He released the album *8701* in 2001. The album earned Usher earned two Grammy Awards for the singles "U Remind Me" and "U Don't Have to Call."

Around the same time, Usher began a high-profile relationship with singer Rozonda "Chilli" Thomas from the musical group TLC. In addition to his role in the film *Texas Rangers* (2001), he made guest appearances on the several television shows, including *7th Heaven, American Dreams,* and *Sabrina, the Teenage Witch* in 2002.

Usher (bottom) and Stevie Wonder perform at the Lincoln Memorial. (©iStockphoto.com/Justin Sullivan)

After a public split from Thomas in 2004, Usher released his fourth album, *Confessions,* which produced the singles "Confessions," "Burn," and "Yeah!" The album earned him two more Grammys. The singer then began a relationship with model Naomi Campbell, but the couple did not stay together for very long. Also in 2004, Usher shared a Grammy with singer Alicia Keys for their performance of the single "My Boo." The following year, Usher returned to acting with a role in the film *In the Mix.* He made his Broadway debut in a production of *Chicago* in 2006.

In 2007, Usher announced his impending nuptials to his former stylist, Tameka Foster. After months of media attention following the couple's engagement, Usher and Foster married in August of that year. The couple's first child, Usher Raymond V, was born in November 2007. In 2008, Usher released his fifth studio album, *Here I Stand,* which features songs about his marriage to Foster. In late 2008, Usher and Foster welcomed another son, Naviyd Ely Raymond. However, the couple divorced in 2009. Usher released the album *Raymond v. Raymond* in 2010.

Impact

In addition to being one of the most popular singers of the decade, Usher also helped foster new talent. In 2009, Usher signed Justin Bieber to his record label. Bieber went on to release two successful albums and become a pop superstar in his own right.

Further Reading

Nickson, Chris. *Usher: The Godson of Soul.* New York: Simon Spotlight, 2005. Print.

Peisner, David. "The Rumors Say Usher's Making a Comeback." *New York Times.* New York Times Company, 26 Mar. 2010. Web. 11 July 2012.

Wang, Julia, ed. "Usher Biography." *People.* Time Inc., 2012. Web. 11 July 2012.

Angela Harmon

■ USS *Cole* bombing

The Event: The bombing of US Navy destroyer USS *Cole* by al-Qaeda, resulting in the deaths of seventeen American sailors and injuring of thirty-nine others

Date: October 12, 2000
Place: Aden, Yemen

As the US Navy destroyer USS Cole *refueled in the port of Aden, Yemen, in October of 2000, a large explosion alongside the vessel killed or injured many sailors on board. An investigation revealed that the terrorist attack was planned by the militant Islamist organization al-Qaeda.*

The USS *Cole* docked in Aden harbor on Thursday, October 12, 2000, in need of fuel. The ship was on its way to the Persian Gulf to assist in imposing an oil embargo against Iraq, then controlled by dictator Saddam Hussein. As the vessel refueled, a

Cole Attack Galvanizes al-Qaeda

According to a source from the 9/11 Commission Report, excerpted below, Osama bin Laden anticipated that the United States would retaliate following the attack on the USS Cole *and that if it did not, "he would launch something bigger." The* Cole *attack invigorated al-Qaeda recruitment efforts:*

Back in Afghanistan, Osama bin Laden anticipated U.S. military retaliation. He ordered the evacuation of al-Qaeda's Kandahar airport compound and fled the desert area near Kabul, then to Khowst and Jalalabad, and eventually back to Kandahar. In Kandahar, he rotated between five to six residences, spending one night at each residence. He sent his senior advisor, Mohammed Atef, to a different part of Kandahar and his deputy, Ayman al-Zawahiri, to Kabul so that all three could not be killed in one attack.

There was no American strike. In February 2001, a source reported that an individual he referred to as the big instructor (probably a reference to bin Laden) complained frequently that the United States had not yet attacked. According to the source, Osama bin Laden wanted the United States to attack, and if it did not, "he would launch something bigger."

The attack on the USS *Cole* galvanized al-Qaeda's recruitment efforts. Following the attack, Osama bin Laden instructed the media committee, then headed by Khalid Sheikh Mohammed, to produce a propaganda video that included a reenactment of the attack along with images of the al-Qaeda training camps and training methods. The video also highlighted Muslim suffering in Palestine, Kashmir, Indonesia, and Chechnya. Al-Qaeda's image was very important to Osama bin Laden, and the video was widely disseminated. Portions were aired on Al Jazeera, CNN, and other television outlets. It was also disseminated among many young men in Saudi Arabia and Yemen, and caused many extremists to travel to Afghanistan for training and jihad, a war against evil and nonbelievers. Al-Qaeda members considered the video an effective tool in their struggle for preeminence among other Islamist and jihadist movements.

Kirk Lippold, commanding officer of the USS Cole. (Courtesy U.S. Naval War College/Photograph by Mass Communication Specialist First Class Eric Dietrich)

small motorboat carrying hundreds of pounds of C-4 explosives came alongside it. At 11:18 a.m., as crew members began to line up in the galley for lunch, suicide bombers blasted a forty-foot hole in the ship's hull. The blast killed seventeen sailors and injured thirty-nine others.

The incident was the most deadly attack against a US naval ship since an Iraqi air force plane attacked the USS *Stark* in 1987. The terrorist organization al-Qaeda later took credit for the assault on the *Cole*. The organization's leader, Osama bin Laden,

praised his followers for the strike in a videotaped statement.

In early 2007, a federal judge ruled that the Sudanese government was partly responsible for the attacks. Several families of the sailors killed in the attack filed lawsuits against Sudan, claiming that the government's complicity enabled the terrorists to complete their mission. Terrorism experts testified in court that Sudan allowed terrorists to set up training camps inside its borders and supplied al-Qaeda with diplomatic passports and materiel so they could ship explosives without drawing attention. The court held Sudan liable for the damages and awarded the families $13 million from account of frozen Sudanese assets.

Impact

Per the ship's rules of engagement, sailors on the USS *Cole* were forbidden from firing any weapons unless the ship was fired upon first. Some argued that this policy encourage terrorists to engage the vessel. This criticism, along with an independent investigation into the cause of the attack, prompted a reassessment of US naval security procedures and led to such precautions as booms to protect ships in port. Following the attack, the USS *Cole* was repaired and returned to service.

Further Reading

Associated Press. "Judge: Sudan Responsible for USS Cole Attack." *NBC News*. NBCNews.com, 14 Mar. 2007. Web. 9 Aug. 2012.

Lippold, Kirk. *Front Burner: Al-Qaeda's Attack on the USS* Cole. New York: PublicAffairs, 2012. Print.

"Pentagon Panel Urges Tighter Overseas Security for U.S. Military." *CNN*. Cable News Network, 2 Jan. 2001. Web. 9 Aug. 2012.

Cait Caffrey

V

■ Vaccinations

Definition: Substances, often inactivated or laboratory-synthesized infectious particles, that are administered to patients in order to turn on an immune protective response against disease

First developed for widespread use in 1796, when Edward Jenner promulgated the protective benefits of cowpox exposure into prevention of smallpox, vaccinations are ubiquitous health tools offering lifelong protection against infectious diseases, cancers, and more.

Youth vaccination changed the outlook of public health and infectious disease morbidity and mortality in only a few generations, completely or nearly eradicating numerous diseases and saving billions of lives. In the 2000s, as research evolved toward new targets and mechanisms, consumer response to vaccination burdens became less one-sided in support and spurred action to categorize adverse effects.

Targets and Techniques

The US Centers for Disease Control and Prevention (CDC) touts youth vaccination against diseases such as polio as the greatest public health success of the twentieth century. Continuing that effort in the 2000s, vaccines nearly eradicated many dangerous diseases. In the United States by 2010, occurrences of polio, diphtheria, and smallpox had decreased 100 percent from twentieth-century rates; measles, mumps, rubella, *Haemophilus influenza* type B (Hib), and tetanus decreased 98 percent to 99 percent. Hospitalizations declined noticeably in 2008 with the expanded use of vaccination for new disease targets, including varicella (chicken pox), childhood pneumococcus, and rotavirus, which were associated with decreased mortality. For example, in 2009, rotavirus vaccination reduced US hospitalizations by 88 percent in infants aged six to eleven months when compared to hospitalization rates for 2006.

New administration methods also complement injections for old disease targets. In 2003, the first intranasal administration of an influenza vaccine was approved in the United States. Also called live attenuated influenza vaccine (LAIV), the weakened live virus offered protection against the annual flu strains and, in 2007, was approved for use in healthy, nonasthmatic patients between the ages of two years and forty-nine years. In 2009, the pandemic outbreak of H1N1 influenza (popularly mislabeled "swine flu") involved enormous national surveillance and vaccination efforts, which afforded public health officials the opportunity to quickly develop, distribute, and evaluation a new vaccine. Teenage vaccinations expanded during the early twenty-first century as well, as pertussis and meningococcal boosters were introduced to maintain childhood immunity. In addition, the first approved vaccine against human papillomavirus (HPV) was approved in 2006 for use in girls and young women between the ages of nine and twenty-six to prevent cervical cancer in adulthood. Use of the HPV vaccine was approved for boys as well to prevent penile, anal, and oral cancers in adulthood. According to the Institute of Medicine (IOM), these new vaccines given during puberty warranted special encouragement and education to ensure public acceptance, especially among parents.

Marketing and Safety

The decision to bring vaccines to market is evaluated in part by the IOM, which determined by 2009 that vaccines have compelling public health benefits. Although an ideal vaccine will save costs and lives, both industry and government leaders acknowledge that many costly vaccines are worthwhile to prevent morbidity and mortality.

However, vaccine development remains highly empiric; professionals rely on postmarket administration to verify long-term efficacy and safety. Adverse effects are primarily noticed after vaccines are administered in vast numbers and are most often coincidental, not causal, in relation. After a review of data from 1994 through the 2000s, the IOM reported on the tenuous link between vaccines and serious morbidity and declared that most vaccination adverse reactions—except anaphylaxis in patients allergic to vaccine components—have no evidence for or against a causal relationship.

Since 1990, the Vaccine Adverse Event Reporting System (VAERS) program within the US Department of Health and Human Services has collected data on all adverse vaccine reactions. Although up to 90 percent of these reactions are considered mild, VAERS has been critical to identifying increased risks in large populations quickly. For example, 2007 surveillance identified a rare connection of increased febrile convulsions when measles-mumps-rubella (MMR) and varicella vaccines were administered together in one injection rather than in separate injections on the same day. Early awareness changed administration methods and prevented more widespread complications in at-risk children with existing immune deficiencies.

Consumer Concerns

As entire populations have become vaccinated against recently dangerous infectious diseases, and as vaccines have turned to protection against milder diseases like varicella, the consumer mindset has shifted from unquestioning approval to concern, inspiring citizen groups to organize. As a result, the herd immunity cultivated in the 1990s has been shaken.

Childhood vaccination reactions receive particular attention in connection to neurologic morbidities, including autism and attention disorders purportedly caused by thimerosal-containing vaccines in the 1990s. Rigorous evaluation of available reports in 2001 by the IOM identified no connections between the preservative and these effects, but thimerosal was reduced or eliminated in all vaccines intended for infants and for many vaccines intended for older children. A connection between MMR vaccination and autism was advanced in 1998 by Andrew Wakefield in the United Kingdom. An overwhelming number of parents chose to refuse at least some protective doses of the vaccine and continued to do so even after Wakefield's study methods and publication in *The Lancet* were discredited in 2010.

Parental fears of unknown ingredients in and reactions to vaccines are deep seated and require partnership by all parties. In February 2009, the US Department of Health and Human Services' National Vaccine Plan public health initiative was instituted to coordinate efforts to safely administer vaccines and effectively communicate with the public.

Impact

Though vaccinations have protected against communicable diseases for centuries, their success has reduced perceived dangers of infection and has turned the tide against youth immunization schedules and herd immunity. Vaccination against modern-day plagues like mutated influenza or cancers nonetheless remain at the forefront, and health professionals are seeking to assuage fears about vaccination safety.

Further Reading

Offit, Paul, and Louis Bell. *Vaccines: What You Should Know.* 3rd ed. Hoboken: Wiley, 2003. Print. A consumer-oriented introduction to vaccination risks and benefits from a physician's perspective.

Riedel, Stefan. "Edward Jenner and the History of Smallpox and Vaccination." *Proc. (Bayl. Univ. Med. Cent.)* 18.1 (2005): 21–25. Print. Modern-day review of vaccination development.

Sears, Robert W. *The Vaccine Book: Making the Right Decision for Your Child.* New York: Little, 2007. Print. Describes an alternative approach to vaccination that revises scheduling tenets of the twentieth century.

"Thimerosal in Vaccines Questions and Answers." *US Food and Drug Administration: Vaccines, Blood, and Biologics.* US Food and Drug Administration, 30 Apr. 2009. Web. 4 Dec. 2012. A succinct resource for consumers about adverse event updates.

United States. Centers for Disease Control and Prevention. *Epidemiology and Prevention of Vaccine-Preventable Diseases (The Pink Book: Course Textbook).* 12th ed. Atlanta: Dept. of Health and Human Services, 2012. Print. The official medical resource on vaccine ingredients, administrations, and more.

Nicole Van Hoey, PharmD

■ Venter, Craig

Identification: American biochemist
Born: October 14, 1946; Salt Lake City, Utah

When biochemist Craig Venter founded Celera Genomics, a private company dedicated to decoding the human genome, he was racing against the publicly funded Human Genome

Craig Venter (left) at a New America Foundation event with Steve Coll. (Courtesy New America Foundation)

Project (HGP). Soon after, Venter claimed to be the first to discover the sequence.

Craig Venter was a member of a team of researchers competing against the Human Genome Project team in the 1990s to be the first to sequence the entire human genome. In 1998, he started a private company, Celera Genomics, with the goal of being the first to map the human genetic blueprint. The Celera researchers were using a technique known as "shotgun sequencing," which was much faster and cheaper than the approach used by the HGP, but far less accurate. He published a draft sequence two years later, several months ahead of the HGP. President Bill Clinton publicly announced the publication of the complete sequences by both groups in 2000, and Venter shared credit with the HGP.

In 2001, Venter helped the federal government solve a suspected case of terrorism, in which five people who received envelopes containing anthrax died. Venter and his coworkers at the Institute for Genomic Research, a nonprofit organization that he founded in 1992, worked with the Federal Bureau of Investigation to identify the source of the anthrax strain and enabled the bureau to narrow the field of suspects to a government scientist, Bruce E. Ivins.

After leaving Celera Genomics in 2002, Venter used funds from his investments to found his own research centers. In 2004 he began a two-year expedition to Nova Scotia seeking microscopic species for DNA sequencing. He then became intent on ending climate change by ending human dependence on oil and decided to focus his research efforts on exploring alternative energy sources. To this end, he founded Synthetic Genomic Inc. in 2005. In 2009 the Exxon Mobil Corporation announced it was providing Venter's company with $300 billion to fund research focused on developing algae cells capable of turning sunlight and carbon dioxide into usable energy.

Venter founded the J. Craig Venter Institute in 2006 and became the first person to have his genome sequenced. His sequencing determined that his hereditary tendencies include blue eyes, heart disease, and attention-deficit disorder. Venter wrote a memoir, *A Life Decoded: My Genome, My Life*, which was released in 2007. In it, he wrote in depth about his background and scientific research. The book also addressed some of the controversy surrounding the human genome research race.

Impact

Venter's groundbreaking work in genomic sequencing was just the beginning of his contributions to American science. His controversial "shotgun sequencing" technique is now widely used in genomic research. His competitive research efforts have accelerated the pace of medical advancement and scientific development. He continues to pioneer some of the most innovative research of the century, though his embrace of private funds to foster research has generated controversy in the scientific community.

Further Reading

Chreeve, Jamie. "The Blueprint of Life." *US News*. US News and World Report, 31 Oct. 2005. Web. 13 July 2012.

Douthat, Ross. "The God of Small Things." *Atlantic*. Atlantic Monthly Group, Jan./Feb. 2007. Web. 13 July 2012.

Venter, Craig. *A Life Decoded: My Genome, My Life*. New York: Viking, 2007. Print.

Ward, Logan. "J. Craig Venter's Amazing Decade." *Popular Mechanics*. Hearst Communications Inc., 4 Oct. 2010. Web. 13 July 2012.

Cait Caffrey

■ Vick, Michael

Identification: American professional football player
Born: June 26, 1980; Newport News, Virginia

Vick rose to prominence as a quarterback at Virginia Tech. The Atlanta Falcons selected him as the first overall pick of the 2001 National Football League (NFL) Draft. In 2007, he experienced legal and financial difficulties because of his involvement in illegal dog fighting. After serving a prison term, Vick returned to the NFL in 2009.

Michael Vick joined the NFL before completing his final two years at Virginia Tech. The Atlanta Falcons signed him in 2002 for six years, offering him a contract worth $62 million. He became the team's starting quarterback the following year, and earned a spot on the 2003 Pro Bowl team. Two years later, the Falcons extended Vick's contract for another ten years with an offer of $130 million—making him the highest paid player in the NFL.

In 2005, a woman accused Vick of giving her a sexually transmitted disease. Vick settled the case before it went to court. Two years later, police searched Vick's Virginia home while investigating his cousin's drug activities, and discovered that Vick was operating an illegal dog-fighting ring. Vick initially denied any involvement, but in August 2007, he pleaded guilty to charges, admitting that he had funded and participated in illegal dog fighting and gambling activity. The NFL suspended him, and his contract with the Falcons was cancelled. Vick later admitted he had killed some dogs. Although Vick expressed remorse for his actions, he was sentenced to twenty-three months in prison and fined almost $1 million in December 2007.

In May 2009, Vick paid $2.5 million for a defaulted real estate loan, and $1.1 million on another loan. The following year, he was accused of illegally using $1.3 million from one of his own company's pension plans. He filed for Chapter 11 bankruptcy. Vick remained imprisoned at Leavenworth, Kansas, for eighteen months. In 2009, he was released to home confinement and given three years of probation.

In July 2009, it was reported that the NFL considering Vick's reinstatement to the league. In August, the Philadelphia Eagles offered him a $1.6 million, one-year contract. He immediately began practicing with the team and soon returned to professional play.

Impact

In 2006, Vick and his family started the Vick Foundation to support at-risk youths in Virginia. In 2007, Vick donated $10,000 to the United Way to help families and victims of the Virginia Tech shootings, and he collected additional funds through the Vick Foundation for the families. Since his release from prison, Vick has worked with the Humane Society of the United States, supporting the Pets for Life program, which advocates ending dog fighting.

Further Reading

Associated Press. "Former QB Vick Makes Donation for Victims Families." *ESPN*. ESPN. Web. 13 July 2012.

Gorant, Jim. *The Lost Dogs: Michael Vick's Dogs and Their Tale of Rescue and Redemption.* New York: Gotham, 2010. Print.

Strouse, Kathy. *Badd Newz: The Untold Story of the Michael Vick Dog Fighting Case.* Charleston: BookSurge, 2009. Print.

Gina Kuchta

■ Video games

Definition: Electronic interactive media usually played on a computer, handheld device, or a gaming console that connects to a television. Video games offer different experiences that include puzzle solving, role playing, and simulations, along with an array of artistic styles ranging from realistic to cartoonish

In the 2000s, the video game industry was the fastest growing sector of media in North America and surpassed the film industry's total revenue in the United States at roughly twenty-two billion dollars in 2008. Gaming culture transitioned from a fringe hobby to mainstream culture with the success of console titles such as Halo and the online role-playing game World of Warcraft (WoW), the latter boasting nearly twelve million active subscribers by the end of the decade.

The 2000s heralded the birth of the sixth and seventh generations of video game consoles. Video game titles generally come in two formats, optical discs or cartridges, and each console has a library of available games developed by console manufacturers and third-party developers. The sixth generation created a competition between four key companies for control of the rapidly growing entertainment industry; this competition was named the console wars.

The Console Wars

The sixth generation of consoles included the Sega Dreamcast, Microsoft Xbox, Sony Playstation 2 (PS2), and Nintendo Gamecube. Sega initiated the sixth-generation era with the Dreamcast, which launched in 1999. Sony, however, released the PS2 the following year, crippling the Dreamcast's sales. Sega discontinued the Dreamcast in 2001 and bowed out of console development. The Xbox and Gamecube also launched in the same year but met greater success than the Dreamcast.

Sony, Nintendo, and Microsoft continued to compete against each other during the seventh console

generation, initiated when Microsoft released the Xbox 360 in 2005, a year ahead of its competitors. Nintendo and Sony released their consoles, the Wii and Playstation 3 (PS3), in 2006. All three consoles sold well during their launch time frames and beyond, but the Wii outsold both the PS3 and Xbox 360 at nearly thirty million copies in the United States alone.

In addition to the major consoles, both Nintendo and Sony released handheld gaming devices. The Nintendo DS was released in November 2004 as a successor to the Advance series, which was debuted in 2001. The DS used two screens and had built-in support for a stylus. Sony's handheld device, the Playstation Portable (PSP), which was available in 2005, featured a large screen, online capabilities, and used optical discs instead of cartridges. Nintendo's DS line had sold about fifty million units by the end of the decade, making it the second highest-selling system of all time behind the PS2.

Growth and Sales

With the rise in popularity of games in the 2000s dozens of titles or series broke sales records and expectations. The best-selling games for each console, discounting bundles, are Mario Kart Wii for Nintendo Wii (32.4 million copies), Halo 3 for Xbox 360 (8.1 million), Gran Turismo 5 for PS3 (7.4 million), Sonic Adventure for Sega Dreamcast (2.5 million), Grand Theft Auto: San Andreas for PS2 (17.3 million), Super Smash Bros. Melee for Nintendo Gamecube (7 million), and Halo 2 for Xbox (8 million). The best-selling games for handhelds include Pokemon: Ruby & Sapphire for Gameboy Advance (13 million), New Super Mario Bros. for Nintendo DS (29 million), and Gran Turismo for PSP (3.6 million). The highest-grossing PC game of the 2000s was The Sims 2 with more than 20 million copies sold.

The popularity of PC gaming exploded with the rise of subscription-based massive multiplayer online role-playing games (MMOs). Everquest launched in 1999 and rapidly gained a large subscriber base, surpassing Ultima Online in 2000 and peaking at about a half million users by the middle of the decade. Everquest is one of the longest running games with nineteen official expansions, but it lost most of its population with the release of Everquest II and World of Warcraft (WoW) in 2004. WoW gained massive popularity in the burgeoning MMO scene and is one of the best-known video games of all time, with a peak subscriber base of twelve million.

Criticism and Controversy

As video games transitioned into mainstream culture, they began to draw negative attention and controversy for both their subject matter and their effect on players. Tragedies, such as the Columbine shootings in 1999 and the Virginia Tech massacre in 2007, cite the violence displayed in video games as a contributing factor. Addiction to games has become a concern as well, due to reported cases of binge-playing resulting in death, such as the Guangzhou resident who died after three consecutive days of playing video games at an Internet cafe in 2007. There are, however, few scientific studies conducted on the psychological and physiological effects of video games; the effects remain inconclusive.

Impact

The video game industry is the largest and fastest growing division of entertainment media in North America, with 72 percent of American households containing games in 2010. Despite an ailing economy, video games have generated more than 120,000 jobs and $25.1 billion in sales. The spectrum of participants ranges from children to senior citizens; the average gamer is thirty-seven years old and has been playing video games for twelve years. Over the last decade, the gender disparity has begun to equalize: 58 percent of the gamer population is male, and 42 percent is female. The industry is predicted to maintain steady growth as new applications are being found and tested, such as military training and medical rehabilitation.

Further Reading

Bissell, Tome. *Extra Lives: Why Video Games Matter.* New York: Vintage, 2010. Print. A perspective on the art and meaning of video games.

Jones, Gerard. *Killing Monsters: Why Children Need Fantasy, Super Heroes, and Make-Believe Violence.* New York: Basic, 2003. Print. Persuasive book on the merits of make-believe violence for children.

Kent, Stephen. *The Ultimate History of Video Games: From Pong to Pokemon—The Story Behind the Craze That Touched Our Lives and Changed the World.* New York: Three Rivers, 2001. Print. A comprehensive walk through the history of video games.

McGonigal, Jane. *Reality is Broken: Why Games Make Us Better and How They Can Change the World.* New York: Penguin, 2011. Print. An engaging study on the effects of video games by a renowned designer.

"Sales, Demographic and Usage Data 2011: Essential Facts about the Computer and Video Game Industry." *Entertainment and Software Association.* ESA, 12 June 2011. PDF file. Offers recent sales data and statistics released by the Entertainment and Software Association.

Andrew Maul

■ Virginia Tech massacre

The Event: A shooting rampage at the Virginia Tech college campus that left thirty-three people dead
Date: April 16, 2007
Place: Blacksburg, Virginia

The shooting at Virginia Tech was the deadliest rampage by a single shooter in US history. Seung-Hui Cho, a student at the university, killed twenty-seven of his fellow students and five faculty members before committing suicide. At least seventeen others were injured in the shooting.

The massacre at Virginia Tech began in the early hours of Monday, April 16, 2007. Around 7:00 a.m., senior English major Seung-Hui Cho entered West Ambler Johnston Hall, a dormitory, armed with several firearms. Cho encountered Emily Hilscher, a freshman who lived in the dormitory, and killed her. Resident assistant Ryan Clark went to investigate noise when he encountered Cho, who shot and killed Clark before fleeing the building.

Fifteen minutes later, police responded to a 911 call about the shootings. Police believed the shootings at the dormitory were an isolated incident. They secured the location and began their investigation. By 8:00 a.m., students were headed to class, but campus officials had not yet informed them about the killings that had occurred at the dorm.

Meanwhile, Cho briefly returned to his dormitory. He then stopped at the post office to mail a package and proceeded to Norris Hall, a building housing numerous classrooms, carrying two handguns and a bag of ammunition.

Around 9:30 a.m., campus officials sent out an e-mail notifying students about the first shooting. More than two hours after the first incident, another shooting continued on the second floor of Norris Hall. Police responded to a 911 call about the shooting around 9:45 a.m. When they arrived at the building, they found the doors chained shut from the inside. The police broke into the building and followed the sounds of gunfire to the second floor, where they found that Cho had committed suicide. Before taking his own life, Cho had killed more than thirty people. It was not until after the second shooting that campus officials sent out e-mails announcing the cancellation of classes, and warning students to stay indoors.

The following day, NBC News received a package from Cho that included videos and a statement in which he claimed he was forced into his actions.

Warning Signs

After the massacre, it was revealed that mental health professionals had deemed Cho a potential threat to himself due to signs of psychological illness. Almost two years prior, Cho was evaluated by a psychiatric hospital after several female classmates told police they had received unsettling messages from him, and another classmate suggested Cho was suicidal. However, he was not deemed a threat to others at the time. It was recommended that Cho seek counseling on an outpatient basis.

Around this time, author Nikki Giovanni, a teacher at Virginia Tech, asked that Cho be removed from her poetry class after he turned in disturbing writings. Classmates accused him of secretly taking pictures of them. Lucinda Roy, then a director of the creative writing department, started teaching Cho one-on-one. She too found Cho's writings upsetting, and she contacted campus police and university administrators. However, because Cho did not make any explicit threats, no official reports were filed. Cho passed a criminal background check and purchased two guns early in 2007.

Aftermath

Virginia Tech officials were widely criticized for their response to the shootings. After the massacre, a review panel was convened to assess the actions taken by the university in response to the shootings. The report showed that the university failed to alert students that there was a shooter on campus for more than two hours. It determined the university's reaction to the first shooting contributed to the loss of life in the second shooting. Virginia Tech, along with the state government, paid an $11.1 million settlement to the families of the victims. The university also made major renovations to the buildings where the shootings occurred, upgraded the campus security program, and set up an online Office of Emergency Management.

Impact

The tragedy of the Virginia Tech massacre caused colleges and universities across the United States to reassess their safety systems and review existing programs for helping students with mental illnesses. After a state panel investigated the incident, a law was passed requiring Virginia's public universities to set up teams to examine students' medical, criminal, and academic records to assess possible threats. The state's private universities were exempted from the law, but many set up similar teams in the effort to prevent future acts of violence.

The Virginia Tech shootings also led to a change in gun-control laws. In 2008, President George W. Bush signed legislation that would provide incentives for states to report mentally ill and other potentially dangerous individuals to the National Instant Criminal Background Check System, an FBI database used to determine whether a person should be barred from purchasing a firearm.

Further Reading

Carter, Shan, et al. "Deadly Rampage at Virginia Tech." *New York Times.* New York Times, 23 Apr. 2007. Web. 9 Oct. 2012. Provides an interactive timeline and map of the events that occurred during the Virginia Tech massacre.

Chen Sampson, Zinie. "5 Years after the Virginia Tech Massacre, Colleges Gauge Threats." *Huffington Post.* HuffingtonPost.com, 14 Apr. 2012. Web. 9 Oct. 2012. Discusses and evaluates the safety and emergency-response changes made on college campuses in the wake of the Virginia Tech massacre.

Du Lac, J. Freedom. "A Massacre's Survivors: Recovery and Resilience at Va. Tech." *Washington Post.* Washington Post, 14 Apr. 2012. Web. 9 Oct. 2012. Examines the lives of Virginia Tech shooting survivors five years after the shooting.

"Killer's Manifesto: 'You Forced Me into a Corner.'" *CNN.* Cable News Network, 18 Apr. 2007. Web. 9 Oct. 2012. Details the contents of the video Cho sent to NBC News and his manifesto. Provides video clips from Cho's recording and from interviews with students, officials, and authorities.

Potter, Ned. "Va. Tech Killer Ruled Mentally Ill by Court; Let Go after Hospital Visit." *ABC News.* ABC News Internet Ventures, 18 Apr. 2007. Web. 9 Oct. 2012. Details Cho's erratic behavior prior to the shooting rampage, including quotes from fellow students who knew him, and gives an overview of Cho's video recording.

Roy, Lucinda. *No Right to Remain Silent: The Tragedy at Virginia Tech.* New York: Crown, 2009. Print. Written by a professor who worked with Cho and tried to warn campus officials and mental health counselors about his mental state prior to the shootings.

Rebecca Sparling

■ Wales, Jimmy

Identification: American Internet entrepreneur
Born: August 7, 1966; Huntsville, Alabama

Jimmy Wales is an American Internet entrepreneur best known for cocreating the Internet encyclopedia Wikipedia *and for founding the web hosting company Wikia. Wales is considered a pioneer in the use of open-community software platforms to collaboratively create and catalogue information online.*

In 1998, former financial trader James Wales founded his first Internet company, a web portal firm named Bomis, in San Diego. The firm's modest success allowed Wales to explore his first vision for an online encyclopedia, *Nupedia*, in 2001. The project stalled due to a lack of content growth as voluntary submissions by academics were dogged from scrutiny by a multifaceted editorial review process.

The failure of *Nupedia* to generate trustworthy content at a rapid pace led Wales and his colleague Larry Sanger to conceive of a new kind of feeder encyclopedia, in which articles could be hosted prior to peer review. They dubbed the new encyclopedia *Wikipedia*, after the software used to construct it. The new encyclopedia's open source content contribution system, helmed and policed by thousands of volunteer editorial contributors, quickly became one of the Internet's most popular sites in the 2000s.

In 2002, Wales would found the nonprofit Wikimedia Foundation to oversee *Wikipedia* and a myriad of other collaborative online projects utilizing wiki software. In 2004, Wales founded Wikia, a for-profit web hosting service for wiki content.

Impact

As one of the key figures behind the founding of *Wikipedia*, Jimmy Wales has been instrumental in the initialization, construction, and maintenance of a permanent and freely accessible electronic archive for human knowledge. More importantly, his projects

Jimmy Wales. (Courtesy William Brawley)

throughout the 2000s proved how effective digital technology could be as a collaborative tool for the benefit of the common good on a global scale.

Further Reading

"Jimmy Wales on the Birth of Wikipedia." *Ted Talks.* Ted Conferences LLC, Aug. 2006. Web. 8 Oct. 2012.

Mangu-Ward, Katherine. "Wikipedia and Beyond: Jimmy Wales' Sprawling Vision." *Reason.com.* Reason Foundation, June 2007. Web. 8 Oct. 2012.

Poe, Marshall. "The Hive." *Atlantic.* Atlantic Monthly Group, Sept. 2006. Web. 8 Oct. 2012.

John Pritchard

■ Wallace, David Foster

Identification: American author and educator
Born: February 21, 1962; Ithaca, New York
Died: September 12, 2008; Claremont, California

David Foster Wallace was a highly influential and versatile writer known especially for his dark humor, verbosity, and philosophical insight.

During the 2000s, David Foster Wallace continued to prove himself as one of America's most masterful writers while focusing more on essays and nonfiction than on novels and short stories, genres that brought him accolades during the 1990s. While many general readers were intimidated by the 1,079-page length of *Infinite Jest* (1996), which was nominated in 2005 by *Time* magazine as one of the "100 best English-language novels published since 1923" and which earned him a MacArthur Foundation Fellowship (the "genius grant"), he also demonstrated his powerful wit, intellect, and grip of the English language in magazine articles that were accessible to a mainstream audience. Among his most memorable essays are "The Weasel, Twelve Monkeys, and the Shrub," about John McCain's 2000 presidential campaign, published in *Rolling Stone* in April 2000; "Consider the Lobster," published in *Gourmet* in August 2004; and "Federer as Religious Experience," published in the New *York Times* in August 2006.

In 2002, Wallace accepted the Roy Edward Disney Professorship in Creative Writing and a professorship in English at Pomona College in Claremont, California. The following year, he published *Everything and More: A Compact History of Infinity*, a treatise on mathematics, one of his many intellectual passions. He followed that with the critically acclaimed collection of stories, *Oblivion* (2004).

In 2005, Wallace gave a commencement speech at Kenyon College on the importance of leading a compassionate life. The impassioned speech reverberated throughout the wider academic community and was reprinted in the *Wall Street Journal* and the *Times* (London) before being published in book form as *This Is Water* (2009).

After publishing a collection of essays, *Consider the Lobster* (2006), Wallace returned to novels, writing *The Pale King* (published posthumously in 2011), his first since *Infinite Jest*. However, the depression that he had suffered throughout most of his adult life began to consume his everyday existence, and on September 12, 2008, he committed suicide by hanging himself.

David Foster Wallace. (Courtesy of Steve Rhodes)

Impact

Wallace's greatest contribution to literature is his style of writing: self-conscious, witty, and verbose, marked by a keen sense of observation as he pursues and documents truth. His essays, short stories, novels, and nonfiction are studied in writing and literature programs and have impacted the work of many modern writers. Critics believe that Wallace's legacy will be defined better in time, as his writing seems to represent the end of the period of postmodernism and the beginning of something else, often referred to as post-postmodernism.

Further Reading

Boswell, Marshall. *Understanding David Foster Wallace.* Columbia: U of South Carolina P, 2003. Print.

Harris, Charles B. "David Foster Wallace: That Distinctive Singular Stamp of Himself." *Critique* 51.2 (2010): 168. Print.

Lipsky, David. *Although of Course You End up Becoming Yourself: A Road Trip with David Foster Wallace.* New York: Broadway, 2010. Print.

Sally Driscoll

■ War in Afghanistan

Definition: The US-led military campaign in Afghanistan to oust the Taliban regime and dismantle the al-Qaeda network operating in that country

The September 11, 2001, attacks on the United States were perpetrated by the international terrorist network al-Qaeda. This network was believed to have trained the terrorists who carried out the attack, as well as planned and implemented the attack itself, in a remote region in Afghanistan. The ruling regime in that country, the Taliban, gave safe haven to al-Qaeda, enabling it to conduct its operations. Shortly after the attacks, the United States and its North Atlantic Treaty Organization (NATO) allies launched a campaign designed to destroy al-Qaeda and topple the regime that protected it. This campaign continued throughout the 2000s, costing the lives of thousands of American soldiers as they engaged not only the Taliban and al-Qaeda but other regional insurgents and warlords while attempting to rebuild Afghanistan's infrastructure and stabilize the nation.

When the terrorist network known as al-Qaeda launched its multifarious attacks against US targets on September 11, 2001, it did so from a secure location in Afghanistan. Al-Qaeda leader Osama bin Laden and his leadership team were believed to be operating in a remote region of that country, where they plotted the attack, trained the perpetrators, and organized the transfer of funds to enable their operatives to carry out the plot. Al-Qaeda was able to do so because it was operating without interference, thanks to the support of the Taliban, a radical Islamic militant regime that had seized power in Afghanistan only a short time before.

In order to truly impact al-Qaeda, therefore, the United States needed to engage the Taliban as well. The Taliban would need to be removed from power for the United States to launch a full-scale attack on the regions in which al-Qaeda was operating. Furthermore, Afghanistan itself would then need to be stabilized, with the Taliban's government replaced by a balanced infrastructure that would not support al-Qaeda. These objectives proved extremely daunting, requiring a significant investment of US military technology, money, and lives.

Toppling the Taliban

The Taliban was born from the Soviet occupation of Afghanistan in the 1980s, emerging from the US-supported resistance organizations that fought against the Russians. When the Soviet Union withdrew from Afghanistan during the 1990s, various parties within the Afghan population began fighting with one another in the resulting power vacuum. The Taliban took advantage of the infighting and seized power in 1996, installing an ultraconservative Islamic form of government in the Afghan capital of Kabul.

In order to move on al-Qaeda, the US-led forces needed safe passage, unimpeded by the ruling government. Unfortunately, the Taliban was unwilling to allow the United States to operate in Afghanistan. Not long after they took power, a senior member of the Taliban's leadership, Mullah Mohammed Omar, formed a relationship with Saudi Arabian–born terrorist Osama bin Laden after the latter moved his base of operations from Sudan to Kandahar, Afghanistan. After the September 11 attacks, the United States demanded that the Taliban hand over bin Laden for his actions; Omar and his regime declined the ultimatum, instead offering to try bin Laden in an Afghan court. The United States thus launched a major bombing campaign, followed by a full-scale invasion by American and British forces that routed the Taliban in Kabul and Kandahar, driving them away but not defeating them. The Taliban regrouped in the Afghan wilderness, gaining support as an insurgency group and coordinating with al-Qaeda to launch suicide bombings, car-bomb attacks, and other operations against the international coalition, including the use of improvised explosive devices (IEDs).

Compounding the issue was the fact that the Taliban had close, albeit undefined and unofficial, relations with the government of Pakistan, a partner of the United States in the war on terrorism. Although the Pakistani government was known to engage and capture al-Qaeda members on and within its borders, it did not launch a full offensive against the Taliban insurgency, making the US effort in remote Afghanistan more difficult. In fact, many experts believe that Omar himself moved to Pakistan, along with other members of the Taliban's leadership, and was safeguarded there after the Taliban ouster. Although al-Qaeda was the main goal of the US-and-NATO-led campaign, the flexibility and continued strength of the Taliban outside of the cities made both attacking al-Qaeda and establishing order in post-Taliban Afghanistan highly difficult.

U.S. Army First Lieutenant Robert Wolfe, security force platoon leader, provides rooftop security during an engagement in Farah City, Afghanistan. (U.S.Navy/Photograph by Lieutenant j.g. Matthew Stroup)

Engaging al-Qaeda

As US leadership had anticipated, the main target of the war in Afghanistan, al-Qaeda, proved an elusive foe. To be sure, al-Qaeda was frequently a collaborator in suicide bombings and other terrorist-style attacks against US and international forces. However, Osama bin Laden and his central leadership team were largely unseen during the 2000s. Most experts believed them to be in the mountain stronghold of Tora Bora, in a rugged region in the White Mountains in eastern Afghanistan, near the city of Jalalabad. Tora Bora was a perfect hiding place, a network of caves and tunnels carved deep into the mountains. The mujahideen, Afghan freedom fighters who had united against the Soviets during the 1980s, had used this network to evade Soviet bombings during the war. Osama bin Laden arrived in this region in 1996 after being forced out of Sudan, and he and al-Qaeda used the stronghold to plot their attacks, conduct training

exercises, and perform other operations without satellite detection.

As American and allied forces battled al-Qaeda forces in the area and relentlessly bombed the mountain stronghold, a campaign dubbed the battle of Tora Bora, they continued to find themselves at least a step behind bin Laden and his closest leaders. Rumors abounded that once the United States began to target Tora Bora, bin Laden fled the area to Jalalabad, into nearby Pakistan, or even back to the Middle East or Africa. Despite a substantial reward for information leading to bin Laden's capture, information about his whereabouts always seemed to arrive a day too late, as forces would arrive at a suspected hiding spot only to find that he had already moved on.

The effort was further confounded by the fact that the Afghan people living in the eastern region, a collective of clans and tribes known as the Pashtun, refused to give up their foreign-born "guests" to the

Americans. It is a Pashtun tradition to provide sanctuary to a guest who asks for it and to protect that guest with passion. Reward or no, the allied forces hunting bin Laden found little help from the local tribes.

Meanwhile, al-Qaeda was doing its best to convince the Afghan people that they were of the same heritage. Al-Qaeda operatives were distributing propaganda to the Afghans, appealing to their shared Muslim faith and drawing comparisons between the Americans and the country's last occupying force, the Soviet Union. In this area, the United States was not just battling al-Qaeda; it was competing with al-Qaeda for the support of the people who could help it capture bin Laden and his cadre.

Restoring Order in Afghanistan

The general goal of the war in Afghanistan was to thoroughly defeat al-Qaeda and subsequently prevent that network from reestablishing itself in the region. While ousting the Taliban and capturing the al-Qaeda leadership in the eastern part of the country were important components of this pursuit, it was critical for the success of the operation that the United States and its allies in the region work to stabilize the country, rebuild government infrastructure, and create an environment in which al-Qaeda and the Taliban could not return and thrive.

This element of the war in Afghanistan proved extremely daunting in light of a wide range of factors. One of these issues was a power struggle that had existed since the Soviets were forced out. The Taliban had previously won such a struggle during the vacuum years following Soviet occupation; in its absence, many other groups emerged as would-be leaders in this diverse and fractured country. The most prominent of these groups were ethnic in nature, such as the Pashtuns (members of which made up the majority of the Taliban), Tajiks, Hazaras, and Uzbeks. Others were regional and tribal, although often distinguished by ethnicity, dominating smaller regions outside of Kabul and Kandahar. The Taliban's victory disenfranchised these groups, creating even greater divides between them.

During the 2000s, a difficult task for Americans and the international community was to reach out to these groups and attempt to bring them back to the table in a spirit of cooperation. In December 2001, under the terms of the United Nations–sponsored Bonn Agreement, an interim government was established in Kabul in which the Pashtun majority was no longer the dominant group, although the provisional government's leader, Hamid Karzai, was a Pashtun. In 2002, the interim government was replaced by a transitional government, still led by Karzai, in which Pashtuns made up a greater proportion of the administration, though still not a majority. The new government's ethnic diversity, a positive attribute in the minds of the international commission that developed it, in many ways worked to the detriment of the government; because the various factions represented had previously operated independent of and in direct competition with one another, the government ministries under their control were frequently incapable of operating effectively.

Outside of Kabul and the cities, the stabilization of post-Taliban Afghanistan was even more difficult for the Americans. The ethnic divisions that existed in Kabul were magnified in rural regions. Compounding the issue was the inherent distrust many of these groups felt for the Americans who had invaded their country. Some of these ethnic groups and tribes were suspicious of any outsiders, a fact al-Qaeda took advantage of as they competed with the Americans for the hearts and minds of the tribes, clans, and even warlords in rural Afghanistan.

Still another destabilizing element in the country was the drug trade. Afghanistan has long been a major producer of opium, but the drug trade during the pre-invasion years was limited somewhat by the Taliban regime, which regarded drugs as counter to the values of Islam. After being driven out of Kabul in 2001, however, the very same Taliban looked on the drug trade as a means by which it could continue its effort against the Americans. Even al-Qaeda was rumored to be involved in opium production, using the money to finance its own operations both in-country and abroad. During the 2000s, opium and heroin production skyrocketed, as without a viable alternative source of industry, Afghans continued to embrace the drug trade, undercutting the American effort to restore order to post-Taliban Afghanistan.

Impact

The United States and its NATO allies launched the war in Afghanistan in order to make a definitive statement to international terrorists that they were serious about eradicating terrorism wherever it could be found. After the events of September 11, the United States decided that a limited series of air-strikes or operations against perceived al-Qaeda targets in Afghanistan was would not be enough; al-Qaeda's home base needed to be destroyed, and Osama bin Laden and the other leaders of al-Qaeda were to be captured or killed. Any parties who stood in the way of the American forces were to be treated as enemies in league with al-Qaeda.

The war in Afghanistan required a significant investment on a number of fronts. First, the regime that gave al-Qaeda safe haven, the Taliban, had to be removed. This goal was reached in relatively quick fashion early in the campaign. However, the Taliban might have been ousted from Kabul, but it was far from eliminated; it became a legitimate threat to the allied forces, engaging them both on the battlefield and in terroristic attacks.

The primary target of the war, al-Qaeda, also proved vexing. Bin Laden and his leadership team continued to move throughout the tunnels and caves of Tora Bora and the rest of the region, seemingly always just ahead of their pursuers. Al-Qaeda took advantage of the protection of their hosts in the region, and in addition to helping the Taliban launch frequent attacks against American and coalition targets in Afghanistan, they reached out to native Afghans for support.

In addition to the military effort, the United States needed to rebuild Afghanistan after driving out the Taliban. In Kabul, the inclusiveness of the new government proved problematic because of persistent divides between ethnic groups. Outside of the cities, the diversity of disparate clans, groups, and tribes made it difficult to unify Afghanistan, especially because the force seeking to do so was a foreign one. Finally, the major growth of the drug trade in post-Taliban Afghanistan helped support the Taliban and al-Qaeda and undermine the efforts of the United States and its allies to rebuild the country as a stable, antiterrorist nation.

Further Reading

Anderson, Ben. *No Worse Enemy: The Inside Story of the Chaotic Struggle for Afghanistan.* Oxford: Oneworld, 2012. Print. Provides an eyewitness account of the challenges facing the international coalition in restoring order to Afghanistan, including training Afghan police and engaging warlords and drug producers.

Bahmanyar, Mir. *Afghanistan Cave Complexes, 1979–2004: Mountain Strongholds of the Mujahideen, Taliban & Al Qaeda.* Illus. Ian Palmer. Colchester: Osprey, 2004. Print. Provides views and descriptions of the complex subterranean mountain strongholds used by al-Qaeda to withstand US-led bombing attacks.

Cole, Juan. "Pakistan and Afghanistan: Beyond the Taliban." *Political Science Quarterly* 124.2 (2009): 221–49. Describes the relationship between the government of Pakistan and the Taliban. Print.

McGirk, Tim. "Tracking the Ghost of bin Laden in the Land of the Pashtun." *National Geographic* 206.6 (2004): 2–27. Print. A firsthand account of efforts to hunt down Osama bin Laden in eastern Afghanistan, focusing on both the geography and the Afghans living there.

Rupp, Richard. "High Hopes and Limited Prospects: Washington's Security and Nation-Building Aims in Afghanistan." *Cambridge Review of International Affairs* 19.2 (2006): 285–98. Print. Discusses the formidable issues that stand in the way of a stable post-Taliban Afghanistan, including the presence of competing clans and tribes and the ongoing drug trade.

Strick van Linschoten, Alex, and Felix Kuehn. *An Enemy We Created: The Myth of the Taliban-Al Qaeda Merger in Afghanistan.* New York: Oxford UP, 2012. Print. Describes the complex and complicated relationship between al-Qaeda and the Taliban militia in Afghanistan.

Michael P. Auerbach, MA

■ War on Terrorism

Definition: The comprehensive campaign waged by the United States and its allies against al-Qaeda and other terrorist groups during the 2000s

Although the United States had faced international terrorism before, the bold and devastating terrorist attacks of September 11, 2001, prompted the United States to launch a comprehensive, multifaceted "war" on international terrorism. The main focus of the campaign was Osama bin Laden's al-Qaeda terrorist network, which had carried out the September 11 attacks, but the War on Terrorism expanded to include efforts to combat other brands of terrorism in both the domestic and international arenas. Military, law enforcement, regulatory, and public safety resources were utilized during the War on Terrorism that continued throughout the decade.

On September 11, 2001, the international terrorist network known as al-Qaeda launched a massive assault on American soil, destroying the World Trade Center, severely damaging the Pentagon, and killing thousands of people. Although the United States had been confronted by international and domestic terrorists before, the September 11 attacks sent shockwaves throughout the world, injuring the American economy and instilling a sense of fear that Americans had not felt since the Second World War. As rescuers sifted through the rubble of the World Trade Center and the wreckage sites in Washington, DC, and Pennsylvania, President George W. Bush and Congress collectively called for a "war on terrorism."

The "war"—which continued throughout the 2000s—would be fought on multiple fronts and in multiple arenas, using a wide range of military, law enforcement, emergency, and civilian resources. While the War on Terrorism's immediate target was al-Qaeda, any other potential threats to American interests—both foreign and domestic—were also targeted.

Military Deployment

One of the immediate responses to the September 11 attacks was the deployment of American troops (and their allies) to Afghanistan. That country, which was at the time operating under the regime of the Taliban, a conservative Muslim militia, was believed to be the location of al-Qaeda leader Osama bin Laden and his lieutenants as well as the staging area for the September 11 attacks. Less than a month after September 11, the United States launched Operation Enduring Freedom, a military campaign designed to remove the Taliban—which the United States maintained was giving safe haven to al-Qaeda—from power; disrupt and dismantle al-Qaeda; and capture Osama bin Laden.

The Taliban was quickly removed from power in Kabul, but it was not eradicated. American leaders maintained that Operation Enduring Freedom would not be an easy victory, nor would it be short-lived, as al-Qaeda leaders were believed to be hidden in bunkers and other secure locations in Afghanistan's most remote mountain regions. The Taliban, meanwhile, continued to engage American forces throughout the decade, while regional warlords and other factions fought with one another and the new government that was installed in Kabul. Afghanistan, especially areas outside of the capital, remained

unstable throughout the 2000s, and American forces continually remained targets for roadside bombs, sniper attacks, and other violence. Thousands of American soldiers were killed during Operation Enduring Freedom between 2001 and 2010, while only one of the mission's priorities—the ouster of the Taliban—had been fully accomplished.

As stated earlier, the War on Terrorism's immediate target was al-Qaeda. However, it quickly expanded to include all international terrorists that posed a genuine threat to American interests in the United States and abroad. In 2003, President Bush announced intelligence that Iraqi leader Saddam Hussein was defying the international community and developing weapons of mass destruction. These weapons, the administration argued, could be used against the United States and its allies in the Middle East and/or sold to terrorist organizations.

Based on this perceived threat, Bush was authorized by Congress to launch Operation Iraqi Freedom, a military campaign whose goal was the ouster of Saddam Hussein and the reconstruction of a stable Iraq. The removal and capture of Hussein proved successful, but the complete stabilization of that country post-Saddam involved a much greater investment of military, civilian, and monetary resources. Operation Iraqi Freedom also placed a strain on the military as well as the federal budget—the United States was now operating military campaigns in two separate and distant theaters, a trend that continued through the end of the 2000s.

Department of Homeland Security

The September 11 attacks were neither simple nor impulsive. Al-Qaeda planned the operation for a long period of time, training the perpetrators, utilizing resources, channeling money, and developing an infrastructure that enabled their hijackers to enter the United States and move into position. As federal investigators came to grips with the scope of this terrorist operation, they also became aware of a series of disconnects between federal, state, and local law enforcement, as well as between law enforcement, intelligence resources, and public safety. Had better connections existed between the intelligence community and law enforcement, or between the government and airports and airlines, al-Qaeda's plan might have been undercut or even thwarted altogether.

Less than two weeks after September 11, Pennsylvania Governor Tom Ridge was appointed to head up the Office of Homeland Security. His task was to create a comprehensive national strategy toward identifying and thwarting terrorist threats and ensuring national security. A year later, the Department of Homeland Security (DHS) was established, integrating the operations of twenty-two previously separated federal agencies in order to create a single public safety network. The agencies included those focused on law enforcement, immigration, transportation, public health, energy, agriculture, and emergency management. In 2005, DHS was expanded again, this time to include in its network public and private partners, state and local law enforcement, and public safety organizations, as well as tribal groups and international allies.

DHS would have an extremely complex set of jurisdictions. For example, it would be responsible for establishing and modifying a wide range of emergency response actions for terrorist attacks, including nuclear, chemical, and biological weapons–based attacks. Considerable responsibility for immigration and visas were also given to DHS in order to ensure that foreign visitors to the United States did not have ties to terrorist organizations. Even the Secret Service, Federal Bureau of Investigation (FBI), and other law enforcement agencies were required to collaborate with DHS.

The expansion of DHS over the years has proven challenging in many ways. Although few argued against the need for an integrated approach to combating terrorist threats against the United States, some agencies were reluctant to either give up their budgetary funding, perceived autonomy, or operational controls to DHS. Advocates for the Department of State, for example, expressed reluctance to hand over management of visas to DHS, as the former agency had long operated this program, which includes diplomatic personnel. Despite these growing pains, the establishment of the DHS has been seen by most leaders as an effective (and perhaps long-overdue) resource for combating terrorism.

The USA PATRIOT Act

A month after September 11, 2001, Congress moved quickly to introduce legislation that would make it easier for law enforcement to investigate, detain, and prosecute suspected terrorists. Arguably the most well-known of these legislative initiatives was the Uniting and Strengthening America by Providing Appropriate Tools Required to Intercept and Obstruct Terrorism (USA PATRIOT) Act, also known as the Patriot Act. Among the Patriot Act's provisions was language that loosened restrictions on the monitoring of telephone conversations, voicemail messages, and e-mail between suspected terrorists and/or criminals. Previously, the intercept of these communications was only permitted during serious investigations and only under the strict provisions of a court order—the process of obtaining such an order was often difficult. However, the Patriot Act loosened those requirements, giving greater flexibility to law enforcement to pursue such court orders as well as conduct intercepts. The act also loosened restrictions on foreign intelligence-gathering, search warrants, and detention of immigrants suspected of participating in terrorist activities.

The Patriot Act famously expanded US law to account for terrorism-related crimes, including such areas as computer abuse, racketeering, and money laundering. Put simply, the act made pursuit of terrorists and their accomplices much easier for prosecutors and law enforcement officials.

The Patriot Act was not without controversy, however. Despite moving quickly through Congress and being signed by President Bush into law, many Americans voiced concerns about perceived civil rights violations the act seemed to allow. By lowering the strict standards by which law enforcement could acquire a search warrant, for example, opponents argued that Americans' privacy was at risk. One hotly-contested area was Section 215, which allowed law enforcement to review the books a suspect might take out of the library or purchase at a store. Librarians spoke out against this provision, arguing that it would discourage people from reading or speaking out in public. Despite this backlash, however, Section 215 and other controversial elements of the Patriot Act were retained when the act was reauthorized in 2005.

Local Emergency Systems

The September 11 attacks and the subsequent War on Terrorism instilled in the American population a desire to be more vigilant. According to post–September 11 reports, for example, the hijackers went on dry run flights to get a better feel for the planes, airline procedures, and airports before the actual attacks. They also paid for hotel rooms with cash, which at the time helped them avoid using identification.

When, in 2004, al-Qaeda suicide bombers detonated devices in Madrid, and did so again in London in 2005, it was revealed that the perpetrators were captured on camera observing stations in which they could inflict maximum damage. Had security personnel—and even private citizens—who were in those facilities during these reconnaissance actions observed and reported the perpetrators' atypical actions, it is possible that these attacks might have been thwarted, according to experts.

The leaders of the War on Terrorism therefore enlisted the help of all Americans to demonstrate greater vigilance when traveling, commuting to work, or simply going about their daily lives. Local commuter transit systems introduced programs encouraging customers to report any unattended bags or unusual behavior. The original goal of these local programs was not to instill a sense of panic among commuters but to make vigilance a part of Americans' daily routine. As the panic of September 11 settled down, public information campaigns proved effective even if they did not specifically cite the threat of terrorism. The attacks on Madrid and London, however, reignited American fears of another terrorist attack—law enforcement and transit authorities drew from this sense of urgency a renewed call for Americans to be more vigilant in the face of terrorism, asking people to be on the lookout for bombs and would-be terrorists.

Local vigilance campaigns proved to be an effective resource in the War on Terrorism during the 2000s. Aided somewhat by a color-coded alert system implemented by the Bush administration, civilians were reminded on a daily basis to be cognizant of their surroundings and responsible for their belongings. Such behavior enabled security personnel in airports and train stations to better monitor suspicious behavior and intervene when necessary.

Impact

The War on Terrorism, launched by the United States immediately after the September 11 attacks, was fought on a variety of fronts and with many resources. Some of these resources were military, directly targeting those who launched the attacks from Afghanistan. Although this theater was not completely stabilized by the end of the 2000s, the United States could declare success at least in terms of disrupting al-Qaeda by ousting the regime that gave it safe haven. The campaign in Iraq, also a part of the

War on Terrorism, did succeed in toppling a dangerous regional dictator, although the effectiveness of the US presence there was subject to great debate.

On the home front, one of the most effective elements of the War on Terrorism was the establishment of the DHS. For the first time in the era of international terrorism, the United States had, in the DHS, a comprehensive and interconnected set of resources to seek, identify, track, and act against terrorist attacks at home and abroad. The DHS did experience some growing pains during the latter 2000s, as agencies engaged in minor disagreements with one another over budget dollars. Still, the agency's formation has been welcomed as a useful tool in the ongoing fight against terrorism.

The war also involved expansion of law enforcement's legal authority to investigate suspicious activity as well as to deputize private citizens in monitoring suspicious behavior. The expansion of legal authority—specifically the provisions of the Patriot Act—was initially well-received but later heavily debated on the issue of civil rights. The war instilled a sense of vigilance in all Americans, calling upon them to be citizen soldiers and use their eyes and ears to safeguard against terrorist activity.

Further Reading
Amin, Rooh Ul, et al. "Post-9/11 Reconstruction and Rehabilitation in Afghanistan, A Challenge for International Community." *Interdisciplinary Journal of Contemporary Research in Business*, 3.3 (2011): 365–377. Print. Discusses the challenges the international community faced as it worked to stabilize Afghanistan by combating the Taliban, warlords, and al-Qaeda during Operation Enduring Freedom.

Brattberg, Erik. "Coordinating for Contingencies: Taking Stock of Post-9/11 Homeland Security Reforms." *Journal of Contingencies and Crisis Management*, 20.2 (2012): 77–89. Print. Discusses how the infrastructures and frameworks of different government agencies have changed to address the homeland security issues raised by the terrorist attacks of September 11.

Dale, Catherine. "Operation Iraqi Freedom: Strategies, Approaches, Results, and Issues for Congress." *CRS Report for Congress*. Congressional Research Service, 2 Apr. 2009. Web. 5 Dec. 2012. Outlines the strategies and issues involved with the military campaign in Iraq.

Ibbetson, Paul A. *Living Under the Patriot Act: Educating a Society.* Bloomington: Author House, 2007. Print. Provides a review of the Patriot Act, including the forces that helped create and, later, renew this bill. Also shares opinions from both sides of this controversial law.

Robb, John. *Brave New War: The Next Stage of Terrorism and the End of Globalization.* New York: Wiley, 2007. Print. Describes how the tactics of insurgent groups in Iraq during Operation Iraqi Freedom, as well as groups like al-Qaeda, have achieved success against the United States and other large nations.

White, Richard A., Tina Markowski, and Kevin Collins, eds. *The United States Department of Homeland Security: An Overview.* 2nd ed. Boston: Pearson, 2010. Print. Provides a comprehensive review of the War on Terrorism and the wide range of agencies and resources that combined to form the DHS in response to the terrorist threat of the 2000s.

Zakheim, Dov S. "What 9/11 Has Wrought." *Middle East Quarterly* 18.4 (2011): 3–13. Print. Discusses the changes made in the United States as a response to the terrorist attacks of September 11. Reviews the development of the DHS and the operations in Afghanistan and Iraq.

Michael P. Auerbach, MA

Rick Warren. (© Sarah Aaskov, WEBN News 2009)

■ Warren, Rick

Identification: American pastor and best-selling author
Born: January 28, 1954; San Jose, California

Through his ministry at Saddleback Church, his best-selling books, his Internet presence, and his widespread appearances at conferences, Rick Warren has become one of the most influential evangelical Protestant ministers in the United States.

After graduating from California Baptist College and Southwest Baptist Theological Seminary, Rick Warren and his wife, Kay, founded the Saddleback Church in 1980, beginning with a Bible study with one other family. An ordained Southern Baptist minister who also earned a doctor of ministry degree from Fuller Theological Seminary, Warren was determined to begin a congregation that would attract "seekers" unfamiliar with Christian worship.

The church met in temporary facilities before building on a 120-acre campus in Lake Forest, California, an Orange County suburb, in 1995. Saddleback has grown to become one of the largest churches in the United States, with more than twenty thousand people attending weekend services at the original location and at several branch locations.

In addition to his ministry at the Saddleback Church, Warren has published numerous books and publishes a weekly email newsletter for pastors with a circulation of 150,000. Unlike many popular pastors of evangelical megachurches (large-attendance congregations designed to attract people with little or no experience with Christianity), Warren has no regular television program. His website receives more than 400,000 hits per day. His book *The Purpose Driven Life* (2002) became the best-selling hardback book in the history of American publishing and has sold more than 20 million copies worldwide.

In August 2008, Warren hosted a Civil Forum on the Presidency at his church, which featured appearances by candidates Barack Obama and John

McCain. Warren gave one of the prayers at President Obama's inauguration in January 2009.

Warren has also been involved in many social reform ministries, working with children in Africa orphaned by warfare or the AIDS epidemic. He promotes a "peace plan" that encourages Christians worldwide to help combat what he has called "five global giants": "poverty, disease, spiritual emptiness, self-serving leadership, and illiteracy."

Impact

Widely identified as one of most influential evangelical Protestant ministers in the United States, Rick Warren is a preeminent example of a megachurch pastor. Though he has become a celebrity of sorts because of the impact of *The Purpose Driven Life* and his association with President Obama, Warren focuses his ministry on spreading the Gospel to those unfamiliar with traditional American church services and encourages his congregation to help fight global problems.

Further Reading

Abanes, Richard. *Rick Warren and the Purpose That Drives Him: An Insider Looks at the Phenomenal Bestseller.* Eugene: Harvest, 2005. Print.

Lee, Shayne, and Phillip Luke Sinitiere. "Surfing Spiritual Waves: Rick Warren and the Purpose-Driven Church." *Holy Mavericks: Evangelical Innovators and the Spiritual Marketplace.* New York: NYU P, 2009. 129–48. Print.

Van Diema, David. "The Global Ambition of Rick Warren." *Time* 18 Aug. 2008: 36–42. Print.

Mark S. Joy

Denzel Washington. (©iStockphoto.com/Giulio Marcocchi)

■ Washington, Denzel

Identification: American actor and director
Born: December 28, 1954; Mount Vernon, New York

Celebrated for his portrayals of tough guys and historical heroes, Washington is one of the most well known actors of his generation. Besides being a critical favorite, he is also a hit with audiences. Washington is one of the most commercially successful actors in the entertainment industry.

Denzel Washington began the decade playing real-life high school football coach Herman Boone in the hit *Remember the Titans* (2000). The film became the highest grossing of his career, earning more than $115 million at the box office. Washington followed this up by playing a crooked cop in the 2001 film *Training Day*. His performance earned him an Academy Award for best actor.

In *John Q* (2002), Washington plays a father who holds an emergency room hostage to secure a heart transplant for his son. The movie was not a favorite of critics, and did not perform well at the box office. Washington made his directorial debut with 2002's *Antwone Fisher*. Although audiences responded well to the tale of a young US Navy officer who becomes a successful Hollywood screenwriter, the movie made little money.

The actor's next film, *Out of Time* (2003), was another commercial disappointment. However, 2004's *Man on Fire* proved more successful. In the movie, Washington plays a bodyguard who is hired to protect a child from kidnappers. That same year, Washington received critical acclaim for his role in the remake of the thriller *The Manchurian Candidate.* The actor took on the role of a disturbed war veteran, which was performed by Frank Sinatra in the original film. After the lukewarm reception of his films *Deja Vu* and *Inside Man* in 2006, Washington published the book *A Hand to Guide Me* (2006), a collection of celebrities' stories about mentors. The book made the New York Times Best Sellers list, and all proceeds went to the Boys & Girls Club of America.

For his next role, Washington played a chauffeur turned drug kingpin in 2007's *American Gangster.* The part earned him a Golden Globe nomination for best actor. Washington then directed and starred in *The Great Debaters* (2007), the true story of a teacher and his debate team at an African American college in the 1930s. *The Great Debaters* was named best film at the NAACP Image Awards. Washington's final film of the decade was a remake of the thriller *The Taking of Pelham 123* (2009), in which he plays a subway operator who negotiates with a criminal who has hijacked a train.

Impact

During the 2000s, Washington took on new challenges behind the camera. However, he continued to hone his acting skills by taking on a variety of roles. His dedication to his craft earned him critical praise and the distinction of becoming just the second African American actor in history to win an Oscar for best actor.

Further Reading

People. "Denzel Washington Biography." *People.* Time Inc., 2012. Web. 11 July 2012.

Washington, Denzel. *A Hand to Guide Me.* Des Moines: Meredith, 2006. Print.

Cait Caffrey

■ Waterboarding

Definition: An interrogation technique that involves pouring water onto the subject's face, often over a wet cloth, simulating the experience of being drowned

After the terrorist attacks against the United States in 2001, the Central Intelligence Agency (CIA) adopted se- *vere interrogation methods while trying to extract information from al-Qaeda operatives. One of those techniques, waterboarding, was considered by most to be a form of torture. Once its use by US authorities became public, waterboarding fueled a strong reaction in the media.*

In 2002, Assistant Attorney General Jay S. Bybee signed a memorandum that approved certain interrogation procedures to be used against members of al-Qaeda, including waterboarding. In 2008, CIA Director Michael V. Hayden confirmed that waterboarding was used by his agency on three al-Qaeda captives from 2002 through 2003: Abu Zubaydah, Khalid Shaikh Mohammed, and Abd al-Rahim al-Nashiri. Zubaydah had been subjected to the method eighty-three times, and Mohammed 183 times. Hayden stated that the method had not been used again since that period. The use of the procedure was personally endorsed by President George W. Bush and Vice President Dick Cheney, who remained proponents of waterboarding even after the torture accusations were made public.

In spite of its severity, waterboarding might not be very effective in obtaining reliable information. Bush administration officials claimed that using the interrogation method on Zubaydah provided information leading to the capture of Mohammed, and waterboarding Mohammed helped prevent future terror attacks. Many experts on torture, however, said that the harshness of the interrogation technique would lead to false confessions and fabricated terror plots, as the subjects desperately tried to avoid further suffering.

In January of 2009, President Barack Obama signed Executive Order 13491, which effectively banned the use of any questionable interrogation methods, including waterboarding. The order revoked any privileges and loopholes left by the Bush administration that allowed the CIA to use such methods, which was meant to ensure full compliance with international treaty obligations regarding the treatment of individuals in custody.

Impact

The news that the CIA, backed by the White House, had used waterboarding had a negative impact on the international image of the United States, especially in the Islamic world. Although the majority of the population considered the harsh interrogation method a form of torture, many high-ranking government officials and political figures thought its use was justified. Distancing himself from the morally questionable decisions of the previous administration, Obama adopted a firm stance against waterboarding early in his presidency.

Further Reading

Bybee, Jay S. "Interrogation of al Qaeda Operative." *US Department of Justice.* Federation of American Scientists, 1 Aug. 2002. Web. 5 Dec. 2012.

Karl, Jonathan. "'This Week' Transcript: Former Vice President Dick Cheney." *ABC.* ABC News Network, 14 Feb. 2010. Web. 5 Dec. 2012.

Thompson, Mark, and Bobby Ghosh. "Did Waterboarding Prevent Terrorism Attacks?" *Time.* Time Inc, 21 Apr. 2009. Web. 5 Dec. 2012.

Miroslav Farina

■ West Virginia/Kentucky coal sludge spill

The Event: An environmental disaster in which nearly 300 million gallons of toxic coal slurry was released into streams and rivers in Kentucky and West Virginia

Date: October 11, 2000

Place: Martin County, Kentucky, and parts of West Virginia

In the early hours of October 11, 2000, in Martin County, Kentucky, a seventy-two-acre coal-slurry holding pond experienced a structural failure that sent approximately 300 million gallons of slurry flowing into local streams, creeks, and rivers, polluting more than one hundred miles of waterways.

Coal slurry is a by-product of the process typically used to purify coal in order to increase its burning potential. The waste minerals that are removed from coal during the cleaning process are combined with water to form slurry; at most coal-mining facilities, this slurry is stored in large containment ponds until it evaporates.

At the Martin County Coal Corporation (MCCC) in Martin County, Kentucky, a slurry pond approximately eighty feet deep had been built on top of an old mine that had openings leading directly to several local waterways. Early on October 11, 2000, part of the bottom of the holding pond gave way and sent 250 to 300 million gallons of slurry flowing into the abandoned mine below. As the slurry continued to flow inside the mine, it eventually exited through several openings that led to nearby waterways. The spill ultimately spread through and contaminated more than one hundred miles of waterways before reaching the Ohio River.

Although the incident did not result in any human deaths or serious injuries, the effects of the spill were environmentally disastrous. During the course of its journey, the toxic slurry flow polluted local water supplies and flooded onto approximately thirty residential properties near Inez, Kentucky. The spill also proved to be deadly to wildlife, killing nearly all the fish and other aquatic animals in the local ecosystem.

Impact

As a result of the role it played in the spill, MCCC's parent company, Massey Energy, was forced to pay $46 million in cleanup costs and an additional $3.5 million in fines. Massey was also required to pay an undisclosed amount to cover the damage-related costs incurred by residents whose properties were in the path of the slurry flow.

In the wake of the disaster, the Mine Safety and Health Administration took steps to help prevent similar incidents from happening again. These steps included the introduction of improved training methods, the publication of a special handbook for those responsible for the management of slurry impoundments, and the implementation of a new regulation requiring mining companies to complete thorough investigations of any underground mines located near slurry ponds.

Further Reading

Lovan, Dylan. "Kentucky Town a Decade after Disaster." *Huffington Post.* HuffingtonPost.com, 10 Oct. 2010. Web. 9 Aug. 2012.

Sealey, Geraldine. "Sludge Spill Pollutes Ky., W. Va. Waters." *ABC News.* ABC News Network, 23 Oct. 2000. Web. 9 Aug. 2012.

US Department of Labor, Mine Safety and Health Administration. *Internal Review of MSHA's Actions at the Big Branch Refuse Impoundment Martin County Coal Corporation Inez, Martin County, Kentucky.* Washington: US Department of Labor, Mine Safety and Health Administration, 21 Jan. 2003. PDF file.

Jack Lasky

■ West, Kanye

Identification: American rapper and producer
Born: June 8, 1977; Atlanta, Georgia

Best known for his outspoken and controversial public persona, Kanye West rose to fame as a groundbreaking hip-hop artist, label executive, and producer in the mid-2000s.

After producing songs for a number of artists in the 1990s, Kanye West gained significant attention when he was given the opportunity to contribute four tracks to multiplatinum hip-hop artist Jay-Z's album *The Blueprint* in 2001. West launched his solo rap career in 2004 with the release of his album *The College Dropout*, which featured the debut single "Through the Wire" as well as the award-winning song "Jesus Walks." Praised for its self-aware and intelligent content, *The College Dropout* achieved platinum status and garnered several Grammy Award nominations, including album of the year; West won the awards for best rap album and best rap song. West followed *The College Dropout* with *Late Registration* (2005), *Graduation* (2007), and *808s and Heartbreak* (2008), each the recipient of several awards and nominations. He also continued to produce songs for artists such as Jay-Z, Mariah Carey, and John Legend.

As West's success grew, so did his larger-than-life persona. West's notoriety spiked when he made unscripted comments criticizing President George W. Bush during a 2005 telethon to aid victims of Hurricane Katrina. Both praised and condemned for his opinionated outbursts, West became as well known for his off-the-cuff remarks as for his acclaimed music.

Throughout the decade, West used hip-hop as a platform to draw attention to issues he believed in. He spoke out against homophobia in hip-hop, a genre known for unbridled machismo, and produced music for artists through his G.O.O.D (Getting Out Our Dreams) Music label. He also established the Kanye West Foundation. The foundation's initiatives include Loop Dreams, which teaches at-risk youths how to write and produce music, and the College Drop In Program, in association with the Dr. Ralph Bunche Center for African American Studies at the University of California, Los Angeles (UCLA), which introduces local middle school students to college courses, faculty, and campus life.

Kanye West. (©iStockphoto.com/Kevin Winter)

Impact

Kanye West's introspective lyrics, fashion sense, and middle-class background set him apart from other popular hip-hop artists whose work was largely influenced by inner-city culture. His work broached subjects largely untouched in mainstream hip-hop, such as religion, homophobia, and family relationships. Although he was notorious for his controversial comments by the end of the decade, West continued to build his reputation through musical talent and philanthropy.

Further Reading

Tyrangiel, Josh. "Why You Can't Ignore Kanye." *Time* 29 Aug. 2005: 54–61. Print.

Weicker, Gretchen. *Kanye West.* Berkeley Heights: Enslow, 2009. Print.

West, Donda. *Raising Kanye: Life Lessons From the Mother of a Hip-Hop Superstar.* New York: Pocket, 2007. Print.

Tamela N. Chambers

■ White, Jack

Identification: American musician
Born: July 9, 1975; Detroit, Michigan

As a member of three different bands, musician Jack White was prolific in the 2000s, releasing a total of eight albums during the decade.

In 2000, the ex-spouse duo of Jack and Meg White, known as the White Stripes, released their second album, entitled *De Stijl*. Although the album was not a giant commercial success, it was highly praised by music critics. In 2001, the band released *White Blood Cells*. Propelled by the second single, "Fell in Love with a Girl," the album went platinum.

The White Stripes' next album, *Elephant*, was preceded by the release of the single "Seven Nation Army" in 2003. The song reached number one on the US Billboard Hot Modern Rock Tracks chart and would go on to appear in Top 10 positions on many major publications' lists of best songs of the decade. *Elephant* was nominated for the 2004 Grammy Award for Best Alternative Music Album. *Rolling Stone* named *Elephant* the fifth best release of the 2000s.

In addition to his work as a musician, White has appeared in several films. He makes an appearance with Meg White in director Jim Jarmusch's film *Coffee and Cigarettes* (2003). White also has a small role in the film *Cold Mountain* (2003) playing a troubadour. Performing as a solo artist, he contributed five songs to the film's soundtrack.

The White Stripes released *Get Behind Me Satan* in 2005. The album moved away from the garage rock sound that made them popular, focusing instead on piano-driven songs. Despite the change, the album was still a success. The single "The Denial Twist" hit number five on the US Alt Rock charts, and the band won yet another Best Alternative Music Album Grammy Award in 2006.

Later that year, White started a new band with singer/songwriter Brendan Benson called the Raconteurs. Their debut release, *Broken Boy Soldiers* (2006), earned a nomination for Best Rock Album. White, however, was not done with the White Stripes. *Icky Thump* (2007) featured a return to the band's previous sound; album's title track went to number twenty-six on the Billboard Hot 100. In 2008, the White Stripes were awarded their third Best Alternative Music Grammy.

In 2008, White released a second album with the Raconteurs, entitled *Consolers of the Lonely*. The album reached number seven on the Billboard charts. Later that year, White collaborated with R&B singer Alicia Keyes on the theme song "Another Way To Die" for the James Bond film *Quantum of Solace* (2008). White formed the band The Dead Weather in 2009. Composed of band members from the Kills, Queens of the Stone Age, and the Raconteurs, the super group released its debut, *Horehound* in 2009.

Impact

Although the White Stripes broke up in February 2011, songs from their back catalog continue to be released. The duo's minimalist style and use of outdated instruments were essential in creating their award-winning music and influenced other alternative bands during the decade. Since the band's breakup, White has worked on other projects, including a collaborative effort with producer Danger Mouse, and composer Daniele Luppi, entitled *Home* (2011). In 2012, White released his first solo album, *Blunderbuss*.

Further Reading

Sullivan, Denise. *The White Stripes: Sweethearts of the Blues*. San Francisco: Backbeat, 2004. Print.
True, Everett. *The White Stripes and the Sound of Mutant Blues*. London: Omnibus, 2004. Print.

Leland Spencer

■ Wi-Fi

Definition: Wireless local-area network technology that allows users to connect to the Internet with electronic devices

The spread of Wi-Fi technology in the 2000s made it possible for people to conduct business, communicate, and explore the Internet from anywhere a wireless Wi-Fi signal was available, without the use of a modem cable. The technology rapidly became popular and was soon made available in public spaces such as cafes, airports, and libraries. Concerns over the security of electronic devices connected to a Wi-Fi network quickly arose and forced the technology to evolve over the decade.

Wi-Fi (wireless-fidelity) technology constantly transmits a high-frequency radio signal over a limited range. Wi-Fi transmits and receives data, creating a local-area network to which electronic devices within range can connect. Wi-Fi is a trademarked name created by the Wi-Fi Alliance, a trade association that promotes Wi-Fi technology. Other wireless technologies were developed after Wi-Fi, but only wireless technology that meets the standards of the Institute of Electrical and Electronics Engineers is allowed to use the name Wi-Fi.

Wi-Fi technology was first utilized in laptop computers. This allowed users to connect to the Internet outside of their home or office anywhere in the range of a Wi-Fi router transmitting a signal. Soon after the technology was made available, laptops with built-in wireless capabilities were introduced. Prior to built-in technology, users had to purchase a wireless network card adaptor to insert into a universal serial bus (USB) port on their laptop. The demand for Wi-Fi technology increased and soon mobile phones were developed with built-in wireless capabilities.

Concerns over network safety and access to personal information led to the development of several security encryptions. When Wi-Fi technology was first introduced, computer hackers found it easy to break into wireless networks. The most common kind of security is the Wired Equivalent Privacy, which comes standard on most Wi-Fi routers. In 2003 the Wi-Fi Alliance introduced Wi-Fi Protected Access, which allowed users to attach a password to their network, preventing unauthorized users from joining.

Despite concerns over security issues, cities and towns experimented with municipal wireless networks in the 2000s. In a municipal wireless network, local governments provided Wi-Fi to the public as a service, so that individuals and businesses did not have to pay private firms for access. Several cities in the United States successfully implemented free Wi-Fi networks for their citizens. The city of Sunnyvale in California was the first city to provide this service, which began in 2005 and was discontinued in 2008.

Impact

By the end of the decade, Wi-Fi technology was integrated into a large variety of electronic devices such as televisions, Blu-ray players, and radios. Mobile phones equipped with built-in Wi-Fi were nearly ubiquitous by 2010. Wi-Fi became the default network in homes, offices, and public places where a

network was offered. Throughout the decade an increasing number of college campuses and cities offered the public free Wi-Fi.

Further Reading

Hayes, Vic, et al. *The Innovation Journey of Wi-Fi: The Road to Global Success*. Cambridge: Cambridge UP, 2010. Print.

Hills, Alex. *Wi-Fi and the Bad Boys of Radio: Dawn of a Wireless Technology*. Indianapolis: Dog Ear, 2011. Print.

Patrick G. Cooper

■ WikiLeaks

Definition: WikiLeaks is a highly controversial organization that publishes documents and videos intended primarily to expose injustices or promote transparency in government and business

As the first and largest repository in the world for documents obtained by hacking or leaks, WikiLeaks has been at the center of a flurry of controversy and lawsuits while establishing itself as a premier source for investigative journalists.

WikiLeaks is a nonprofit, activist organization founded in 2007 by Australian computer hacker and journalist Julian Assange and run by an international group of computer programmers, dissidents, journalists, academics, and other volunteers. Although its name resembles that of Wikipedia, there is no affiliation between the organizations. WikiLeaks' stated mission at first was to expose oppression and injustices in the regimes of countries in Asia, the former Soviet Union, sub-Saharan Africa, and the Middle East; the organization also wanted to provide assistance to whistle-blowers who were willing to expose unethical behavior in their respective governments and businesses. It later revised its mission statement to reference Article 19 of the United Nation's 1948 Universal Declaration of Human Rights, which states the "right to freedom of opinion and expression," and "to seek, receive and impart information and ideas through any media." WikiLeaks also specified that it was open to receiving documents from the United States and elsewhere. Anyone could upload documents anonymously to WikiLeaks' encrypted computers. The documents would then be reviewed

Julian Assange leaving the Royal Court of Justice after losing all appeals in the United Kingdom. (Courtesy Olga Talalay)

for authenticity by a team of legal experts before being published on WikiLeaks.org.

Early Scandals

The first major collection of sensitive documents posted on WikiLeaks.org detailed corruption by the former Kenyan leader Daniel arap Moi. In 2008, WikiLeaks posted confidential operating manuals for the treatment of detainees at the US detention facility at Guantanamo Bay, as well as classified documents from the US military that detailed guidelines for the Iraq War. The organization also published leaked documents from an Icelandic bank that revealed sensitive information regarding its collapse. In addition to publishing government and business secrets, WikiLeaks published sensitive documents from the Church of Scientology and the Church of Jesus Christ of Latter-day Saints.

In September 2008, WikiLeaks posted a log of e-mails from vice-presidential candidate Sarah Palin's personal Yahoo account, which had been hacked by a member of Anonymous (an anonymous activist group). While mostly personal e-mails, the log included some political e-mails that allegedly evaded public records laws. In November 2009, WikiLeaks posted e-mails and other documents composed by scientists at England's East Anglia University Climatic Research Unit that appeared to expose unethical behavior over global warming research. The information was used by skeptics of global warming and led to major investigations of the researchers, although in the end they were cleared.

By February 2008, WikiLeaks had been targeted with a few lawsuits, but it maintained its right to publish documents based on freedom of the press and free speech, and the cases were dropped. That month, however, a California federal judge forced Dynadot, the Internet host of Wikileaks.org in the United States, to shut down the site after they refused to remove documents that allegedly revealed offshore money laundering and tax evasion by customers of the Swiss Julius Baer Bank and Trust Company. After the American Civil Liberties Union (ACLU), Electronic Frontier Foundation (EFF), and others intervened, the judge lifted the injunction and allowed WikiLeaks.org back online. As WikiLeaks hosted mirror sites at other locations in the world and its site at Dynadot could still be accessed by savvy computer users, duplicate copies quickly spread among supporters, demonstrating the challenges of removing documents in the cyber world.

A Behind-the-Scenes Glimpse of September 11, 2001

In November 2009, Wikileaks published 573,000 lines of transcribed text that were sent on September 11 and 12, 2001, prior to, during, and after the terrorist attacks on the World Trade Center and the Pentagon. The collection includes personal messages from individuals, work-related texts from a variety of businesses, and alerts from the military, United States Secret Service, Federal Bureau of Investigation (FBI), and other government agencies as they responded to the emergency. The messages were probably intercepted illegally by a scanner, although the source remains anonymous. Some of the messages are anonymous requests for their recipients to phone home, remember a doctor appointment, or pick up a child after school, eerily oblivious to the events that would unfold. Those written later refer frantically to the planes crashing, smoke-filled rooms, or equipment malfunctioning. Some of the more personal messages were probably the last text messages sent from the victims. Others are more cryptic, sent from government personnel in code and later translated by investigative journalists. Overall, the text messages represent a valuable collection for historians and a moving glimpse into humanity on a very tragic day, a departure from the incriminating or classified documents for which WikiLeaks had become known.

Impact

WikiLeaks' pursuit of truth, transparency, and free speech has posed an unprecedented and formidable threat to governments, individuals, and businesses worldwide. By exposing immoral or illegal behavior, they have risked not only incurring the wrath of numerous people and organizations, but also igniting large-scale diplomatic debacles that could lead to serious conflicts between countries or factions. The organization's support for hacking and whistle-blowing has caused organizations to tighten security for computer systems and to implement measures that safeguard printed documents. WikiLeaks has also tested international law, influencing investigative journalism, and changing history with their collection of provocative documents.

Further Reading

Duchschere, Kevin. "Website Describes How It Got Donor List." *Star Tribune* [Minneapolis] 18 Mar. 2009: B5. Print. Details WikiLeaks' publication of Republican Norm Coleman's donor list while he was challenging Democrat Al Franken's win in the US Senatorial race.

Liptak, Adam, and Brad Stone. "Judge Orders Wikileaks Web Site Shut." *New York Times.* New York Times, 19 Feb. 2008. Web. 9 Nov. 2012. Provides the facts and an analysis of the erroneous decision made by a federal judge in the Julius Baer Bank–WikiLeaks lawsuit.

Ludlow, Peter. "WikiLeaks and Hacktivist Culture." *Nation* 4 Oct. 2010: 25–26. Print. Discusses the Ethics of Julian Assange and the International Hacking Culture.

Ottosen, Rune. "WikiLeaks: Ethical Minefield or a Democratic Revolution in Journalism?" *Journalism Studies* 13.5–6 (2012): 836–46. Print. Examines the ethical issues surrounding the use of WikiLeaks as a source in reporting.

Singel, Ryan. "Immune to Critics, Secret-Spilling Wikileaks Plans to Save Journalism . . . and the World." *Wired.* Condé Nast, 3 July 2008. Web. 9 Nov. 2012. Explores the effects of WikiLeaks on investigative journalism and the idealistic motivations behind the organization.

Sally Driscoll

■ *Wikipedia*

Definition: A free, online encyclopedia comprised of anonymously contributed, peer-edited entries available in more than 275 languages

The online encyclopedia Wikipedia *was founded by Internet entrepreneur Jimmy Wales and philosophy professor Lawrence Sanger in 2001. The website was the result of the failure of the duo's first Internet-based encyclopedia concept,* Nupedia, *a year earlier.* Wikipedia *was founded under the philosophy of an open-source contribution process, sparking worldwide enthusiasm that helped it become one of the most visited websites of the 2000s.*

American Internet entrepreneur Jimmy Wales launched his first online encyclopedia concept, *Nupedia*, with funding from his web directory company Bomis in March 2000. Wales enlisted the assistance of philosophy professor Lawrence Sanger in order to add academic authority to the project.

Encyclopedic entries on *Nupedia* were created through a multistep editorial process, in which expert volunteers contributed articles that would then undergo a lengthy, seven-step peer review. The growth of *Nupedia* was slowed by a lack of flexibility in its interface and by the peer-editing process required of all articles prior to publication on the site, which resulted in a lack of published content.

Wikipedia was originally conceived of by Sanger and Wales in 2001 as a collaborative platform with which users could create encyclopedic entries for consideration for *Nupedia* that would eventually undergo the peer-editing process. The platform was created based on the software known as Wiki, invented by the American computer programmer Ward Cunningham in 1994, which allows for multiple users to create and edit content for a web page collaboratively. The software's name is derived from the Hawaiian word meaning "quick." Wiki's easily modifiable, text-based interface would make it one of the Internet's most revolutionary collaborative tools. Many of *Nupedia*'s volunteer editors, however, were uninterested in reviewing open-sourced content, so Wales and Sanger launched a separate website, called *Wikipedia*, in January 2001.

Wikipedia's revolutionary concept was that articles could be contributed without approval by any overarching editorial guideline or governance and then peer edited, all by volunteers. As a result of its ease of use, its open-ended platform, and the freedom from harsh peer review, *Wikipedia*'s popularity soon dwarfed that of its predecessor. *Nupedia* was consequently shut down in 2003.

Although he was instrumental in developing *Wikipedia*'s open-community philosophy, Sanger departed *Wikipedia* about a year after its launch, largely due to his belief that the site should be still regulated by some authoritative peer-editing process. In 2003, Jimmy Wales transferred control of *Wikipedia* to the nonprofit Wikimedia Foundation, which maintains the site's operations. Wales nevertheless stayed involved in the project, serving as a member of the foundation's board.

Editorial Process

Wikipedia was founded on several non-negotiable principles, including mandatory adherence to a neutral point of view in all articles, the maintenance of a welcoming editing environment, and the capability of all articles to be contributed to and edited by anyone with an Internet connection. The idea was for *Wikipedia*'s contributors to act as a self-policing community against inaccurate and unscholarly content. From its inception, however, *Wikipedia* was marred by articles that were poorly written or that contained gross factual inaccuracies or deliberate distortions. Similarly, quality article contributions would fall victim to vandalism, hoaxes, and other acts of editorial malice. As the site and its popularity expanded, *Wikipedia*'s community underwent a wide variety of changes to increase the quality of articles and to decrease instances of vandalism through the implementation of semi-automated editing processes completed by software programs.

In 2005, *Wikipedia* added the editorial flag "citation needed" for users to mark questionable statements that had not been cited to a credible source.

Oft-vandalized and controversial articles would remain on the site, but would be accessible for editing only to specific, experienced *Wikipedia* editors with administrative privileges (though still acting as volunteers). In 2009, *Wikipedia* announced that, in its efforts to limit libel from appearing on the site, edits made to the biographies of living people would now be marked as "flagged revisions," which would have to be vetted by an authorized editor before the updates were made visible to the public.

Criticism

Wikipedia drew criticism throughout the decade from numerous sources. Many within the publishing industry disagreed with the community-based contributions on which the project was founded, frequently citing the potential for the publication of erroneous information. Academics, too, decried the unscholarly submission process and instances of poorly constructed and inaccurate articles.

Wikipedia has also been criticized for the significant gender gap that exists among its editors. In 2011, *Wikipedia* conducted a survey of its contributors and found that only 9 percent of its editors were women. This has contributed to topic bias on *Wikipedia*, in which topics that typically have a male-dominated following frequently receive more thorough coverage than topics with a predominantly female following.

Despite these criticisms, *Wikipedia*'s growth continued throughout the decade. The encyclopedia grew from a total number of approximately 250,000 entries in 2003 to an estimated twenty-three million articles in 2012, with more than four million articles in its English-language edition.

Impact

By decade's end, the value of *Wikipedia* as a reference tool was still a topic of debate among writers, scholars, and publishers alike. Though the safeguards against vandalism, plagiarism, and bias had vastly improved its reputation by 2009, the site was still widely considered unreliable when compared to traditional reference sites.

Wikipedia's most notable achievement may be the creation of the Internet-based community which acts as its steward. Though its status as a verifiable and academically accepted reference volume remained in question, the site's pioneer philosophy of neutrality and revolutionary, open-sourced collaboration opened several new horizons for the potential of the Internet worldwide.

Further Reading

Bosch, Torie. "How Kate Middleton's Wedding Gown Demonstrates Wikipedia's Woman Problem." *Slate.* Slate Group, 13 July 2012. Web. 6 August 2012. Discusses *Wikipedia*'s gender gap among its editors and examines how this disparity affects topic coverage.

Cohen, Noah. "Wikipedia." *New York Times.* New York Times Company, 23 May 2011. Web. 9 Aug. 2012. Summarizes *Wikipedia*'s history and development. n. pag. Print.

O'Sullivan, Dan. *Wikipedia: A New Community of Practice?* Burlington: Ashgate, 2009. Print. Describes the history of efforts to compile human knowledge in one place, with a focus on *Wikipedia.*

Poe, Marshall. "The Hive." *Atlantic.* Atlantic Monthly Group, Sept. 2006. Web. 9 Aug. 2012. Describes *Wikipedia*'s editorial processes and provides a history of the site's development.

Wales, Jimmy. "Jimmy Wales on the birth of Wikipedia." Oxford, England. Ted Global 2005. July 2005. Speech. The founder of *Wikipedia*, Jimmy Wales, speaks about its development, evolution, and maintenance.

John Pritchard

■ Wilco

Definition: American alternative rock band from Chicago, Illinois.

The Chicago rock band Wilco, led by singer-songwriter Jeff Tweedy, achieved widespread popularity in the 2000s with the release of three critically acclaimed studio albums, a live concert album, and a documentary feature film. Their 2002 album Yankee Hotel Foxtrot, *is ranked as one of the top five hundred albums of all time by* Rolling Stone *magazine. The band also received a Grammy Award for best alternative music album for their 2004 record* A Ghost is Born.

The American rock band Wilco was founded in Chicago, Illinois, in 1994. The group's first three records garnered minor critical interest while attracting an allegiant fan base, positioning Wilco in the early 2000s as up-and-coming alternative country artists who blended country music–style songwriting and instrumentation with experimental rock and pop influences. After extensive touring for their 1999 album *Summerteeth*, Wilco prepared to release their fifth full-length album, *Yankee Hotel Foxtrot*.

Following production, a dispute erupted between Wilco and their then label Reprise Records, a facet of Warner Music Group, who refused to release *Yankee* due to a perceived lack of commercial viability. After extensive litigation, the band purchased the album's release rights from Reprise, subsequently selling them to another Warner Music Group subsidiary label, Nonesuch Records, where it debuted on April 23, 2002. Many of the logistical, creative, and internal disputes surrounding the release of *Yankee* would be captured in director Sam Jones's documentary film from that same year, *I Am Trying to Break Your Heart: A Film about Wilco.*

National music publications such as *Pitchfork*, *PopMatters*, and *Rolling Stone* all heaped effusive praise on *Yankee,* lauding the album's mix of melodic complexity and experimentation with catchy rock hooks. The equally experimental and atmospheric of their Grammy Award–winning *A Ghost Is Born,* released two years later, further propelled Wilco to higher critical and popular recognition, winning praise from fans in country, folk, rock, and avant-garde genres. Material from both *Yankee* and *Ghost* was prominently featured in the band's 2005 live album *Kicking Television,* recorded in front of rapt audiences in the band's native Chicago.

Venerated rock and jazz guitarist Nels Cline joined the band as a full-time member prior to the release of 2007's *Sky Blue Sky.* The commercial success of *Sky Blue Sky* would surpass any previous Wilco release, firmly establishing the group as one of America's premier bands.

Impact

Wilco's pairing of traditional country music with avant-garde experimentation solidified them as a genre-defining staple of the alternative country milieu. Additionally, their very public conflicts with the commercial interests of major recording labels in the 2000s would become an apt microcosm of the changing music industry, most notably exemplifying the increasing priority placed on artist independence and creative expression over profit and commercial distribution.

Further Reading

Kot, Greg. *Wilco: Learning How to Die.* New York: Broadway, 2004. Print.

"Wilco: Album Guide." *Rolling Stone.* Rolling Stone, 2009. Web. 10 June 2012.

John Pritchard

■ Williams, Serena

Identification: American tennis player, entrepreneur, and philanthropist
Born: September 26, 1981; Saginaw, Michigan

Williams is one of the most influential African American women in the United States. While dominating the sport of women's tennis throughout the 2000s, she founded her own clothing company, and established a charitable foundation that helps children and families around the world.

Serena Williams won a gold medal in the women's singles and doubles events at the 2000 Olympic Games in Sydney, Australia, teaming with her sister Venus in the doubles match. In 2002, Williams won the French Open, the US Open, and Wimbledon, defeating Venus in the final round of each. That year, the Associated Press named Serena Williams its Female Athlete of the Year, and Best Sports Woman in the World. She won her first Australian Open in 2003, becoming one of five women in tennis history to win all four grand-slam tournaments. She ranked number one for fifty-seven consecutive weeks from 2002–2003, and was named Female Athlete of the Year and Female Tennis Player of the Year at the annual ESPY Awards in 2003. Two years later, Williams again won the Australian Open. Injuries plagued her in 2006, but the following year, she won the Australian Open and the Sony Ericsson Open. In 2008, Williams regained the number one position for four weeks, and won the US Open for the third time. The following year, she won her fourth Australian Open and her third Wimbledon.

In addition to her success on the court, Williams is also an actor, author, and entrepreneur. In 2001, she appeared in the movie *My Wife and Kid.* The next year, she was named one of *People*'s 25 Most Intriguing People, and she was recognized in *Essence* magazine as one of the 50 Most Inspiring African Americans. In June 2004, Williams started a clothing company, Aneres. In 2009, she published a memoir, *On the Line.* That same year, Williams opened a secondary school in Kenya for children whose parents could not afford to send them to school.

Throughout her career, Williams has also faced adversity. In 2003, Williams's sister Yetunde Price was murdered in Los Angeles, California. During the final match of the US Open in 2009, Williams lost her temper with a lineswoman, and the US Tennis Association fined her $10,000. Two months later, Williams was fined an additional $82,500 and was placed on probation for two years.

Impact

Williams's success has inspired countless young women to pursue tennis. Her foundation strives to help children and families who have been victimized by violent crimes and to assist underprivileged children around the world.

Further Reading

Christopher, Matt. *On the Court with Venus and Serena Williams.* New York: Little, 2002. Print.

Williams, Serena, and Daniel Paisner. *On the Line.* New York: Grand Central, 2009. Print.

Gina Kuchta

■ Winfrey, Oprah

Identification: American business mogul and philanthropist
Born: January 29, 1954; Kosciusko, Mississippi

Raised in rural poverty and self-propelled to extreme wealth and accomplishment, talk show host, actress, author, producer, and businesswoman Oprah Winfrey was a multimedia powerhouse by the 2000s. Her daily Oprah Winfrey Show *was seen in nearly 150 countries and was the number-1 talk show in the United States throughout the decade.*

Oprah Winfrey began her career in media during her senior year of high school, when she secured a part-time position with Nashville's WVOL radio station. While a sophomore at Tennessee State University, she left radio to become a television reporter for the local CBS affiliate. In 1976 she was hired as a reporter and coanchor of the ABC news station in Baltimore, Maryland, but she soon moved

Oprah Winfrey and Jesse Jackson attend the Alvin Ailey American Dance Theater's 50th anniversary performance. (©iStockphoto.com/Astrid Stawiarz)

on to cohosting the station's new morning show, *People Are Talking*. After six years at that job, Winfrey moved to Chicago, Illinois, where she hosted the ABC talk show *AM Chicago*. Within weeks, she turned a program that had been receiving poor ratings into a success. In 1985, after one year with Winfrey at the helm, the show was expanded to an hour and renamed *The Oprah Winfrey Show*. The show was a phenomenal success, and it was syndicated nationally beginning in 1986.

Television

By 2000, *The Oprah Winfrey Show* was the most popular talk show in the world as well as the highest rated television talk show ever. While the show had at one time featured confrontational, titillating topics, Winfrey had since the mid-1990s sought to focus on areas of self-help and personal improvement, giving the show a more lifestyle-oriented format. By the first decade of the twenty-first century, the show, and Oprah herself, had developed a reputation as a trusted source of information and advice

among viewers in the United States and abroad.

In addition to making her one of the world's most widely recognizable figures, Winfrey's appearance on millions of television sets around the world brought fame and celebrity to new faces, such as Phil McGraw. Known as Dr. Phil, the motivational psychologist made weekly appearances on *The Oprah Winfrey Show* and eventually began to host a popular weekly show of his own, produced by Winfrey's Harpo Studios. Winfrey was also an early supporter of Barack Obama's candidacy in the 2008 presidential election. She invited him to appear on her show on October 19, 2006, and voiced her support during the Democratic primaries but stepped back during the general election, claiming that she did not want to use her fame to influence politics.

Winfrey was involved in a number of other television-related endeavors during the decade. In 2000, Winfrey expanded her influence into cable television with her cofounding of Oxygen Media, a company that operated a cable television channel geared toward women. In 2008, she partnered with Discovery Communications to create OWN, the Oprah Winfrey Network, which began broadcasting late in 2009. In 2008, Winfrey announced that *The Oprah Winfrey Show* would air its last episode in September of 2011.

Other Projects

While Winfrey was best known for her television program, she pursued ventures in other areas of media as well. In 2000, she launched *O, The Oprah Magazine*. A companion magazine, *O at Home*, followed in 2004. In October of that year, the *Chicago Sun-Times* estimated Winfrey's wealth at $800 million.

In 2006, the media mogul expanded her empire still further, this time into satellite radio. That year, she signed a multimillion-dollar deal with XM Satellite Radio, launching the Oprah and Friends channel. XM later merged with Sirius Satellite Radio, becoming Sirius-XM, and Winfrey's channel was later renamed Oprah Radio.

A strong supporter of reading, Winfrey created an indelible link between television and books through her on-air endorsements of books she enjoyed. Begun in 1996, the "Oprah's Book Club" segment of *The Oprah Winfrey Show* brought new and classic books to the attention of millions of viewers, reviving interest in the joy of reading. However, the segment sparked controversy in 2006 when journalists revealed that author James Frey's 2003 memoir, *A Million Little Pieces*, which Winfrey had selected for her book club the previous year, was more fictional than autobiographical. Winfrey initially backed Frey, but she later confronted him on her show and publicly admonished him for distorting the truth.

Winfrey was also well known for her philanthropy during the 2000s. She urged her viewers to donate money and time to charities, both those she created, such as Oprah's Angel Network, and independent charities such as the international housing charity Habitat for Humanity. Funded largely by Winfrey's $40 million donation, the Oprah Winfrey Leadership Academy for Girls opened in South Africa in 2007.

Impact

Winfrey has been named the world's most powerful woman and celebrity by *Forbes*, CNN, and *Time*. At the peak of her success, her talk show was the most popular show of its kind on television, with approximately fourteen million viewers every day. Although *The Oprah Winfrey Show* aired its last episode on May 25, 2011, Winfrey remained a successful and influential figure in American media into the second decade of the twenty-first century.

Further Reading

Cooper, Ilene. *Up Close: Oprah Winfrey*. New York: Penguin, 2007. Print.

Davis, Deborah. *The Oprah Winfrey Show: Reflections on an American Legacy*. New York: Abrams, 2011. Print.

Harris, Jennifer, and Elwood Watson, eds. *The Oprah Phenomenon*. Lexington: UP of Kentucky, 2007. Print.

Rooney, Kathleen. *Reading with Oprah: The Book Club That Changed America*. Fayetteville: U of Arkansas P, 2005. Print.

Westen, Robin. *Oprah Winfrey: I Don't Believe in Failure*. Berkeley Heights: Enslow, 2005. Print.

Hope L. Killcoyne

■ *The Wire*

Identification: Television drama set in Baltimore, Maryland
Executive Producer: David Simon (b. 1960)
Date: June 22, 2002–March 9, 2008

Although it never won any major awards and did not receive high ratings, many critics consider The Wire *to be a landmark television series. Some have called it the greatest television series of all time.* The Wire *is celebrated for its realist portrayal of the drug trade in urban America, and its effects on public institutions.* The Wire *aired in sixty episodes over five seasons on HBO, ending in March 2008.*

Journalist and author David Simon teamed up with former Baltimore homicide detective Ed Burns to create *The Wire*. The two had formerly collaborated to produce the 2000 HBO miniseries *The Corner*, based on a book they had written about a poor family living in West Baltimore and how their lives are impacted by illegal drugs. For *The Wire*, Simon and Burns extended their scope, exploring how the illegal drug trade affected neighborhoods, schools, law enforcement agencies, and government.

The Wire was shot on location in Baltimore. The cast was comprised of character actors who were relatively unknown when filming began. Each of the series' five seasons highlighted a different aspect of Baltimore: the drug dealers and police officers, the stevedores and the shipping industry, politics, the public education system, and the media—specifically *The Baltimore Sun* newspaper. Through all of the seasons, the fictional drug operation known as the "Barksdale Organization" remains central to the story. Led by Avon Barksdale (Wood Harris) and Russell "Stringer" Bell (Idris Elba), the gang is the target of a special police detail that includes detectives James McNulty (Dominic West) and William "Bunk" Moreland (Wendell Pierce). One of the series' most popular characters is Omar Little (Michael K. Williams), an openly homosexual man who survives on the streets by robbing drug dealers. The show also cast real life ex-felons for roles, such as Felicia Pearson, who played a Barksdale Organization soldier named Snoop.

Corruption is a key theme in *The Wire*. The story explores the presence and impact of corruption in institutions such as law enforcement and politics. Other themes addressed in the series include the decline of American industry, the struggle to reform corrupt institutions and individuals, and the reciprocity of crime.

Impact

Each character in *The Wire*, including drug dealers, cops, and politicians, are depicted as unglamorous, morally conflicted people. The show presents a challenging, realistic look into the world of drugs, violence and law enforcement that exists in many cities in the United States. The show helped bring attention to the drug-related issues and crime in Baltimore, as well as the rest of America, engendering discussion about how social problems might be effectively addressed.

Further Reading

Alvarez, Rafael. *The Wire: Truth Be Told*. New York: Simon, 2010. Print.

Potter, Tiffany, and C. W. Marshall, eds. *The Wire: Urban Decay and American Television*. New York and London: Continuum, 2009. Print.

Patrick G. Cooper

Paul Wolfowitz (left), Agustín Carstens (center) and Rodrigo de Rato (right) at IMF headquarters. (IMF Staff Photo/Stephen Jaffe)

■ Wolfwitz, Paul

Identification: US deputy secretary of defense, 2001–5 and president of the World Bank, 2005–7
Born: December 22, 1943; New York, New York

Paul Wolfowitz was the former Deputy Secretary of Defense for the Bush Administration, and the former President of the World Bank. Wolfowitz has a long career history with the federal government, including two previous positions in the United States Department of Defense and a stint as ambassador to Indonesia. One of the leaders of the neoconservative movement in the United States, Wolfowitz was the key player in the planning of the war in Iraq and an adviser to President Bush on defense issues.

Paul Wolfowitz began working for then presidential candidate and Texas governor George W. Bush in 1999, serving as a foreign policy advisor. In March 2001, President Bush made Wolfowitz the nation's twenty-eighth Deputy Secretary of Defense after Wolfowitz twice turned down an offer to direct the Central Intelligence Agency. Early in the Bush administration, Wolfowitz advocated a sharp increase in defense spending and argued before the US Senate in favor of a ballistic missile-defense system.

Two days after the September 11, 2001, terrorist attacks against the United States, Wolfowitz announced the emergency allocation of $20 billion to repair the damage done in New York and to the Pentagon, and to assist the US military in fighting terrorism. He stated that the military would be given all the support it needed to win the war of terror. Wolfowitz supported and encouraged the president in his efforts to topple the Taliban in Afghanistan, and was one of the first to suggest an attempt to oust Saddam Hussein in Iraq.

As the United States prepared to invade Iraq in 2003, Wolfowitz was instrumental in gaining the support from other nations and making the case for removing Saddam. He played a role in the development of US policy in post-Saddam Iraq, and advised the president on international matters such as the possible nuclear threat from North Korea.

Wolfowitz was named president of the World Bank in January of 2005. His nomination to the office was criticized by many. Although Wolfowitz's stated aim as World Bank president was to fight corruption and increase aid to African countries, his tenure ended up being overshadowed by the controversy that led to his exit.

Allegations that he provided special treatment and salary increases to his girlfriend Shaha Riza eventually forced Wolfowitz to resign from his post. Although supporters of Wolfowitz argued that his actions paled in comparison to other acts of internal corruption at the organization, an ethics investigation into Wolfowitz's office led to his resignation on May 17, 2007.

Impact

Paul Wolfowitz held many high ranking positions in his extensive political career. He played a significant role in diplomacy, intelligence and policy-relations, and exercised a considerable influence as president of the World Bank during the Bush Administration. In addition to his successful career in politics, Wolfowitz was also a professor of International Relations at John Hopkins University. He was also the dean of the Paul H. School of Advanced International Studies at John Hopkins.

Further Reading

Crane, Lee. *Wolfowitz on Point.* Douglas, MI: Pavilion, 2003. Print.

Immerman, Richard H. *Empire for Liberty: A History of American Imperialism from Benjamin Franklin to Paul Wolfowitz.* Princeton: Princeton UP, 2012. Print.

Solomon, Lewis, D. *Paul D. Wolfowitz: Visionary Intellectual, Policymaker, and Strategist (Praeger Security International).* Santa Barbara: Praeger, 2007. Print.

Matt Pearce

■ Women's rights

Definition: Refers to the privileges, entitlements, rights, and protections afforded to women. Also refers to the global movement to equalize political and social treatment between men and women

In the first decade of the twenty-first century, efforts to address women's rights generally focused on closely related is- *sues including reproductive rights, abortion and family planning, the right to protection from sexual violence, and workplace discrimination and equality. Women's rights have been among the most important human rights issues of the modern era, as many women still face significant social and political inequities.*

Reproductive Rights

Reproductive rights include the social and legal rights surrounding reproduction, as well as access to reproductive health care information and services. Controversial facets of this issue include the debate over abortion and birth control. Abortion is the most widely contested issue within the reproductive rights sphere, as a significant percentage of the global population opposes abortion on religious/spiritual or moral grounds.

As of 2012, fifty countries including the United States allow abortions "on demand," meaning at the woman's request, while the vast majority of countries require certain circumstances, such as a threat to the woman's life or pregnancy resulting from rape or sexual abuse. Thirty-five countries ban abortions entirely, mostly for religious or moral reasons.

During the 2000s the abortion policy of the United States was based on the landmark Supreme Court case *Roe v. Wade*, settled in 1973. The ruling can be summarized in four key principles: 1) women have a constitutional right to have an abortion; 2) federal and state laws cannot force women to make a choice for or against an abortion; 3) abortion before the fetus is viable can only be prohibited to protect the health of the mother; 4) the government may prohibit abortion after the fetus is viable, but must make exceptions to protect a woman's health.

The abortion debate in the United States has been one of the central issues of the twenty-first century and a polarizing force in politics. According to a 2011 Gallup Poll, over 70 percent of Americans believe that abortion should remain legal in some circumstances, while 22 percent favor a general ban. A slight majority of respondents described themselves as "pro-life" rather than "pro-choice."

In the 2000 case of *Stenberg v. Carhart*, the Supreme Court struck down a Nebraska law banning "partial birth abortions," otherwise known as "intact dilation and extraction." The court found that the Nebraska ruling placed an "undue burden" on a woman's choice, and objected to the fact that the law did not

Thousands of abortion rights activists crowd Pennsylvania Avenue. (Paul J. Richards/AFP/Getty Images)

number of women's rights organizations, such as Planned Parenthood, the American Civil Liberties Union (ACLU), and the National Organization for Women (NOW). The 2007 Supreme Court ruling essentially overturned its 2000 ruling on the same issue.

Further debate during the decade considered the issue of funding for clinics and health care centers that provide either abortions or information about abortion options. In 2001, the Bush administration's Mexico City Policy outlawed federal funding for any health care organization providing abortions or "promoting" abortion services. The legislation was first introduced under Ronald Reagan and officially reinstated under George W. Bush, after having been reversed during the Clinton administration of the 1990s. In 2009, the Obama administration reversed the Mexico City Policy again.

In 2004, the Bush administration passed the Unborn Victims of Violence Act, which allows courts to prosecute individuals for killing or damaging a fetus during a violent crime against a pregnant woman. Opponents of the act argued that according to *Roe v. Wade*, a fetus is not considered a person. Opponents also accused the Bush administration of attempting to further legislation that could be used to place future restrictions on abortion rights.

While the early Bush administration restricted abortion rights in the United States, abortion rights expanded globally in several key areas. In 2005, the government of Ethiopia legalized abortions for the first time in the country's history—for cases of rape, sexual abuse, and fetal impairment. The governments of Portugal, Mexico, and Australia passed legislation granting abortion rights to women during the early stages of pregnancy. Also during the decade, Mexico, Colombia, and Nepal passed legislation requiring state funding for abortion services.

Contraception funding and availability is another controversial facet of reproductive rights. Some organizations that are morally opposed to contraception contest the use of federal/government funding to promote or provide contraception. Under the Health

include any exceptions to protect a woman's health. Intact dilation and extraction became a central issue of the debate, though it accounts for less than 1 percent of abortions performed worldwide. Opponents of a ban on the procedure contested that pro-life activists were using the issue to introduce subtle legislation that would eventually place further restrictions on all forms of abortion.

In 2003, the Bush administration passed a federal ban on intact dilation and extraction, despite the Supreme Court's decision in 2000. The law was challenged in the courts and upheld by the Supreme Court in the 2007 case of *Gonzalez v. Carhart*. The 2003 ban was the first federal restriction on abortion passed since *Roe v. Wade*. It was opposed by a

Care and Education Reconciliation Act of 2010, amended in 2012, insurance providers became required to fund contraceptive coverage in the United States, though this act has faced opposition from groups that oppose contraception on moral or religious grounds.

According to United Nations and World Health Organization data, the number of abortions worldwide has declined as contraceptive use has increased. Between 2005 and 2007, the percentage of women using contraceptives around the world rose from 54 to 63 percent. In Africa, contraceptive use rose from 17 to 28 percent, while in Central America and the Caribbean, the rate rose from 62 to 72 percent. Since the 2000s, contraceptive education and availability have remained major issues in the United States and around the world.

Violence against Women

Another major facet of women's rights is violence against women, including various types of rape, sexual abuse, molestation, domestic violence, and spousal abuse. While violence against women is legally prohibited in many countries, women's rights organizations still work to address legal and social inequities and to strengthen and amend legislation believed to be discriminatory against women seeking aid or protection.

During the 1990s, several key legislative measures were introduced to specifically address the issue, including the Violence Against Women Act (VAWA) of 1994, which dedicated $1.5 billion to investigate and prosecute cases involving violent crimes against women. The VAWA was renewed in 2000 and 2005, with additional provisions adopted at each stage. Opponents of the act targeted a provision allowing women to sue their assailants in federal courts. This opposition resulted in the 2000 Supreme Court case of *United States v. Morrison*, in which the court ruled 5–4 that this provision violated states' rights and that the states had the right to oversee civil cases of this nature.

According to 2010 data from the United Nations Convention on the Elimination of all forms of Discrimination Against Women (CEDAW), violence against women varies widely depending on geographic location. Sociological factors play a major role, as violence against women is more common in patriarchal societies and in impoverished areas. Throughout the 2000s, Zambia had one of the

highest rates of violence against women, with almost 60 percent of women reporting an incident of violence or rape during their lifetime. In Australia, Mozambique, and the Czech Republic, the rate is between 48 and 52 percent. By contrast, Chinese women in Hong Kong reported among the lowest rates in the world, approximately 11 to 12 percent. In Zambia, Peru, and Ethiopia, nearly 50 percent of women were abused by a sexual partner or spouse, while other countries, notably China, had rates as low as 7 percent.

The United States is at the lower end of international trends regarding violence against women, but experienced a significant rise in rates of domestic violence and rape during the 2000s, with nearly 20 percent of women reporting one or more instances. According to research by the Center for Disease Control (CDC) in 2010, more than 22 million women in the United States have been raped at least once, more than 60 percent of which involved a former sexual partner or spouse. These statistics may be conservative, however, as Department of Justice reports released in 1998 estimate that less than half of domestic violence incidents are reported, while the Federal Bureau of Investigation estimates that only between 20 to 30 percent of rapes are reported in the United States.

Employment and Educational Achievement

Another significant issue in women's rights is the equalization of employment opportunities and compensation for women compared to men in similar occupations. In most countries, women are statistically more likely to be unemployed or to spend more time engaged in domestic activities and/or child rearing. Women in many countries, including the United States, face employment discrimination and are typically paid significantly less.

According to the 2011 survey *Women in America*, a joint project of the Department of Commerce Economics and Statistics Division and the Executive Office of the President, women have made significant gains in educational attainment. Approximately 87 percent of women graduate from high school, compared to approximately 59 percent of men. In 2009, about 29 percent of both women and men had obtained a college degree, marking a significant increase for women during the 2000s.

Women have also made significant gains in obtaining compensation commensurate with men in similar occupations. In 1979, women earned roughly

62 percent of the average salary of a man in the same position, whereas in 2009, this had increased to 80 percent. The number of women holding full-time employment did not increase during the 2000s, remaining at about 61 percent, which was roughly the same as the late 1990s.

Internationally, the percentage of women in the workplace remained close to 52 percent during the decade. In terms of educational attainment, women lagged significantly behind men in terms of both basic and secondary education. For instance, in terms of literacy, more than two-thirds of the world's illiterate population were women in 2009. Overall, rates of educational attainment showed slight gains around the world, as did participation in the workforce.

Impact

During the 2000s, women's rights issues remained controversial and contentious internationally, especially with regard to reproductive rights. In 2010, the debate over the legality and morality of abortion was a central issue around the world. In the United States, abortion debates played a major role in political developments and were the cause of numerous violent episodes, especially violence against physicians involved in performing abortions, perpetrated by radical anti-abortion activists.

While violence against women, educational rights, and inequities in employment were also major issues facing the world's female population in the first decade of the twenty-first century, none of these issues received as much political and media coverage as the debate over abortion. The decade from 2000 to 2010 saw significant increases in domestic violence and rape in the United States, while violence against women overall decreased globally. The 2000s also saw an unprecedented involvement of women in politics, the broader implications of which may not be fully realized for some time, as the political and social changes initiated by female leaders take hold in global society.

Further Reading

Black, M.C., et al. "The National Intimate Partner and Sexual Violence Survey (NISVS): 2010 Summary Report". *Division of Violence Prevention.* Centers for Disease Control and Prevention, 2011. Web. 14 Aug. 2012. This CDC study discusses instances of rape and violence in the United States, with 2010 statistics reported for rape and sexual violence.

"Crime in the United States." *Federal Bureau of Investigation.* US Department of Justice, 2012. Web. 14 Aug. 2012. Database of statistics, collected by US state and federal crime prevention and control organizations. Provides estimates of crime, divided by year, type of crime, and other characteristics.

Department of Economic and Social Affairs. *The World's Women 2010: Trends and Statistics.* New York: United Nations, 2010. E-book. Annual report produced by the United Nations, based on global statistics related to women's issues. Provides statistics on educational and employment achievement, as well as other characteristics of the global female population.

Evans, John H. *Reproduction: Genetic Technologies, Religion, and the Public Debate.* Chicago: U of Chicago P, 2011. Print. Overview of numerous issues surrounding the abortion and reproductive technology debate of the twentieth and early twenty-first centuries. Written for the general reader to provide an overview of issues, rather than to support a single viewpoint.

US Department of Commerce, and Executive Office of the President. *Women in America: Indicators of Social and Economic Well-Being.* Washington, DC: White House Council on Women and Girls, 2011. E-book. Annual report, written for media and general readers, providing basic statistics and a description of the current state of women's achievements and rights in the United States.

Micah Issitt

■ Woods, Tiger

Identification: American professional golfer
Born: December 30, 1975; Cyprus, California

Considered to be one of the most successful golfers in the history of the game, Tiger Woods was the highest paid athlete in the world and broke numerous world records throughout the 2000s. Woods was named PGA Player of the Year eight times over the course of the decade.

Eldrick "Tiger" Woods began his golf career at an early age, setting records while in his early teens. After becoming the youngest player to win the Insurance

Tiger Woods. (Courtesy Keith Allison)

Youth Golf Classic, Woods was crowned the Southern California Player of the Year. At age fifteen, he was named *Golf World*'s Player of the Year. After graduating from high school, Woods attended Stanford University, where he joined the golf team. However, after two years, Woods left Stanford in order to dedicate himself entirely to professional golf, launching his professional career on August 27, 1996. He competed in numerous tournaments, including the Professional Golfers' Association (PGA) Tour, the Masters, and the PGA Championship. He was also a member of the victorious 1999 US Ryder Cup team.

Career Grand Slam

In 2000, Woods achieved a series of victories that overshadowed his previous extraordinary achievements. After just four seasons on the PGA Tour, Woods became only the fifth golfer in history to complete the career Grand Slam of golf, winning all four

prestigious major tournaments: the Masters Tournament, the US Open, the British Open, and the PGA Championship. He had won the Masters in 1997 and the PGA Championship in 1999, so by 2000, he had only two titles left to attain.

The excitement began on June 18, 2000, when Woods finished in first place at the US Open. He finished at twelve under par with a score of 272. His score in relation to par broke a record, and he won by an astonishing fifteen-stroke lead. This broke the US Open margin record set by Willie Smith in 1899 with eleven strokes. It was also the largest lead in any major-championship victory since Old Tom Morris set the record in 1862 with thirteen strokes in the British Open.

The following month, Woods won his next major championship of the year, the British Open. He finished nineteen under par with a score of 269, another low score record in relation to par. With a stroke margin of eight, he broke the record set by J. H. Taylor in 1913.

Other Victories

Woods won his second straight PGA Championship in August of 2000, becoming only the second player to win back-to-back PGA Championships since Denny Shute in 1936 and 1937. Woods finished the PGA Championship eighteen under par with a score of 270, tying Bob May's record score. In addition to these major tournaments, Woods won an additional six tour victories in 2000. He took first place at the Mercedes Championships, the AT&T Pebble Beach National Pro-Am, the Bay Hill Invitational, the Memorial Tournament, the WGC-NEC Invitational, and the Bell Canadian Open.

In December of 2000, Woods was named Sports Illustrated Sportsman of the Year for a second time. In the forty-six years that the award had been given out, no other athlete has ever been honored twice. The following year, he won his second Masters Tournament.

Woods won the US Open for a second time in 2002 and the British Open in 2005 and 2006. He also won his third and fourth Masters championships in 2002 and 2005, respectively. In 2007, he won his fourth PGA Championship. However, his 2008 season was cut short by a knee injury that required surgery.

In 2009, Woods returned to the PGA tour. He played well in the WGC-Accenture Match Play Championship and the WGC-CA Championship but did not win either event, and he finished in sixth place at the Masters. However, Woods won the PGA Championship, the WGC-Bridgestone Invitational, and the FedEx Cup title and went on to be named the PGA Tour Player of the Year for 2009.

Impact

The most decorated golfer in PGA history, Woods has broken records once thought insurmountable, achieved more than seventy PGA Tour victories, and been honored with such titles as Male Athlete of the Year and World Sportsman of the Year. Although Woods took a brief leave of absence from professional golf in early 2010, following a scandal regarding his personal life, he returned to professional golf in the 2010 Masters, finishing in fourth place.

Further Reading

Barbie, Donna. *The Tiger Woods Phenomenon: Essays on the Cultural Impact of Golf's Fallible Superman.* Jefferson: McFarland, 2012. Print.

Callahan, Tom. *His Father's Son: Earl and Tiger Woods.* New York: Gotham, 2010. Print.

Helling, Steve. *Tiger: The Real Story.* New York: Perseus, 2010. Print.

Lusetich, Robert. *Unplayable: An Inside Account of Tiger's Most Tumultuous Season.* New York: Atria, 2010. Print.

Starn, Orin. *The Passion of Tiger Woods: An Anthropologist Reports on Golf, Race, and Celebrity Scandal.* Durham: Duke UP, 2011. Print.

Woods, Tiger. *How I Play Golf.* New York: Warner, 2001. Print.

Veronica Bray

■ World of Warcraft

Definition: Massive multiplayer online role-playing game (MMO) developed by Blizzard Entertainment in which players create and control an avatar character. Players progress through the game by fighting monsters, completing quests, and engaging in both competitive and cooperative play with other people in a fantasy-themed world.

World of Warcraft) was released in 2004 as Blizzard's entry into the MMO market. World of Warcraft improved on the genre's traditional gameplay by offering a robust player-versus-player experience, and introducing a system that allowed players to complete quests on their own. The game earned the Guinness World Record in 2009 for largest subscription base at 11.6 million subscribers.

World of Warcraft (WoW) was released on the tenth anniversary of Blizzard's Warcraft series to capitalize on the burgeoning MMO market. The game featured the series' signature hand-painted art style and lore familiar to fans of the Warcraft universe, which helped it establish a strong subscriber base shortly after its release. In order to play the game, a monthly subscription fee is required, in addition to the retail or downloadable installation content. Players create a character by selecting from a pool of races and classes, or professions, and engage in a varied set of features to gain experience points. These features include player-versus-everything (PvE) content such

World of Warcraft display at San Diego Comic Con International. (Courtesy Matt Chan)

as completing quests for non-player characters, or teaming up with other players in a party to defeat a dungeon, and player-versus-player (PvP) content in which players fight each other. WoW set the standards for the MMO genre by streamlining the game mechanics to make it accessible to a broader audience. To keep players interested beyond the original game, Blizzard released three expansion packs by the end of the decade: The Burning Crusade (2007), Wrath of the Lich King (2008), and Cataclysm (2010).

Impact

World of Warcraft built upon the foundations of the niche MMO genre, and its popularity propelled the genre into mainstream popular culture. At its peak, the game had twelve million active subscribers. The success of the WoW has spawned a board and trading card game, as well as fantasy novels and comics. Real world markets developed for gold (the in-game currency) and high-level player accounts, which both sold for real-life currencies. In one marketing campaign, World of Warcraft was endorsed by famous actors like Mr. T and Chuck Norris. *South Park*, a cartoon on Comedy Central, had an entire episode focused around the characters playing World of Warcraft.

Further Reading

Corneliussen, Hilde, and Jill Walker Rettberg. *Digital Culture, Play, and Identity: A World of Warcraft® Reader.* Cambridge: MIT P, 2011. Print.

Cuddy, Luke, and John Nordlinger. *World of Warcraft and Philosophy: Wrath of the Philosopher King.* Chicago: Open Court, 2009. Print.

Nardi, Bonnie. *My Life as a Night Elf Priest: An Anthropological Account of World of Warcraft.* Ann Arbor: U of Michigan P, 2010. Print.

◼ WorldCom scandal

Definition: On June 25, 2002, WorldCom, the second largest telecommunications company in the United States, admitted that its accountants had overstated its 2001 and first quarter 2002 earnings by $3.8 billion. On July 21 of the same year, WorldCom filed for bankruptcy. On August 8, 2002, the company admitted that it had misclassified at least another $3.8 billion.

In the investigation that followed the initial revelations by WorldCom, it was revealed that the company had misstated earnings by approximately $11 billion. This remains one of the largest accounting scandals in United States history. The fall in the value of WorldCom stock after revelations about the massive accounting fraud led to over $180 billion in losses by WorldCom's investors.

WorldCom, which began operating under the name Long Distance Discount Services in 1983, was led by one of its founders, CEO Bernard Ebbers, from 1985 to 2002. Under Ebbers's leadership, the company engaged in a series of acquisitions, becoming one of the largest American telecommunications companies. In 1997, the company merged with MCI, making it the second largest telecom company after AT&T. In 1999, it attempted to merge with Sprint, which would have made it the largest in the industry. However, this merger was scrapped due to the intervention of the Department of Justice, which feared a WorldCom monopoly.

WorldCom stock, which rose more than 50 percent on rumors of this merger, began to fall. Ebbers then tried to grow his company through new customers rather than corporate mergers, but was unable to do so because the sector was oversaturated in 2000. He borrowed significantly so that WorldCom would have enough cash to cover anticipated margin calls, commonly used to prove that a company has funds to cover potential speculative losses. Desperate to keep his company's stock prices high, Ebbers pressured company accountants to show robust growth on earnings statements.

The WorldCom accounting scandal was ultimately uncovered by a team of WorldCom whistleblowers led by accountant Cynthia Cooper. Their secret investigation revealed evidence that ordinary business expenses were being counted as capital expenses, inflating the company's record of assets. The whistleblowers informed the WorldCom board of directors, who then went public with the story. As a result, several WorldCom executives were arrested for orchestrating the fraud. On July 13, 2005, Ebbers was sentenced to twenty-five years in federal prison.

Impact

When it broke, the WorldCom scandal was the largest instance of accounting fraud in American history. Moreover, it happened soon after a similar case involving the energy company Enron. As a result, the scandal created enormous public pressure to pass legislation targeting similar forms of fraud. This came in the form of the Sarbanes-Oxley Act of 2002. Among other things, the new law increased criminal penalties for executives involved with fraud, required companies to use external auditors, and called for more transparent asset disclosures. However, the law did not prevent even larger instances of accounting fraud revealed by the financial crisis of 2008.

Further Reading

Beresford, Dennis, Nicholas Katzenbach, and C. B. Rogers Jr. "Report of Investigation by the Special Investigative Committee of the Board of Directors of WorldCom, Inc." *US Securities and Exchange Commission.* US SEC, 31 Mar. 2003. Web. 5 Dec. 2012.

Lyke, Bob, and Mark Jickling. "WorldCom: The Accounting Scandal." *CRS Report for Congress.* Congressional Research Service, 29 Aug. 2002. Web. 5 Dec. 2012.

Adam J. Berger, PhD

■ Wright, Jeremiah

Identification: American religious leader
Born: September 22, 1941; Philadelphia, Pennsylvania

Jeremiah A. Wright Jr., the senior pastor at Trinity United Church of Christ in Chicago from 1972 to 2008, was a spiritual advisor to presidential candidate Barack Obama. He gained notoriety after segments of his sermons were publicized during the 2008 presidential race.

When Reverend Jeremiah Wright took over Trinity United Church of Christ in 1972, the small church was failing to serve the economic, social, and spiritual needs of the black community, in Wright's opinion. Seeking to make connections between Christianity and the "black experience," he began to deliver sermons from the perspective of black liberation theology, a social justice–oriented theology that embraced hope and courage and that linked Christianity with politics and government actions at a time when the civil rights movement and the Vietnam War dominated public opinion.

In March 2008, Wright and then presidential candidate Barack Obama found themselves at the center of a controversy when segments from some of Wright's sermons were released through the media during the presidential primary. In one segment taken from a sermon Wright delivered following the September 11, 2001, attacks, he appeared to blame the United States for the terrorist acts when he stated, "America's chickens are coming home to roost."

Many were offended and called Wright "anti-American" or a "fanatic." Bomb threats were made against Wright and the church. Further, the fact that Obama had bonded with Wright led many people to believe that Obama was too radical to become president.

Wright defended his sermons in an April 2008 interview with journalist Bill Moyers. He admonished the media for airing "snippets" of his sermons out of context. In his full sermon, for example, he had attributed the "chicken" quote to Ambassador Edward Peck, a white man who had quoted black activist Malcolm X on Fox News. Wright had also referred to violent actions undertaken by other governments, including the United Kingdom, Russia, Japan, and Germany, and condemned their policies, not the countries. His anger at the US government stemmed from its history of aggressive policies toward minorities. Wright also found policies that he felt sought revenge, such as the atomic bombing of Japan during World War II, to be inconsistent with Christian faith, and he blamed the past policies of white governments for the ongoing poverty of urban blacks.

To counter the backlash, Obama delivered a speech in Philadelphia on race titled "A More Perfect Union," in which he criticized Wright's comments as "inexcusable" and "divisive." However, he defended Wright as a caring minister who uplifted the poor and tended to the sick, and he stood by his longtime association with Wright's church.

Other snippets of Wright's sermons caused additional controversy, especially his charge that the US government deliberately introduced AIDS into the black community. After these additional video clips aired, Obama held a press conference to denounce Wright and formally announced his decision to separate himself from Wright.

Impact

Despite the negative press Wright and his church received during the 2008 presidential race, Wright has been recognized as an important leader for African Americans and the religious community. Wright has received numerous awards, including seven honorary doctorate degrees, a Rockefeller Fellowship, and the Carver Medal by Simpson College.

Further Reading

Walker, Clarence E., and Gregory D. Smithers. *The Preacher and the Politician: Jeremiah Wright, Barack Obama, and Race in America.* Charlottesville: U of Virginia P, 2009. Print.

Wright, Jeremiah A., Jr., and Jini Kilgore Ross. *What Makes You So Strong?: Sermons of Joy and Strength from Jeremiah A. Wright, Jr.* Valley Forge: Judson, 1993. Print.

—. *A Sankofa Moment: The History of the Trinity Church of Christ.* Dallas: Saint Paul, 2010. Print.

Sally Driscoll

■ Writers Guild of America strike

Definition: A one-hundred-day labor strike over profit sharing that pitted film and television writers against studios

Between November 5, 2007, and February 13, 2008, the members of the Writers Guild of America went on strike as a result of their inability to come to terms on a new contract with the Alliance of Motion Picture and Television Producers. The main point of contention was the writers' demand for an increase in residual payments related to content delivered online and through other forms of new media.

On November 5, 2007, the approximately twelve thousand members of the Writers Guild of America's (WGA) eastern and western divisions went on strike after talks to complete a new contract with the Alliance of Motion Picture and Television Producers (AMPTP) failed to produce an agreement that both sides were willing to accept. During the strike, which ultimately lasted one hundred days, production of most scripted television shows and some motion pictures came to a halt. The dispute was finally settled on February 12, 2008, at which point the entertainment industry returned to normal operations.

The WGA strike was primarily centered on the issue of residual payments associated with content streamed online and released through other forms of new media. The WGA argued that writers were entitled to a larger portion of the profits that studios were making on such releases of the content that writers created. Conversely, the AMPTP and the studios held that they needed the profits from new media and online releases to meet their ever-rising expenses.

The strike continued into February 2008 before the WGA and AMPTP were able to reach an agreement that satisfied both sides. On February 12, the WGA's members voted almost unanimously to accept the new agreement. As a result of this vote, the strike was formally ended on February 13, and the writers returned to work.

Impact

During the strike, production on a large number of scripted television shows and films was suspended. Among the first programs affected by the strike were late-night talk shows, many of which were forced off the air due to the loss of their writing staffs. As the number of previously produced episodes of sitcoms and prime-time dramas dwindled, these programs were also either forced off the air or into reruns.

With the acceptance of its new agreement with the AMPTP and the end of the strike, the WGA succeeded in achieving many of its goals. Both the rates at which writers are paid for their work and the amount they receive in residual payments for content used and written for online and new media outlets increased. Though the WGA was forced to make some concessions, the strike substantially altered the relationship between writers and studios and the way that both benefit from content released online and through other forms of new media.

Further Reading

"Q&A: Hollywood Writers' Strike." *BBC News.* British Broadcasting Co., 13 Feb. 2008. Web. 26 Nov. 2012.

"Strike Over, Hollywood Writers Head Back to Work." *CNN.* Cable News Network, 13 Feb. 2008. Web 26 Nov. 2012.

"Writers Guild of America." *New York Times.* New York Times Co., 10 Feb. 2008. Web. 26 Nov. 2012.

Jack Lasky

■ YouTube

Definition: A popular video-hosting website that allows users to watch, share, and upload their own videos

Since its launch in November 2005, the video-hosting website YouTube has become highly influential in shaping Internet trends in the realms of social media and popular culture. Thousands of hours of new content are uploaded to the site every day, and YouTube's strong Internet presence has created celebrity status for individuals who garner worldwide publicity from their videos. The site has also become a popular marketing and political tool.

History of YouTube

Chad Hurley, Steve Chen, and Jawed Karim began developing YouTube in 2005. All three individuals were former employees of PayPal, an electronic-commerce website that allows people to transfer money via the Internet. The three men wanted to create a site that would allow individuals to easily share videos. They purchased the domain YouTube.com in February 2005 and uploaded the first video in April. It was titled "Me at the Zoo" and featured Karim at California's San Diego Zoo.

A beta test for the public began in May 2005 and the site was officially launched six months later in November 2005, becoming popular within its first few months of service. By the summer of 2006, it was one of the fastest growing websites on the Internet. The web-tracking service Alexa ranked YouTube the fifth most popular website in July 2006 when more than sixty thousand new videos were uploaded and over one hundred million were viewed each day.

In June 2006, YouTube entered a partnership with the National Broadcasting Company (NBC), which allowed the broadcaster to market and promote their programs on YouTube. Over the next few years, several other media companies partnered with YouTube, which enabled them to post television shows, films, and advertisements in order to reach a wider online audience. The online search engine Google purchased YouTube in October 2006 for $1.65 billion in stock. The agreement reached between the two companies allows YouTube to run as an independent unit of Google.

Internet Stardom and Viral Videos

Due to the popularity of YouTube and the ease in which individuals can publicize their videos for free, the website has created several Internet celebrities, including musicians, actors, and comedians who have crossed over into mainstream popular culture. Previously, there was no easy or inexpensive way for artists to promote their craft. With YouTube's simple interface, however, videos can be posted and then shared with the world within minutes.

Canadian singer-songwriter Justin Bieber was discovered on YouTube by a talent manager who happened upon Bieber's videos and later arranged for him to sign a record deal with Island Records in the United States. Bieber had already amassed a large fan base on YouTube before releasing his first album, which debuted in November 2009 and went on to sell over one million copies.

YouTube videos have also created celebrities out of people who post shocking, real-life events that are oftentimes humorous. One of the earliest examples is "The Bus Uncle," which was uploaded in April 2006. The video features a quarrel between a youth and an older man on a bus in Hong Kong. The video received over one million views (also called "hits") in its first three weeks on YouTube, becoming the site's most viewed video in May 2006. In Hong Kong, the video became the centerpiece of a discussion concerning etiquette and media ethics.

When a video receives a large number of hits in a short amount of time, it is said to have "gone viral," and with the launch of YouTube, users were then able to rapidly share videos via email, blogs, and other social media outlets. Companies recognized the marketing power of viral videos and began producing their own YouTube videos to promote specific products, televisions shows, and movies. This approach, known as "viral marketing," is used by advertisers in what has become known as "viral campaigns."

YouTube and Politics

The impact of YouTube on politics became evident during the 2008 campaign for president of the United States. The Internet had already been used successfully for political fundraising, but during the 2008 election campaign, presidential candidate Barack Obama and his team utilized YouTube and other social-media outlets to organize and communicate with supporters, respond to criticism, and to advertise to voters—without any additional cost to the campaign. After the election, political consultant Joe Trippi stated that the Obama YouTube videos were watched for over 14.5 million hours. Buying an equal amount of advertising time on television would have cost the campaign an estimated $47 million.

YouTube has also negatively affected political careers. In 2006, Virginia Republican senate candidate George Allen was unknowingly filmed while he uttered an ethnic slur toward a campaign worker. The video was uploaded to YouTube, and Allen, who had been winning in the polls prior to the video's posting, lost the election to his Democratic opponent. Many blame the video for Allen's senate loss.

Offensive Content

Although YouTube prohibits the posting of videos containing pornography, slander, or illegal activity, many have criticized the website for its controversial material. YouTube has explained that due to the high volume of videos that are uploaded every day, it's nearly impossible to catch and remove all offensive content in a timely manner. They claim that their best defense is through their reviewers who monitor videos as they are uploaded. The site also has a flagging system in place, which allows users to notify YouTube of any video they find objectionable.

Copyright Issues

Since YouTube does not review videos before they are posted to the site, many have been uploaded that contain copyrighted material. If a copyright holder finds a video using their material, it is up to the holder to notify YouTube. Several media companies, such as Viacom, have filed lawsuits against YouTube

that argue the website has not done enough to prevent copyright infringement. Viacom stated that YouTube was profiting from pirated content, and during the Viacom trial in 2007, YouTube was ordered to hand over large amounts of data that detailed users' viewing habits. Many saw this court ruling as an invasion of privacy.

To help prevent the uploading of copyrighted material, YouTube implemented a system in June 2007 they called Content ID. The system uses a database to detect if uploaded content contains copyrighted audio or video material. If the video is flagged for copyright infringement, the user can then either block the video or allow YouTube to add advertisements to it. The Content ID system has proved effective and has also served to generate advertising revenue for the site.

Impact

What began as a way for Internet users to efficiently upload, view, and share videos turned into a powerful communication, marketing, activism, and political tool. YouTube has been central in creating celebrities out of everyday people and in helping artists propel their careers. The site has become an international forum for people to voice their opinions on the media, religion, and politics. It has also changed the way political campaigns are managed and promoted. YouTube affected nearly every facet of popular culture in the 2000s.

Further Reading

Burgess, Jean, et al. *YouTube: Online Video and Participatory Culture.* Cambridge: Polity, 2009. Print. This book examines the social, cultural, and political contexts in which YouTube is used.

Goo, Sara Kehaulani. "Ready for Its Close-Up." *Washington Post.* Washington Post, 7 Oct. 2006. Web. 22 Oct. 2012. This article was written in the early days of YouTube and features interviews with the founders.

Helft, Miguel. "Google Told to Turn Over User Data of YouTube." *New York Times.* New York Times Company, 4 July 2008. Web. 22 Oct. 2012. This article discusses the lawsuit against YouTube filed by Viacom Inc. and looks at privacy issues concerning the court order requiring Google to hand over user information to Viacom.

Lacy, Sarah. *The Stories of Facebook, YouTube & MySpace.* Richmond, Eng.: Crimson, 2009. Print. This book explores the origins and popularity of YouTube and other popular social media websites.

Lowensohn, Josh. "YouTube Bumps Video Limit to 15 Minutes." *CNET*. CBS Interactive Inc., 29 July 2010. Web. 22 Oct. 2012. This article discusses copyright infringement issues on YouTube and looks at how the site limited the length of uploaded videos to help prevent copyright violations.

Patrick G. Cooper

Z

◼ *Zelman v. Simmons-Harris*

The Case: US Supreme Court ruling that found an Ohio school-voucher program did not violate the separation of church and state
Date: Decided on June 27, 2002

In 1995, Cleveland, Ohio, began participating in the Pilot Project Scholarship Program to offer low-income families a choice of schools for their children to attend. A group of residents filed a lawsuit challenging the validity of the program, citing the state's violation of the First Amendment of the US Constitution.

Due to the poor performance of public schools in Cleveland, Ohio, the state established the Pilot Project Scholarship Program in 1995. The program provided low-income families of students in the Cleveland City School District with vouchers that enabled them to send their children to schools of their choice. The vouchers were distributed by lottery and could be used for Cleveland public or private schools—including religiously affiliated schools—that were participating in the program. Ohio's was the first voucher program in the United States to include religious schools; in fact, the majority of participating schools in 1999–2000 were religiously affiliated, and nearly all of the vouchers were redeemed for private schools with religious affiliations. This angered many groups throughout the state.

Doris Simmons-Harris and other Cleveland residents filed a lawsuit against the state, including Ohio superintendent of public instruction Susan Tave Zelman, claiming that the program aided religiously affiliated schools and violated the First Amendment's establishment clause, which enforces the separation of church and state. The case began in 1996, making its way to the US District Court for the Northern District of Ohio in 1997. The US Supreme Court refused to hear the case in the summer of 1999. The following year, the voucher program was challenged again in court, and in 2001, the US Supreme Court agreed to hear the case of *Zelman v. Simmons-Harris.*

On June 27, 2002, the Supreme Court ruled five to four in favor of the voucher program, stating that the program remained "entirely neutral with respect to religion." The court reaffirmed that the program afforded educational opportunities to all children and that the state of Ohio did not interfere with the students' choice of schools, therefore it did not violate the establishment clause.

Impact

The Supreme Court's decision in *Zelman v. Simmons-Harris* enabled the voucher program to remain in place in Cleveland, Ohio, and reinforced similar programs in Florida and Milwaukee, Wisconsin. Cleveland's voucher program became so popular that it led to a statewide voucher program in 2005. Other states responded by initiating voucher programs as well.

Further Reading

Carl, Jim. *Freedom of Choice: Vouchers in American Education.* New York: Praeger, 2011. Print.
"Zelman v. Simmons-Harris." Oyez Project. IIT Chicago-Kent College of Law, 6 Nov. 2012. Web. 8 Nov. 2012.
"Zelman v. Simmons-Harris, 536 U.S. 639 (2002)." *First Amendment Schools.* First Amendment Schools, 8 Nov. 2012. Web. 8 Nov. 2012.

Angela Harmon

◼ Zuckerberg, Mark

Identification: American Internet entrepreneur
Born: May 14, 1984; Dobbs Ferry, New York

Internet entrepreneur Mark Zuckerberg initially designed computer network software as a novel way to stay in touch with college classmates. The venture grew and expanded throughout the 2000s. By the end of the decade, 350 million people worldwide were using his Facebook website. Zuckerberg's creation helped introduce the concept of social networking in the early twenty-first century.

Mark Zuckerberg had such a strong interest in computers that his father, a dentist, hired a private computer tutor for his son. While attending Phillips Exeter Academy in New Hampshire, the teen developed Synapse, a music program that provided recommendations based on listeners' tastes. Zuckerberg fielded job offers from such companies as AOL and Microsoft before he graduated from the academy in 2002.

Zuckerberg majored in computer science and psychology at Harvard University, where he impressed classmates with his technical skills. During his sophomore year, Zuckerberg built CourseMatch, a program that used information about course selections to help students choose classes. He also found tremendous (though fleeting) success among his peers with Facemash, a program that compared photos of students and allowed classmates to rate their attractiveness. Harvard administrators shut down the program, stating that it was inappropriate.

Classmates Divya Narendra and Cameron and Tyler Winklevoss sought out Zuckerberg for help in developing a dating site they called Harvard Connection. Though Zuckerberg initially joined them, he later began working with Chris Hughes, Dustin Moskovitz, and Eduardo Saverin on a different social networking site called The Facebook. This site allowed users to create profiles and interact with friends online. Zuckerberg quit college in 2004 after his sophomore year and moved to Palo Alto, California, to build Facebook. The site, which at the time welcomed only Ivy League students to join, had one million members by the end of the year.

The following year, Accel Partners, a venture capital firm, invested more than $12 million in Facebook. Zuckerberg opened Facebook to students from other colleges, as well as international schools and high schools. Members numbered more than 5.5 million by the end of 2005. Advertisers took notice of the company, but Zuckerberg rebuffed their interests at first. The following year, his former collaborators, Narendra and the Winklevoss brothers, accused him of stealing their idea. He denied stealing anything, but lawyers found evidence that some intellectual property from the Harvard Connection had been used for the Facebook project. Zuckerberg apologized, but the parties argued over the settlement for several years.

Zuckerberg endured more scrutiny when Ben Mezrich's book *The Accidental Billionaires* was published

Mark Zuckerberg. (©iStockphoto.com/Justin Sullivan)

in 2009. Though much of the work was fictional, screenwriter Aaron Sorkin bought the rights to the book and later developed a film, *The Social Network* (2010).

Meanwhile, Zuckerberg continued to expand Facebook's reach. He opened membership to workplaces in 2006. By the end of that year, Facebook had 12 million members. After extending membership to the general public, Facebook had 350 million users by 2009. The company's continued success drew attention, and soon other companies were interested in buying Facebook. However, Zuckerberg refused to sell, turning down a billion-dollar offer from Yahoo!.

As Facebook expanded, the company relocated several times to accommodate its growing staff. Its office culture reflected the preferences of its young chief executive. The open work space included desks but no offices, though there were conference rooms. Doodles and skateboards dotted the company headquarters, and employees enjoyed perks such as free meals and snacks and free dry cleaning.

In the early years, the company had a number of executives that left quickly. The high turnover changed when Zuckerberg hired a new chief executive officer, Sheryl Sandberg, in 2008. With Sandberg's help, Zuckerberg continued to grow Facebook. Sandberg had a solid background in business, having worked for Google and other computer companies, and her presence attracted other competent executives to Facebook.

From the beginning, Zuckerberg avoided intrusive ads on Facebook, instead relying on small ads on the side of the site. Advertising revenue was low before Sandberg joined the company. Sandberg leveraged Facebook's vast database of user information to target them with relevant ads and draw in top advertisers. The "Like" button, added in 2009, also attracted advertisers, who realized that products approved by a person's circle of friends were more interesting to users.

Though Facebook used and compiled information about its users, the company insisted it did not sell the information to advertisers. In similar fashion, when authorities presented Facebook with subpoenas for information about users, the company went to court to avoid complying.

Facebook's Success

Some experts attribute the success of Zuckerberg's idea to its similarity to real-life social interaction. Whereas some websites allow users to remain anonymous or create false profiles, Facebook encourages users to be recognized for who they are. The Facebook approach, rooted in Zuckerberg's background in psychology, is based on the idea that anonymity encourages antisocial behavior, while honesty fosters civility. Facebook even reminds users that it is against the social network's policy to present false information when creating a profile. On the other hand, critics of Facebook claim that it represents a potential danger to children, putting them at risk of contact with bullies or predators. Other critics have theorized that the supplanting of real-life interaction with online interaction is detrimental to society as a whole.

Zuckerberg's ability to anticipate what people want also contributed to Facebook's rise. By taking such desires and creating new applications, he answered these needs. For example, in 2005, Internet sites such as Photobucket and Flickr were offering photo uploading and sharing services. Facebook was not designed for high-resolution images, but Zuckerberg understood that users did not want to organize and catalog their photos online—they wanted to group images by who appeared in the pictures. Once Facebook gave users the ability to tag photos with friends' names, they soon uploaded millions of images.

When games were added to Facebook, they were designed to be social activities, rather than individual experiences. FarmVille encourages friendship and cooperation—users "help" one another by doing chores on friends' farms and exchanging gifts. Another game allows users to give and receive animals as they build and expand their zoos.

At times, Zuckerberg has endured widespread complaints about changes implemented to Facebook. Though users initially complained about the addition of the News Feed feature in 2006, Zuckerberg did not change course. The updating list of stories from users' friends remained and became a permanent fixture on the website.

Through all of its successes, however, Facebook has also endured challenges. Developments in 2007 and 2009 upset many Facebook users who were concerned about privacy. The first, Beacon, alerted friends about purchases, which ruined Christmas surprises and alarmed many users. In December 2009, Facebook incensed users by making some of their information public without notifying them first. Users felt the site's privacy settings were complicated to understand and control. As a result, the Federal Trade Commission (FTC) conducted an investigation into the company's practices. After scrutinizing such issues as privacy controls and third-party access to users' information, the agency found that the company did not share user information with advertisers.

In the spirit of Zuckerberg's vision for Facebook, openness and sharing are the norm. Users disagreed, however, at least when it came to the company's privacy settings. Zuckerberg uses the words "open" and "connected" when he describes his vision for social networking. He has indicated that he does not understand others' concerns about keeping secrets.

Facebook's openness has not been welcomed by some foreign governments. Many countries, among them Saudi Arabia and Iran, have occasionally issued bans of the social networking site. In 2009, the Chinese government blocked Facebook, though workarounds and facsimiles have flourished.

Personal Life

Zuckerberg hired his sister, Randi, as marketing director. He also offered a job to Priscilla Chan, his longtime girlfriend, when he was recruiting classmates to join his fledgling Facebook venture. The pair met at a party at Harvard at Zuckerberg's Jewish fraternity, Alpha Epsilon Pi. After her graduation in 2007, Chan moved to California to attend medical school at the University of California, San Francisco. The couple saw each other on weekends.

Chan, recognizing Zuckerberg's devotion to Facebook, insisted on some relationship rules, including a date each week. She also played a part in Zuckerberg's business decisions. For example, she reminded him about his goals when Yahoo! offered to buy the company. The couple married in 2012.

Impact

Through the development and advancement of Facebook, Zuckerberg changed the way people interact online by tapping into people's desire for connection. Facebook allows users to connect with people they know in the real world and share their everyday experiences with friends and family members. By the end of the decade, Facebook had connected users all around the world and became one of the most popular sites on the Internet.

Further Reading

Grossman, Lev. "Person of the Year 2010, Mark Zuckerberg." *Time.* Time Inc., 15 Dec. 2010. Web. 9 Oct. 2012. Details Mark Zuckerberg's youth and early years, describes his personality, and examines the social context and effects of his signature creation, Facebook.

Hill, Kashmir. "Facebook's Mark Zuckerberg: 'We've Made a Bunch of Mistakes.'" *Forbes.* Forbes.com, 29 Nov. 2011. Web. 9 Oct. 2012. Includes a list of the privacy-related problems uncovered by the FTC investigation of Facebook.

Kirkpatrick, David. *The Facebook Effect: The Inside Story of the Company That Is Connecting the World.* New York: Simon, 2010. Print. An authorized company history of Facebook that analyzes its origins, successes and failures, and plans for the future.

"Mark Zuckerberg Biography." *Biography.* A+E Television Networks, 2012. Web. 9 Oct. 2012. Provides an overview of Zuckerberg's life and the development of Facebook from Harvard onward.

Vargas, Jose Antonio. "The Face of Facebook." *New Yorker.* Condé Nast, 20 Sept. 2010. Web. 9 Oct. 2012. A personality sketch of Mark Zuckerberg including quotes from Zuckerberg himself, friends and acquaintances, and former collaborators. Written just prior to the release of the semibiographical film *The Social Network.*

Josephine Campbell

Appendixes

■ Entertainment: Major Films of the 2000s

The one hundred films from the 2000s (through 2010) listed here are a representative sampling of films regarded as significant because of their box-office success, their Academy Award honors, their influence, or their critical reputations. All references to best-acting and other awards refer to the Oscars awarded annually (beginning in 1928) by the Academy of Motion Picture Arts and Sciences. A title followed by an asterisk (*) indicates the presence of a full-length essay within *The 2000s in America*.

2000

Almost Famous (Columbia Pictures/DreamWorks, dir: Cameron Crowe) Comedy/drama depicts an emerging teenage reporter for *Rolling Stone* magazine encountering musicians and fans in the 1960s. Won Oscar for best original screenplay and was nominated for best supporting actress (Kate Hudson).

Castaway (Twentieth Century Fox/DreamWorks, dir: Robert Zemeckis) Drama about a FedEx employee who becomes stranded on a desert island and learns to survive was one of the highest grossing films of the year and won an Oscar nomination for best actor (Tom Hanks).

Crouching Tiger, Hidden Dragon (Asian Union Film & Entertainment/Columbia Pictures Film Production Asia, dir: Ang Lee) Martial Arts action film depicts two aging heroes (Chow Yun-fat and Michelle Yeoh) investigating the crimes of a long wanted villain. Won Oscar for best score (Tan Dun) and best foreign language film.

Erin Brockovich (Jersey Films/Universal Pictures, dir: Steven Soderbergh) Dramatization of the life of Erin Brockovich who initiated a legal battle against the Pacific Gas and Electric Company. Won Oscar for best actress (Julia Roberts) as well as nominations for best picture and best director.

*Gladiator** (DreamWorks/Universal Pictures, dir: Ridley Scott) Historical action film depicts the life of a fictional gladiator who fights to unseat the despotic son (Joaquin Phoenix) of a murdered emperor. Won Oscars for best picture, actor (Russell Crowe), visual effects, costume design and sound.

Meet the Parents (Universal Pictures/DreamWorks/TriBeCa, dir: Jay Roach) Comedy about a recently engaged man meeting the parents of his fiancée was one of the highest grossing films of the year and the beginning of a successful multi-film series.

Mission Impossible 2 (Paramount Pictures, dir: John Woo) Action film loosely based on a 60s and 70s television series, depicts Agent Ethan Hunt (Tom Cruise) investigating a biological weapons threat in the highest grossing film of 2000 and the second in the three film series.

Pollock (Brant-Allen/Sony Pictures, dir: Ed Harris) Biography of the life of twentieth century painter Jackson Pollock won an Oscar for best supporting actress (Marcia Gay Harden) and was nominated for best actor (Harris).

Traffic (Bedford Falls Productions, dir: Steven Soderbergh) Crime drama exploring different aspects of the illegal drug trade in the United States and Mexico. Won Oscars for best director, best supporting actor (Benicio Del Toro), and best screenplay adaptation.

X-Men (Twentieth Century Fox/Marvel Entertainment, dir: Bryan Singer) Action film adapted from a famed comic book series depicts a group of superheroes battling to determine the fate of mankind in one of the highest grossing films of the year and the first in a three-part franchise.

2001

A Beautiful Mind (Imagine Entertainment/Universal Pictures, dir: Ron Howard) Biographical drama based on the life of a Nobel Prize–winning economist who suffered from schizophrenia, won four Oscars for best adapted screenplay, best director, best supporting actress, and best picture.

Amélie (France 3 Cinema/Miramax Films, dir: Jean-Pierre Jeunet) French comedy about a young woman with an active imagination searching for love received five Oscar nominations including best original screenplay, best foreign language film, and best cinematography.

*Harry Potter and the Sorcerer's Stone** (Heyday Films/Warner Bros. Pictures, dir: Chris Columbus) The first of an eight-part film series, based on the best-selling book series, depicting young witches and wizards making their way through schooling in magic was the highest grossing film of the year and was nominated for three academy awards.

*The Lord of the Rings: The Fellowship of the Rings** (New Line Cinema/Wing Nut Films, dir: Peter Jackson) First of three films based on the fantasy novels of J. R. R. Tolkien was the second highest grossing film of the year and won four Oscars for best cinematography, best visual effects, best makeup, and best original score.

Monster's Ball (Lee Daniels Entertainment/Lions Gate Films, dir: Marc Foster) Drama about a man and woman with tragic family histories forming a relationship won Oscars for best actress (Halle Berry) and best original screenplay.

Moulin Rouge! (Twentieth Century Fox Films/Bazmark Films, dir: Baz Luhrmann) Musical comedy about a young writer who falls in love with a cabaret dancer was nominated for six Oscars including best picture, best actress (Nicole Kidman), and best cinematography.

Ocean's 11 (Village Roadshow Pictures/Warner Brothers Pictures, dir: Steven Soderbergh) Remake of the 1960 crime comedy film features a group of criminal friends cooperating to rob a casino in one of the top grossing films of the year and the first in a successful three-film franchise.

Pearl Harbor (Jerry Bruckheimer Films, Touchstone Pictures, dir: Michael Bay) Drama based on a dramatic interpretation of the events surrounding the Japanese attack on Pearl Harbor was one of the highest grossing films of the year and was nominated for four Oscars including best sound editing and best visual effects.

*Shrek** (DreamWorks Animation, dir: Andrew Adamson and Vicky Jenson) Animated comedy about an ogre who pursues romance and fights against a villainous lord was one of the highest grossing films of the year and was the first film to win the newly created Oscar for best animated feature film.

Training Day (Village Roadshow, Warner Bros. Pictures, dir: Antoine Fuqua) Crime drama featuring Denzel Washington as a crooked LAPD drug enforcement officer training a new recruit won an Oscar for best actor (Washington) and a nomination for best supporting actor.

2002

Adaptation (Good Machine/Beverly Detroit/Columbia Pictures, dir: Spike Jonze) Comedic drama centering around the efforts of an author to adapt a book into a film won the Oscar for best supporting actor (Chris Cooper) and garnered two additional nominations including best actor (Nicolas Cage) and best supporting actress (Meryl Streep).

Chicago (Miramax Films, Producers Circle, dir: Rob Marshall) Musical comedy adapted from a successful Broadway Musical won Oscars for best picture, art direction, costume design, film editing, and sound editing, as well as an Oscar for best supporting actress (Catherine Zeta-Jones).

*Harry Potter and the Chamber of Secrets** (Heyday Films/Warner Bros. Pictures, dir: Chris Columbus) The second installment of the popular Harry Potter fantasy franchise was the second highest grossing film in the United States and the top grossing film internationally.

The Hours (Paramount Pictures/Miramax Films, dir: Stephen Daldry) Drama about three women whose lives are linked through the Virginia Woolf novel *Mrs. Dalloway* won the Oscar for best actress (Kidman) as well as eight additional Oscar nominations.

*The Lord of the Rings: The Two Towers** (WingNut Films/New Line Cinema, dir: Peter Jackson) Epic fantasy adventure adapted from the second book in J. R. R. Tolkien's famous novels was the highest grossing film in the United States and won Oscars for best visual effects and best sound editing in addition to four Oscar nominations including best picture.

The Pianist (Studio Canal+/Focus Pictures/Universal Pictures, dir: Roman Polanski) Biographical film about a Jewish Polish pianist attempting to survive during World War II won the Oscar for best actor (Adrien Brody), best director, and best adapted screenplay.

Signs (Touchstone Pictures/Blinding Edge Pictures, dir: M. Night Shyamalan) Extraterrestrial suspense film was one of the top grossing films of the year.

Spider Man (Marvel Enterprises/Columbia Pictures, dir: Sam Raimi) Superhero adventure film based on the popular comic book hero was one of the highest grossing films of the year and received two Oscar nominations for best visual effects and best sound mixing.

Spirited Away (Studio Ghibli, dir: Hayao Miyazaki) Animated Japanese fantasy/adventure film won the Oscar for best animated feature film and was at the top of many critics' lists for best foreign films of the year.

Star Wars Episode II: Attack of the Clones (Lucasfilm/ Twentieth Century Fox, dir: George Lucas) Second edition of the prequel trilogy set in Lucas's iconic Star Wars universe received an Oscar nomination for best visual effects and was one of the top grossing films internationally.

2003

Cold Mountain (Miramax Films/Mirage Enterprises/ Bona Fide Productions, dir: Anthony Minghella) Civil War drama about a soldier trying to return to the woman he loves won an Oscar for Best Supporting Actress (Renee Zellweger) and was one of the year's best box office successes.

Finding Nemo (Walt Disney Pictures/Pixar Studios, dir: Andrew Stanton) Animated adventure/ comedy about a father fish searching for his lost son was one of the year's highest grossing films and earned the Oscar for best animated film.

The Last Samurai (Warner Brothers/Radar Pictures, dir: Edward Zwick) Historical drama about an American soldier coming into contact with Japanese samurai culture in the late 1800s was nominated for four Academy Awards including best supporting actor (Ken Watanabe).

The Lord of the Rings: Return of the King* (WingNut Films/New Line Cinema, dir: Peter Jackson) Final part in the fantasy trilogy based on J. R. R. Tolkien's seminal books won eleven Oscar awards, including best picture, best director, best visual effects and best adapted screenplay, making it the most successful film in Academy Award history at the time.

Lost in Translation* (American Zoetrope/Focus Features, dir: Sofia Coppola) Comedic drama about a friendship between two Americans meeting while traveling in Tokyo received the Oscar for best original screenplay as well as nominations for best picture and best director.

The Matrix Reloaded (Warner Brothers/Village Roadshow, dir: Andy and Larry Wachowski) Second in the science fiction/action series was one of the year's highest grossing films of the year and one of two *Matrix* films to be released in 2003.

Monster (Media 8 Entertainment/DEJ Productions/ Newmarket Films, dir: Patty Jenkins) Crime drama about an abused prostitute who becomes a serial killer won the Oscar for best actress (Charlize Theron).

Mystic River (Village Roadshow/Warner Brothers Pictures, dir: Clint Eastwood) Crime drama dealing with sexual abuse and murder won the Oscars for best actor (Sean Penn) and best supporting actor (Tim Robbins).

Pirates of the Caribbean: The Curse of the Black Pearl* (Jerry Bruckheimer Films/Walt Disney Pictures, dir: Gore Verbinski) First in a successful series of action/adventure films was one of the year's highest grossing films and earned Oscar nominations for best supporting actor and best visual effects.

X2 (Marvel Enterprises/Twentieth Century Fox, dir: Bryan Singer) Second in the popular superhero series based on the well-known Marvel comic book franchise was one of the highest grossing films of the year.

2004

The Aviator (Warner Brothers Pictures/Miramax, dir: Martin Scorsese) Biographical drama about the life of Howard Hughes received the Oscar for best supporting actress (Cate Blanchett) as well as nominations for eleven Academy Awards including best picture, best director, and best actor.

Harry Potter and the Prisoner of Azkaban* (Warner Brothers/Heyday Pictures, dir: Alfonso Cuarón) Third film in the eight-film fantasy series based on the books of J. K. Rowling was one of the year's highest grossing films and received Oscar nominations for best score and best visual effects.

Hotel Rwanda (United Artists/Lions Gate Films, dir: Terry George) Drama about the Rwandan Genocide of 2004 was nominated for three Academy Awards including best actor (Cheadle) and best supporting actress.

The Incredibles (Walt Disney Pictures/Pixar, dir: Brad Bird) Animated film about a married couple of aging superheroes trying to raise a family in a world that no longer values superheroes won the Oscar for best animated film as well as a nomination for best original screenplay.

Million Dollar Baby (Lakeshore Entertainment/ Warner Brothers Pictures, dir: Clint Eastwood) Drama about a struggling boxing trainer and a woman trying to become a professional boxer won four Oscars including best picture, best director, best actress (Hilary Swank), and best supporting actor (Morgan Freeman).

Ray (Bristol Bay Productions/Universal Pictures, dir: Taylor Hackford) Biopic of the life of singer/musician Ray Charles received the Oscar for best actor (Jamie Foxx) as well as nominations for best director and best picture.

Shrek 2* (DreamWorks, dir: Andrew Adamson, Kelly Asbury and Conrad Vernon) Animated comedy about the life and relationships of an ogre living in a fantasy realm was the highest grossing film of the year and was nominated for an Academy Award for best animated feature film.

Sideways (Fox Searchlight/Michael London Productions, dir: Alexander Payne) Comedy/drama about a group of friends and their various obsessions with wine was nominated for four Academy Awards and won the Oscar for best adapted screenplay.

Spider Man 2 (Marvel Enterprises/Columbia Pictures, dir: Sam Raimi) Second in the popular three-part film series about the comic book superhero was one of the year's highest grossing films and won the Oscar for best visual effects.

Troy (Warner Brothers Pictures/Helena Productions, dir: Wolfgang Petersen) Historical war drama set against the backdrop of the ancient war between Troy and Sparta was one of the year's highest grossing films and was nominated for the Academy Award for best costume design.

2005

Batman Begins (Warner Entertainment/D.C. Comics, dir: Christopher Nolan) First in a series of films based on the Dark Knight comic book series was one of the highest grossing films of the year and the beginning of a successful three-film franchise.

Brokeback Mountain* (River Road Entertainment/Focus Features, dir: Ang Lee) Romantic drama became one of the most lauded and controversial films of the year due to its portrayal of a same sex relationship between two conflicted ranch hands. Won the Oscars for best director, best original score, and best adapted screenplay as well as nominations for best picture, best actor, best supporting actor, and best supporting actress.

Capote (United Artists/A-Line Pictures/Sony Pictures Classics, dir: Bennett Miller) Biographical drama about the life of writer Truman Capote was nomi-

nated for five Academy Awards, including best picture and best director, and received the Oscar for best actor (Phillip Seymour Hoffman).

Crash (Bob Yari Productions/DEJ Productions/Lionsgate, dir: Paul Haggis) Drama about racial and social tension in Los Angeles following a carjacking incident won Oscars for best picture and best original screenplay.

Good Night, and Good Luck (Warner Independent Pictures/2929 Entertainment, dir: George Clooney) Biographical drama depicts the efforts of broadcast legend Edward R. Murrow to discredit the anti-Communist propaganda of Senator Joseph McCarthy. Nominated for six Academy Awards including best actor, best director, best original screenplay, and best picture.

Harry Potter and the Goblet of Fire* (Heydey Entertainment/Warner Bros. Films, dir: Mike Newell) Fourth installment in the hit fantasy franchise was the highest grossing film of the year and one of the biggest box office hits internationally.

King Kong (WingNut Films/Universal Pictures, dir: Peter Jackson) Fantasy adventure film based on the life of a monstrous gorilla won the Oscars for best visual effects, sound editing, and sound mixing, and was one of the highest grossing films of the year.

Munich (Amblin Entertainment/Universal Studios, dir: Steven Spielberg) Drama about the Israeli government's retaliation for the Black September massacre during the 1972 Olympics was nominated for five Academy Awards including best picture and best director.

Star Wars III: Revenge of the Sith (Lucasfilm/Twentieth Century Fox, dir: George Lucas) The conclusion to the epic prequel trilogy set in the Star Wars universe was one of the highest grossing films of the year and was nominated for an Academy Award for best makeup.

Walk the Line (Fox 2000 Pictures/Tree Line Films, dir: James Mangold) Biographical drama about the life of musician Johnny Cash received an Academy Award nomination for best actor (Joaquin Phoenix) and won the Oscar for best actress (Reese Witherspoon).

2006

Babel (Paramount Pictures/Paramount Vantage, dir: Alejandro Gonzalez Inarritu) Drama depicting interrelated events linking the lives of characters in

Morocco, Japan, the United States, and Mexico received seven Academy Award nominations, including best picture, best director, and best supporting actress and was awarded the Oscar for best original score.

Casino Royale (Metro Goldwyn Mayer/Columbia Pictures, dir: Martin Campbell) Action/adventure based on the Ian Flemming character James Bond was one of the highest grossing films of the year and the beginning of Daniel Craig's film series portraying the famed British secret agent.

The Da Vinci Code (Imagine Entertainment/Columbia Pictures, dir: Ron Howard) Suspense film based on the best-selling novel about conspiracies within religious Christian and Catholic culture was the second highest grossing film of the year.

The Departed (Warner Bros. Pictures/Plan B Entertainment, dir: Martin Scorsese) Crime drama about police and organized crime in Boston won four Academy Awards including best picture, best director, best adapted screenplay, and best editing.

Dreamgirls (Paramount Pictures/DreamWorks, dir: Bill Condon) Musical drama based on the Motown Records industry received eight nominations for Academy Awards and won the Oscar for best supporting actress (Jennifer Hudson).

Happy Feet (Warner Bros. Pictures/Village Roadshow Pictures, dir: George Miller, Warren Coleman, and Judy Morris) Animated musical comedy about a penguin with an urge to be a dancer was one of the year's top grossing films and received the Oscar for best animated feature.

Letters from Iwo Jima (Amblin Entertainment/Warner Bros. Pictures/DreamWorks Pictures/Malpaso Productions, dir: Clint Eastwood) World War II drama depicting the Battle of Iwo Jima from the perspective of Japanese soldiers was nominated for four Academy Awards including best picture, best director, and best original screenplay and won the Oscar for best sound editing.

Pirates of the Caribbean: Dead Man's Chest* (Jerry Bruckheimer Films/Walt Disney Pictures, dir: Gore Verbinski) Second in the series of comedy/adventure films about pirate lore was the top grossing film of the year and won the Oscar for best visual effects.

The Queen (Canal+/Miramax Films, dir: Stephen Frears) Biographical drama about the life of Queen Elizabeth II following the death of Princess Diana won the Oscar for best actress (Helen Mirren) as well as a nomination for best picture.

X-Men: The Last Stand (Twentieth Century Fox/Marvel Entertainment, dir: Brett Ratner) Final film in the series based on the popular line of Marvel comic books was one of the highest grossing films worldwide and was one of the most expensive films in history at the time of its release.

2007

Harry Potter and the Order of the Phoenix* (Heydey Films/Warner Bros. Pictures, dir: David Yates) Fifth installment of the popular fantasy film series was the second highest grossing film of the year and one of the top grossing films worldwide.

Juno (Fox Searchlight/Mandate Pictures, dir: Jason Reitman) Comedic drama about a teenager coping with an unplanned pregnancy won the Oscar for best original screenplay and was nominated for three additional Academy Awards including best picture, best director, and best actress.

La Vie En Rose (Legende Films/Picturehouse, dir: Olivier Dahan) Biopic drama about the life of French singer Edith Piaf won the Oscars for best actress (Marion Cotillard) and best makeup in addition to a nomination for best costume design.

Michael Clayton (Castle Rock/Warner Bros., dir: Tony Gilroy) Suspenseful drama about a lawyer dealing with corruption and deceit surrounding a controversial class action suit was nominated for seven Academy Awards including best picture, best director, and best actor (George Clooney), and won the Oscar for best supporting actress (Tilda Swinton).

No Country for Old Men (Miramax Films/Paramount Vantage, dir: Joel Cohen and Ethan Cohen) Crime drama about a collection of characters competing for possession of a lost fortune was one of the highest rated films of the year and received Oscars for best picture, best director, best supporting actor (Javier Bardem), and best adapted screenplay.

Pirates of the Caribbean: At World's End* (Jerry Bruckheimer Films/Warner Bros. Pictures, dir: Gore Verbinski) Third in the popular fantasy series involving pirates and nautical action was the highest grossing film of the year and was nominated for two Academy Awards in best visual effects and best makeup.

Ratatouille (Pixar/Walt Disney Pictures, dir: Brad Bird) Animated comedy about a rat seeking to become a chef won the Oscar for best animated feature and was one of the top grossing films of the year.

Spider Man 3 (Columbia Pictures/Marvel Entertainment, dir: Sam Raimi) The final installment in the superhero adventure series based on the popular comic book was one of the highest grossing films of the year.

There Will Be Blood* (Miramax Films/Paramount Vantage, dir: Paul Thomas Anderson) Drama about the life of a ruthless oil prospector during the California oil rush won the Oscar for best actor (Daniel Day Lewis) and was nominated for seven additional Academy Awards including best picture, best director, and best adapted screenplay.

Transformers (DreamWorks Pictures/Paramount Pictures, dir: Michael Bay) Fantasy action film based on the poplar line of Hasbro action figures was one of the highest grossing films of the year and was nominated for three Academy Awards including best visual effects.

2008

The Curious Case of Benjamin Button (Paramount Pictures/Warner Bros. Pictures, dir: David Fincher) Romantic drama about a man who ages in reverse won thirteen Academy Award nominations, including best picture, best actor, and best director and won Oscars for best art direction, best visual effects, and best makeup.

The Dark Knight* (Legendary Pictures/Warner Brothers Pictures/D.C. Comics, dir: Christopher Nolan) The second in the series of superhero adventure films based on the popular comic book character was the highest grossing film of the year and received the Oscars for best supporting actor (Heath Ledger) and best sound editing, in addition to six other nominations.

Doubt (Miramax Films, dir: John Patrick Shanley) Drama about child molestation in a Brooklyn church community was nominated for five Academy Awards including best actress, best supporting actress, and best supporting actor.

Frost/Nixon (Imagine Entertainment/StudioCanal/Universal Pictures, dir: Ron Howard) Political drama about a series of interviews between reporter David Frost and former President Richard Nixon was awarded five Academy Award nominations including best picture, best director, and best actor.

Indiana Jones and the Kingdom of the Crystal Skull (Lucasfilm/Paramount Pictures, dir: Steven Spielberg) Fourth film in the popular action/adventure franchise about a treasure hunting archaeologist was the second highest grossing film of the year despite receiving only mediocre reviews.

Kung Fu Panda (DreamWorks Pictures/Paramount Pictures, dir: John Wayne Stevenson and Mark Osborne) Animated action comedy about a panda learning to become a kung fu fighter to save a threatened kingdom was one of the year's highest grossing films and was nominated for an Academy Award for best animated feature.

Milk (Gus Van Sant Films/Focus Features, dir: Gus Van Sant) Biopic drama about the life of San Francisco politician Harvey Milk was nominated for eight Academy Awards, including best picture and best director, and won the Oscars for best actor (Sean Penn) and best original screenplay.

The Reader (Mirage Enterprises/The Weinstein Company, dir: Stephen Daldry) Drama about individuals whose lives cross romantically against the backdrop of World War II war crimes trials received Academy Award nominations for best picture and best director and won the Oscar for best actress (Kate Winslet).

Slumdog Millionaire* (Pathe/Fox Searchlight Pictures/Warner Bros. Pictures, dir: Danny Boyle) Drama about a poor Indian man attempting to win a game show in order to save the woman he loves was nominated for ten Academy Awards and won eight Oscars, including best director and best picture.

WALL-E (Pixar/Walt Disney Pictures, dir: Andrew Stanton) Animated comedy about a romance between two robots was one of the highest grossing films of the year and received six Academy Award nominations, winning the Oscar for best animated feature.

2009

Avatar* (Lightstorm Entertainment/Twentieth Century Fox, dir: James Cameron) Epic science fiction/action film widely lauded for its innovative special effects was the highest grossing movie of the year and was nominated for nine Academy Awards, winning Oscars for best art direction, best cinematography, and best visual effects.

The Blind Side (Warner Bros., dir: John Lee Hancock) Drama about a troubled teen football player and his adopted family was nominated for two Academy Awards and won the Oscar for best actress (Sandra Bullock).

Crazy Heart (Fox Searchlight Pictures, dir: Scott Cooper) Drama about an aging country western musician involved in a new romance was nominated for three Academy Awards and won the Oscars for best actor (Jeff Bridges) and best original song.

*Harry Potter and the Half Blood Prince** (Heyday Films/Warner Bros. Pictures, dir: David Yates) The sixth film in the epic fantasy series was the second highest grossing film of the year and was nominated for the Academy Award for best cinematography.

*The Hurt Locker** (Voltage Pictures/Warner Bros., dir: Kathryn Bigelow) War drama about a team of bomb disposal officers working during the Iraq War was nominated for nine Academy Awards and won six, including best picture, best director, and best original screenplay.

Inglorious Basterds (The Weinstein Company/Universal Pictures, dir: Quentin Tarantino) World War II drama about a group of soldiers attempting to assassinate Nazi leaders was nominated for eight Academy Awards and received the Oscar for best supporting actor (Christoph Waltz).

Precious (Lee Daniels Entertainment/Lionsgate, dir: Lee Daniels) Drama about a the life of a poor teenaged mother living in a New York tenement building was nominated for six Academy Awards and won the Oscars for best supporting actress (Mo'Nique) and best adapted screenplay.

Transformers: Revenge of the Fallen (DreamWorks/Paramount, dir: Michael Bay) Action/adventure sequel to the 2007 film based on the popular line of Hasbro toys was the second highest grossing film in the United States despite mediocre reviews.

UP (Pixar/Walt Disney Pictures, dir: Pete Docter) Animated adventure film about an elderly widower and young boy was one of the year's highest grossing films and was the second animated film to be nominated for the Academy Award for best picture. *UP* won the Oscar for best animated feature.

Up In The Air (DW Studios/Paramount Pictures) Comedy drama focusing on the relationships of a traveling corporate consultant (Clooney) was nominated for six Academy Awards including

nominations for Best Picture, Best Actor, Best Director and Best Supporting Actress.

2010

Alice in Wonderland (Tim Burton Productions/Walt Disney Pictures, dir: Tim Burton) Fantasy adventure film derived from the writings of British author Lewis Carol was the second highest grossing film in the United States and was nominated for three Academy Awards, winning the Oscars for best art direction and best costume design.

Black Swan (Fox Searchlight, Cross Creek Pictures, dir: Darren Aronofsky) Psychological thriller following the life of a professional ballet dancer was nominated for five Academy Awards and won the Oscar for best actress (Natalie Portman).

The Fighter (Relativity Media/Paramount Pictures, dir: David O. Russell) Family drama focuses on the lives of professional boxers Mickey Ward and his half-brother Dickey Ecklund was nominated for seven Academy Awards and won two Oscars for best supporting actor (Christian Bale) and best supporting actress (Melissa Leo).

*Harry Potter and the Deathly Hallows Part I** (Heyday Films/Warner Bros. Pictures, dir: David Yates) The seventh film in the popular fantasy franchise was the third highest grossing film worldwide and won two Academy Award nominations for best visual effects and best art direction.

Inception (Legendary Pictures/Warner Bros. Pictures, dir: Christopher Nolan) Psychological adventure film about espionage utilizing a target's dreams was one of the highest grossing films of the year. *Inception* was nominated for eight Academy Awards and won four, including best cinematography and best visual effects.

Iron Man 2 (Marvel Studios/Paramount Pictures, dir: Jon Favreau) Sequel to the 2008 superhero action film was the third-highest grossing film of the year and was nominated for the Academy Award for best visual effects.

The King's Speech (The Weinstein Company, dir: Tom Hooper) Historical drama about King George VI's struggle to overcome a speech impediment was nominated for twelve Academy Awards and won four, including best picture, best director, best actor (Colin Firth), and best original screenplay.

127 Hours (Cloud Eight Films/Fox Searchlight, dir: Danny Boyle) Drama about a rock climber caught in the mountains after an accident was nominated for six Academy Awards including best picture, best actor, and best adapted screenplay.

Toy Story 3 (Pixar/Walt Disney Pictures, dir: Lee Unkrich) Animated film about the adventures of a group of toys competing for the love of their aging owner was the highest grossing film in North America and was nominated for five Academy Awards, including best picture, and won the Oscars for best animated feature and best original song.

True Grit (Skydance Productions/Paramount Pictures, dir: Joel & Ethan Coen) Western drama derived from a 1968 classic novel by Charles Portis was nominated for ten Academy Awards including best picture, best director, best actor, and best supporting actress.

■ Entertainment: Academy Awards

A title or name followed by an asterisk (*) indicates the presence of a full-length essay within *The 2000s in America*.

2000
Best Picture: *Gladiator**
Best Actor: Russell Crowe, *Gladiator**
Best Actress: Julia Roberts, *Erin Brockovich*
Best Supporting Actor: Benicio Del Toro, *Traffic*
Best Supporting Actress: Marcia Gay Harden, *Pollock*
Best Director: Steven Soderbergh, *Traffic*
Best Original Screenplay: Cameron Crowe, *Almost Famous*
Best Adapted Screenplay: Stephen Gaghan, *Traffic*
Best Cinematography: Peter Pau, *Crouching Tiger, Hidden Dragon*

2001
Best Picture: *A Beautiful Mind*
Best Actor: Denzel Washington, *Training Day*
Best Actress: Halle Berry, *Monster's Ball*
Best Supporting Actor: Jim Broadbent, *Iris*
Best Supporting Actress: Jennifer Connelly, *A Beautiful Mind*
Best Director: Ron Howard, *A Beautiful Mind*
Best Original Screenplay: Julian Fellowes, *Gosford Park*
Best Adapted Screenplay: Akiva Goldsman, *A Beautiful Mind*
Best Cinematography: Andrew Lesnie, *The Lord of the Rings: The Fellowship of the Ring**

2002
Best Picture: *Chicago*
Best Actor: Adrien Brody, *The Pianist*
Best Actress: Nicole Kidman, *The Hours*
Best Supporting Actor: Chris Cooper, *Adaptation*
Best Supporting Actress: Catherine Zeta-Jones, *Chicago*
Best Director: Roman Polanski, *The Pianist*
Best Original Screenplay: Pedro Almodóvar, *Talk to Her*
Best Adapted Screenplay: Ronald Harwood, *The Pianist*
Best Cinematography: Conrad L. Hall, *Road to Perdition*

2003
Best Picture: *The Lord of the Rings: The Return of the King**
Best Actor: Sean Penn, *Mystic River*
Best Actress: Charlize Theron, *Monster*
Best Supporting Actor: Tim Robbins, *Mystic River*
Best Supporting Actress: Renee Zellweger, *Cold Mountain*
Best Director: Peter Jackson, *The Lord of the Rings: The Return of the King**
Best Original Screenplay: Sofia Coppola, *Lost in Translation**
Best Adapted Screenplay: Fran Walsh, Philippa Boyens, and Peter Jackson, *The Lord of the Rings: The Return of the King*
Best Cinematography: Russell Boyd, *Master and Commander: The Far Side of the World*

2004
Best Picture: *Million Dollar Baby*
Best Actor: Jamie Foxx, *Ray*
Best Actress: Hillary Swank, *Million Dollar Baby*
Best Supporting Actor: Morgan Freeman, *Million Dollar Baby*
Best Supporting Actress: Cate Blanchett, *The Aviator*
Best Director: Clint Eastwood, *Million Dollar Baby*
Best Original Screenplay: Charlie Kaufman, Michel Gondry, and Pierre Bismuth, *Eternal Sunshine of the Spotless Mind*
Best Adapted Screenplay: Alexander Payne and Jim Taylor, *Sideways*
Best Cinematography: Robert Richardson, *The Aviator*

2005
Best Picture: *Crash*
Best Actor: Philip Seymour Hoffman, *Capote*
Best Actress: Reese Witherspoon, *Walk the Line*
Best Supporting Actor: George Clooney, *Syriana*
Best Supporting Actress: Rachel Weisz, *The Constant Gardener*
Best Director: Ang Lee, *Brokeback Mountain**
Best Original Screenplay: Paul Haggis and Bobby Moresco, *Crash*

Best Adapted Screenplay: Larry McMurtry and Diana Ossana, *Brokeback Mountain**
Best Cinematography: Dion Beebe, *Memoirs of a Geisha*

2006

Best Picture: *The Departed*
Best Actor: Forest Whitaker, *The Last King of Scotland*
Best Actress: Helen Mirren, *The Queen*
Best Supporting Actor: Alan Arkin, *Little Miss Sunshine*
Best Supporting Actress: Jennifer Hudson, *Dreamgirls*
Best Director: Martin Scorsese, *The Departed*
Best Original Screenplay: Michael Arndt, *Little Miss Sunshine*
Best Adapted Screenplay: William Monahan, *The Departed*
Best Cinematography: Guillermo Navarro, *Pan's Labyrinth*

2007

Best Picture: *No Country for Old Men*
Best Actor: Daniel Day-Lewis, *There Will Be Blood**
Best Actress: Marion Cotillard, *La Vie en Rose*
Best Supporting Actor: Javier Bardem, *No Country for Old Men*
Best Supporting Actress: Tilda Swinton, *Michael Clayton*
Best Director: Joel Coen and Ethan Coen, *No Country for Old Men*
Best Original Screenplay: Diablo Cody, *Juno*
Best Adapted Screenplay: Joel Coen and Ethan Coen, *No Country for Old Men*

Best Cinematography: Robert Elswit, *There Will Be Blood**

2008

Best Picture: *Slumdog Millionaire**
Best Actor: Sean Penn, *Milk*
Best Actress: Kate Winslet, *The Reader*
Best Supporting Actor: Heath Ledger, *The Dark Knight**
Best Supporting Actress: Penélope Cruz, *Vicky Cristina Barcelona*
Best Director: Danny Boyle, *Slumdog Millionaire**
Best Original Screenplay: Dustin Lance Black, *Milk*
Best Adapted Screenplay: Simon Beaufoy, *Slumdog Millionaire**
Best Cinematography: Anthony Dod Mantle, *Slumdog Millionaire**

2009

Best Picture: *The Hurt Locker**
Best Actor: Jeff Bridges, *Crazy Heart*
Best Actress: Sandra Bullock, *The Blind Side*
Best Supporting Actor: Christoph Waltz, *Inglourious Basterds*
Best Supporting Actress: Mo'Nique, *Precious*
Best Director: Kathryn Bigelow, *The Hurt Locker**
Best Original Screenplay: Mark Boal, *The Hurt Locker**
Best Adapted Screenplay: Geoffrey Fletcher, *Precious: Based on the Novel 'Push' by Sapphire*
Best Cinematography: Mauro Fiore, *Avatar**

■ Entertainment: Major Broadway Plays and Awards

This list contains all Broadway plays that ran for at least one full month between January 1, 2000, and December 31, 2009, and that had total runs of at least two hundred performances. It also includes plays with shorter runs that received major awards.

Shows Opening in 2000

Aida (opened March 23, 2000) 1,852 performances
  – 2000 Tony Awards: Best Original Musical Score, Elton John (music) and Tim Rice (lyrics)
Contact (opened March 30, 2000) 1,010 performances
  – 2000 Tony Awards: Best Featured Actor in a Musical, Boyd Gaines; Best Featured Actress in a Musical, Karen Ziemba; Choreographer, Susan Stroman; Best Musical, Lincoln Center Theater, André Bishop, Bernard Gersten
  – 2000 New York Drama Critics' Circle Award: Best Musical Runner-Up, John Weidman
Copenhagen (opened April 11, 2000) 326 performances
  – 2000 Tony Awards: Best Actress in a Musical, Heather Headley; Best Director of a Play, Michael Blakemore; Best Play, Michael Frayn (author), Michael Codron, Lee Dean, Royal National Theatre, James M. Nederlander, Roger Berlind, Scott Rudin, Elizabeth I. McCann, Ray Larsen, Jon B. Platt, Byron Goldman, and Scott Nederlander (producers)
  – 2000 New York Drama Critics' Circle Award: Best Foreign Play, Michael Frayn
The Dinner Party (opened October 19, 2000) 364 performances
Dirty Blonde (opened May 1, 2000) 352 performances
The Full Monty (opened September 25, 2000) 770 performances
James Joyce's The Dead (opened January 11, 2000) 120 performances
  – 2000 Tony Awards: Best Book of a Musical, Richard Nelson
  – 2000 New York Drama Critics' Circle Award: Best Musical, Shaun Davey and Richard Nelson
Jane Eyre (opened November 9, 2000) 209 performances
A Moon for the Misbegotten (opened March 19, 2000) 120 performances
  – 2000 Tony Awards: Best Featured Actor in a Play, Roy Dotrice
The Music Man (opened April 27, 2000) 699 performances

Proof (opened October 24, 2000) 917 performances
The Real Thing (opened April 17, 2000) 136 performances
  – 2000 Tony Awards: Best Actor in a Play, Stephen Dillane; Best Actress in a Play, Jennifer Ehle; Best Revival of a Play, Anita Waxman, Elizabeth Williams, Rob Kastner, Miramax Films, and The Donmar Warehouse (producers)
Riverdance (opened March 16, 2000) 605 performances
The Rocky Horror Show (opened November 15, 2000) 437 performances

Shows Opening in 2001

42nd Street (opened April 4, 2001) 1,524 performances
  – 2001 Tony Awards: Best Actress in a Musical, Christine Ebersole; Best Revival of a Musical, Dodger Theatricals, Joop van den Ende, Stage Holding
The Invention of Love (opened March 29, 2001) 108 performances
  – 2001 Tony Awards: Best Featured Actor in a Play, Robert Sean Leonard; Best Actor in a Play, Richard Easton
  – 2001 New York Drama Critics' Circle Award: Best Play, Tom Stoppard
King Hedley II (opened May 1, 2001) 72 performances
  – 2001 Tony Awards: Best Featured Actress in a Play, Viola Davis
Noises Off (opened November 1, 2001) 348 performances
One Flew Over the Cuckoos' Nest (opened April 8, 2001) 121 performances
  – 2001 Tony Awards: Best Revival of a Play, Michael Leavitt, Fox Theatricals, Anita Waxman, Elizabeth Williams, John York Noble, Randall L. Wreghitt, Dori Berinstein, and The Steppenwolf Theatre Company (producers)
The Producers (opened April 19, 2001) 2,502 performances
  – 2001 Tony Awards: Best Featured Actor in a Musical, Gary Beach; Best Actor in a Musical,

Nathan Lane; Best Featured Actress in a Musical, Cady Huffman; Best Book of a Musical, Mel Brooks and Thomas Meehan; Best Choreographer, Susan Stroman; Best Director of a Musical, Susan Stroman; Best Musical, Rocco Landesman, SFX Theatrical Group, The Frankel-Baruch-Viertel-Routh Group, Bob and Harvey Weinstein, Rick Steiner, Robert F.X. Sillerman, Mel Brooks, and James D. Stern/Douglas Meyer (producers); Best Original Musical Score, Mel Brooks
  –2001 New York Drama Critics' Circle Award: Best Musical, Mel Brooks and Thomas Meehan
Urinetown (opened September 20, 2001) 965 performances
  –2002 Tony Awards: Best Book of a Musical; Best Director for a Musical, John Rando; Best Original Musical Score, Mark Hollmann (music and lyrics) and Greg Kotis (lyrics)

Shows Opening in 2002

Edward Albee's The Goat, or Who Is Sylvia? (opened March 10, 2002) 309 performances
  –2002 Tony Awards: Best Play, Edward Albee (author), Elizabeth Ireland McCann, Daryl Roth, Carole Shorenstein Hays, Terry Allen Kramer, Scott Rudin, Bob Boyett, Scott Nederlander, and Sine/ZPI (producers)
  –2002 New York Drama Critics' Circle Award: Best Play, Richard Greenberg
Fortune's Fool (opened April 2, 2002) 127 performances
  –2002 Best Featured Actor in a Play, Frank Langella; Best Actor in a Play, Alan Bates
Frankie and Johnny in the Clair de Lune (opened August 8, 2002) 242 performances
The Graduate (opened April 4, 2002) 380 performances
Hairspray (opened August 15, 2002) 2,642 performances
  –2003 Tony Awards: Best Actor in a Musical, Harvey Fierstein; Best Actress in a Musical, Marissa Jaret Winokur; Best Featured Actor in a Musical, Dick Latessa; Best Musical, Margo Lion, Adam Epstein, The Baruch-Viertel-Routh-Frankel Group, James D. Stern/Douglas L. Meyer, Rick Steiner/Frederic H. Mayerson, SEL & GFO, New Line Cinema, Clear Channel Entertainment, A. Gordon/E. McAllister, D. Harris/M. Swinsky, and J. & B. Osher (pro-

ducers); Best Director of a Musical, Jack O'Brien; Best Book of a Musical, Mark O'Donnell and Thomas Meehan; Best Original Musical Score, Marc Shaiman (music and lyrics) and Scott Wittman (lyrics)
  –2003 New York Drama Critics' Circle Award: Best Musical
Into the Woods (opened April 30, 2002) 279 performances
  –2002 Tony Awards: Best Revival of a Musical, Dodger Theatricals, Stage Holding/Joop van den Ende and TheatreDreams (producers)
La Bohéme (opened December 8, 2002) 228 performances
Man of La Mancha (opened December 5, 2002) 304 performances
Metamorphoses (opened March 4, 2002) 400 performances
Movin' Out (opened October 24, 2002) 1,303 performances
  –2003 Tony Awards: Best Orchestrations, Billy Joel and Stuart Malina; Best Choreographer, Twyla Tharp
Oklahoma! (opened March 21, 2002) 388 performances
  –2002 Tony Awards: Best Featured Actor in a Musical, Shuler Hensley
Private Lives (opened April 28, 2002) 127 performances
  –2002 Tony Awards: Best Actress in a Play, Lindsay Duncan; Best Revival of a Play, Emanuel Azenberg, Ira Pittelman, Scott Nederlander, Frederick Zollo, Nicholas Paleologos, Broccoli/Sine, James Nederlander, Kevin McCollum, Jeffrey Seller, and Duncan C. Weldon and Paul Elliott for Triumph Entertainment Partners Ltd. (producers)
Say Goodnight, Gracie (opened October 10, 2002) 364 performances
Sweet Smell of Success (opened March 14, 2002) 109 performances
  –2002 Tony Awards: Best Actor in a Musical, John Lithgow
Thoroughly Modern Millie (opened April 18, 2002) 903 performances
  –2002 Tony Awards: Best Featured Actress in a Musical, Harriet Harris; Best Actress in a Musical, Sutton Foster; Best Choreographer, Rob Ashford; Best Musical, Michael Leavitt, Fox Theatricals, Hal Luftig, Stewart F. Lane,

James L. Nederlander, Independent Presenters Network, L. Mages/M. Glick, Berinstein/Manocherian/Dramatic Forces, John York Noble, and Whoopi Goldberg (producers); Best Orchestrations, Doug Besterman and Ralph Burns

Shows Opening in 2003

Anna in the Tropics (opened November 16, 2003) 113 performances
  –2003 Pulitzer Prize
Avenue Q (opened July 31, 2003)
  –2004 Tony Awards: Best Book of a Musical, Jeff Whitty; Best Musical, Kevin McCollum, Robyn Goodman, Jeffrey Seller, Vineyard Theatre, and The New Group (producers)
The Boy From Oz (opened October 16, 2003) 364 performances
Golda's Balcony (opened October 15, 2003) 493 performances
Henry IV (opened November 20, 2003) 58 performances
  –2004 Tony Awards: Best Director of a Play, Jack O'Brien; Best Revival of a Play, Lincoln Center Theater, André Bishop, and Bernard Gersten (producers)
I Am My Own Wife (opened December 3, 2003) 360 performances
  –2004 Tony Awards: Best Play, Doug Wright (author), Delphi Productions and Playwrights Horizons (producers)
Little Shop of Horrors (opened October 2, 2003) 372 performances
Long Day's Journey Into Night (opened May 6, 2003) 117 performances
  –2003 Tony Awards: Best Actor in a Play, Brian Dennehy; Best Actress in a Play, Vanessa Redgrave; Best Revival of a Play, David Richenthal, Max Cooper, Eric Falkenstein, Anthony and Charlene Marshall, Darren Bagert, Kara Medoff, Lisa Vioni, and Gene Korf (producers)
Nine (opened April 10, 2003) 283 performances
  –2003 Tony Awards: Best Featured Actress in a Play, Jane Krakowski; Best Revival of a Musical, Roundabout Theatre Company, Todd Haimes, Ellen Richard, and Julia C. Levy (producers)
Take Me Out (opened February 27, 2003) 355 performances
  –2003 Tony Awards: Best Featured Actor in a Play, Denis O'Hare; Best Play, Richard Greenberg (author), Carole Shorenstein Hays, Frederick DeMann, The Donmar Warehouse and The Public Theater (producers); Best Director of a play, Joe Mantello
  –2003 New York Drama Critics' Circle Award: Best Play, Richard Greenberg
Wicked (opened October 30, 2003)
  –2004 Tony Awards: Best Actress in a Musical, Idina Menzel; Best Costume Designer, Susan Hilferty
Wonderful Town (opened November 23, 2003) 497 performances

Shows Opening in 2004

Assassins (opened April 22, 2004) 101 performances
  –2004 Tony Awards: Best Featured Actor in a Musical, Michael Cerveris; Best Director of a Musical, Joe Mantello; Best Orchestrations, Michael Starobin; Best Revival of a Musical, Roundabout Theatre Company, Todd Haimes, Ellen Richard, and Julia C. Levy (producers)
Bombay Dreams (opened April 29, 2004) 284 performances
Brooklyn (opened October 21, 2004) 284 performances
Caroline, or Change (opened May 2, 2004) 136 performances
  –2004 Tony Awards: Best Featured Actress in a Musical, Anika Noni Rose
Fiddler on the Roof (opened February 26, 2004) 781 performances
Frozen (opened May 4, 2004) 128 performances
  –2004 Tony Awards: Best Featured Actor in a Play, Brían F. O'Byrne
La Cage aux Folles (opened December 9, 2004) 229 performances
  –2005 Tony Awards: Best Revival of a Musical, James L. Nederlander, Clear Channel Entertainment, Kenneth Greenblatt, Terry Allen Kramer, and Martin Richards (producers); Best Choreographer, Jerry Mitchell
A Raisin in the Sun (opened April 26, 2004) 88 performances
  –2004 Tony Awards: Best Featured Actress in a Play, Audra McDonald; Best Actress in a Play, Phylicia Rashad
Twelve Angry Men (opened October 28, 2004) 228 performances

Shows Opening in 2005

All Shook Up (opened March 24, 2005) 213 performances

Chitty Chitty Bang Bang (opened April 28, 2005) 285 performances

The Color Purple (opened December 1, 2005) 910 performances
  - 2006 Tony Awards: Best Actress in a Musical, LaChanze

Dirty Rotten Scoundrels (opened March 3, 2005) 627 performances
  - 2005 Tony Awards: Best Actor in a Musical, Norbert Leo Butz

Doubt (opened March 31, 2005) 525 performances
  - 2005 Tony Awards: Best Play, John Patrick Shanley(author), Carole Shorenstein Hays, MTC Productions, Inc., Lynne Meadow, Barry Grove, Roger Berlind, and Scott Rudin (producers); Best Actress in a Play, Cherry Jones; Best Featured Actress in a Play, Adriane Lenox; Best Director of a Play, Doug Hughes
  - 2005 New York Drama Critics' Circle Award: Best Play, John Patrick Shanley
  - 2005 Pulitzer Prize

Glengarry Glen Ross (opened May 1, 2005) 137 performances
  - 2005 Tony Awards: Best Revival of a Play, Jeffrey Richards, Jerry Frankel, Jam Theatricals, Boyett Ostar Productions, Ronald Frankel, Philip Lacerte, Stephanie P. McClelland/CJM Productions, Barry Weisbord, Zendog Productions, Herbert Goldsmith Productions, Roundabout Theatre Company, Todd Haimes, Ellen Richard, and Julia C. Levy (producers); Best Featured Actor in a Play, Live Schreiber

Jersey Boys (opened November 6, 2005) 2,241 performances (as of 2011)
  - 2006 Tony Awards: Best Musical, Dodger Theatricals, Joseph J. Grano, Pelican Group, Tamara and Kevin Kinsella, Latitude Link, and Rick Steiner/Osher/Staton/Bell/Mayerson Group (producers); Best Actor in a Musical, John Lloyd Young; Best Featured Actor in a Musical, Christian Hoff

The Light in the Piazza (opened April 18, 2005) 504 performances
  - 2005 Tony Awards: Best Score, Adam Guettel; Best Actress in a Musical, Victoria Clark

Monty Python's Spamalot (opened March 17, 2005) 1,574 performances
  - 2005 Tony Awards: Best Musical, Boyett Ostar Productions, The Shubert Organization, Arielle Tepper, Stephanie McClelland/Lawrence Horowitz, Élan V. McAllister/Allan S. Gordon, Independent Presenters Network, Roy Furman, GRS Associates, Jam Theatricals, TGA Entertainment, Clear Channel Entertainment (producers); Best Featured Actress in a Musical, Sara Ramirez; Best Director of a Musical, Mike Nichols

The Odd Couple (opened October 27, 2005) 249 performances

The Pillowman (opened April 10, 2005) 185 performances
  - 2005 New York Drama Critics' Circle Award: Best Foreign Play, Martin McDonagh

Sweeney Todd (opened November 3, 2005) 349 performances
  - 2006 Tony Awards: Best Director of a Musical, John Doyle

Sweet Charity (opened May 4, 2005) 279 performances

The 25th Annual Putnam County Spelling Bee (opened May 2, 2005) 1,136 performances
  - 2005 Tony Awards: Best Book of a Musical, Rachel Sheinkin; Best Featured Actor in a Musical, Dan Fogler

Shows Opening in 2006

Awake and Sing! (opened April 17, 2006) 80 performances
  - 2006 Tony Awards: Best Revival of a Play, Lincoln Center Theater, André Bishop, and Bernard Gersten (producers)

Bridge & Tunnel (opened January 26, 2006) 213 performances

A Chorus Line (opened October 5, 2006) 759 performances

Company (opened November 29, 2006) 246 performances
  - 2007 Tony Awards: Best Revival of a Musical, Marc Routh, Richard Frankel, Tom Viertel, Steven Baruch, Ambassador Theatre Group, Tulchin/Bartner Productions, Darren Bagert, and Cincinnati Playhouse in the Park (producers)

The Drowsy Chaperone (opened May 1, 2006) 674 performances
  - 2006 Tony Awards: Best Book of a Musical, Bob Martin and Don McKellar; Best Score, Lisa

Lambert and Greg Morrison; Best Featured Actress in a Musical, Beth Leavel
- 2006 New York Drama Critics' Circle Award: Best Musical, Roundabout Theatre Company, Todd Haimes, Harold Wolpert, Julia C. Levy, Jeffrey Richards, James Fuld Jr., and Scott Landis (producers)

Faith Healer (opened May 4, 2006) 117 performances
- 2006 Tony Awards: Best Featured Actor in a Play, Ian McDiarmid

Grey Gardens (opened November 2, 2006) 308 performances
- 2007 Tony Awards: Best Actress in a Musical, Christine Ebersole; Best Featured Actress in a Musical, Maro Louise Wilson

The History Boys (opened April 23, 2006) 185 performances
- 2006 Tony Awards: Best Play, Alan Bennett (author), Boyett Ostar Productions, Roger Berlind, Debra Black, Eric Falkenstein, Roy Furman, Jam Theatricals, Stephanie P. McClelland, Judith Resnick, Scott Rudin, Jon Avnet/Ralph Guild, Dede Harris/Mort Swinsky, and The National Theatre of Great Britain (producers); Best Actor in a Play, Richard Griffiths; Best Featured Actress in a play, Frances de la Tour; Best Director of a Play, Nicholas Hytner
- 2006 New York Drama Critics' Circle Award: Best Play, Alan Bennet

Les Misérables (opened November 9, 2006) 463 performances

The Little Dog Laughed (opened November 13, 2006) 112 performances
- 2007 Tony Awards: Best Actress in a Play, Julie White

The Pajama Game (opened February 23, 2006) 129 performances
- 2006 Tony Awards: Best Revival of a Musical, Roundabout Theatre Company, Todd Haimes, Harold Wolpert, Julia C. Levy, Jeffrey Richards, James Fuld Jr., and Scott Landis (producers); Best Choreographer, Kathleen Marshall

Rabbit Hole (opened February 2, 2006) 77 performances
- 2006 Tony Awards: Best Actress in a Play
- 2007 Pulitzer Prize

Spring Awakening (opened December 10, 2006) 888 performances
- 2007 Tony Awards: Best Musical, Ira Pittelman, Tom Hulce, Jeffrey Richards, Jerry Frankel, Atlantic Theater Company, Jeffrey Sine, Freddy DeMann, Max Cooper, Mort Swinsky/Cindy and Jay Gutterman/Joe McGinnis/Judith Ann Abrams, ZenDog Productions/CarJac Productions, Aron Bergson Productions/Jennifer Manocherian/Ted Snowdon, Harold Thau/Terry Schnuck/Cold Spring Productions, Amanda Dubois/Elizabeth Eynon Wetherell, and Jennifer Maloney/Tamara Tunie/Joe Cilibrasi/StyleFour Productions (producers); Best Book of a Musical, Steven Slater; Best Score, Duncan Sheik and Steven Sater; Best Featured Actor in a Musical, John Gallagher Jr.; Best Director of a Musical, Michael Mayer; Best Choreographer, Bill T. Jones
- 2007 New York Drama Critics' Circle Award: Best Musical, Duncan Sheik and Steven Slater

Tarzan (opened May 10, 2006) 486 performances

The Wedding Singer (opened April 27, 2006) 285 performances

Shows Opening in 2007

August: Osage County (opened December 4, 2007) 648 performances
- 2008 Tony Awards: Best Play, Tracy Letts (author), Jeffrey Richards, Jean Doumanian, Steve Traxler, Jerry Frankel, Ostar Productions, Jennifer Manocherian, The Weinstein Company, Debra Black/Daryl Roth, Ronald & Marc Frankel/Barbara Freitag, Rick Steiner/Staton Bell Group, and The Steppenwolf Theatre Company (producers); Best Actress in a Play, Deanna Dunagan; Best Featured Actress in a Play, Rondi Reed; Best Director of a Play, Anna D. Shapiro
- 2008 New York Drama Critics' Circle Award: Best Play
- 2008 Pulitzer Prize

The Coast of Utopia (opened February 18, 2007) 34 performances
- 2007 Tony Awards: Best Play, Tom Stoppard (author), Lincoln Center Theater, André Bishop, Bernard Gersten, and Bob Boyett (producers); Best Featured Actor in a Play, Billy Crudup; Best Featured Actress in a Play, Jennifer Ehle; Best Director of a Play, Jack O'Brien
- 2007 New York Drama Critics' Circle Award: Best Play, Tom Stoppard

Curtains (opened March 22, 2007) 511 performances
  –2007 Tony Awards: Best Actor in a Musical, David Hyde Pierce
Frost/Nixon (opened April 22, 2007) 137 performances
  –2007 Tony Awards: Best Actor in a Play, Frank Langella
Journey's End (opened February 22, 2007) 125 performances
  –2007 Tony Awards: Best Revival of a Play, Boyett Ostar Productions, Stephanie P. McClelland, Bill Rollick, James Dora, and Philip Geiger (producers)
Landau (opened July 10, 2007) 528 performances
Legally Blonde (opened April 29, 2007) 595 performances
Radio Golf (opened May 8, 2007) 64 performances
  –2007 New York Drama Critics' Circle Award: Best American Play
The Seafarer (opened December 6, 2007) 133 performances
  –2008 Tony Awards: Best Featured Actor in a Play, Jim Norton

Shows Opening in 2008

Billy Elliot (opened November 13, 2008) 1,304 performances
  –2009 Tony Awards: Best Musical, Universal Pictures Stage Productions, Working Title Films, Old Vic Productions, and Weinstein Live Entertainment (producers); Best Book of a Musical, Lee Hall; Best Actor in a Musical, David Alvarez, Trent Kowalik, and Kiril Kulish; Best Featured Actor in a Musical, Gregory Jbara; Best Director of a Musical, Stephen Daldry; Best Choreographer, Peter Darling
  –2009 New York Drama Critics' Circle Award: Best Musical, Elton John and Lee Hall
Boeing-Boeing (opened May 4, 2008) 279 performances
  –2008 Tony Awards: Best Revival of a Play, Sonia Friedman Productions, Bob Boyett, Act Productions, Matthew Byam Shaw, Robert G. Bartner, The Weinstein Company, Susan Gallin/Mary Lu Roffe, Broadway Across America, Tulchin/Jenkins/DSM, and The Areca Group (producers); Best Actor in a Play, Mark Rylance
Gypsy (opened March 9, 2008) 332 performances
  –2008 Tony Awards: Best Actress in a Musical, Patti LuPone; Best Featured Actor in a Musical,

Boyd Gaines; Best Featured Actress in a Musical, Laura Benanti
In the Heights (opened March 9, 2008) 1,185 performances
  –2008 Tony Awards: Best Musical, Kevin McCollum, Jeffrey Seller, Jill Furman, Sander Jacobs, Goodman/Grossman, Peter Fine, Everett/Skipper (producers); Best Score, Lin-Manuel Miranda; Best Choreographer, Andy Blankenbuehler
November (opened January 17, 2008) 205 performances
Passing Strange (opened February 28, 2008) 165 performances
  –2008 New York Drama Critics' Circle Award: Best Musical, Stew and Heidi Rodewald
Shrek the Musical (opened December 14, 2008) 441 performances
South Pacific (opened April 3, 2008) 996 performances
  –2008 Tony Awards: Best Revival of a Musical, Lincoln Center Theater, André Bishop, Bernard Gersten, and Bob Boyett (producers); Best Actor in a Musical, Paulo Szot; Best Director of a Musical, Bartlett Sher

Shows Opening in 2009

Blithe Spirit (opened March 15, 2009)
  –2009 Tony Awards: Best Featured Actress in a Play, Angela Lansbury
Exit the King (opened March 26, 2009)
  –2009 Tony Awards: Best Actor in a Play, Geoffrey Rush
God of Carnage (opened March 22, 2009) 452 performances
  –2009 Tony Awards: Best Play, Yamuna Reza (author), Robert Fox, David Pugh & Dafydd Rogers, Stuart Thompson, Scott Rudin, Jon B. Platt, The Weinstein Company, and The Shubert Organization (producers); Best Actress in a Play, Marcia Gay Harden; Best Director of a Play, Matthew Watches
Hair (opened March 31, 2009) 519 performances
  –2009 Tony Awards: Best Revival of a Musical, The Public Theater, Oskar Eustis, Andrew D. Hamingson, Jeffrey Richards, Jerry Frankel, Gary Goddard Entertainment, Kathleen K. Johnson, Nederlander Productions, Inc., Fran Kirmser Productions/Jed Bernstein, Marc Frankel, Broadway Across America, Barbara Manocherian/Wencarlar Productions, JK

Productions/Terry Schnuck, Andy Sandberg, Jam Theatricals, The Weinstein Company/ Norton Herrick, Jujamcyn Theaters, Joey Panes, and Elizabeth Ireland McCann (producers)

Joe Turner's Come and Gone (opened April 16, 2009) 69 performances
　　–2009 Tony Awards: Best Featured Actor in a Play, Roger Robinson

Memphis: A New Musical (opened October 19, 2009) 1,166 performances

Next to Normal (opened April 15, 2009) 733 performances
　　–2009 Tony Awards: Best Score, Tom Kitt and Brian Yorkey; Best Actress in a Musical, Alice Ripley

The Norman Conquests (opened April 25, 2009) 28 performances
　　–2009 Tony Awards: Best Revival of a Play, Sonia Friedman Productions, Steven Baruch, Marc Routh, Richard Frankel, Tom Viertel, Dede Harris, Tulchin/Bartner/Lauren Doll, Jamie deRoy, Eric Falkenstein, Harriet Newman Leve, Probo Productions, Douglas G. Smith, Michael Filerman/Jennifer Manocherian, Richard Winkler, Dan Frishwasser, Pam Laudenslager/ Remmel T. Dickinson, Jane Dubin/True Love Productions, Barbara Manocherian/Jennifer Isaacson, and The Old Vic Theatre Company (producers)

West Side Story (opened March 19, 2009) 748 performances
　　–2009 Tony Awards: Best Featured Actress in a Musical, Karen Olivo

■ Entertainment: Most-Watched US Television Shows

This appendix lists the top ten American television programs of each year (based on each September–April or September–May season) as ranked by the Nielsen Media Company. Titles followed by an asterisk (*) indicate that the program or series has its own full-length essay within *The 2000s in America*.

2000–2001
1. *Survivor: The Australian Outback** CBS
2. *ER* NBC
3. *Who Wants to Be a Millionaire* (Wednesday) ABC
4. *Friends* NBC
5. *Who Wants to Be a Millionaire* (Sunday) ABC
6. *Everybody Loves Raymond* CBS
7. *Who Wants to Be a Millionaire* (Tuesday) ABC
8. *NFL Monday Night Football* ABC
9. *The Practice* ABC
10. *CSI* *CBS

2001–2002
1. *Friends* NBC
2. *CSI** CBS
3. *ER* NBC
4. *Survivor: Marquesas** CBS
5. *Survivor: Africa** CBS
6. *Everybody Loves Raymond* CBS
7. *Law & Order* NBC
8. *Friends* (8:30 p.m.) NBC
9. *Will & Grace* NBC
10. *The West Wing* NBC

2002–2003
1. *CSI** CBS
2. *Joe Millionaire* Fox
3. *American Idol** (Wednesday) Fox
4. *Friends* NBC
5. *American Idol** (Tuesday) Fox
6. *Survivor: Thailand** CBS
7. *ER* NBC
8. *Survivor: Amazon** CBS
9. *Everybody Loves Raymond* CBS
10. *Law & Order* NBC

2003–2004
1. *American Idol** Fox
2. *CSI** CBS
3. *American Idol Results** Fox
4. *Survivor: All Stars** CBS

5. *Friends* NBC
6. *Survivor: Pearl Islands** CBS
7. *The Apprentice* NBC
8. *ER* NBC
9. *CSI: Miami** CBS
10. *Everybody Loves Raymond* CBS

2004–2005
1. *American Idol** Fox
2. *CSI** CBS
3. *American Idol Results** Fox
4. *Desperate Housewives** ABC
5. *Survivor: Palau** CBS
6. *Survivor: Vanuatu** CBS
7. *CSI: Miami** CBS
8. *Without a Trace* CBS
9. *Grey's Anatomy* ABC
10. *Everybody Loves Raymond* CBS

2005–2006
1. *American Idol** Fox
2. *American Idol Results** Fox
3. *CSI** CBS
4. *Desperate Housewives** ABC
5. *Grey's Anatomy* ABC
6. *Without a Trace* CBS
7. *Dancing with the Stars* ABC
8. *Survivor: Guatemala** CBS
9. *CSI: Miami** CBS
10. *House* Fox

2006–2007
1. *American Idol Results** Fox
2. *American Idol** Fox
3. *Dancing with the Stars* (Fall) ABC
4. *CSI** CBS
5. *Dancing with the Stars* (Spring) ABC
6. *Dancing with the Stars Results* (Fall) ABC
7. *Grey's Anatomy* ABC
8. *House* Fox
9. *Dancing with the Stars Results* (Spring) ABC
10. *Sunday Night Football* NBC

2007–2008

1. *American Idol* * Fox
2. *American Idol Results* * Fox
3. *Dancing with the Stars* (Fall) ABC
4. *Dancing with the Stars* (Spring) ABC
5. *Dancing with the Stars Results* (Fall) ABC
6. *Dancing with the Stars Results* (Spring) ABC
7. *Desperate Housewives* * ABC
8. *House* Fox
9. CSI* CBS
10. *Grey's Anatomy* ABC

2008–2009

1. *American Idol Results* * Fox
2. *American Idol* * Fox
3. *Dancing with the Stars* ABC
4. *CSI* * CBS
5. *NCIS* CBS

6. *The Mentalist* CBS
7. *Dancing with the Stars Results* ABC
8. *Sunday Night Football* NBC
9. *Desperate Housewives* * ABC
10. *Two and a Half Men* CBS

2009–2010

1. *NCIS* CBS
2. *Sunday Night Football* NBC
3. *Dancing with the Stars* ABC
4. *The Mentalist* CBS
5. *NCIS: Los Angeles* CBS
6. *CSI* * CBS
7. *Dancing with the Stars Results* ABC
8. *Desperate Housewives* * ABC
9. *Grey's Anatomy* ABC
10. *House* Fox

■ Entertainment: Emmy Awards

The categories and titles of the Emmy Awards changed almost every year. This list contains a selection of the television awards generally considered to be the most important. Programs followed by an asterisk (*) are the subject of their own full-length essay within *The 2000s in America*.

2000 (1999–2000)
Outstanding Drama Series: *The West Wing* (NBC)
Outstanding Comedy Series: *Will and Grace* (NBC)
Outstanding Miniseries: *The Corner* (HBO)
Outstanding Drama/Comedy Special: *Saturday Night Live: The Twenty-Fifth Anniversary Special* (NBC)
Outstanding Variety, Music, or Comedy Series: *Late Show with David Letterman* (CBS)
Outstanding Lead Actor in a Drama Series: James Gandolfini, *The Sopranos** (HBO)
Outstanding Lead Actress in a Drama Series: Sela Ward, *Once and Again* (ABC)
Outstanding Lead Actor in a Comedy Series: Michael J. Fox, *Spin City* (ABC)
Outstanding Lead Actress in a Comedy Series: Patricia Heaton, *Everybody Loves Raymond* (CBS)
Outstanding Supporting Actor in a Drama Series: Richard Schiff, *The West Wing* (NBC)
Outstanding Supporting Actress in a Drama Series: Allison Janney, *The West Wing* (NBC)
Outstanding Supporting Actor in a Comedy Series: Sean Hayes, *Will and Grace* (NBC)
Outstanding Supporting Actress in a Comedy Series: Megan Mullally, *Will and Grace* (NBC)
Outstanding Directing for a Drama Series: Thomas Schlamme, *The West Wing* (NBC)
Outstanding Directing for a Comedy Series: Todd Holland, *Malcolm in the Middle* (Fox)
Outstanding Directing for a Variety or Music Program: Louis J. Horvitz, *The Seventy-Second Annual Academy Awards* (ABC)

2001 (2000–2001)
Outstanding Drama Series: *The West Wing* (NBC)
Outstanding Comedy Series: *Sex and the City* (HBO)
Outstanding Miniseries: *Anne Frank* (ABC)
Outstanding Drama/Comedy Special: *Cirque Du Soleil's Dralion* (BRV)
Outstanding Variety, Music, or Comedy Series: *Late Show with David Letterman* (CBS)
Outstanding Lead Actor in a Drama Series: James Gandolfini, *The Sopranos** (HBO)

Outstanding Lead Actress in a Drama Series: Edie Falco, *The Sopranos** (HBO)
Outstanding Lead Actor in a Comedy Series: Eric McCormack, *Will & Grace* (NBC)
Outstanding Lead Actress in a Comedy Series: Patricia Heaton, *Everybody Loves Raymond* (CBS)
Outstanding Supporting Actor in a Drama Series: Bradley Whitford, *The West Wing* (NBC)
Outstanding Supporting Actress in a Drama Series: Allison Janney, *The West Wing* (NBC)
Outstanding Supporting Actor in a Comedy Series: Peter MacNicol, *Ally McBeal* (FOX)
Outstanding Supporting Actress in a Comedy Series: Doris Roberts, *Marie Barone* (CBS)
Outstanding Directing for a Drama Series: *The West Wing* (NBC)
Outstanding Directing for a Comedy Series: *Malcolm in the Middle* (FOX)
Outstanding Directing for a Variety or Music Program: David Mallet, *Cirque Du Soleil's Dralion* (BRV)

2002 (2001–2002)
Outstanding Drama Series: *The West Wing* (NBC)
Outstanding Comedy Series: *Friends* (NBC)
Outstanding Miniseries: *Band of Brothers* (HBO)
Outstanding Drama/Comedy Special: *America: A Tribute to Heroes*
Outstanding Variety, Music, or Comedy Series: *Late Show with David Letterman* (CBS)
Outstanding Lead Actor in a Drama Series: Michael Chiklis, *The Shield* (FX)
Outstanding Lead Actress in a Drama Series: Allison Janney, *The West Wing* (NBC)
Outstanding Lead Actor in a Comedy Series: Ray Romano, *Everybody Loves Raymond* (CBS)
Outstanding Lead Actress in a Comedy Series: Jennifer Aniston, *Friends* (NBC)
Outstanding Supporting Actor in a Drama Series: John Spencer, *The West Wing* (NBC)
Outstanding Supporting Actress in a Drama Series: Stockard Channing, *The West Wing* (NBC)

Outstanding Supporting Actor in a Comedy Series: Brad Garrett, *Everybody Loves Raymond* (CBS)

Outstanding Supporting Actress in a Comedy Series: Doris Roberts, *Everybody Loves Raymond* (CBS)

Outstanding Directing for a Drama Series: *Six Feet Under* (HBO)

Outstanding Directing for a Comedy Series: *Sex and the City* (HBO)

Outstanding Directing for a Variety or Music Program: Ron de Moraes, Bucky Gunts, and Kenny Ortega, *Opening Ceremony Salt Lake 2002 Olympic Winter Games*

2003 (2002–2003)

Outstanding Drama Series: *The West Wing* (NBC)

Outstanding Comedy Series: *Everybody Loves Raymond* (CBS)

Outstanding Miniseries: *Steven Spielberg Presents Taken* (Sci Fi)

Outstanding Drama/Comedy Special: *Cher— The Farewell Tour*

Outstanding Variety, Music, or Comedy Series: *The Daily Show with Jon Stewart*

Outstanding Lead Actor in a Drama Series: James Gandolfini, *The Sopranos** (HBO)

Outstanding Lead Actress in a Drama Series: Edie Falco, *The Sopranos** (HBO)

Outstanding Lead Actor in a Comedy Series: Tony Shalhoub, *Monk* (USA)

Outstanding Lead Actress in a Comedy Series: Debra Messing, *Will & Grace* (NBC)

Outstanding Supporting Actor in a Drama Series: Joe Pantoliano, *The Sopranos** (HBO)

Outstanding Supporting Actress in a Drama Series: Tyne Daly, *Judging Amy* (CBS)

Outstanding Supporting Actor in a Comedy Series: Brad Garrett, *Everybody Loves Raymond* (CBS)

Outstanding Supporting Actress in a Comedy Series: Doris Roberts, *Everybody Loves Raymond* (CBS)

Outstanding Directing for a Drama Series: Christopher Misiano, *The West Wing* (NBC)

Outstanding Directing for a Comedy Series: Robert B. Weide, *Curb Your Enthusiasm* (HBO)

Outstanding Directing for a Variety or Music Program: Glenn Weiss, *The Fifty-Sixth Annual Tony Awards* (CBS)

2004 (2003–2004)

Outstanding Drama Series: *The Sopranos** (HBO)

Outstanding Comedy Series: *Arrested Development** (FOX)

Outstanding Miniseries: *Angels in America* (HBO)

Outstanding Drama/Comedy Special: *Elaine Stritch: At Liberty* (HBO)

Outstanding Variety, Music, or Comedy Series: *The Daily Show with Jon Stewart* (Comedy Central)

Outstanding Lead Actor in a Drama Series: James Spader, *The Practice* (ABC)

Outstanding Lead Actress in a Drama Series: Allison Janney, *The West Wing* (NBC)

Outstanding Lead Actor in a Comedy Series: Kelsey Grammer, *Frasier* (NBC)

Outstanding Lead Actress in a Comedy Series: Sarah Jessica Parker, *Sex and the City* (HBO)

Outstanding Supporting Actor in a Drama Series: Michael Imperioli, *The Sopranos** (HBO)

Outstanding Supporting Actress in a Drama Series: Drea de Matteo, *The Sopranos** (HBO)

Outstanding Supporting Actor in a Comedy Series: David Hyde Pierce, *Frasier* (NBC)

Outstanding Supporting Actress in a Comedy Series: Cynthia Nixon, *Sex and the City* (HBO)

Outstanding Directing for a Drama Series: Walter Hill, *Deadwood* (HBO)

Outstanding Directing for a Comedy Series: Joe and Anthony Russo, *Arrested Development** (FOX)

Outstanding Directing for a Variety or Music Program: Louis J. Horvitz, *The Seventy-Sixth Annual Academy Awards*

2005 (2004–2005)

Outstanding Drama Series: *Lost** (ABC)

Outstanding Comedy Series: *Everybody Loves Raymond* (CBS)

Outstanding Miniseries: *The Lost Prince (Masterpiece Theatre)* (PBS)

Outstanding Drama/Comedy Special: *The Fifty-Eighth Annual Tony Awards* (CBS)

Outstanding Variety, Music, or Comedy Series: *The Daily Show with Jon Stewart* (Comedy Central)

Outstanding Lead Actor in a Drama Series: James Spader, *Boston Legal* (ABC)

Outstanding Lead Actress in a Drama Series: Patricia Arquette, *Medium* (NBC)

Outstanding Lead Actor in a Comedy Series: Tony Shalhoub, *Monk* (USA)

Outstanding Lead Actress in a Comedy Series: Felicity Huffman, *Desperate Housewives** (ABC)

Outstanding Supporting Actor in a Drama Series: William Shatner, *Boston Legal* (ABC)

Outstanding Supporting Actress in a Drama Series: Blythe Danner, *Huff* (Showtime)

Outstanding Supporting Actor in a Comedy Series: Brad Garrett, *Everybody Loves Raymond* (CBS)

Outstanding Supporting Actress in a Comedy Series: Doris Roberts, *Everybody Loves Raymond* (CBS)

Outstanding Directing for a Drama Series: J. J. Abrams, *Lost** (ABC)

Outstanding Directing for a Comedy Series: Charles McDougall, *Desperate Housewives** (ABC)

Outstanding Directing for a Variety or Music Program: Bucky Gunts, *Games of the XXVIII Olympiad—Opening Ceremony*

2006 (2005–2006)

Outstanding Drama Series: *24** (FOX)

Outstanding Comedy Series: *The Office** (NBC)

Outstanding Miniseries: *Elizabeth I* (HBO)

Outstanding Drama/Comedy Special: *The XX Olympic Winter Games—Opening Ceremony* (NBC)

Outstanding Variety, Music, or Comedy Series: *The Daily Show with Jon Stewart* (Comedy Central)

Outstanding Lead Actor in a Drama Series: Kiefer Sutherland, *24** (FOX)

Outstanding Lead Actress in a Drama Series: Mariska Hargitay, *Law & Order: Special Victims Unit* (NBC)

Outstanding Lead Actor in a Comedy Series: Tony Shalhoub, *Monk* (USA)

Outstanding Lead Actress in a Comedy Series: Julia Louis-Dreyfus, *The New Adventures of Old Christine* (CBS)

Outstanding Supporting Actor in a Drama Series: Alan Alda, *The West Wing* (NBC)

Outstanding Supporting Actress in a Drama Series: Blythe Danner, *Huff* (Showtime)

Outstanding Supporting Actor in a Comedy Series: Jeremy Piven, *Entourage* (HBO)

Outstanding Supporting Actress in a Comedy Series: Megan Mullally, *Will & Grace*

Outstanding Directing for a Drama Series: *24** (FOX)

Outstanding Directing for a Comedy Series: *My Name Is Earl* (NBC)

Outstanding Directing for a Variety or Music Program: Louis J. Horvitz, *The Seventy-Eighth Annual Academy Awards* (ABC)

2007 (2006–2007)

Outstanding Drama Series: *The Sopranos** (HBO)

Outstanding Comedy Series: *30 Rock* (NBC)

Outstanding Miniseries: *Broken Trail* (AMC)

Outstanding Drama/Comedy Special: Prime Suspect: *The Final Act (Masterpiece Theatre)* (PBS)

Outstanding Variety, Music, or Comedy Series: *The Daily Show with Jon Stewart* (Comedy Central)

Outstanding Lead Actor in a Drama Series: James Spader, *Boston Legal* (ABC)

Outstanding Lead Actress in a Drama Series: Sally Field, *Brothers & Sisters* (ABC)

Outstanding Lead Actor in a Comedy Series: Ricky Gervais, *Extras* (HBO)

Outstanding Lead Actress in a Comedy Series: America Ferrera, *Ugly Betty* (ABC)

Outstanding Supporting Actor in a Drama Series: Terry O'Quinn, *Lost** (ABC)

Outstanding Supporting Actress in a Drama Series: Katherine Heigl, *Grey's Anatomy* (ABC)

Outstanding Supporting Actor in a Comedy Series: Jeremy Piven, *Entourage* (HBO)

Outstanding Supporting Actress in a Comedy Series: Jaime Pressly, *My Name Is Earl* (NBC)

Outstanding Directing for a Drama Series: Richard Shepard, *Ugly Betty* (ABC)

Outstanding Directing for a Comedy Series: Alan Taylor, *The Sopranos** (HBO)

Outstanding Directing for a Variety or Music Program: Rob Marshall, *Tony Bennett: An American Classic* (NBC)

2008 (2007–2008)

Outstanding Drama Series: *Mad Men** (AMC)

Outstanding Comedy Series: *30 Rock* (NBC)

Outstanding Miniseries: *John Adams* (HBO)

Outstanding Drama/Comedy Special: *Mr. Warmth: The Don Rickles Project* (HBO)

Outstanding Variety, Music, or Comedy Series: *The Daily Show with Jon Stewart* (Comedy Central)

Outstanding Lead Actor in a Drama Series: Bryan Cranston, *Breaking Bad* (AMC)

Outstanding Lead Actress in a Drama Series: Glenn Close, *Damages* (FX)

Outstanding Lead Actor in a Comedy Series: Alec Baldwin, *30 Rock* (NBC)

Outstanding Lead Actress in a Comedy Series: Tina Fey*, *30 Rock* (NBC)

Outstanding Supporting Actor in a Drama Series: Zeljko Ivanek, *Damages* (FX)

Outstanding Supporting Actress in a Drama Series: Dianne Wiest, *In Treatment* (HBO)

Outstanding Supporting Actor in a Comedy Series: Jeremy Piven, *Entourage* (HBO)

Outstanding Supporting Actress in a Comedy Series: Jean Smart, *Samantha Who?* (ABC)

Outstanding Directing for a Drama Series: Greg Yaitanes, *House* (FOX)

Outstanding Directing for a Comedy Series: Barry Sonnenfeld, *Pushing Daisies* (ABC)

Outstanding Directing for a Variety or Music Program: Louis J. Horvitz, *The Eightieth Annual Academy Awards* (ABC)

2009 (2008–2009)

Outstanding Drama Series: *Mad Men** (AMC)

Outstanding Comedy Series: *30 Rock* (NBC)

Outstanding Miniseries: *Little Dorrit (Masterpiece)* (PBS)

Outstanding Drama/Comedy Special: *The Kennedy Center Honors* (CBS)

Outstanding Variety, Music, or Comedy Series: *The Daily Show with Jon Stewart* (Comedy Central)

Outstanding Lead Actor in a Drama Series: Bryan Cranston, *Breaking Bad* (AMC)

Outstanding Lead Actress in a Drama Series: Glenn Close, *Damages* (FX)

Outstanding Lead Actor in a Comedy Series: Alec Baldwin, *30 Rock* (NBC)

Outstanding Lead Actress in a Comedy Series: Toni Collette, *United States of Tara* (Showtime)

Outstanding Supporting Actor in a Drama Series: Michael Emerson, *Lost** (ABC)

Outstanding Supporting Actress in a Drama Series: Cherry Jones, *24** (FOX)

Outstanding Supporting Actor in a Comedy Series: Jon Cryer, *Two and a Half Men* (CBS)

Outstanding Supporting Actress in a Comedy Series: Kristin Chenoweth, *Pushing Daisies* (ABC)

Outstanding Directing for a Drama Series: Rod Holcomb, *ER* (NBC)

Outstanding Directing for a Comedy Series: Jeff Blitz, *The Office** (NBC)

2010 (2009–2010)

Outstanding Drama Series: *Mad Men** (AMC)

Outstanding Comedy Series: *Modern Family** (ABC)

Outstanding Miniseries: *The Pacific* (HBO)

Outstanding Drama/Comedy Special: *The Kennedy Center Honors* (CBS)

Outstanding Variety, Music, or Comedy Series: *The Daily Show with Jon Stewart* (Comedy Central)

Outstanding Lead Actor in a Drama Series: Bryan Cranston, *Breaking Bad* (AMC)

Outstanding Lead Actress in a Drama Series: Kyra Sedgwick, *The Closer* (TNT)

Outstanding Lead Actor in a Comedy Series: Jim Parsons, *The Big Bang Theory* (CBS)

Outstanding Lead Actress in a Comedy Series: Edie Falco, *Nurse Jackie* (Showtime)

Outstanding Supporting Actor in a Drama Series: Aaron Paul, *Breaking Bad* (AMC)

Outstanding Supporting Actress in a Drama Series: Archie Panjabi, *The Good Wife* (CBS)

Outstanding Supporting Actor in a Comedy Series: Eric Stonestreet, *Modern Family** (ABC)

Outstanding Supporting Actress in a Comedy Series: Jane Lynch, *Glee* (FOX)

Outstanding Directing for a Drama Series: Steve Shill, *Dexter* (Showtime)

Outstanding Directing for a Comedy Series: Ryan Murphy, *Glee* (FOX)

■ Entertainment: Top Selling Video Games of the 2000s

This appendix lists the ten best-selling video games for each year of the 2000s (between January 1, 2000 and December 31, 2009). Entries include PC games as well as console games. Games are listed from highest sales to lowest for each year.

Best-Selling Video Games of 2000

Title	Console	Publisher	Year Released*
Pokémon Silver	Game Boy Color	Nintendo	
Pokémon Gold	Game Boy Color	Nintendo	
Pokémon Yellow	Game Boy	Nintendo	1999
Pokémon Stadium	N64	Nintendo	
Tony Hawk's Pro Skater 2	Playstation	Activision	1999
Legend of Zelda: Majora's Mask	N64	Nintendo	
Tony Hawk's Pro Skater	Playstation	Activision	1999
Gran Turismo 2	Playstation	Sony	1999
Pokémon Blue	Game Boy	Nintendo	1998
Pokémon Red	Game Boy	Nintendo	1998

*In the event the publication year is different

Best-Selling Video Games of 2001

Title	Console	Publisher	Year Released
Grand Theft Auto 3	Playstation 2	Rockstar Games	
Madden NFL 2002	Playstation 2	Electronic Arts	
Pokémon Crystal	Gameboy Color	Nintendo	
Metal Gear Solid 2: Sons of Liberty	Playstation 2	Konami	
Super Mario Advance	Gameboy Advance	Nintendo	
Gran Turismo 3: A-Spec	Playstation 2	Sony	
Tony Hawk's Pro Skater 3	Playstation 2	Activision	
Tony Hawk's Pro Skater 2	Playstation	Activision	2000
Pokémon Silver	Gameboy Color	Nintendo	2000
Driver 2	Playstation	Infogames	2000

Best-Selling Video Games of 2002

Title	Console	Publisher	Year Released
Grand Theft Auto: Vice City	Playstation 2	Rockstar Games	
Grand Theft Auto 3	Playstation 2	Rockstar Games	2001
Madden NFL 2003	Playstation 2	Electronic Arts	
Super Mario Advance 2	Game Boy Advance	Nintendo	
Gran Turismo 3: A-Spec	Playstation 2	Sony	2001
Medal of Honor Frontline	Playstation 2	Electronic Arts	
Spider-Man: The Movie	Playstation 2	Activision	
Kingdom Hearts	Playstation 2	Square EA	
Halo	Xbox	Microsoft	2001
Super Mario Sunshine	Gamecube	Nintendo	

Best-Selling Video Games of 2003

Title	Console	Publisher	Year Released
Madden NFL 2004	Playstation 2	Electronic Arts	
Pokémon Ruby	Gameboy Advance	Nintendo	
Pokémon Sapphire	Gameboy Advance	Nintendo	
Need for Speed: Underground	Playstation 2	Electronic Arts	
Zelda: The Wind Waker	Gamecube	Nintendo	
Grand Theft Auto: Vice City	Playstation 2	Rockstar Games	2002
Mario Kart: Double Dash	Gamecube	Nintendo	
Tony Hawk's Underground	Playstation 2	Activision	
Enter the Matrix	Playstation 2	Atari	
Medal of Honor: Rising Sun	Playstation 2	Electronic Arts	

Best-Selling Video Games of 2004

Title	Console	Publisher	Year Released
Grand Theft Auto: San Andreas	Playstation 2	Rockstar Games	
Halo 2	Xbox	Microsoft	
Madden NFL 2005	Playstation 2	Electronic Arts	
ESPN NFL 2K5	Playstation 2	2K Sports	
Need for Speed Underground 2	Playstation 2	Electronic Arts	
Pokémon FireRed	Gameboy Advance	Nintendo	
NBA Live 2005	Playstation 2	Electronic Arts	
Spider-Man 2	Playstation 2	Activision	
Halo: Combat Evolved	Xbox	Microsoft	2001
ESPN NFL 2K5	Xbox	2K Sports	

Best-Selling Video Games of 2005

Title	Console	Publisher	Year Released
Madden NFL 06	Playstation 2	Electronic Arts	
Pokémon Emerald	Gameboy Advance	Nintendo	
Gran Turismo 4	Playstation 2	Sony	
Madden NFL 06	Xbox	Electronic Arts	
NCAA Football 06	Playstation 2	Electronic Arts	
Star Wars: Battlefront II	Playstation 2	Lucas Arts	
MVP Baseball 2005	Playstation 2	Electronic Arts	
Star Wars Episode III: Revenge of the Sith	Playstation 2	Lucas Arts	
NBA Live 06	Playstation 2	Electronic Arts	
LEGO Star Wars	Playstation 2	Eidos	

Best-Selling Video Games of 2006

Title	Console	Publisher	Year Released
Madden NFL 07	Playstation 2	Electronic Arts	
New Super Mario Bros.	DS	Nintendo	
Gears of War	Xbox 360	Microsoft	
Kingdom Hearts II	Playstation 2	Square Enix	
Guitar Hero II	Playstation 2	Activision	
Final Fantasy XII	Playstation 2	Square Enix	
Brain Age: Train Your Brain	DS	Nintendo	
Madden NFL 07	Xbox 360	Electronic Arts	
Ghost Recon: Advanced Warfighter	Xbox 360	Ubisoft	
NCAA Football 07	Playstation 2	Electronic Arts	

Best-Selling Video Games of 2007

Title	Console	Publisher	Year Released
Halo 3	Xbox 360	Microsoft	
Wii Play	Wii	Nintendo	
Call of Duty 4: Modern Warfare	Xbox 360	Activision	
Guitar Hero III: Legends of Rock	Playstation 2	Activision	
Super Mario Galaxy	Wii	Nintendo	
Pokémon Diamond	DS	Nintendo	
Madden NFL 08	Playstation 2	Electronic Arts	
Guitar Hero II	Playstation	Activision	2006
Assassin's Creed	Xbox 360	Ubisoft	
Mario Party 8	Wii	Nintendo	

Best-Selling Video Games of 2008

Title	Console	Publisher	Year Released
Wii Play	Wii	Nintendo	2007
Mario Kart Wii	Wii	Nintendo	
Wii Fit	Wii	Nintendo	
Super Smash Bros. Brawl	Wii	Nintendo	
Grand Theft Auto IV	Xbox 360	Rockstar	
Call of Duty: World at War	Xbox 360	Activision	
Gears of War 2	Xbox 360	Microsoft	
Grand Theft Auto IV	Playstation 3	Rockstar	
Madden NFL 09	Xbox 360	Electronic Arts	
Mario Kart DS	DS	Nintendo	

Best-Selling Video Games of 2009

Title	Console	Publisher	Year Released
Call of Duty: Modern Warfare 2	Xbox 360	Activision	
Call of Duty: Modern Warfare 2	Playstation 3	Activision	
New Super Mario Bros.	Wii	Nintendo	
Assassin's Creed II	Xbox 360	Ubisoft	
Left 4 Dead 2	Xbox 360	Electronic Arts	
Wii Sports Resort	Wii	Nintendo	
Wii Fit Plus	Wii	Nintendo	
Assassin's Creed II	Playstation 3	Ubisoft	
Dragon Age: Origins	Xbox 360	Electronic Arts	
Mario Kart Wii	Wii	Nintendo	

■ Literature: Best-Selling US Books

2000 Fiction
1. *The Brethren*, John Grisham
2. *The Mark*, Jerry B. Jenkins and Tim La Haye
3. *The Bear and the Dragon*, Tom Clancy
4. *The Indwelling*, Jerry B. Jenkins and Tim La Haye
5. *The Last Precinct*, Patricia Cornwell
6. *Journey*, Danielle Steel
7. *The Rescue*, Nicholas Sparks
8. *Roses Are Red*, James Patterson
9. *Cradle and All*, James Patterson
10. *The House on Hope Street*, Danielle Steel

2000 Nonfiction
1. *Who Moved My Cheese?*, Spencer Johnson
2. *Guinness World Records 2001*
3. *Body for Life*, Bill Phillips
4. *Tuesdays with Morrie*, Mitch Albom
5. *The Beatles Anthology*, The Beatles
6. *The O'Reilly Factor*, Bill O'Reilly
7. *Relationship Rescue*, Dr. Phil McGraw
8. *The Millionaire Mind*, Thomas J. Stanley
9. *Ten Things I Wish I'd Known—Before I Went Out into the Real World*, Maria Shriver
10. *Eating Well for Optimum Health*, Andrew Weil, MD

2001 Fiction
1. *Desecration*, Jerry B. Jenkins and Tim La Haye
2. *Skipping Christmas*, John Grisham
3. *A Painted House*, John Grisham
4. *Dreamcatcher*, Stephen King
5. *The Corrections*, Jonathan Franzen
6. *Black House*, Stephen King and Peter Straub
7. *Last Man Standing*, David Baldacci
8. *Valhalla Rising*, Clive Cussler
9. *A Day Late and a Dollar Short*, Terri McMillan
10. *Violets Are Blue*, James Patterson

2001 Nonfiction
1. *The Prayer of Jabez*, Bruce Wilkinson
2. *Secrets of the Vine*, Bruce Wilkinson
3. *Who Moved My Cheese?*, Spencer Johnson
4. *John Adams*, David McCullough
5. *Guinness World Records 2002*
6. *The Prayer of Jabez for Women*, Darlene Wilkinson
7. *The No-Spin Zone*, Bill O'Reilly
8. *Body for Life*, Bill Phillips
9. *How I Play Golf*, Tiger Woods
10. *Jack*, Jack Welch

2002 Fiction
1. *The Summons*, John Grisham
2. *Red Rabbit*, Tom Clancy
3. *The Remnant*, Jerry B. Jenkins and Tim La Haye
4. *The Lovely Bones*, Alice Sebold, Little
5. *Prey*, Michael Crichton
6. *Skipping Christmas*, John Grisham
7. *The Shelters of Stone*, Jean M. Auel
8. *Four Blind Mice*, James Patterson, Little
9. *Everything's Eventual*, Stephen King
10. *The Nanny Diaries*, Emma McLaughlin and Nicola Kraus

2002 Nonfiction
1. *Self Matters*, Dr. Phil McGraw
2. *A Life God Rewards*, Bruce Wilkinson with David Kopp
3. *Let's Roll!*, Lisa Beamer with Ken Abraham
4. *Guinness World Records 2003*
5. *Who Moved My Cheese?*, Spencer Johnson
6. *Leadership*, Rudolph W. Giuliani
7. *The Prayer of Jabez for Women*, Darlene Wilkinson
8. *Bush at War*, Bob Woodward
9. *Portrait of a Killer*, Patricia Cornwell
10. *Body for Life*, Bill Phillips

2003 Fiction
1. *Harry Potter and the Order of the Phoenix*, J. K. Rowling
2. The *Da Vinci Code*, Dan Brown
3. *The Five People You Meet in Heaven*, Mitch Albom
4. *The King of Torts*, John Grisham
5. *Bleachers*, John Grisham
6. *Armageddon*, Tim La Haye and Jerry B. Jenkins
7. *The Teeth of the Tiger*, Tom Clancy
8. *The Big Bad Wolf*, James Patterson
9. *Blow Fly*, Patricia Cornwell
10. *The Lovely Bones*, Alice Sebold

2003 Nonfiction
1. *The Purpose-Driven Life*, Rick Warren
2. *The South Beach Diet*, Arthur Agatston, MD

3. *Atkins for Life*, Robert Atkins, MD
4. *The Ultimate Weight Solution*, Dr. Phil McGraw
5. *Living History*, Hillary Rodham Clinton
6. *Lies: And the Lying Liars Who Tell Them*, Al Franken
7. *Guinness World Records 2004*
8. *Who's Looking Out for You?*, Bill O'Reilly
9. *Dude, Where's My Country?*, Michael Moore
10. *A Royal Duty*, Paul Burrell

2004 Fiction

1. *The Da Vinci Code*, Dan Brown
2. *The Five People You Meet in Heaven*, Mitch Albom
3. *The Last Juror*, John Grisham
4. *Glorious Appearing*, Tim LaHaye and Jerry B. Jenkins
5. *Angels & Demons*, Dan Brown
6. *State of Fear*, Michael Crichton
7. *London Bridges*, James Patterson
8. *Trace*, Patricia Cornwell
9. *The Rule of Four*, Ian Caldwell and Dustin Thomason
10. *The Da Vinci Code: Special Illustrated Collector's Edition*, Dan Brown

2004 Nonfiction

1. *The Purpose-Driven Life*, Rick Warren
2. *The South Beach Diet*, Arthur Agatston, MD
3. *My Life*, Bill Clinton
4. *America (The Book)*, Jon Stewart and the *Daily Show* writers
5. *The South Beach Diet Cookbook*, Arthur Agatston, MD
6. *Family First*, Dr. Phil McGraw
7. *He's Just Not That into You*, Greg Behrendt and Liz Tuccillo
8. *Eats, Shoots & Leaves*, Lynne Truss
9. *Your Best Life Now: 7 Steps to Living at Your Full Potential*, Joel Osteen
10. *Guinness World Records 2005*

2005 Fiction

1. *The Broker*, John Grisham
2. *The Da Vinci Code*, Dan Brown
3. *Mary, Mary*, James Patterson
4. *At First Sight*, Nicholas Sparks
5. *Predator*, Patricia Cornwell
6. *True Believer*, Nicholas Sparks
7. *Light from Heaven*, Jan Karon
8. *The Historian*, Elizabeth Kostova
9. *The Mermaid Chair*, Sue Monk
10. *Eleven on Top*, Janet Evanovich

2005 Nonfiction

1. *Natural Cures "They" Don't Want You to Know About*, Kevin Trudeau
2. *Your Best Life Now: 7 Steps to Living at Your Full Potential*, Joel Osteen
3. *The Purpose-Driven Life*, Rick Warren
4. *You: The Owner's Manual*, Michael F. Roizen, MD, and Mehmet C. Oz, MD
5. *1776*, David McCullough
6. *The World Is Flat*, Thomas L. Friedman
7. *Love Smart: Find the One You Want, Fix the One You Got*, Dr. Phil McGraw
8. *Blink: The Power of Thinking Without Thinking*, Malcolm Gladwell
9. *Freakonomics*, Steven D. Levitt and Stephen J. Dubner
10. *Guinness World Records 2006*

2006 Fiction

1. *For One More Day*, Mitch Albom
2. *Cross*, James Patterson, Little
3. *Dear John*, Nicholas Sparks
4. *Next*, Michael Crichton
5. *Hannibal Rising*, Thomas Harris
6. *Lisey's Story*, Stephen King
7. *Twelve Sharp*, Janet Evanovich
8. *Cell*, Stephen King
9. *Beach Road*, James Patterson and Peter de Jonge
10. *The Fifth Horseman*, James Patterson and Maxine Paetro

2006 Nonfiction

1. *The Innocent Man*, John Grisham
2. *You: On a Diet—The Owner's Manual for Waist Management*, Michael F. Roizen, MD, and Mehmet C. Oz, MD
3. *Marley & Me*, John Grogan
4. *The Audacity of Hope*, Barack Obama
5. *Culture Warrior*, Bill O'Reilly
6. *Guinness World Records 2007*
7. *The Best Life Diet*, Bob Greene
8. *Cesar's Way: The Natural Everyday Guide to Understanding and Correcting Common Dog Problems*, Cesar Millan and Melissa Jo Peltier
9. *The World Is Flat*, Thomas L. Friedman
10. *State of Denial: Bush at War Part III*, Bob Woodward

2007 Fiction

1. *Harry Potter and the Deathly Hallows*, J. K. Rowling
2. *A Thousand Splendid Suns*, Khaled Hosseini
3. *Playing for Pizza*, John Grisham
4. *The Choice*, Nicholas Sparks
5. *Lean Mean Thirteen*, Janet Evanovich
6. *Plum Lovin'*, Janet Evanovich
7. *Book of the Dead*, Patricia Cornwell
8. *The Quickie*, James Patterson and Michael Ledwidge
9. *The 6th Target*, James Patterson and Maxine Paetro
10. *The Darkest Evening of the Year*, Dean Koontz

2007 Nonfiction

1. *The Secret*, Rhonda Byrne
2. *The Dangerous Book for Boys*, Conn and Hal Iggulden
3. *Deceptively Delicious*, Jessica Seinfeld
4. *You: Staying Young—The Owner's Manual for Extending Your Warranty*, Michael F. Roizen, MD, and Mehmet C. Oz, MD
5. *I Am America (and So Can You!)*, Stephen Colbert
6. *Become a Better You: 7 Keys to Improving Your Life Every Day*, Joel Osteen
7. *The Daring Book for Girls*, Andrea J. Buchanan & Miriam Peskowitz
8. *You: On a Diet—The Owner's Manual for Waist Management*, Michael F. Roizen, MD, and Mehmet C. Oz, MD
9. *Guinness World Records 2008*
10. *The Weight Loss Cure "They" Don't Want You to Know About*, Kevin Trudeau

2008 Fiction

1. *The Appeal*, John Grisham
2. *The Story of Edgar Sawtelle*, David Wroblewski
3. *The Host*, Stephenie Meyer
4. *Cross Country*, James Patterson
5. *The Lucky One*, Nicholas Sparks
6. *Fearless Fourteen*, Janet Evanovich
7. *Christmas Sweater*, Glenn Beck
8. *Scarpetta*, Patricia Cornwell
9. *Your Heart Belongs to Me*, Dean Koontz
10. *Plum Lucky*, Janet Evanovich

2008 Nonfiction

1. *How to Live: A Search for Wisdom from Old People(While They Are Still on This Earth)*, Henry Alford
2. *Nothing to Be Frightened of*, Julian Barnes
3. *The Journal of Hélène Berr*, Hélène Berr
4. *The Solitary Vice: Against Reading*, Mikita Brottman
5. *Abraham Lincoln: A Life*, Michael Burlingame
6. *The Forever War*, Dexter Filkins
7. *Outliers: The Story of Success*, Malcolm Gladwell
8. *The Hemingses of Monticello: An American Family*, Annette Gordon-Reed
9. *Standard Operating Procedure*, Philip Gourevitch and Errol Morris
10. *Champlain's Dream*, David Hackett Fischer

2009 Fiction

1. *The Lost Symbol: A Novel*, Dan Brown
2. *The Associate: A Novel*, John Grisham
3. *The Help*, Kathryn Stockett.
4. *I, Alex Cross*, James Patterson
5. *The Last Song*, Nicholas Sparks
6. *Ford County*, John Grisham
7. *Finger Lickin' Fifteen*, Janet Evanovich
8. *The Host*, Stephenie Meyer
9. *Under the Dome*, Stephen King
10. *Pirate Latitudes*, Michael Crichton

2009 Nonfiction

1. *Going Rogue: An American Life*, Sarah Palin
2. *Act Like a Lady, Think Like a Man: What Men Really Think About Love, Relationships, Intimacy, and Commitment*, Steve Harvey
3. *Arguing with Idiots: How to Stop Small Minds and Big Government*, Glenn Beck
4. *Liberty & Tyranny: A Conservative Manifesto*, Mark R. Levin
5. *True Compass: A Memoir*, Edward M. Kennedy
6. *Have a Little Faith: A True Story*, Mitch Albom
7. *It's Your Time: Activate Your Faith, Achieve Your Dreams, and Increase in God's Favor*, Joel Osteen
8. *The Last Lecture*, Randy Pausch with Jeffrey Zaslow
9. *Stones into Schools: Promoting Peace with Books Not Bombs*, Greg Mortenson
10. *Superfreakonomics*, Steven D. Levitt and Stephen J. Dubner

■ Literature: Major Literary Awards

Nobel Prizes in Literature

2000: Gao Xingjian, China
2001: Vidiadhar Surajprasad Naipaul, United Kingdom
2002: Imre Kertész, Hungary
2003: John M. Coetzee, South Africa
2004: Elfriede Jelinek, Austria
2005: Harold Pinter, United Kingdom
2006: Orhan Pamuk, Turkey
2007: Doris Lessing, United Kingdom
2008: Jean-Marie Gustave Le Clézio, France
2009: Herta Müller, Germany

Pulitzer Prizes

2000

Fiction: *Interpreter of Maladies* by Jhumpa Lahiri
Drama: *Dinner with Friends* by Donald Margulies
History: *Freedom from Fear: The American People in Depression and War, 1929–1945* by David M. Kennedy
Biography or Autobiography: *Vera (Mrs. Vladimir Nabokov)* by Stacy Schiff
Poetry: *Repair* by C. K. Williams

2001

Fiction: *The Amazing Adventures of Kavalier & Clay* by Michael Chabon
Drama: *Proof* by David Auburn
History: *Founding Brothers: The Revolutionary Generation* by Joseph J. Ellis
Biography or Autobiography: *W.E.B. Du Bois: The Fight for Equality and the American Century, 1919–1963* by David Levering Lewis
Poetry: *Different Hours* by Stephen Dunn

2002

Fiction: *Empire Falls* by Richard Russo
Drama: *Topdog/Underdog* by Suzan-Lori Parks
History: *The Metaphysical Club: A Story of Ideas in America* by Louis Menand
Biography or Autobiography: *John Adams* by David McCullough
Poetry: *Practical Gods* by Carl Dennis

2003

Fiction: *Middlesex* by Jeffrey Eugenides
Drama: *Anna in the Tropics* by Nilo Cruz
History: *An Army at Dawn: The War in North Africa, 1942–1943* by Rick Atkinson
Biography or Autobiography: *Master of the Senate* by Robert A. Caro
Poetry: *Moy Sand and Gravel* by Paul Muldoon

2004

Fiction: *The Known World* by Edward P. Jones
Drama: *I Am My Own Wife* by Doug Wright
History: *A Nation Under Our Feet: Black Political Struggles in the Rural South from Slavery to the Great Migration* by Steven Hahn
Biography or Autobiography: *Khrushchev: The Man and His Era* by William Taubman
Poetry: *Walking to Martha's Vineyard* by Franz Wright

2005

Fiction: *Gilead* by Marilynne Robinson
Drama: *Doubt, a Parable* by John Patrick Shanley
History: *Washington's Crossing* by David Hackett Fischer
Biography or Autobiography: *De Kooning: An American Master* by Mark Stevens and Annalyn Swan
Poetry: *Delights & Shadows* by Ted Kooser

2006

Fiction: *March* by Geraldine Brooks
Drama: No Award
History: *Polio: An American Story* by David M. Oshinsky
Biography or Autobiography: *American Prometheus: The Triumph and Tragedy of J. Robert Oppenheimer* by Kai Bird and Martin J. Sherwin
Poetry: *Late Wife* by Claudia Emerson

2007

Fiction: *The Road* by Cormac McCarthy
Drama: *Rabbit Hole* by David Lindsay-Abaire
History: *The Race Beat: The Press, the Civil Rights Struggle, and the Awakening of a Nation* by Gene Roberts and Hank Klibanoff

Biography or Autobiography: *The Most Famous Man in America: The Biography of Henry Ward Beecher* by Debby Applegate

Poetry: *Native Guard* by Natasha Trethewey

2008

Fiction: *The Brief Wondrous Life of Oscar Wao* by Junot Diaz

Drama: *August: Osage County* by Tracy Letts

History: *What Hath God Wrought: The Transformation of America, 1815–1848* by Daniel Walker Howe

Biography or Autobiography: *Eden's Outcasts: The Story of Louisa May Alcott and Her Father* by John Matteson

Poetry: *Failure* by Philip Schultz; *Time and Materials* by Robert Hass

2009

Fiction: *Olive Kitteridge* by Elizabeth Strout

Drama: *Ruined* by Lynn Nottage

History: *American Lion: Andrew Jackson in the White House* by Jon Meacham

Biography or Autobiography: *American Lion: Andrew Jackson in the White House* by Jon Meacham

Poetry: *The Shadow of Sirius* by W. S. Merwin

National Book Awards

2000

Fiction: *In America* by Susan Sontag

Nonfiction: *In the Heart of the Sea: The Tragedy of the Whaleship* Essex by Nathaniel Philbrick

Poetry: *Blessing the Boats: New and Selected Poems 1988–2000* by Lucille Clifton

Young People's Literature: *Homeless Bird* by Gloria Whelan

2001

Fiction: *The Corrections* by Jonathan Franzen

Nonfiction: *The Noonday Demon: An Atlas of Depression* by Andrew Solomon

Poetry: *Poems Seven: New and Complete Poetry* by Alan Dugan

Young People's Literature: *True Believer* by Virginia Ewer Wolff

2002

Fiction: *Three Junes* by Julia Glass

Nonfiction: *Master of the Senate: The Years of Lyndon Johnson* by Robert A. Caro

Poetry: *In the Next Galaxy* by Ruth Stone

Young People's Literature: *The House of the Scorpion* by Nancy Farmer

2003

Fiction: *The Great Fire* by Shirley Hazzard

Nonfiction: *Waiting for Snow in Havana: Confessions of a Cuban Boy* by Carlos Eire

Poetry: *The Singing* by C. K Williams

Young People's Literature: *The Canning Season* by Polly Horvath

2004

Fiction: *The News from Paraguay* by Lily Tuck

Nonfiction: *Arc of Justice: A Saga of Race, Civil Rights, and Murder in the Jazz Age* by Kevin Boyle

Poetry: *Door in the Mountain: New and Collected Poems* by Jean Valentine

Young People's Literature: *Godless* by Pete Hautman

2005

Fiction: *Europe Central* by William T. Vollmann

Nonfiction: *The Year of Magical Thinking* by Joan Didion

Poetry: *Migration: New and Selected Poems by W. S. Merwin*

Young People's Literature: *The Penderwicks* by Jeanne Birdsall

2006

Fiction: *The Echo Maker* by Richard Powers

Nonfiction: *The Worst Hard Time: The Untold Story of Those Who Survived the Great American Dust Bowl* by Timothy Egan

Poetry: *Splay Anthem* by Nathaniel Mackey

Young People's Literature: *The Astonishing Life of Octavian Nothing, Traitor to the Nation, Vol. 1: The Pox Party* by M. T. Anderson

2007

Fiction: *Tree of Smoke* by Denis Johnson

Nonfiction: *Legacy of Ashes: The History of the CIA* by Tim Weiner

Poetry: *Time and Materials* by Robert Hass

Young People's Literature: *The Absolutely True Diary of a Part-Time Indian* by Sherman Alexie

2008

Fiction: *Shadow Country by Peter Matthiessen*

Nonfiction: *The Hemingses of Monticello: An American Family* by Annette Gordon-Reed

Poetry: *Fire to Fire: New and Selected Poems* by Mark Doty

Young People's Literature: *What I Saw and How I Lied* by Judy Blundell

2009

Fiction: *Let the Great World Spin by Colum McCann*

Nonfiction: *The First Tycoon: The Epic Life of Cornelius Vanderbilt* by T. J. Stiles

Poetry: *Transcendental Studies: A Trilogy* by Keith Waldrop

Young People's Literature: *Claudette Colvin: Twice toward Justice* by Phillip Hoose

Newbery Medal for Best Children's Book of the Year

2000: *Bud, Not Buddy* by Christopher Paul Curtis

2001: *A Year Down Yonder* by Richard Peck

2002: *A Single Shard* by Linda Sue Park

2003: *Crispin: The Cross of Lead* by Avi

2004: *The Tale of Despereaux: Being the Story of a Mouse, a Princess, Some Soup, and a Spool of Thread* by Kate DiCamillo

2005: *Kira-Kira* by Cynthia Kadohata

2006: *Criss Cross* by Lynne Rae Perkins

2007: *The Higher Power of Lucky* by Susan Patron

2008: *Good Masters! Sweet ladies! Voices from a Medieval Village* by Laura Amy Schlitz

2009: *The Graveyard Book* by Neil Gaiman

Canadian Library Association Book of the Year for Children

2000: *Sunwing* by Kenneth Oppel

2001: *Wild Girl & Gran* by Nan Gregory

2002: *Orphan at My Door: The Home Child Diary of Victoria Cope* by Jean Little

2003: *Hana's Suitcase* by Karen Levine

2004: *Boy O'Boy* by Brian Doyle

2005: *Last Chance Bay* by Anne Laurel Carter

2006: *The Crazy Man* by Pamela Porter

2007: *Johnny Kellock Died Today* by Hadley Dyer

2008: *Elijah of Buxton* by Christopher Paul Curtis

2009: *The Shepherd's Granddaughter* by Anne Laurel Carter

■ Music: Grammy Awards

This list includes winners of Grammy Awards in major categories. An asterisk (*) following a name or group indicates the presence of a full-length entry in *The 2000s in America*.

2000

Album of the Year: *Two against Nature*, Steely Dan, (artist), Richard Rainey and Steve Lillywhite, (engineers/mixers), Brian Eno and Daniel Lanois, (producers)

Record of the Year: "Beautiful Day," U2, (artist), Dave Russell, Elliot Scheiner, Phil Burnett, and Roger Nichols (engineers/mixers), Brian Eno and Daniel Lanois (producers)

Song of the Year: "Beautiful Day," U2 (songwriter)

Best New Artist: Shelby Lynne

Best Pop Vocals Performance, Female: "I Try," Macy Gray

Best Pop Vocals Performance, Male: "She Walks This Earth (Soberana Rosa)," Sting

Best Pop Performance by a Duo or Group with Vocals: "Cousin Dupree," Steely Dan

Best Pop Collaboration with Vocals: "Is You Is, or Is You Ain't (My Baby)," B. B. King and Dr. John

Best Pop Instrumental Performance: "Caravan," Brian Setzer

Best Dance Recording: "Who Let The Dogs Out," Baha Men (artist), Michael Mangini and Steve Greenberg, (producers/mixers)

Best Pop Instrumental Album: *Symphony No. 1*, Joe Jackson (artist), Dan Gellert (engineer/mixer)

Best Pop Vocals Album: *Two against Nature*, Steely Dan (artist), Dave Russell, Elliot Scheiner, Phil Burnett, and Roger Nichols (engineers/mixers)

Best Traditional Pop Vocals Album: *Both Sides Now*, Joni Mitchell (artist), Allen Sides and Geoff Foster (engineers/mixers), Larry Klein (producer)

Best Rock Performance, Female: "There Goes The Neighborhood," Sheryl Crow

Best Rock Performance, Male: "Again," Lenny Kravitz

Best Rock Performance by a Duo or Group with Vocals: "Beautiful Day," U2

Best Hard Rock Performance: "Guerrilla Radio," Rage against the Machine

Best Metal Performance: "Elite," Deftones

Best Rock Instrumental Performance: "The Call of Ktulu," Metallica and Michael Kamen

Best Rock Song: "With Arms Wide Open," Mark Tremonti and Scott Stapp (songwriters)

Best Rock Album: *There is Nothing Left to Lose*, Foo Fighters (artist), Adam Kasper (engineer/mixer), Adam Kasper (producer)

Best Alternative Music Album: *Kid A*, Radiohead* (artist), Nigel Godrich (engineer/mixer), Nigel Godrich (producer)

Best R & B Vocals Performance, Female: "He Wasn't Man Enough," Toni Braxton

Best R & B Vocals Performance, Male: "Untitled (How Does It Feel)," D'Angelo

Best R & B Performance by a Duo or Group with Vocals: "Say My Name," Destiny's Child

Best R & B Song: "Say My Name," Destiny's Child

Best R & B Album: *Voodoo*, D'Angelo (artist), Russell "The Dragon" Elevado (engineer/mixer)

Best Traditional R & B Vocals Album: *Ear-Resistible*, Temptations

Best Rap Solo Performance: "The Real Slim Shady," Eminem*

Best Rap Performance by a Duo or Group: "Forgot about Dre," Dr. Dre and Eminem*

Best Rap Album: *The Marshall Mathers LP*, Eminem* (artist), Dr. Dre and Richard Huredia (engineers/mixers)

Best Country Vocals Performance, Female: "Breathe," Faith Hill

Best Country Vocals Performance, Male: "Solitary Man," Johnny Cash

Best Country Performance by a Duo or Group with Vocals: "Cherokee Maiden," Asleep at the Wheel

Best Country Collaboration with Vocals: "Let's Make Love," Faith Hill and Tim McGraw

Best Country Instrumental Performance: "Leaving Cottondale," Alison Brown and Béla Fleck

Best Country Song: "I Hope You Dance," Mark D. Sanders and Tia Sillers (songwriters)

Best Country Album: *Breathe*, Faith Hill (artist), Julian King and Mike Shipley (engineers/mixers), Byron Gallimore (producer)

Best Contemporary Jazz Album: *Outbound*, Béla Fleck And The Flecktones (artists), Richard Battaglia and Robert Battaglia (engineers/mixers)

Best Jazz Vocals Album: In *The Moment—Live In Concert*, Dianne Reeves (artist), Erik Zobler (engineer/mixer), George Duke (producer)

Best Jazz Instrumental Solo: "(Go) Get It," Pat Metheny

Best Jazz Instrumental Album: Individual or Group: *Contemporary Jazz*, Branford Marsalis Quartet (artist), Rob "Wacko!" Hunter (engineer/mixer and producer)

Best Large Jazz Ensemble: "52nd Street Themes," Joe Lovano, (artist), James Farber (engineer/mixer)

Best Music Video, Short Form: *Learn to Fly*, Foo Fighters (artist), Jesse Peretz (video director), Tina Nakane (video producer)

Best Music Video, Long Form: *Gimme Some Truth—The Making Of John Lennon's Imagine Album*, Andrew Solt (video director), Andrew Solt, Greg Vines, Leslie Tong and Yoko Ono (video producers)

2001

Album of the Year: *O Brother, Where Art Thou?—Soundtrack*, Alison Krauss and Union, Chris Sharp, Chris Thomas King, Emmylou Harris, Gillian Welch, Harley Allen, John Hartford, Mike Compton, Norman Blake, Pat Enright, Peasall Sisters, Ralph Stanley, Sam Bush, Stuart Duncan, The Cox Family, The Fairfield Four, and Tim Blake Nelson (artists), Mike Piersante and Peter Kurland (engineers/mixers), Gavin Lurssen (mastering engineer), T-Bone Burnett (producer)

Record of the Year: "Walk On," U2 (artist), Richard Rainey and Steve Lillywhite (engineers/mixers), Brian Eno and Daniel Lanois (producers)

Song of the Year: "Fallin'," Alicia Keys* (songwriter)

Best New Artist: Alicia Keys*

Best Pop Vocals Performance, Female: "I'm Like a Bird," Nelly Furtado

Best Pop Vocals Performance, Male: "Don't Let Me Be Lonely Tonight," James Taylor

Best Pop Performance by a Duo or Group with Vocals: "Stuck In a Moment You Can't Get Out Of," U2

Best Pop Collaboration with Vocals: "Lady Marmalade," Christina Aguilera, Lil' Kim, Mya, and Pink

Best Pop Instrumental Performance: "Reptile," Eric Clapton

Best Dance Recording: "All For You," Janet Jackson (artist), Steve Hodge (mixer), Janet Jackson, Jimmy Jam and Terry Lewis (producers)

Best Pop Instrumental Album: *No Substitutions - Live in Osaka*, Larry E. Carlton and Steven Lukather (artists), Neil Citron, Steve Vai and Yoshiyasu Kumada (engineers), Steve Vai and Steven Lukather (producers)

Best Pop Vocals Album: *Lovers Rock*, Sade (artist), Mike Pela (engineer and producer)

Best Traditional Pop Vocals Album: *Songs I Heard*, Harry Connick Jr. (artist), Gregg Rubin (engineer), Tracey Freeman (producer)

Best Rock Vocals Performance, Female: "Get Right with God," Lucinda Williams

Best Rock Vocals Performance, Male: "Dig In," Lenny Kravitz

Best Rock Performance by a Duo or Group with Vocals: "Elevation," U2

Best Hard Rock Performance: "Crawling," Linkin Park

Best Metal Performance: "Schism," Tool

Best Rock Instrumental Performance: "Dirty Mind," Jeff Beck

Best Rock Song: "Drops of Jupiter," Charlie Colin, Jimmy Stafford, Pat Monahan, Rob Hotchkiss and Scott Underwood (songwriters)

Best Rock Album: *All That You Can't Leave Behind*, U2 (artist), Richard Rainey (engineer), Brian Eno and Daniel Lanois (producers)

Best Alternative Music Album: *Parachutes*, Coldplay* (artist), Ken Nelson and Michael H. Brauer (engineers), Ken Nelson (producer)

Best R & B Vocals Performance, Female: "Fallin'," Alicia Keys*

Best R & B Vocals Performance, Male: "U Remind Me," Usher*

Best R & B Performance by a Duo or Group with Vocals: "Survivor," Destiny's Child

Best R & B Song: "Fallin'," Alicia Keys*

Best R & B Album: *Songs in a Minor*, Alicia Keys* (artist), Kerry "Krucial" Brothers (engineer)

Best Traditional R & B Vocals Album: *At Last*, Gladys Knight

Best Rap Solo Performance: "Get Ur Freak On," Missy Elliott

Best Rap Performance by a Duo or Group: "Ms. Jackson," OutKast

Best Rap/Sung Collaboration: "Let Me Blow Ya Mind," Eve and Gwen Stefani

Best Rap Album: *Stankonia*, OutKast (artist), John Frye (engineer), David Sheats (producer)

Best Country Vocals Performance, Female: "Shine," Dolly Parton

Best Country Vocals Performance, Male: "O Death," Ralph Stanley

Best Country Performance by a Duo or Group with Vocals: "The Lucky One," Dan Tyminski, Harley Allen, and Pat Enright

Best Country Instrumental Performance: "Foggy Mountain Breakdown," Albert Lee, Earl Scruggs, Gary Scruggs, Glen Duncan, Jerry Douglas, Leon Russell, Marty Stuart, Paul Shaffer, Randy Scruggs, Steve Martin, and Vince Gill (artists)

Best Country Song: "The Lucky One," Robert Lee Castleman (songwriter)

Best Country Album: *Timeless—Hank Williams Tribute*, Bonnie Garner, Luke Lewis, and Mary Martin (producers)

Best Contemporary Jazz Album: *M2*, Marcus Miller (artist) Khaliq-O-Vision and Ray Bardani (engineers), David Isaac (engineer/mixer and producer)

Best Jazz Vocals Album: *The Calling*, Dianne Reeves (artist), Erik Zobler (engineer), George M. Duke (producer)

Best Jazz Instrumental Solo: "Chan's Song," Michael Brecker

Best Jazz Instrumental Album, Individual or Group: *This Is What I Do*, Sonny Rollins (artist), Troy Halderson (engineer), Lucille Rollins (producer)

Best Large Jazz Ensemble Album: *Homage to Count Basie*, Bob Mintzer Big Band (artist), Tom Jung (engineer and producer)

Best Music Video, Short Form: *Weapon of Choice*, Bootsy Collins and Fatboy Slim (artists), Spike Jonze, (video director), Deannie O'Neil and Vincent Landay (video producers)

Best Music Video, Long Form: *Recording* The Producers*: A Musical Romp with Mel Brooks*, Mel Brooks (artist), Susan Froemke (video director), Peter Gelb and Susan Froemke (video producers)

2002

Album of the Year: *Come Away with Me*, Norah Jones* (artist), Jay Newland and S. Husky Höskulds, (engineers/mixer), Ted Jensen (mastering engineer), Arif Mardin, Craig Street, Jay Newland, and Norah Jones* (producers)

Record of the Year: "Don't Know Why", Norah Jones* (artist), Jay Newland (engineer/mixer), Arif Mardin, Jay Newland, and Norah Jones* (producers)

Song of the Year: "Don't Know Why," Jesse Harris (songwriter)

Best New Artist: Norah Jones*

Best Pop Vocals Performance, Female: "Don't Know Why," Norah Jones*

Best Pop Vocals Performance, Male: "Your Body Is a Wonderland," John Mayer

Best Pop Performance by a Duo or Group with Vocals: "Hey Baby," No Doubt

Best Pop Collaboration with Vocals: "The Game of Love," Carlos Santana and Michelle Branch

Best Pop Instrumental Album: *Just Chillin'*, Norman Brown (artist), Paul Brown (engineer/mixer and producer)

Best Pop Vocals Album: *Come Away with Me*: Norah Jones* (artist), Jay Newland and S. Husky Höskulds (engineers/mixers), Arif Mardin and Jay Newland (producers)

Best Dance Recording: "Days Go By," Dirty Vegas (artist), Ben Harris, Paul Harris, and Steve Smith (producers)

Best Traditional Pop Vocals Album: *Playin' With My Friends: Bennett Sings the Blues*, Tony Bennett, (artist), Joel Moss and Tom Young (engineers/mixers), Phil Ramone (producer)

Best Rock Vocals Performance, Female: "Steve McQueen," Sheryl Crow

Best Rock Vocals Performance, Male: "The Rising," Bruce Springsteen

Best Rock Performance by a Duo or Group with Vocals: "In My Place," Coldplay*

Best Hard Rock Performance: "All My Life," Foo Fighters

Best Metal Performance: "Here to Stay," Korn

Best Rock Instrumental Performance: "Approaching Pavonis Mons by Balloon (Utopia Planitia)," The Flaming Lips

Best Rock Song: "The Rising," Bruce Springsteen

Best Rock Album: "The Rising," Bruce Springsteen (artist), Brendan O'Brien and Nick Didia (engineers/mixers), Brendan O'Brien (producer)

Best Alternative Music Album: *A Rush of Blood to the Head*, Coldplay* (artist), Ken Nelson and Mark Phythian (engineers/mixers), Ken Nelson (producer)

Best R & B Vocals Performance, Female: "He Think I Don't Know," Mary J. Blige

Best R & B Vocals Performance, Male: "U Don't Have To Call," Usher*

Best R & B Performance by a Duo or Group with Vocals: "What's Going On," Chaka Khan and The Funk Brothers

Best R & B Song: "Love Of My Life," Erykah Badu, Glenn Standridge, James Poyser, Madukwu Chinwah, Raphael Saadiq, Rashid Lonnie Lynn, and Robert Ozuna (songwriters)

Best R & B Album: *Voyage to India*, India.Arie (artist), Alvin Speights (engineer/mixer), Shannon Sanders (producer)

Best Contemporary R & B Album: *Ashanti*, Ashanti (artist), 7 Aurelius, Brian Springer, and Milwaukee Buck (engineers/mixers), 7 Aurelius and Irv Gotti (producers)

Best Rap Solo Performance, Female: "Scream a.k.a. Itchin'," Missy Elliott

Best Rap Solo Performance, Male: "Hot In Here," Nelly

Best Rap Performance by a Duo or Group: "The Whole World," Killer Mike and OutKast

Best Rap/Sung Collaboration: "Dilemma," Kelendria Rowland and Nelly

Best Rap Album: *The Eminem Show*, Eminem* (artist), Steve King (engineer/mixer)

Best Country Vocals Performance, Female: "Cry," Faith Hill

Best Country Vocals Performance, Male: "Give My Love to Rose," Johnny Cash

Best Country Performance by a Duo or Group with Vocals: "Long Time Gone," Dixie Chicks

Best Country Collaboration with Vocals: "Mendocino County Line," Lee Ann Womack and Willie Nelson

Best Country Instrumental Performance: "Lil' Jack Slade," Dixie Chicks

Best Country Song: "Where Were You (When the World Stopped Turning)," Alan Jackson (songwriter)

Best Country Album: *Home*, Dixie Chicks (artist), Gary Paczosa (engineer/mixer), Lloyd Maines (producer)

Best Music Video, Short Form: *Without Me*, Eminem* (artist), Joseph Kahn (video director), Greg Tharp (video producer)

Best Music Video, Long Form: *Westway to the World*, The Clash (artist), Don Letts (video director)

2003

Album of the Year: *Speakerboxxx/The Love Below*, OutKast (artist), Brian Paturalski, Chris Carmouche, Darrell Thorp, Dexter Simmons, John Frye, Kevin Davis, Matt Still, Moka Nagatani, Neal H. Pogue, Padraic Kernin, Pete Novak, Reggie Dozier, Robert Hannon, Terrence Cash, and Vincent Al-

exander (engineer),s/mixers. Bernie Grundman and Brian "Big Bass" Gardner (mastering engineers), André 3000, Big Boi, and Carl Mo (producers)

Record of the Year: *Clocks*, Coldplay* (artist), Coldplay*, Ken Nelson, and Mark Phythian (engineers/mixers), Coldplay* and Ken Nelson (producers)

Song of the Year: "Dance with My Father," Luther Vandross and Richard Marx (songwriters)

Best New Artist: Evanescence

Best Pop Vocals Performance, Female: "Beautiful," Christina Aguilera

Best Pop Vocals Performance, Male: "Cry Me A River," Justin Timberlake*

Best Pop Performance by a Duo or Group with Vocals: "Underneath It All," No Doubt

Best Pop Collaboration with Vocals: "Whenever I Say Your Name," Mary J. Blige and Sting

Best Pop Instrumental Performance: "Marwa Blues," George Harrison

Best Pop Instrumental Album: *Mambo Siunuendo*, Manuel Galbán and Ry Cooder (artists), Jerry Boys (engineer/mixer)

Best Pop Vocals Album: *Justified*, Justin Timberlake* (artist), Andrew Coleman (engineer), Serban Ghenea (engineer/mixer), Chad Hugo and Rob Davis (producers)

Best Dance Recording: "Come into My World," Kylie Minogue (artist), Bruce Elliott-Smith, Cathy Dennis, Phil Larsen, and Rob Davis (mixers), Cathy Dennis and Rob Davis (producers)

Best Traditional Pop Vocals Album: *A Wonderful World*, Tony Bennett and K. D. Lang (artists), Dae Bennett (engineer/mixer), T-Bone Burnett (producer)

Best Rock Vocals Performance, Female: "Trouble," Pink

Best Rock Vocals Performance, Male: "Gravedigger," Dave Matthews

Best Rock Performance by a Duo or Group with Vocals: "Disorder in the House," Bruce Springsteen and Warren Zevon

Best Hard Rock Performance: "Bring Me to Life," Evanescence

Best Metal Performance: "St. Anger," Metallica

Best Rock Instrumental Performance: "Plan B," Jeff Beck

Best Rock Song: "Seven Nation Army," Jack White*

Best Rock Album: *One By One*, Foo Fighters

Best Alternative Music Album: *Elephant*, White Stripes (artist), Liam Watson (engineer/mixer)

Best R & B Vocals Performance, Female: "Dangerously In Love 2," Beyoncé Knowles*

Best R & B Vocals Performance, Male: "Dance with My Father," Luther Vandross

Best R & B Performance by a Duo or Group with Vocals: "The Closer I Get To You," Beyoncé Knowles* and Luther Vandross

Best Traditional R & B Vocals Performance: "Wonderful," Aretha Franklin

Best Urban/Alternative Performance: "Hey Ya!," OutKast

Best R & B Song: "Crazy in Love," Beyoncé Knowles*, Jay-Z*, and Rich Harrison (songwriters)

Best R & B Album: *Dance with My Father*, Luther Vandross (artist), Ray Bardani (engineer/mixer)

Best Contemporary R&B Album: *Dangerously in Love*, Beyoncé Knowles* (artist), Tony Maserati (engineer/mixer)

Best Rap Solo Performance, Female: "Work It," Missy Elliott

Best Rap Solo Performance, Male: "Lose Yourself," Eminem*

Best Rap Performance by a Duo or Group: "Shake Ya Tailfeather," Murphy Lee, Nelly, and Sean Combs (artists)

Best Rap/Sung Collaboration: "Crazy in Love," Beyoncé Knowles* and Jay-Z* (artists)

Best Rap Song: "Lose Yourself," Eminem*, Jeff Bass, and L Resto (songwriters)

Best Rap Album: *Speakerboxxx/The Love Below*, OutKast (artist), John Frye (engineer/mixer)

Best Country Vocals Performance, Female: "Keep on the Sunny Side," June Carter Cash

Best Country Vocals Performance, Male: "Next Big Thing," Vince Gill

Best Country Performance by a Duo or Group with Vocals: "A Simple Life," Ricky Skaggs and Kentucky Thunder

Best Country Instrumental Performance: "Cluck Old Hen," Alison Krauss and Union Station

Best Country Song: "It's Five O'clock Somewhere," Don Rollins and Jim Brown

Best Country Album: *Livin', Lovin', Losin': Songs of the Louvin Brothers*, Carl Jackson (producer), Luke Wooten (engineer)

Best Contemporary Jazz Album: *34th N Lex,* Randy Brecker (artist), George Whitty (engineer/mixer and producer)

Best Jazz Vocals Album: *A Little Moonlight*, Dianne Reeves (artist), Michael O'Reilly (engineer), Arif Mardin (producer)

Best Jazz Instrumental Solo: "Matrix," Chick Corea

Best Jazz Instrumental Album, Individual or Group: *Alegría*, Wayne Shorter (artist), Clark Germain (engineer), Dave Darlington and Robert Sadin (engineers/mixers), Robert Sadin (producer)

Best Large Jazz Ensemble Album: *Wide Angles*, Michael Brecker Quindectet (artist), Jay Newland (engineer/mixer), Gil Goldstein (producer)

Best Music Video, Short Form: *Hurt*, Johnny Cash (artist), Mark Romanek (video director), Aris McGarry (video producer)

Best Music Video, Long Form: *Legend*, Mary Wharton, Mick Gochanour and Robin Klein (video producers)

2004

Album of the Year: *Genius Loves Company*, Ray Charles (artist), Al Schmitt, Ed Thacker, Joel W. Moss, John Harris, Mark Fleming, Pete Karam, Robert Fernandez, Seth Presant and Terry Howard (engineers/mixers), Doug Sax and Robert Hadley (mastering engineers), Don Mizell, Herbert Waltl, John R. Burk, Phil Ramone and Terry Howard (producers)

Record of the Year: "Here We Go Again," Norah Jones* and Ray Charles (artists), Al Schmitt, Mark Fleming, and Terry Howard (engineers/mixers), John R. Burk (producer)

Song of the Year: "Daughters," John Mayer

Best New Artist: Maroon 5

Best Pop Vocals Performance, Female: "Sunrise," Norah Jones*

Best Pop Vocals Performance, Male: "Daughters," John Mayer

Best Pop Performance by a Duo or Group with Vocals: "Heaven," Los Lonely Boys

Best Pop Collaboration with Vocals: "Here We Go Again," Norah Jones* and Ray Charles

Best Pop Instrumental Performance: "11th Commandment," Ben Harper

Best Pop Vocals Album: *Genius Loves Company*, Ray Charles (artist), Al Schmitt (engineer/mixer), John R. Burk (producer)

Best Dance Recording: "Toxic," Britney Spears* (artist), Niklas Flyckt (mixer), Avant (a.k.a. Pontus Winnberg) and Bloodshy (a.k.a. Christian Karlsson) (producers)

Best Electronica/Dance Album: *Kish Kash*, Basement Jaxx

Best Traditional Pop Vocals Album: *Stardust . . . The Great American Songbook Volume III*, Rod Stewart (artist), Andy Zulla (engineer/mixer), Steve Tyrell (producer)

Best Solo Rock Vocals Performance: "Code of Silence," Bruce Springsteen

Best Rock Performance by a Duo or Group with Vocals: "Vertigo," U2

Best Hard Rock Performance: "Slither," Velvet Revolver

Best Metal Performance: "Whiplash," Motorhead

Best Rock Instrumental Performance: "Mrs. O'Leary's Cow," Brian Wilson

Best Rock Song: "Vertigo," U2

Best Rock Album: *American Idiot*, Green Day (artist), Chris Lord-Alge and Doug McKean (engineers/mixers), Rob Cavallo (producer)

Best Alternative Music Album: *A Ghost Is Born*, Wilco* (artist), Chris Shaw and Jim O'Ruorke (engineers/mixers), Jim O'Rourke (producer)

Best R & B Vocals Performance, Female: "If I Ain't Got You," Alicia Keys*

Best R & B Vocals Performance, Male: "Call My Name," Prince

Best R & B Performance by a Duo or Group with Vocals: "My Boo," Alicia Keys* and Usher*

Best Traditional R & B Vocals Performance "Musicology," Prince

Best Urban/Alternative Performance: "Cross My Mind," Jill Scott

Best R & B Song: "You Don't Know My Name," Alicia Keys*, Harold Lilly, and Kanye West*

Best R & B Album: *The Diary of Alicia Keys*, Alicia Keys* (artist), Ann Mincieli, Anthony Duino, and Manny Marroquin (engineers/mixers)

Best Contemporary R&B Album: *Confessions*, Usher*

Best Rap Solo Performance: "99 Problems," Jay-Z*

Best Rap Performance by a Duo or Group: "Let's Get It Started," Black Eyed Peas

Best Rap/Sung Collaboration: "Yeah!," Lil Jon, Ludacris, and Usher*

Best Rap Song: "Jesus Walks," Che Smith, Kanye West*, and Miri Ben Ari

Best Rap Album: *The College Dropout*, Kanye West* (artist), Manny Marroquin (engineer/mixer)

Best Country Vocals Performance, Female: "Redneck Woman," Gretchen Wilson

Best Country Vocals Performance, Male: "Live Like You Were Dying," Tim McGraw

Best Country Performance by a Duo or Group with Vocals: "Top of the World," Dixie Chicks

Best Country Collaboration with Vocals: "Portland, Oregon," Jack White* and Loretta Lynn

Best Country Instrumental Performance: "Earl's Breakdown," Earl Scruggs, Jerry Douglas, Nitty Gritty Dirt Band (Bob Carpenter, Jimmie Fadden, Jeff Hanna, Jimmy Ibbotson, John McEuen), Randy Scruggs, and Vassar Clements

Best Country Song: "Live like You Were Dying," Craig Wiseman and Tim Nichols (songwriters)

Best Country Album: *Van Lear Rose*, Loretta Lynn (artist), Brendan Benson, Eric McConnell, and Stuart Sikes (engineers/mixers), Jack White* (producer)

Best Contemporary Jazz Album: *Unspeakable*, William Frisell (artist), Eric Liljestrand (engineer/mixer), Hal Willner (producer)

Best Jazz Vocals Album: *R.S.V.P. (Rare Songs, Very Personal)*, Nancy Wilson (artist), Jay Ashby and Jay Dudt (engineers/mixers), Jay Ashby and Martin J. Ashby (producers)

Best Jazz Instrumental Solo: "Speak Like A Child," Herbie Hancock

Best Jazz Instrumental Album, Individual or Group: *Illuminations*, Christian McBride, Gary Bartz, Lewis Nash, McCoy Tyner, and Terence Blanchard (artists), Jack Renner (engineer/mixer), Elaine L. Martone (producer)

Best Large Jazz Ensemble Album: *Concert in the Garden*, Maria Schneider (artist), David Baker and Peter Carini (engineers/mixers)

Best Latin Jazz Album: *Land of the Sun*, Charlie Haden (artist), Jay Newland and Mario Garcia (engineers/mixers), Gonzalo Rubalcaba and Ruth Cameron (producers)

Best Music Video, Short Form: *Vertigo*, U2 (artist), Alex and Martin (Alex Courtes, Martin Fougerol), (video directors), Grace Bodie (video producer)

Best Music Video, Long Form: *Concert for George*, David Leland (video director), Jon Kamen, Olivia Harrison, and Ray Cooper (video producers)

2005

Album of the Year: *How to Dismantle an Atomic Bomb*, U2 (artist), Carl Glanville, Flood, Greg Collins, Jacknife Lee, Nellee Hooper, Simon Gogerly and Steve Lillywhite (engineers/mixers), Arnie Acosta (mastering engineer), Brian Eno, Chris Thomas,

Daniel Lanois, Flood, Jacknife Lee, and Steve Lillywhite (producers)

Record of the Year: "Boulevard of Broken Dreams," Green Day (artist), Chris Lord-Alge and Doug McKean (engineers/mixers), Green Day and Rob Cavallo (producers)

Song of the Year: "Sometimes You Can't Make It on Your Own," U2

Best New Artist: John Legend

Best Pop Vocals Performance, Female: "Since U Been Gone," Kelly Clarkson*

Best Pop Vocals Performance, Male: "From the Bottom of My Heart," Stevie Wonder

Best Pop Performance by a Duo or Group with Vocals: "This Love," Maroon 5

Best Pop Collaboration with Vocals: "Feel Good Inc.," De La Soul and Gorillaz

Best Pop Instrumental Performance: "Caravan," Les Paul

Best Pop Instrumental Album: *At This Time*, Burt Bacharach (artist), Allen Sides (engineer/mixer)

Best Pop Vocals Album: *Breakaway*, Kelly Clarkson* (artist), Serban Ghenea (engineer/mixer), Clive Davis (producer)

Best Dance Recording: "Galvanize," Kamal Fareed and The Chemical Brothers (artists), Steve Dub and The Chemical Brothers (mixers), The Chemical Brothers (producer)

Best Electronic/Dance Album: *Push the Button*, The Chemical Brothers (artist), Steve Dub (engineer)

Best Traditional Pop Vocals Album: *The Art of Romance*, Tony Bennet (artist), Dae Bennet (engineer/mixer), Phil Ramone (producer)

Best Solo Rock Vocals Performance: "Devils and Dust," Bruce Springsteen

Best Rock Performance by a Duo or Group with Vocals: "Sometimes You Can't Make It Your Own," U2

Best Hard Rock Performance: "B.Y.O.B.," System of a Down

Best Metal Performance: "Before I Forget," Slipknot

Best Rock Instrumental Performance: "69 Freedom Special," Les Paul

Best Rock Song: "City of Blinding Lights," U2

Best Rock Album: *How to Dismantle an Atomic Bomb*, U2 (artist), Matthew Kettle (engineer), John P. Hampton (engineer/mixer)

Best R & B Vocals Performance, Female: "We Belong Together," Mariah Carey

Best R & B Vocals Performance, Male: "Ordinary People," John Legend

Best R & B Performance by a Duo or Group with Vocals: "So Amazing," Beyoncé Knowles* and Stevie Wonder

Best Traditional R & B Vocals Performance: "A House Is Not a Home," Aretha Franklin

Best Urban/Alternative Performance: "Welcome to Jamrock," Damian Marley

Best R & B Song: "We Belong Together," Jermaine Dupri, Johnta Austin, Manuel Seal Jr., and Mariah Carey

Best R & B Album: *Get Lifted*, John Legend (artist), Anthony Kilhoffer (engineer), Manny Marroquin (engineer/mixer)

Best Contemporary R & B Album: *The Emancipation of Mimi*, Mariah Carey (artist), Brian Garten and Dana Jon Chappelle (engineers), Philip Tan (engineer/mixer)

Best Rap Solo Performance: "Gold Digger," Kanye West*

Best Rap Performance by a Duo or Group: "Don't Phunk with My Heart," Black Eyed Peas

Best Rap/Sung Collaboration: *Numb/Encore*, Linkin Park and Shawn Carter

Best Rap Song: "Diamond from Sierra Leone," DeVon Harris and Kanye West*

Best Rap Album: *Late Registration*, Kanye West* (artist), Andrew Dawson, Anthony Kilhoffer, and Tom Biller (engineers), Mike Dean (engineer/mixer, Jon Brion (producer)

Best Country Vocals Performance, Female: "The Connection," Emmylou Harris

Best Country Vocals Performance, Male: "You'll Think of me," Keith Urban

Best Country Collaboration with Vocals: "Like We Never Loved at All," Faith Hill and Tim McGraw

Best Country Instrumental Performance: "Unionhouse Branch," Alison Krauss and Union Station

Best Country Song: "Bless the Broken Road," Bobby Boyd, Jeff Hanna, and Marcus Hummon

Best Country Album: *Lovely Runs Both Ways*, Alison Krauss and Union Station

Best Contemporary Jazz Album: *The Way Up*, Pat Metheny Group

Best Jazz Vocals Album: *Good Night, and Good Luck*, Dianne Reeves (artist), Edward Tise (engineer), Charles Paakari and Leslie Ann Jones (engineers/mixers), Allen J. Sviridoff (producer)

Best Jazz Instrumental Solo: "Why Was I Born," Sonny Rollins

Best Jazz Instrumental Album, Individual or Group: *Beyond the Sound Barrier*, Wayne Shorter Quartet (artist), and Rob Griffin (engineer/mixer)

Best Large Jazz Ensemble Album: *Overtime*, Dave Holland (artist), James Farber (engineer), Louise Holland (producer)

Best Music Video, Short Form: *Lose Control*, Ciara Harris, Fat Man Scoop, and Missy Elliott (artists) Dave Meyers and Missy Elliott (video directors), Joseph Sasson (video producer)

Best Music Video, Long Form: *No Direction Home*, Martin Scorsese (video director), Anthony Wall, Jeff Rosen, Margaret Bodde, Martin Scorsese, Nigel Sinclair, and Susan Lacy (video producers)

2006

Album of the Year: *Taking the Long Way*, Dixie Chicks (artist), Chris Testa, Jim Scott, and Richard Dodd (engineers/mixers), Richard Dodd (mastering engineer), Rick Rubin (producer)

Record of the Year: "Not Ready to Make Nice," Dixie Chicks (artist), Chris Testa, Jim Scott, and Richard Dodd (engineers/mixers), Richard Dodd (mastering engineer), Rick Rubin (producer)

Song of the Year: "Not Ready to Make Nice," Dan Wilson, Emily Robinson, Martie Maguire, and Natalie Maines (songwriters)

Best New Artist: Carrie Underwood

Best Pop Vocals Performance, Female: "Ain't No Other Man," Christina Aguilera

Best Pop Vocals Performance, Male: "Waiting On the World to Change," John Mayer

Best Pop Performance by a Duo or Group with Vocals: "My Humps," Black Eyed peas

Best Pop Collaboration with Vocals: "For Once in My Life," Stevie Wonder and Tony Bennett

Best Pop Instrumental Performance: "Mornin'," George Benson

Best Pop Instrumental Album: *Fingerprints*, Peter Frampton (artist), Aaron Swihart and Chuck Ainly (engineers/mixers), Steve Jordan (producer)

Best Pop Vocals Album: *Continuum*, John Mayer (artist), Chad Franscoviak, Joe Ferla, Michael H. Brauer (engineers/mixers), Steve Jordan (producer)

Best Dance Recording: "Sexy Back," Justin Timberlake*, Timbaland (artists), Jimmy Douglass (mixer), Justin Timberlake*, Nate (Danja) Hills, and Timbaland (producers)

Best Electronic/Dance Album: "Confessions on a Dance Floor," Madonna (artist), Mart Stent (engineer/mixer), Stuart Price (producer)

Best Traditional Pop Vocals Album: *Duets: An American Classic*, Tony Bennet (artist), Dae Bennet (engineer/mixer), Phil Ramone (producer)

Best Solo Rock Vocals Performance: "Someday Baby," Bob Dylan

Best Rock Performance by a Duo or Group with Vocals: "Dani California," Red Hot Chili Peppers

Best Hard Rock Performance: "Woman," Wolfmother

Best Metal Performance: "Eyes of the Insane," Slayer

Best Rock Instrumental Performance: "The Wizard Turns On . . . ," The Flaming Lips

Best Rock Song: "Dani California," Red Hot Chili Peppers

Best Rock Album: *Stadium Arcadium*, Red Hot Chili Peppers (artist), Andrew Scheps, Mark Linett, and Ryan Hewitt (engineers/mixers), Rick Rubin (producer)

Best Alternative Music Album: *St. Elsewhere*, Gnarls Barkley (artist), Ben Allen, Kennie Takahashi (engineers/mixers)

Best R & B Vocals Performance, Female: "Be Without You," Mary J. Blige

Best R & B Vocals Performance, Male: "Heaven," John Legend

Best R & B Performance by a Duo or Group with Vocals: "Family Affair," John Legend

Best Traditional R & B Vocals Performance: "God Bless the Child," Al Jarreau, George Benson, and Jill Scott (artists)

Best Urban/Alternative Performance: "Crazy," Gnarls Barkley

Best R & B Song: "Be Without You," Bryan Michael Cox, Jason Perry, Johnta Austin, and Mary J. Blige

Best R & B Album: *The Breakthrough*, Mary J. Blige (artist), Patrick Dillett (engineer/mixer)

Best Contemporary R & B Album: *B'Day*, Beyoncé Knowles* (artist), Jason Goldstein and Jim Caruana (engineers/mixers)

Best Rap Solo Performance: "What You Know," T.I.

Best Rap Performance by a Duo or Group: "Ridin," Chamillionaire, Krayzie Bone

Best Rap/Sung Collaboration: "My Love," Justin Timberlake* and T.I.

Best Rap Song: "Money Maker," Ludacris, Pharrell Williams

694 Music: Grammy Awards

The 2000s in America

Best Rap Album: *Release Therapy*, Ludacris (artist), Joshua Monroy and Phil Tan (engineers/mixers)

Best Country Vocals Performance, Female: "Jesus, Take the Wheel," Carrie Underwood

Best Country Vocals Performance, Male: "The Reason Why," Vince Gill

Best Country Performance by a Duo or Group with Vocals: "Not Ready to Make Nice," Dixie Chicks

Best Country Collaboration with Vocals: "Who Says You Can't Go Home," Bon Jovi and Jennifer Nettles

Best Country Instrumental Performance: "Whiskey before Breakfast," Bryan Sutton and Doc Watson

Best Country Song: "Jesus, Take the Wheel," Brett James, Gordie Sampson, and Hillary Lindsey

Best Country Album: *Taking the Long Way*, Dixie Chicks (artist), Christ Testa, Jim Scott, and Richard Dodd (engineers/mixers), Rick Rubin (producer)

Best Contemporary Jazz Album: *The Hidden Land*, Béla Fleck and the Flecktones (artist), Richard Battaglia and Robert Battaglia (engineers/mixers)

Best Jazz Vocals Album: *Turned to Blue*, Nancy Wilson (artist), Jay Dudt (engineer/mixer), Jay Ashby and Martin J. Ashby (producers)

Best Jazz Instrumental Solo: "Some Skunk Funk," Michael Brecker

Best Jazz Instrumental Album, Individual or Group: *The Ultimate Adventure*, Chick Corea (artist), Al Schmitt, Bernie Kirsh, and Buck Snow (engineers/mixers)

Best Large Jazz Ensemble Album: *Some Skunk Funk*, Jim Beard, Marcio Doctor, Michael Brecker, Peter Erskine, Randy Brecker, Vince Mendoza, WDR Big Band, and Will Lee (artists), Klaus Genuit and Peter Brandt (engineers/mixers), Joachim Becker and Lucas Schmid (producers)

Best Music Video, Short Form: *Here It Goes Again*, Ok Go (artist), Andy Ross, Damian Kulash Jr., Dan Konopka, Timothy Nordwind, and Trish Sie (video directors and video producers)

Best Music Video, Long Form: *Wings For Wheels: The Making of Born to Run*, Bruce Springsteen (artist), Thom Zimny (video director), Thom Zimny (video producer)

2007

Album of the Year: *River: The Joni Letters*, Herbie Hancock (artist), Helik Hadar (engineer/mixer), Corinne Bailey Rae, Joni Mitchell, Leonard Cohen, Luciana Souza, Norah Jones*, and Tina Turner (featured artists), Bernie Grundman (mastering engineer) Herbie Hancock and Larry Klein (producers)

Record of the Year: "Rehab," Amy Winehouse (artist), Dom Morley, Gabriel Roth, Mark Ronson, Samuel "Vaughan" Merrick, and Tom Elmhirst (engineers/mixers), Mark Ronson (producer)

Song of the Year: "Rehab," Amy Winehouse

Best New Artist: Amy Winehouse

Best Pop Vocals Performance, Female: "Rehab," Amy Winehouse

Best Pop Vocals Performance, Male: "What Goes Around . . . Comes Around," Justin Timberlake*

Best Pop Performance by a Duo or Group with Vocals: "Makes Me Wonder," Maroon 5

Best Pop Collaboration with Vocals: "Gone Gone Gone (Done Moved On)," Alison Krauss and Robert Plant

Best Pop Instrumental Performance: "The Mix-Up," Beastie Boys (artist), Adam Horovitz, Adam Yauch, Jon Weiner, and Michael Diamond (engineers and producers)

Best Pop Vocal Album: *Back to Black*, "Amy Winehouse (artist), Mark Ronson, Samuel "Vaughan" Merrick, and Tom Elmhirst (engineers), Mark Ronson (producer)

Best Dance Recording: "LoveStoned/I Think She Knows," The Chemical Brothers (Tom Rowlands, Ed Simons) (artist), Steve Dub (engineer), Ed Simons and Tom Rowlands (producers),

Best Traditional Pop Vocal Album: *Call Me Irresponsible*, Michael Bublé (artist), Humberto Gatica (engineer), David Foster and Humberto Gatica (producers),

Best Solo Rock Vocal Performance: "Radio Nowhere," Bruce Springsteen

Best Rock Performance by a Duo or Group with Vocals: "Icky Thump," White Stripes

Best Hard Rock Performance: "The Pretender," Foo Fighters

Best Metal Performance: "Final Six," Slayer

Best Rock Instrumental Performance: "Once Upon a Time in the West," Bruce Springsteen

Best Rock Song: "Radio Nowhere," Bruce Springsteen

Best Rock Album: *Echoes, Silence, Patience and Grace*, Foo Fighters (David Grohl, Taylor Hawkins, Nate Mendel, Chris Shiflett) (artist), Adrian Bushby and Richard Costey (engineers). Gil Norton (producer)

Best Alternative Music Album, *Icky Thump*, White Stripes (Jack White*, Meg White) (artist), Joseph Chiccarelli (engineer)

Best R & B Vocal Performance, Female: "No One," Alicia Keys*

Best R & B Vocal Performance, Male: "Future Baby Mama," Prince

Best R & B Performance by a Duo or Group with Vocals: "Disrespectful," Chaka Khan and Mary J. Blige

Best Traditional R & B Vocal Performance: "In My Songs," Gerald Levert

Best Urban/Alternative Performance: "Daydreamin'," Jill Scott and Wasalu Muhammad Jaco

Best R & B Song: "No One," Alicia Keys*, Dirty Harry and Kerry "Krucial" Brothers

Best R & B Album: *Funk This*, Chaka Khan (artist), Matt Marrin (engineer), Bobby Ross Avila, Issiah J. Avila, James "Big Jim" Wright, James Harris III, and Terry Lewis (producers)

Best Contemporary R&B Album: *Because of You*, Ne-Yo (artist), Kevin Davis and Mike Tocci (engineers), Ne-Yo (producer)

Best Rap Solo Performance: "Stronger," Kanye West*

Best Rap Performance by a Duo or Group: "Southside," Kanye West* and Rashid Lonnie Lynn

Best Rap/Sung Collaboration: "Umbrella," Rihanna and Shawn Carter

Best Rap Song: "Good Life," Aldrin Davis, Faheem Najm, Kanye West*, and Mike Dean

Best Rap Album: *Graduation*, Kanye West*, Andrew Dawson, Anthony Kilhoffer, and Mike Dean (engineers), Kanye West* (producer)

Best Country Vocal Performance, Female: "Before He Cheats," Carrie Underwood

Best Country Vocal Performance, Male: "Stupid Boy," Keith Urban

Best Country Performance by a Duo or Group with Vocals: "How Long," Eagles

Best Country Collaboration with Vocals: "Lost Highway," Ray Price and Willie Nelson

Best Country Instrumental Performance: "Throttleneck," Brad Paisley

Best Country Song: "Before He Cheats," Chris Tompkins and Josh Kear

Best Country Album: *These Days*, Vince Gill (artist), Justin Niebank (engineer), John N. Hobbs, Justin Niebank, and Vince Gill (producers)

Best Contemporary Jazz Album: *River: the Joni Letters*, Herbie Hancock (artist), Helik Hadar (engineer), Herbie Hancock and Larry Klein (producers)

Best Jazz Vocal Album: *Avant Gershwin*, Patti Austin (artist), Christian Schmitt, Dirk Franken, Don Murray, and Sebastian Roth (engineers), Lucas Schmid, Michael Abene, and Patti Austin (producers)

Best Jazz Instrumental Solo: "Anagram," Michael Brecker

Best Jazz Instrumental Album, Individual or Group: *Pilgrimage*, Michael Brecker (artist), Joe Ferla (engineer), Gil Goldstein, Michael Brecker, Pat Metheny, and Steven Rodby (producers)

Best Large Jazz Ensemble Album: *A Tale of God's Will (A Requiem for Katrina)*, Terence Blanchard (artist), Frank Wolf (engineer), Terence Blanchard (producer)

Best Music Video, Short Form: *God's Gonna Cut You Down*, Johnny Cash (artist), Tony Kaye (video director), Rachel Curl (video producer)

Best Music Video, Long Form: *The Confessions Tour*, Madonna (artist), Jonas Akerlund (video director), David May and Sara Martin (video producers)

2008

Album of the Year: *Raising Sand*, Alison Krauss and Robert Plant (artists), Mike Piersante, (engineer/mixer), Gavin Lurssen (mastering engineer), T-Bone Burnett (producer)

Record of the Year: "Please Read the Letter,"Alison Krauss and Robert Plant (artists), Mike Piersante, (engineer/mixer), T-Bone Burnett (producer)

Song of the Year: "Viva La Vida," Chris Martin, Guy Berryman, Jon Buckland, and Will Champion, songwriters

Best New Artist: Adele

Best Pop Vocal Performance, Female: "Chasing Pavements," Adele

Best Pop Vocal Performance, Male: "Say," John Mayer

Best Pop Performance by a Duo or Group with Vocals: "Viva La Vida," Coldplay*

Best Pop Collaboration with Vocals: "Rich Woman," Alison Krauss and Robert Plant

Best Pop Instrumental Performance: "I Dreamed There Was No War," Eagles

Best Pop Instrumental Album: *Jingle All The Way*, Béla Fleck and The Flecktones (Jeff Coffin, Béla Fleck, Future Man, Victor Lemont Wooten) (artist),

Richard Battaglia and Robert Battaglia (engineers)

Best Pop Vocal Album: *Rockferry*, Duffy

Best Dance Recording: "Harder Better Faster Stronger," Daft Punk (Thomas Bangalter, Guy-Manuel De Homem-Christo) (artist), Guy-Manuel De Homem-Christo and Thomas Bangalter (mixers and producers)

Best Electronic/Dance Album: *Alive 2007*, Daft Punk (Thomas Bangalter, Guy-Manuel De Homem-Christo) (artist), Peter Franco (engineer)

Best Traditional Pop Vocal Album: *Still Unforgettable*, Natalie Cole (artist), Al Schmitt (engineer), Gail Deadrick and Natalie Cole (producers)

Best Solo Rock Vocal Performance: "Gravity," John Mayer

Best Rock Performance by a Duo or Group with Vocals: "Sex on Fire," Kings of Leon

Best Hard Rock Performance: "Wax Simulacra," Mars Volta

Best Metal Performance: "My Apocalypse," Metallica

Best Rock Instrumental Performance: "Peaches En Regalia," Napoleon Brock, Steve Vai, and Zappa Plays Zappa

Best Rock Song: "Girls in Their Summer Clothes," Bruce Springsteen

Best Rock Album: *Viva la Vida or Death and All His Friends*, Coldplay* (artist), Michael H. Brauer and Rik Simpson (engineers). Brian Eno, Markus Dravs, and Rik Simpson (producers)

Best Alternative Music Album: *In Rainbows*, Radiohead *(artist), Dan Grech-Marguerat, Hugo Nicolson, Nigel Godrich, and Richard Woodcraft (engineers), Nigel Godrich(producer),

Best R & B Vocal Performance, Female: "Superwoman," Alicia Keys*

Best R & B Vocal Performance, Male: "Miss Independent," Ne-Yo

Best R & B Performance by a Duo or Group with Vocals: "Stay with Me (by the Sea)," Al Green and John Legend

Best Traditional R & B Vocal Performance: "You've Got the Love I Need," Al Green and Anthony Hamilton

Best Urban/Alternative Performance, "Be OK," Chrisette Michele and will.i.am

Best R & B Song: "Miss Independent," Mikkel Eriksen, Ne-Yo, and Tor Hermansen

Best R & B Album: *Jennifer Hudson*, Jennifer Hudson (artist), Clive Davis and Larry Jackson (producers)

Best Contemporary R & B Album: *Growing Pains*, Mary J. Blige(artist), Dave Pensado, Jaycen Joshua, and Kuk Harrell (engineers)

Best Rap Solo Performance: "A Milli," Lil Wayne

Best Rap Performance by a Duo or Group: "Swagga Like Us," Jay-Z*, Kanye West*, Lil Wayne, and T.I.

Best Rap/Sung Collaboration: "American Boy," Estelle and Kanye West*

Best Rap Song: "Lollipop," Darius "Deezle" Harrison, James Scheffer, Lil Wayne, Rex Zamor, and Static Major (songwriters)

Best Rap Album: *Tha Carter III*, Lil Wayne (artist), Darius "Deezle" Harrison and Fabian Marasciullo (engineers)

Best Country Vocal Performance, Female: "Last Name," Carrie Underwood

Best Country Vocal Performance, Male: "Letter to Me," Brad Paisley

Best Country Performance by a Duo or Group with Vocals: "Stay," Sugarland

Best Country Collaboration with Vocals: "Killing the Blues," Alison Krauss and Robert Plant

Best Country Instrumental Performance: "Cluster Pluck," Albert Lee, Brad Paisley, Brent Mason, James Burton, John Jorgenson, Redd Volkaert, Steve Wariner, and Vince Gill (artists)

Best Country Song: "Stay," Jennifer Nettles

Best Country Album: "Troubadour," George Strait (artist), Chuck Ainlay (engineer), George Strait and Tony Brown (producers)

Best Contemporary Jazz Album: *Randy in Brasil*, Randy Brecker (artist), Eduardo Santos (engineer), Ruriá Duprat (producer),

Best Jazz Vocal Album: *Loverly*, Cassandra Wilson (artist), Jason Wormer and John Fischbach (engineers), Cassandra Wilson (producer),

Best Jazz Instrumental Solo: "Be-Bop," Terence Blanchard

Best Jazz Instrumental Album, Individual or Group: *The New Crystal Silence*, Chick Corea and Gary Burton, (artists), Bernie Kirsh, Brian Vibberts, Buck Snow, Tim Garland, and Tony David Cray (engineers), Chick Corea and Gary Burton (producers)

Best Large Jazz Ensemble Album: *Monday Night Live at the Village Vanguard*, Vanguard Jazz Orchestra (Thomas Bellino, Jim McNeely, John M. Mosca, Dick Oatts, Douglas Purviance) (artist), Ed Reed and Gary Chester (engineers)

Best Music Video, Short Form: "Pork and Beans," Weezer (Brian Bell, Rivers Cuomo, Scott Shriner, Pat Wilson) (artist), Mathew Cullen (video director), Bernard Rahill(video producer)

Best Music Video, Long Form: "Runnin' Down a Dream," Tom Petty And The Heartbreakers (artist), Peter Bogdanovich(video director), George Drakoulias and Skot Bright (video producers)

2009

Album of the Year: *Fearless*, Taylor Swift (artist), Chad Carlson, Justin Niebank, and Nathan Chapman (engineers/mixers), Colbie Caillat (featured artist), Hank Williams (mastering engineer), Nathan Chapman and Taylor Swift (producers)

Record of the Year: "Use Somebody," Kings of Leon (artist), Jacquire King (engineer/mixer) Angelo Petraglia and Jacquire King (producers)

Song of the Year: "Single Ladies (Put a Ring on It)," Beyoncé Knowles*, Chris "Tricky" Stewart, Kuk Harrell, and Terius "Dream" Nash (songwriters)

Best New Artist: Zac Brown Band

Best Pop Vocal Performance, Female: "Halo," Beyoncé Knowles*

Best Pop Vocal Performance, Male: "Make It Mine," Jason Mraz

Best Pop Performance by a Duo or Group with Vocals: "I Gotta Feeling," Black Eyed Peas

Best Pop Collaboration with Vocals: "Lucky," Colbie Caillat and Jason Mraz

Best Pop Instrumental Performance: "Throw Down Your Heart," Béla Fleck

Best Pop Instrumental Album: *Potato Hole*, Booker T. Jones (artist), Doug Boehm and Rob Schnapf (engineers/mixers and producers)

Best Pop Vocal Album: *The E.N.D.*, Black Eyed Peas (artist), Dylan Dresdow and Padraic Kerin (engineers/mixers)

Best Dance Recording: "Poker Face," Lady Gaga* (artist), Dave Russell, RedOne, and Robert Orton (mixers), RedOne (producer)

Best Electronic/Dance Album: *The Fame*, Lady Gaga* (artist), Robert Orton (engineer/mixer)

Best Traditional Pop Vocal Album: *Michael Bublé Meets Madison Square Garden*, Michael Bublé(artist), Humberto Gatica (engineer/mixer and producer)

Best Solo Rock Vocal Performance: "Working on A Dream," Bruce Springsteen

Best Rock Performance by a Duo or Group with Vocals: "Use Somebody," Kings of Leon

Best Hard Rock Performance: "War Machine," AC/DC

Best Metal Performance: "Dissident Aggressor," Judas Priest

Best Rock Instrumental Performance: "A Day in the Life," Jeff Beck

Best Rock Song: "Use Somebody," Kings of Leon

Best Rock Album: *21st Century Breakdown*, Green Day (artist), Philippe Zdar Cerboneschi (engineer/mixer), Philippe Zdar Cerboneschi and Phoenix (Laurent Brancowitz, Deck D'Arcy, Thomas Mars, Christian Mazzalai) (producers)

Best R & B Vocal Performance, Female: "Single Ladies (Put a Ring on It)," Beyoncé Knowles*

Best R & B Vocal Performance, Male: "Pretty Wings," Maxwell

Best Traditional R & B Vocal Performance: "At Last," Beyoncé Knowles*

Best Urban/Alternative Performance: "Pearls," Dobet Gnahore and India.Arie

Best R & B Song: "Single Ladies (Put a Ring on It)," Beyoncé Knowles*, Chris "Tricky" Stewart, Kuk Harrell, and Terius "Dream" Nash (songwriters)

Best R & B Album: *Blacksummers' Night*, Maxwell (artist), Glen Marchese, Hod David, Jesse Gladstone, Maxwell, and Mike Pela (engineers/mixers), Hod David and Maxwell (producers)

Best Contemporary R&B Album: *I Am . . . Sasha Fierce*, Beyoncé Knowles* (artist), Jim Caruana and Mark Stent (engineers/mixers), Beyoncé Knowles* (producer)

Best Rap Solo Performance: "D.O.A. (Death of Auto-Tune)," Jay-Z*

Best Rap Performance by a Duo or Group: "Crack a Bottle," 50 Cent, Dr. Dre, and Eminem* (artists)

Best Rap/Sung Collaboration: "Run This Town," Jay-Z*, Kanye West*, and Rihanna

Best Rap Song: "Run This Town," Ernest Wilson, Jeff Bhasker, Kanye West*, Robyn Fenty, and Shawn Carter (songwriters)

Best Rap Album: *Relapse*, Eminem* (artist), Andre Young, Mauricio "Veto" Iragorri, and Michael Strange (engineers/mixers), Andre Young (producer)

Best Country Vocal Performance, Female: "White Horse," Taylor Swift

Best Country Vocal Performance, Male: "Sweet Thing," Keith Urban

Best Country Performance by a Duo or Group with Vocals: "I Run To You," Lady Antebellum

Best Country Collaboration with Vocals: "I Told You So," Carrie Underwood and Randy Travis

Best Country Instrumental Performance: "Producer's Medley," Steve Wariner

Best Country Song: "White Horse," Liz Rose and Taylor Swift

Best Country Album: *Fearless,* Taylor Swift (artist), Chad Carlson and Justin Niebank (engineers/mixers), Nathan Chapman and Taylor Swift (producers)

Best Contemporary Jazz Album: *75,* Joe Zawinul and The Zawinul Syndicate (Jorge Bezerra, Alegre Correa, Sabine Kabongo, Linley Marthe, Aziz Sahmaoui, Paco Sery, Joe Zawinul) (artist), Joachim Becker, Klaus Genuit, and Wladi Turkewitsch (engineers/mixers), Joachim Becker (producer),

Best Jazz Vocal Album: *Dedicated to You: Kurt Elling Sings the Music of Coltrane and Hartman,* Kurt Elling (artist), Dave O'Donnell and Rob Macomber (engineers/mixers), Kurt Elling and Laurence Hobgood (producers)

Best Improvised Jazz Solo: "Dancin' 4 Chicken," Terence Blanchard

Best Jazz Instrumental Album, Individual or Group: *Five Peace Band—Live,* Five Peace Band (Chick Corea, John McLaughlin, Kenny Garrett, Christian McBride, Vinnie Colaiuta) (artists), Bernie Kirsh, Brian Vibberts and Sven Hoffman (engineers/mixers),

Best Large Jazz Ensemble Album: *Book One,* New Orleans Jazz Orchestra and Irvin Mayfield (artists), Masanori Yura (engineer/mixer)

Best Music Video, Short Form: *Boom Boom Pow,* Black Eyed (artist), Mark Kudsi and Mathew Cullen (video directors) Anna Joseph, Javier Jimenez, and Patrick Nugent (video producers)

Best Music Video, Long Form: *The Beatles Love—All Together Now,* Adrian Wills (video director), Jonathan Clyde and Martin Bolduc (video producers)

■ Sports: Winners of Major Events

Athletes whose names appear with an asterisk (*) are subjects of their own full-length essays within *The 2000s in America.*

MAJOR LEAGUE BASEBALL

World Series
2000: New York Yankees (American League) 4, New York Mets (National League) 1
2001: Arizona Diamondbacks (NL) 4, New York Yankees (AL) 3
2002: Anaheim Angels (AL) 4, San Francisco Giants (NL) 3
2003: Florida Marlins (NL) 4, New York Yankees (AL) 2
2004: Boston Red Sox (AL) 4, St. Louis Cardinals (NL) 0
2005: Chicago White Sox (AL) 4, Houston Astros (NL) 0
2006: St. Louis Cardinals (NL) 4, Detroit Tigers (AL) 1
2007: Boston Red Sox (AL) 4, Colorado Rockies (NL) 0
2008: Philadelphia Phillies (NL) 4, Tampa Bay Rays (AL) 1
2009: New York Yankees (AL) 4, Philadelphia Phillies (NL) 2

All-Star Games
2000: American League 6, National League 3
2001: American League 4, National League 1
2002: American League 7, National League 7
2003: American League 7, National League 6
2004: American League 9, National League 4
2005: American League 7, National League 5
2006: American League 3, National League 2
2007: American League 5, National League 4
2008: American League 4, National League 3
2009: American League 4, National League 3

American League Most Valuable Players
2000: Jason Giambi, Oakland Athletics
2001: Ichiro Suzuki, Seattle Mariners
2002: Miguel Tejada, Oakland Athletics
2003: Alex Rodriguez, Texas Rangers
2004: Vladimir Guerrero, Anaheim Angels
2005: Alex Rodriguez, New York Yankees
2006: Justin Morneau, Minnesota Twins
2007: Alex Rodriguez, New York Yankees
2008: Dustin Pedroia, Boston Red Sox
2009: Joe Mauer, Minnesota Twins

National League Most Valuable Players
2000: Jeff Kent, San Francisco Giants
2001: Barry Bonds*, San Francisco Giants
2002: Barry Bonds*, San Francisco Giants
2003: Barry Bonds*, San Francisco Giants
2004: Barry Bonds*, San Francisco Giants
2005: Albert Pujols, St. Louis Cardinals
2006: Ryan Howard, Philadelphia Phillies
2007: Jimmy Rollins, Philadelphia Phillies
2008: Albert Pujols, St. Louis Cardinals
2009: Albert Pujols, St. Louis Cardinals

American League Rookie of the Year
2000: Kazuhiro Sasaki, Seattle Mariners
2001: Ichiro Suzuki, Seattle Mariners
2002: Eric Hinske, Toronto Blue Jays
2003: Angel Berroa, Kansas City Royals
2004: Bobby Crosby, Oakland Athletics
2005: Huston Street, Oakland Athletics
2006: Justin Verlander, Detroit Tigers
2007: Dustin Pedroia, Boston Red Sox
2008: Evan Longoria, Tampa Bay Rays
2009: Andrew Bailey, Oakland Athletics

National League Rookie of the Year
2000: Rafael Furcal, Atlanta Braves
2001: Albert Pujols, St. Louis Cardinals
2002: Jason Jennings, Colorado Rockies
2003: Dontrelle Willis, Florida Marlins
2004: Jason Bay, Pittsburgh Pirates
2005: Ryan Howard, Philadelphia Phillies
2006: Hanley Ramirez, Florida Marlins
2007: Ryan Braun, Milwaukee Braves
2008: Geovany Soto, Chicago White Sox
2009: Chris Coghlan, Florida Marlins

NATIONAL BASKETBALL ASSOCIATION (NBA)

Championships
2000: Los Angeles Lakers 4, Indiana Pacers 2
2001: Los Angeles Lakers 4, Philadelphia 76ers 1
2002: Los Angeles Lakers 4, New Jersey Nets 0
2003: San Antonio Spurs 4, New Jersey Nets 2
2004: Detroit Pistons 4, Los Angeles Lakers 1
2005: San Antonio Spurs 4, Detroit Pistons 3
2006: Miami Heat 4, Dallas Mavericks 2
2007: San Antonio Spurs 4, Cleveland Cavaliers 0
2008: Boston Celtics 4, Los Angeles Lakers 2
2009: Los Angeles Lakers 4, Orlando Magic 1

NBA Most Valuable Players
2000: Shaquille O'Neal, Los Angeles Lakers
2001: Shaquille O'Neal, Los Angeles Lakers
2002: Shaquille O'Neal, Los Angeles Lakers
2003: Tim Duncan, San Antonio Spurs
2004: Chauncey Billups, Detroit Pistons
2005: Tim Duncan, San Antonio Spurs
2006: Dwyane Wade, Miami Heat
2007: Tony Parker, San Antonio Spurs
2008: Paul Pierce, Boston Celtics
2009: Kobe Bryant, Los Angeles Lakers

NBA Rookie of the Year
2000: Elton Brand, Chicago Bulls; Steve Francis, Houston Rockets
2001: Mike Miller, Orlando Magic
2002: Pau Gasol, Memphis Grizzlies
2003: Amare Stoudemire, Phoenix Suns
2004: LeBron James*, Cleveland Cavaliers
2005: Emeka Okafor, Charlotte Bobcats
2006: Chris Paul, New Orleans Hornets/Oklahoma City Thunder
2007: Brandon Roy, Portland Trailblazers
2008: Kevin Durant, Seattle SuperSonics
2009: Derrick Rose, Chicago Bulls

WOMEN'S NATIONAL BASKETBALL ASSOCIATION (WNBA)

Championships
2000: Houston Comets 2, New York Liberty 0
2001: Los Angeles Sparks 2, Charlotte Sting 0
2002: Los Angeles Sparks 2, New York Liberty 0
2003: Detroit Shock 2, Los Angeles Sparks 1
2004: Seattle Storm 2, Connecticut Sun 1
2005: Sacramento Monarchs 3, Connecticut Sun 1
2006: Detroit Shock 3, Sacramento Monarchs 2
2007: Phoenix Mercury 3, Detroit Shock 2
2008: Detroit Shock 3, San Antonio Silver Stars
2009: Phoenix Mercury 3, Indiana Fever 2

COLLEGE BASKETBALL

National Collegiate Athletic Association (NCAA) Championships
2000: Michigan State 89, Florida 76
2001: Duke 82, Arizona 72
2002: Maryland 64, Indiana 52
2003: Syracuse 81, Kansas 78
2004: Connecticut 82, Georgia Tech 73
2005: North Carolina 75, Illinois 70
2006: Florida 73, UCLA 57
2007: Florida 84, Ohio State 75
2008: Kansas 75, Memphis 68
2009: North Carolina 89, Michigan State 72

National Invitational Tournament (NIT)
2000: Wake Forest 71, Notre Dame 61
2001: Tulsa 79, Alabama 60
2002: Memphis 72, South Carolina 62
2003: St. John's 70, Georgetown 67
2004: Michigan 62, Rutgers 55
2005: South Carolina 60, St. Joe's 57
2006: South Carolina 76, Michigan 64
2007: West Virginia 78, Clemson 73
2008: Ohio State 92, Massachusetts 85
2009: Penn State 69, Baylor 63

PROFESSIONAL FOOTBALL

National Football League (NFL) Championships
2000: Baltimore Ravens 34, New York Giants 7
2001: New England Patriots 20, St. Louis Rams 17
2002: Tampa Bay Buccaneers 48, Oakland Raiders 21
2003: New England Patriots 32, Carolina Panthers 29
2004: New England Patriots 24, Philadelphia Eagles 21
2005: Pittsburgh Steelers 21, Seattle Seahawks 10
2006: Indianapolis Colts 29, Chicago Bears 17
2007: New York Giants 17, New England Patriots 14
2008: Pittsburgh Steelers 27, Arizona Cardinals 23
2009: New Orleans Saints 31, Indianapolis Colts 17

NFL Most Valuable Players
2000: Marshall Faulk, St. Louis Rams; Rich Gannon, Oakland Raiders
2001: Kurt Warner, St. Louis Rams; Marshall Faulk, St. Louis Rams
2002: Rich Gannon, Oakland Raiders
2003: Peyton Manning, Indianapolis Colts; Steve McNair, Tennessee Titans
2004: Peyton Manning, Indianapolis Colts

2005: Shaun Alexander, Seattle Seahawks
2006: LaDainian Tomlinson, San Diego Chargers
2007: Tom Brady*, New England Patriots
2008: Peyton Manning, Indianapolis Colts
2009: Peyton Manning, Indianapolis Colts

Canadian Football League (CFL) Gray Cup Winners
2000: British Columbia Lions 28, Montreal Alouettes 26
2001: Calgary Stampeders 27, Winnipeg Blue Bombers 19
2002: Montreal Alouettes 25, Edmonton Eskimos 16
2003: Edmonton Eskimos 34, Montreal Alouettes 22
2004: Toronto Argonauts 27, British Columbia Lions 19
2005: Edmonton Eskimos 34, Montreal Alouettes 22
2006: British Columbia Lions 25, Montreal Alouettes 14
2007: Saskatchewan Roughriders 23, Winnipeg Blue Bombers 19
2008: Calgary Stampeders 22, Montreal Alouettes 14
2009: Montreal Alouettes 28, Saskatchewan Roughriders 27

COLLEGE FOOTBALL

Heisman Trophy Winners
2000: Chris Weinke, Florida State
2001: Eric Crouch, Nebraska
2002: Carson Palmer, USC
2003: Jason White, Oklahoma

2004: Matt Leinart, USC
2006: Troy Smith, Ohio State
2007: Tim Tebow, Florida
2008: Sam Bradford, Oklahoma
2009: Mark Ingram, Alabama

NATIONAL HOCKEY LEAGUE

Stanley Cup Winners
2000: New Jersey Devils 4, Dallas Stars 2
2001: Colorado Avalanche 4, New Jersey Devils 3
2002: Detroit Red Wings 4, Carolina Hurricanes 1
2003: New Jersey Devils 4, Mighty Ducks of Anaheim 3
2004: Tampa Bay Lightning 4, Calgary Flames 3
2006: Carolina Hurricanes 4, Edmonton Oilers 3
2007: Anaheim Ducks 4, Ottawa Senators 1
2008: Detroit Red Wings 4, Pittsburgh Penguins 2
2009: Pittsburgh Penguins 4, Detroit Red Wings 3

Hart Memorial Trophy (NHL MVP)
2000: Chris Pronger, St. Louis Blues
2001: Joe Sakic, Colorado Avalanche
2002: Jose Theodore, Montreal Canadiens
2003: Peter Forsberg, Colorado Avalanche
2004: Martin St. Louis, Tampa Bay Lightning
2006: Joe Thornton, San Jose Sharks
2007: Sidney Crosby, Pittsburgh Penguins
2008: Alexander Ovechkin, Washington Capitals
2009: Alexander Ovechkin, Washington Capitals

SOCCER

Major League Soccer (MLS) Cup Winners
2000: Sporting Kansas City 1, Chicago Fire 0
2001: San Jose Earthquakes 2, Los Angeles Galaxy 1, OT
2002: Los Angeles Galaxy 1, New England Revolution 0, OT
2003: San Jose Earthquakes 4, Chicago Fire 2
2004: DC United 3, Sporting Kansas City 2
2005: Los Angeles Galaxy 1, New England Revolution 0, OT
2006: Houston Dynamo 1 (4), New England Revolution 1 (3), PK
2007: Houston 2, New England 1
2008: Columbus 3, New York Red Bulls 1
2009: Real Salt Lake 1 (5), Los Angeles 1 (4), PK

BOXING

World Heavyweight Champions (World Boxing Association)
August 12, 2000–March 3, 2001: Evander Holyfield
March 3, 2001–March 1, 2003: John Ruiz
March 1, 2003–February 20, 2004: Roy Jones Jr.
February 20, 2004–December 17, 2005: John Ruiz
December 17, 2005–April 14, 2007: Nikolai Valuev
April 14, 2007–July 18, 2008: Ruslan Chagaev
August 30, 2008–November 7, 2009: Nikolai Valuev
November 7, 2009–July 2, 2011: David Haye

AUTO RACING

Indianapolis 500 Winners
2000: Juan Montoya
2001: Hélio Castroneves
2002: Hélio Castroneves
2003: Gil De Ferran
2004: Buddy Rice
2005: Dan Wheldon
2006: Sam Hornish Jr.
2007: Dario Franchitti
2008: Scott Dixon
2009: Hélio Castroneves

TENNIS

Major Tournament Champions (Men)

Year	Australian Open	French Open	Wimbledon	U.S. Open
2000	Andre Agassi	Gustavo Kuerten	Pete Sampras	Marat Safin
2001	Andre Agassi	Gustavo Kuerten	Goran Ivanisevic	Lleyton Hewitt
2002	Thomas Johansson	Albert Costa	Lleyton Hewitt	Pete Sampras
2003	Andre Agassi	Juan Carlos Ferrero	Roger Federer*	Andy Roddick
2004	Roger Federer*	Gasón Gaudio	Roger Federer*	Roger Federer*
2005	Marat Safin	Rafael Nadal	Roger Federer*	Roger Federer*
2006	Roger Federer*	Rafael Nadal	Roger Federer*	Roger Federer*
2007	Roger Federer*	Rafael Nadal	Roger Federer*	Roger Federer*
2008	Novak Djokovic	Rafael Nadal	Rafael Nadal	Roger Federer*
2009	Rafael Nadal	Roger Federer*	Roger Federer*	Juan Martin Del Potro

Major Tournament Champions (Women)

Year	Australian Open	French Open	Wimbledon	U.S. Open
2000	Lindsay Davenport	Mary Pierce	Venus Williams	Venus Williams
2001	Jennifer Capriati	Jennifer Capriati	Venus Williams	Venus Williams
2002	Jennifer Capriati	Serena Williams*	Serena Williams*	Serena Williams*
2003	Serena Williams*	Justine Henin-Hardenne	Serena Williams*	Justine Henin-Hardenne
2004	Justine Henin	Anastasia Myskina	Maria Sharapova	Svetlana Kuznetsova
2005	Serena Williams*	Justine Henin-Hardenne	Venus Williams	Kim Clijsters
2006	Amélie Mauresmo	Justine Henin-Hardenne	Amélie Mauresmo	Maria Sharapova
2007	Serena Williams*	Justine Henin-Hardenne	Venus Williams	Justine Henin
2008	Maria Sharapova	Ana Ivanovic	Venus Williams	Serena Williams*
2009	Serena Williams*	Svetlana Kuznetsova	Serena Williams*	Kim Clijsters

GOLF

Major Tournament Champions (Men)

Year	British Open	Professional Golf Association (PGA) Championship	The Masters	U.S. Open	FedEx Cup
2000	Tiger Woods*	Tiger Woods*	Vijay Singh	Tiger Woods*	
2001	David Duval	David Toms	Tiger Woods*	Retief Goosen	
2002	Ernie Els	Rich Beem	Tiger Woods*	Tiger Woods*	
2003	Ben Curtis	Shaun Micheel	Mike Weir	Jim Furyk	
2004	Todd Hamilton	Vijay Singh	Phil Mickelson	Retief Goosen	
2005	Tiger Woods*	Phil Mickelson	Tiger Woods*	Michael Campbell	
2006	Tiger Woods*	Tiger Woods*	Phil Mickelson	Geoff Ogilvy	
2007	Pádraig Harrington	Tiger Woods*	Zach Johnson	Ángel Cabrera	Tiger Woods*
2008	Pádraig Harrington	Pádraig Harrington	Trevor Immelman	Tiger Woods*	Vijay Singh
2009	Stewart Cink	Yang Yong-eun	Ángel Cabrera	Lucas Glover	Tiger Woods*

Major Tournament Champions (Women)

Year	U.S. Open	Ladies Professional Golf Association (LPGA) Championship
2000	Karrie Webb	Juli Inkster
2001	Karrie Webb	Karrie Webb
2002	Juli Inkster	Se Ri Pak
2003	Hillary Lunke	Annika Sorenstam
2004	Meg Mallon	Annika Sorenstam
2005	Birdie Kim	Annika Sorenstam
2006	Annika Sorenstam	Se Ri Pak
2007	Cristie Kerr	Suzann Pettersen
2008	Inbee Park	Yani Tseng
2009	Eun-Hee Ji	Anna Nordqvist

HORSE RACING

Triple Crown Races

Year	Kentucky Derby	Preakness	Belmont Stakes
2000	Fusaichi Pegasus	Red Bullet	Commendable
2001	Monarchos	Point Given	Point Given
2002	War Emblem	War Emblem	Sarava
2003	Funny Cide	Funny Cide	Empire Maker
2004	Smarty Jones	Smarty Jones	Bird Stone
2005	Giacomo	Afleet Alex	Afleet Alex
2006	Barbaro	Bernardini	Jazil
2007	Street Sense	Curlin	Rags to Riches
2008	Big Brown	Big Brown	Da' Tara
2009	Mine That Bird	Rachel Alexandra	Summer Bird

■ Popular Names of the 2000s

The following table shows the 100 most popular given names for male and female babies born during the 2000s. For each rank and sex, the table shows the name and the number of occurrences of that name.

Rank	MALES		FEMALES	
	Name	Number	Name	Number
1	Jacob	273,309	Emily	223,420
2	Michael	250,031	Madison	192,914
3	Joshua	231,482	Emma	180,976
4	Matthew	221,163	Olivia	155,795
5	Daniel	203,294	Hannah	155,463
6	Christopher	202,899	Abigail	150,694
7	Andrew	202,110	Isabella	149,241
8	Ethan	201,552	Samantha	134,094
9	Joseph	194,238	Elizabeth	133,084
10	William	193,990	Ashley	132,899
11	Anthony	191,502	Alexis	130,564
12	David	179,367	Sarah	124,076
13	Alexander	178,517	Sophia	119,028
14	Nicholas	177,359	Alyssa	114,310
15	Ryan	173,024	Grace	110,535
16	Tyler	165,311	Ava	104,384
17	James	162,738	Taylor	100,856
18	John	160,612	Brianna	99,612
19	Jonathan	144,495	Lauren	97,075
20	Noah	143,168	Chloe	96,305
21	Brandon	142,753	Natalie	94,948
22	Christian	142,111	Kayla	94,195
23	Dylan	139,920	Jessica	90,522
24	Samuel	138,143	Anna	89,976
25	Benjamin	136,991	Victoria	84,778
26	Nathan	134,588	Mia	83,367
27	Zachary	134,566	Hailey	81,830
28	Logan	133,835	Sydney	76,385
29	Justin	122,779	Jasmine	75,871
30	Gabriel	119,551	Julia	70,787
31	Jose	115,587	Morgan	70,687

| Rank | MALES | | FEMALES | |
	Name	Number	Name	Number
32	Austin	112,591	Destiny	69,577
33	Kevin	110,933	Rachel	68,106
34	Elijah	110,055	Ella	67,360
35	Caleb	109,838	Kaitlyn	66,828
36	Robert	106,367	Megan	66,759
37	Thomas	101,931	Katherine	65,266
38	Jordan	100,932	Savannah	64,584
39	Cameron	95,728	Jennifer	63,437
40	Jack	95,415	Alexandra	61,176
41	Hunter	94,705	Allison	59,906
42	Jackson	94,341	Haley	56,946
43	Angel	94,168	Maria	56,841
44	Isaiah	92,418	Kaylee	56,318
45	Evan	92,035	Lily	56,075
46	Isaac	90,499	Makayla	54,859
47	Mason	90,362	Brooke	54,621
48	Luke	90,351	Mackenzie	54,481
49	Jason	88,384	Nicole	54,461
50	Gavin	88,329	Addison	51,305
51	Jayden	88,286	Stephanie	49,892
52	Aaron	86,738	Lillian	49,267
53	Connor	85,900	Andrea	49,106
54	Aiden	83,341	Zoe	48,654
55	Aidan	76,412	Faith	48,626
56	Kyle	76,060	Kimberly	48,418
57	Juan	75,745	Madeline	48,236
58	Charles	75,202	Alexa	48,049
59	Luis	74,223	Katelyn	47,760
60	Adam	70,859	Gabriella	47,262
61	Lucas	70,842	Gabrielle	46,947
62	Brian	69,657	Trinity	46,774
63	Eric	69,373	Amanda	46,476
64	Adrian	66,000	Kylie	46,369
65	Nathaniel	64,101	Mary	45,903
66	Sean	64,021	Paige	45,510
67	Alex	63,660	Riley	45,475

Rank	MALES		FEMALES	
	Name	Number	Name	Number
68	Carlos	63,079	Leah	45,266
69	Bryan	61,852	Jenna	45,240
70	Ian	61,849	Sara	43,929
71	Owen	61,800	Rebecca	43,504
72	Jesus	61,244	Michelle	43,461
73	Landon	61,015	Sofia	43,318
74	Julian	60,273	Vanessa	43,163
75	Chase	57,082	Jordan	43,116
76	Cole	56,785	Angelina	42,695
77	Diego	55,979	Caroline	41,784
78	Jeremiah	55,424	Avery	41,656
79	Steven	53,777	Audrey	41,460
80	Sebastian	53,776	Evelyn	40,678
81	Xavier	52,341	Maya	39,960
82	Timothy	52,277	Claire	38,975
83	Carter	52,264	Autumn	38,418
84	Wyatt	51,274	Jocelyn	38,339
85	Brayden	50,264	Ariana	37,923
86	Blake	50,025	Nevaeh	37,823
87	Hayden	49,970	Arianna	37,740
88	Devin	49,324	Jada	36,996
89	Cody	48,775	Bailey	36,819
90	Richard	48,491	Brooklyn	36,742
91	Seth	48,080	Aaliyah	36,282
92	Dominic	48,025	Amber	36,147
93	Jaden	46,163	Isabel	35,981
94	Antonio	46,136	Mariah	35,565
95	Miguel	46,010	Danielle	35,551
96	Liam	44,850	Melanie	35,175
97	Patrick	44,691	Sierra	34,448
98	Carson	44,591	Erin	33,334
99	Jesse	43,250	Molly	33,233
100	Tristan	43,210	Amelia	33,199

Source: US Social Security Administration (Sample based on Social Security card application data as of the end of February 2011)

■ Chronological List of Scandals

John Spano Is Sentenced for Fraudulent Purchase of Ice Hockey Team	January 28, 2000	Businessman John A. Spano began negotiations in 1996 to purchase the New York Islanders ice hockey team. He represented himself as the owner of a large company and as an inheritor of substantial wealth. When Spano failed to pay for the club he just bought, investigators found that his company was much smaller than claimed to be and that he had no inherited wealth. Spano was convicted of fraud and forgery.
New York Mayor Rudy Giuliani's Extramarital Affair Is Revealed	May 2, 2000	Rudy Giuliani was married to Donna Hanover when he began an extramarital affair with Judith Nathan. The media's exposure of the affair set off a firestorm of coverage by New York City's tabloid press and television stations. After a public and very contentious divorce, Giuliani married Nathan.
Former Louisiana Governor Edwin Edwards Is Convicted on Corruption Charges	May 9, 2000	The administration of Edwin Edwards, the three-term governor of Louisiana, was marred by allegations of corruption for decades. In 2001, Edwards was sentenced to ten years in federal prison for corrupt practices, including extortion and money laundering, related to the issuance of contracts and licenses for riverboat casino gambling.
American Scientists Are Accused of Starting a Measles Epidemic in the Amazon	September, 2000	Patrick Tierney claimed that two renowned researchers, anthropologist Napoleon A. Chagnon and geneticist James V. Neel, started or exacerbated a measles epidemic among the indigenous Yanomami people of the Amazon in 1968. Conflicting accounts of what actually happened call into question some of Tierney's accusations, which were made in his book *Darkness in El Dorado* (2000).
Ex-gay Leader John Paulk Is Photographed Leaving a Gay Bar	September 19, 2000	John Paulk, chairman of the board for the conservative, Christian, "ex-gay" movement group Exodus International, was photographed leaving a Washington, DC, gay bar in the fall of 2000. A former drag queen, Paulk married a woman after his experiences with Exodus and became its spokesperson. He also was a spokesperson for the conservative group Focus on the Family. Paulk claimed to have stopped at the bar to use the restroom, but not many believed him. He lost his position as Exodus board chairman.
CIA Agent Robert Hanssen Is Arrested for Spying for the Russians	February 18, 2001	As one of the most effective spies in US history, FBI agent Robert Hanssen sold secrets to the Soviet Union and Russia for more than twenty years. His espionage led to one of the most damaging cases of the breaching of national security in the history of the United States. Hanssen was sentenced to life imprisonment, avoiding the death penalty for treason, by pleading guilty to fifteen counts of espionage and conspiracy.
Washington Intern Chandra Levy Disappears	April 30, 2001	Chandra Levy, an intern with the Federal Bureau of Prisons, disappeared just days before she was to return home to California. US Congress member Gary Condit later admitted to having had a sexual relationship with Levy while she was in Washington, DC, but he was never officially named a suspect in her disappearance. Levy's body was found in a park close to her DC apartment, one year after she disappeared. Condit's political career was ruined by the scandal.

Award-Winning Historian Joseph J. Ellis Is Accused of Lying	June 18, 2001	The *Boston Globe* reported that American historian Joseph J. Ellis had frequently lied to his students and others about serving in the Vietnam War. Ellis also lied about, or greatly exaggerated, his participation in other major events of the 1960s, including the peace and Civil Rights movements. The Ellis scandal sparked a heated debate about ethical issues of personal and professional integrity for academics.
Little League Baseball Star Danny Almonte Is Found to Be Over Age	August 27, 2001	Danny Almonte gained fame for exceptional pitching in the 2001 Little League Baseball World Series. Sports reporters soon discovered that he was fourteen years old, two years over the age limit for players. His team was stripped of its records for the season. Both the team's founder and Almonte's father were banned from Little League for life.
Enron Bankruptcy Reveals Massive Financial Fraud	December 2, 2001	When the Texas energy corporation Enron suddenly went bankrupt, it took with it the life savings and pensions of many of its employees and revealed systematic financial corruption and mismanagement that went beyond the company's walls to a respectable accounting firm and the halls of government.
Notre Dame Football Coach Resigns for Falsifying His Résumé	December 14, 2001	George O'Leary, former head football coach for the Georgia Institute of Technology, resigned as head football coach of the University of Notre Dame after only five days on the job. A reporter covering his appointment as Notre Dame's head coach found inaccuracies and falsehoods on his résumé. Upon resigning, O'Leary admitted to including fabricated athletic and academic credentials on his résumé. His resignation, however, did not negatively affect his coaching career, which prospered nonetheless.
Historian Stephen E. Ambrose Is Accused of Plagiarism	January 4, 2002	The *Weekly Standard* reported that Stephen E. Ambrose, one of the most widely read scholars of American history, had plagiarized material from a closely related historical work for one of his own bestselling military histories, *The Wild Blue* (2001). Subsequent investigations revealing that Ambrose had plagiarized other works damaged his reputation as an academic historian but had little negative impact on his popularity with general readers.
Boston Globe Reports on Child Sexual Abuse by Roman Catholic Priests	January 6, 2002	A series of articles in the *Boston Globe* revealed the systematic efforts of the Roman Catholic archdiocese to cover up incidents of sexual abuse by priests and to silence victims wishing to bring these crimes to the attention of authorities and the public. The revelations touched off a nationwide flurry of accusations by others claiming of similar abuse, some of whom were molested decades earlier, as children.
Historian Doris Kearns Goodwin Is Accused of Plagiarism	January 18, 2002	Doris Kearns Goodwin, a Harvard University professor and author of several award-winning books, was accused of plagiarizing another author's work for her best-selling and award-winning history *The Fitzgeralds and the Kennedys* (1987). Goodwin created further scandal when it was revealed that in 1987, she had paid off the author whose work she plagiarized.

French Judge Admits Favoring Russian Figure Skaters in Winter Olympics	February 11, 2002	During the 2002 Winter Olympic Games in Utah, judges awarded the Russian figure skating pair the gold medal in a decision that led to major controversy, as many thought the Canadian silver medalists deserved to win gold instead. The French judge soon admitted that her federation had pressured her to vote for the Russians in a deal designed to help the French ice dancing couple. The scandal resulted in the awarding of a second gold medal and the creation of a new judging system for figure skating at the international level of competition.
Rotting Human Bodies Are Found at Georgia Crematory	February 17, 2002	More than three hundred rotting human bodies that should have been cremated were found unceremoniously dumped on the grounds of Tri-State Crematory in Noble, Georgia. Most of the corpses had to be identified using either forensic methods or the shipping records of the funeral homes that worked with Tri-State. Some of the bodies never were identified. At the time of the discovery, Georgia state funeral laws were lax on cremation requirements, licensing, and inspections, thus the dumping went unnoticed.
Georgia Basketball Coach Jim Harrick, Sr., Resigns over Fraud Allegations	March 27, 2002	University of Georgia basketball coach Jim Harrick, Sr., resigned following accusations of fraud and misconduct against himself and his assistant coach Jim Harrick, Jr., his son. Many people were left wondering who to blame for the scandal after the Harricks had been hired to coach at Georgia even though they had a record of misconduct while coaching at two other universities—UCLA and Rhode Island.
Internal Corruption Forces Adelphia Communications to Declare Bankruptcy	June 25, 2002	At the time of its collapse, Adelphia Communications Corporation was one of the largest cable providers in the United States. In June of 2002, the company declared bankruptcy as a result of the multibillion-dollar defrauding of its own executives. John Rigas, Adelphia founder, and his son, Timothy Rigas, were convicted on charges of conspiracy, bank fraud, and securities violations and were sentenced to prison terms of fifteen and twenty years respectively. The bankruptcy was one of the largest in the history of the United States.
Immunologist Resigns After Being Accused of Falsifying Research	August, 2002	Ranjit Kumar Chandra, a well-respected Canadian immunologist and nutritionist, shocked the scientific world with the revelation that he had falsified data and fabricated research results in several published papers, particularly in papers detailing studies on infant formula and on vitamin therapy in the elderly.
Historian Michael A. Bellesiles Resigns After Academic Fraud Accusations	October 25, 2002	Scandal followed the publication of Michael A. Bellesiles's 2000 book *Arming America*, a study claiming that guns were relatively rare in the American colonies and the United States before the Civil War. Although he was accused of research falsification and distortion, Bellesiles still received the coveted Bancroft Prize for American history. However, in October, 2002, he was forced to resign his professorship after a panel of historians found him guilty of scholarly misconduct.
Senator Trent Lott Praises Strom Thurmond's 1948 Presidential Campaign	December 5, 2002	A speech delivered by Mississippi senator and Senate majority leader Trent Lott on the occasion of the one hundredth birthday of South Carolina senator Strom Thurmond praised Thurmond's 1948 so-called Dixiecrat segregationist campaign for the presidency. The resulting political fallout led to Lott's resignation as majority leader.

333333

33333333333

333333

E-mail Message Prompts Inquiry into Air Force Academy Sexual Assaults	January 2, 2003	An e-mail message alleging a pattern of sexual assaults at the US Air Force Academy and official cover-ups of the assaults prompted a series of investigations and changes in academy policy. The response to the scandal, while substantive, was the subject of controversy and drew criticism both from those who found it excessive and those who considered it insufficient.
US National Security Agency Is Found to Have Spied on UN Officials	March 2, 2003	According to an investigative report by the British newspaper The Observer, the US National Security Agency had been engaging in wiretapping and other forms of spying on United Nations personnel, including Secretary-General Kofi Annan, in preparation for seeking UN Security Council support for the US-British invasion of Iraq in 2003.
New York Times Reporter Jayson Blair Is Exposed as a Fraud	April 29, 2003	The *New York Times* discovered that reporter Jayson Blair had plagiarized a story about an anguished mother of a missing US soldier in Iraq, setting off an investigation that uncovered four years of Blair's fabrications and deceit. Although Blair was fired, and the newspaper took responsibility, the credibility of not only the newspaper but all news sources was questioned.
University of Alabama Fires New Football Coach in Sex Scandal	May 3, 2003	Four months after agreeing to a seven-year, $10 million contract to become the new head football coach at the University of Alabama, Mike Price was fired for inappropriate behavior. An article in *Sports Illustrated* magazine one week later revealed that Price—who was in Florida for a golf tournament—had spent lavishly on alcohol and private dances at a strip club and had consensual sex with two of the dancers in his hotel room. In turn, Price sued the university, Time, Inc., and the reporter for libel and defamation, and he won his case.
Sexually Provocative Film *The Brown Bunny* Premieres at Cannes Film Festival	May 21, 2003	*The Brown Bunny*, a disturbing film by iconoclastic auteur Vincent Gallo that includes a provocative sequence showing fellatio, received a mixed reception from the international film community at the prestigious Cannes Film Festival. Nominated for the Palme d'Or, the film touched off a heated debate over the relationship between filmmakers and critics and ultimately between filmmakers and their audiences.
Basketball Star Kobe Bryant Is Accused of Rape	July 1, 2003	Professional basketball player Kobe Bryant was accused of sexually assaulting a nineteen-year-old concierge at a hotel resort. He denied the accusation and claimed that the sexual encounter was consensual. The prosecution dropped the criminal charges after the accuser, Katelyn Faber, refused to testify on grounds that her sexual history would fuel further media attention. Faber filed a civil suit against Bryant and settled out of court for an undisclosed amount of money.
Columnist Robert Novak Leaks the Name of CIA Operative Valerie Plame	July 14, 2003	CIA operative Valerie Plame's husband, Joseph Wilson, was a former US ambassador who had investigated claims of sales of uranium to Iraq before the US-led invasion of Iraq in 2003. Wilson publicly claimed that Iraq had not obtained uranium from Niger and that Iraq did not have weapons of mass destruction. Newspaper columnist Robert Novak then identified Plame as a CIA agent. Critics said that Plame's name was revealed to Novak by a White House official as revenge against Wilson.

Mutual Fund Companies Are Implicated in Shady Trading Practices	September 3, 2003	New York State attorney general Eliot L. Spitzer filed a legal complaint against Canary Capital Partners, a hedge fund, for fraudulent late trading and time-zone arbitrage, practices that favored select clients over ordinary customers. Investigators looked at twenty-five fund companies, which led to settlements with regulators totaling over $3.1 billion, private civil lawsuits, congressional hearings and legislative proposals, and US Securities and Exchange Commission oversight reforms.
Newspaper Claims That Arnold Schwarzenegger Groped Women	October 2, 2003	As former bodybuilder and popular film actor Arnold Schwarzenegger was running for governor of California, a number of women told reporters that he had harassed or abused them years before. The *Los Angeles Times* published a series about the accusations, but Schwarzenegger won the election nevertheless. He promised to have the charges investigated but did not follow through on his plan.
Paris Hilton Sex-Tape Appears on the Web	Early November, 2003	Paris Hilton, an heir to the Hilton Hotels fortune and actor and businessperson in her own right, became a celebrity for her famous name, beauty, and relentless partying in trendy clubs. Rick Salomon, the son of a film studio vice president, was most famous for a brief, tempestuous marriage to actor Shannon Doherty. When clips from an amateur sex tape of Salomon and Hilton appeared online, it generated the first in a long line of scandals for Hilton.
Senator Strom Thurmond's Biracial Daughter Is Revealed	December 17, 2003	US senator Strom Thurmond, a long-time proponent of racial segregation, had a daughter named Essie Mae Washington-Williams with an African American woman in 1925, a revelation made public on the CBS television news show *60 Minutes* in late 2003. Correspondent Dan Rather interviewed Washington-Williams, closing the book on decades-long rumors that Thurmond had a biracial child out of wedlock.
Pop Star Michael Jackson Is Charged with Child Molestation	December 18, 2003	In 2003, pop-music star Michael Jackson was charged with child molestation and administering an intoxicating agent to commit that felony. Jackson was later acquitted, but his career was negatively affected.
Former United Way Charity Chief Pleads Guilty to Embezzlement	March 4, 2004	Oral Suer, the former chief executive officer and head of United Way in Washington, DC, pleaded guilty to having embezzled from the organization for nearly three decades. For many years, Suer stole from the charity, taking about half a million dollars. He was sentenced to federal prison and ordered by a judge to make full restitution to United Way. The scandal led the charity to make policy changes and institute a new code of ethics.
Martha Stewart Is Convicted in Insider-Trading Scandal	March 5, 2004	In a stunning, but temporary, fall from grace, home-design guru Martha Stewart was convicted of multiple federal felonies for selling stocks immediately before those stocks were expected to decrease in value. Stewart was convicted not of insider trading but rather of lying to government agents about a trade that was not illegal.

CBS Broadcasts Photos of Abused and Tortured Prisoners at Abu Ghraib	April 28, 2004	The CBS news program *60 Minutes II* broadcast photographs of US soldiers abusing and humiliating Iraqi prisoners at Abu Ghraib prison. US officials characterized the abuse as the isolated acts of renegade soldiers. Later evidence showed that "enhanced interrogation techniques" had been approved at the highest levels of the US government, leading many to believe that prisoner abuse was common US military practice. Also, critics claim that US officials knew about and tried to cover up the abuse months before the photos were made public.
Blog "Outs" Antigay Congressman Edward Schrock	August 19, 2004	Political activist Michael Rogers claimed on his blog that US representative Edward Schrock was gay or bisexual. The blog entry linked to a recording alleged to be of Schrock speaking on a phone line for men seeking other men for gay sex. The outing led Schrock to end his 2004 reelection bid.
60 Minutes II Reports on George W. Bush's Evasion of Wartime Duty	September 8, 2004	CBS News correspondent Dan Rather presented documents in a 2004 report on *60 Minutes II* that questioned US president George W. Bush's Air National Guard service during the 1970s. The Killian documents, as they came to be called, accused Bush of having received favors to make his military record look better than it was. The documents were widely considered fakes, permanently damaging the reputations of both Rather and CBS.
Television Producer Files Sex Harassment Suit Against Bill O'Reilly	October 13, 2004	Bill O'Reilly, a conservative political commentator best known for his Fox News television show *The O'Reilly Factor*, was sued by his show's producer, Andrea Mackris, for sexual harassment. O'Reilly was first to sue Mackris, however, claiming in his preemptive suit filed the same day that Mackris and her attorney were extorting him. The matter was settled out of court for an undisclosed amount of money. In the long term, the suits had little impact on O'Reilly's or Mackris's careers in broadcasting.
Insurance Brokerage Marsh & McLennan Is Charged with Fraud	October 14, 2004	Marsh & McLennan, an international insurance brokerage and professional services company, was charged with fraud in 2004 by Eliot L. Spitzer, the attorney general of New York. Confronted by pages of testimony affirming its illegal actions, the company settled out of court, paying a fine of $850 million.
Former Baseball Star Mark McGwire Evades Congressional Questions on Steroid Use	March 17, 2005	After being identified as a steroid user by former teammate José Canseco, Mark McGwire was asked to testify at a US House of Representatives hearing on steroid use in Major League Baseball. At the hearing, McGwire refused to answer questions about his own history with performance-enhancing drugs or their use by baseball players in general.
US Air Force Investigates Religious Intolerance at Its Academy	June 22, 2005	Claims that cadets and staff at the US Air Force Academy were pushing cadets to accept evangelical Christianity prompted an official inquiry into the allegations. Investigators concluded that the academy faced religious insensitivity, but not discrimination. These conclusions were controversial, and debate continues over religious diversity in the military.

Federal Agents Raid Congressman Randall Cunningham's Home	July 1, 2005	A raid by federal agents of the home of US representative Randall Cunningham in an exclusive suburb north of San Diego, California, led to Cunningham's resignation from Congress and to his criminal conviction for bribery, mail and wire fraud, and income tax evasion. He pleaded guilty to accepting bribes amounting to at least $2.4 million from several defense contractors. He was sent to prison for eight years and four months, the longest prison sentence ever for a former member of Congress.
Government Incompetence Mars Hurricane Katrina Relief Efforts	Beginning August 29, 2005	As Hurricane Katrina came ashore along the Gulf coast—most specifically near the city of New Orleans, Louisiana—an ill-prepared local, state, and federal bureaucracy was deeply criticized for its failed response to the devastation. Because many of the victims were African American, critics also claimed that racism was at the heart of government ineffectiveness and inaction. The incompetence led to reform in emergency management at all levels of government and to further questions about the role of racism in how help is administered.
Westar Energy Executives Are Found Guilty of Looting Their Company	September 12, 2005	David Wittig, the former chief executive officer of Westar Energy, Inc., was convicted, along with a company vice president, Douglas Lake, of stealing millions of dollars from the company for personal gain. For their crimes, in which they paid themselves millions of dollars in benefits and used company-owned property for personal matters, Wittig and Lake were heavily fined and sent to prison.
Liberian Workers Sue Bridgestone Firestone over Slave Labor	November 17, 2005	Workers at the world's largest rubber plantation, in Liberia, brought a federal lawsuit against their employer, Bridgestone Firestone, in a US court. Organized by the International Labor Rights Fund on behalf of some six thousand people who lived and worked on the plantation, the suit alleged a litany of abuses including low wages and poor working conditions, forced labor, and the use of children as workers.
Spokane, Washington, Mayor Recalled in Gay-Sex Scandal Spokane	December 6, 2005	Spokane mayor James E. West was a conservative Republican Washington State senator and a staunch leader against gay and lesbian rights while in the legislature. In May, 2005, local media reported that West had chatted online with a seventeen-year-old boy about having sex with him. The media also said that West had sexually molested boys years earlier and that he had been having sex with young men whom he met online. West was recalled from office in 2005.
Author James Frey's Memoir of Addiction Found to Have Been Fictionalized	January, 2006	Frey's gained celebrity status after his memoir or addiction, *A Million Little Pieces*, is selected by Oprah Winfrey for her book club in 2005, but an investigation led to the revelation in early 2006 that some parts of the book were fictionalized, leading to immense public humiliation and a class-action lawsuit for the author.
Duke Lacrosse Players Are Accused of Gang Rape	March 14, 2006	The Duke University men's lacrosse team received scandalous national attention when an exotic dancer accused three of the team's players of raping her during a party. The case led to heated public debate about rape, racism, and press coverage. It also led to the firing of the team's head coach, to the cancellation of the lacrosse team's season, to the disbarring and public disgrace of the prosecutor, to the exoneration of the three indicted players, and to civil lawsuits.

Manufacturer Recalls Pet Food That Killed Thousands of American Pets	Summer, 2006-March 16, 2007	In response to reports of the deaths of thousands of pets in the United States who consumed tainted pet food, the Chinese government and the US Food and Drug Administration identified two Chinese companies that manufactured adulterated food additives with harmful chemicals to maximize their profits.
New York Times Exposes Grading Scandal at Auburn University	July 14, 2006	A sociology professor at Auburn University contacted the *New York Times* to report that his colleague was granting directed-study classes to athletes so that they could raise their grade point averages and remain eligible to play. The student athletes were given inflated grades in courses with virtually no academic work—a practice that also led to a misleading academic ranking of the university by the NCAA.
Actor Mel Gibson Is Caught Making Anti-Semitic Remarks	July 28, 2006	Star film actor Mel Gibson was stopped for erratic driving and speeding and then arrested for drunk driving on Pacific Coast Highway in Malibu. During the traffic stop, he made anti-Semitic remarks to the sheriff's deputy who detained him. Gibson's arrest and vulgar rants were detailed by the media within hours of his arrest. The actor made several public apologies, but the scandal did not affect his career.
Newsweek Reveals That Hewlett-Packard Spied on Its Own Board	September 18, 2006	*Newsweek* magazine revealed that Patricia Dunn, the chairperson of technology giant Hewlett-Packard, had arranged for electronic surveillance of board members and journalists to stop corporate leaks to the press. Through the use of pretexting, company investigators lied to illegally obtain telephone records. The resulting scandal led to a criminal case in California, a congressional investigation, federal criminal charges, and several company resignations.
Congressman Mark Foley Resigns in Sex Scandal Involving a Teenage Page	September 29, 2006	Congressman Mark Foley resigned from the US House of Representatives when it was discovered that he sent sexually explicit e-mails and text messages to at least one teenage boy who was serving as a congressional page. The resignation triggered investigations into how House leadership addressed earlier accusations. Dennis Hastert, Speaker of the House, did not return for another term, and Republican seats in the House may have been lost because of the scandal.
Evangelist Kent Hovind Is Convicted of Federal Tax Violations	November 2, 2006	American evangelist Kent Hovind, who founded Creation Science Evangelism in 1989 but never paid payroll or income taxes despite his lucrative income, was found guilty of tax fraud. After an investigation by the US Internal Revenue Service that included a raid of his home and business, he was convicted of fifty-eight tax-related offenses and sentenced to ten years in federal prison.
Male Escort Reveals Sexual Liaisons with Evangelist Ted Haggard	November 2, 2006	Ted Haggard, the founder and senior pastor of New Life Church in Colorado, was disgraced after a male escort revealed on television that Haggard had sex with him over a three-year period. Haggard, asked by the church to leave his ministry and the Colorado Springs area, also resigned his leadership position with the influential National Association of Evangelicals. A church overseer claimed Haggard was "completely heterosexual" following three weeks of "restorative" therapy.

News Corp Abandons Plan to Publish O. J. Simpson's Book	November 20, 2006	News Corp announced plans to publish a book by the notorious former football star O. J. Simpson called *If I Did It*, an allegedly speculative account of how Simpson would have murdered his former wife, Nicole Brown Simpson, and her friend, Ronald Goldman. Public reaction was so overwhelmingly negative that News Corp canceled both its planned television special and the book's release. Goldman's family received legal title to the book and published it in 2007 as Simpson's actual confession.
Subprime Mortgage Industry Begins to Collapse	Early 2007	During the 2000-2006 housing boom, American lenders issued a staggering total of $1.5 trillion in risky subprime mortgages, relying on rapidly appreciating home values to protect their investments. As home prices began declining in 2006, record numbers of debtors defaulted, leading to soaring home foreclosure rates, lender bankruptcies, and a general weakening of the US economy. Mismanagement and outright fraud at all levels created a cascading national and international financial crisis leading to industry and government reform.
Washington Post Exposes Decline of Walter Reed Army Hospital	February 18, 2007	The *Washington Post* published the first in a series of exposés on the medical neglect and deplorable living conditions of wounded soldiers at Walter Reed Army Medical Center, the Army's major hospital. The exposé led to a national scandal and public condemnation, the resignations of top government and military officials, the formation of a presidential commission to investigate the matter, and new, focused programs for soldier-patients systemwide.
Shock Jock Don Imus Loses His Radio Show over Sexist and Racist Remarks	April 11, 2007	On his morning radio show, notorious shock jock Don Imus referred to members of the Rutgers University women's basketball team as "nappy-headed hos" after his cohost said they were "hardcore hos," creating a national furor. The scandal cost Imus his job, temporarily, and prompted a nationwide discussion of racist and sexist speech on the radio.
Congressman William J. Jefferson Is Indicted for Corruption	June 4, 2007	In March, 2005, the Federal Bureau of Investigation began investigating Louisiana congressman William J. Jefferson for corrupt business dealings. Jefferson had been videotaped receiving $100,000 from an investor-informer to establish business contacts in Nigeria. The FBI searched Jefferson's home and found $90,000 of the cash in his refrigerator freezer. The agency later raided his office in Washington, DC, which provoked intense debate about the right of law enforcement to search congressional offices.
Senator David Vitter's Name Is Found in DC Madam's Address Book	July 9, 2007	Deborah Jeane Palfrey was convicted of racketeering for running a Washington, DC, prostitution ring. One of her clients was David Vitter, a conservative Republican senator from Louisiana famed for long-time public dedication to traditional family values. His name, and the names of her other clients, was released by Palfrey, and Vitter admitted to having sinned. The scandal embarrassed Vitter but cost Palfrey her life; Palfrey committed suicide in 2008.
Florida Politician Is Arrested for Soliciting an Undercover Male Police Officer	July 11, 2007	Elected to the Florida House of Representatives in 2000, Bob Allen attempted to pay a male undercover police officer twenty dollars to perform oral sex on the officer in a public restroom at a Florida park. The arrest drew national attention for its tawdriness and hypocrisy, and for Allen's connections to Republican presidential candidate John McCain.

University of Colorado Fires Professor for Plagiarism and Research Falsification	July 24, 2007	Under intense public and academic scrutiny for writing an inflammatory essay about the September 11, 2001, terrorist attacks in the United States, university professor Ward Churchill was subjected to an academic misconduct investigation and subsequently fired for plagiarism and for fabricating and falsifying information. He filed a lawsuit seeking reinstatement.
Football Star Michael Vick Pleads Guilty to Financing a Dogfighting Ring	August 20, 2007	Michael Vick, a star quarterback in the National Football League, and three other men were convicted and imprisoned for their roles in a dogfighting ring on property owned by Vick in rural Virginia. Vick was suspended from the NFL, lost lucrative commercial contracts, was sued for millions of dollars by his creditors, and was ordered to pay for the long-term care of the dogs rescued from his property.
New England Patriots Football Team Is Fined for Spying on Other Teams	September 13, 2007	The National Football League levied the highest fines in league history against the New England Patriots after collecting evidence that Patriots coaches had violated league rules against videotaping opponents' private signals. Coach Bill Belichick and the team were fined. The unprecedented penalties underlined the severity of the misconduct, damaged the credibility of three league championships, and helped foster public cynicism about ethics in professional sports.
Olympic Champion Marion Jones Admits Steroid Use	October 5, 2007	Olympic track star Marion Jones admitted in court to having lied to federal investigators in 2003 about her use of performance-enhancing drugs and about her knowledge of the involvement of a former boyfriend and former coach in a scheme to cash millions of dollars worth of stolen and forged checks. Jones was jailed and ordered to forfeit her Olympic medals.
New York Governor Eliot Spitzer Resigns in Prostitution Scandal	March 12, 2008	Eliot L. Spitzer a former New York attorney general who built his reputation by crusading aggressively against Wall Street corruption, resigned as the governor of New York following news reports that he had spent tens of thousands of dollars patronizing prostitutes with an escort service.
Singer R. Kelly Is Acquitted on Child Pornography Charges	June 13, 2008	American singer Robert Kelly, better known as R. Kelly, was indicted for sexual molestation and child pornography after a videotape surfaced that appeared to show him having sex with an underage girl. The tape was widely circulated. The sexual molestation charges were dropped and Kelly was ultimately found not guilty on charges of soliciting a minor for child pornography.
NBA Referee Tim Donaghy Is Sentenced to Prison for Betting on Games	July 29, 2008	A veteran referee, Tim Donaghy put the integrity of the National Basketball Association at risk by gambling on basketball games, including those in the postseason, and making calls that may have affected games. Professional basketball referees in the United States are not permitted to gamble, except at racetracks during the NBA off-season. Donaghy was sentenced to fifteen months in federal prison.
Senator John Edwards Confirms Rumors of Extramarital Affair	August 8, 2008	On August 8, 2008, former presidential candidate John Edwards confirmed long-running rumors that he engaged in an extramarital affair with a former campaign staff member, videographer Rielle Hunter. It was later confirmed that the couple had a child together.

Detroit Mayor Kwame Kilpatrick Resigns in Corruption Scandal	September 4, 2008	Detroit Mayor Kwame Kilpatrick resigned in September after pleading guilty to obstruction of justice. He was also charged with numerous other felony accounts and served ninety-nine days in jail.
Financial Institutions and Markets Begin to Collapse	September 7, 2008	Led by a complex web of actions that included a drive to maximize profits and an abandonment of prudence and responsibility, major financial institutions in the United States began to fail. By September, 2008, excessive risk-taking, inadequate cash reserves, excessive debt levels, and the subprime mortgage crisis led to financial collapse. The dire financial condition, coupled with an economic recession in the United States, forced US government interventions that, by November 24, totaled $7.7 trillion in bailouts for these financial institutions.
Bernie Madoff is Arrested and Charged with Running a Massive Ponzi Scheme	December 11, 2008	Investment consultant Bernard L. Madoff is charged with running a criminal enterprise known as a Ponzi scheme which defrauded countless nonprofit organizations and businesses, costing them nearly $50 billion.
Chicago Governor Rod Blagojevich is Impeached and Removed from Office	January 29, 2009	In a complex case of bribery and corruption, Blagojevich is ultimately charged with attempting to use the US Senate seat being vacated by former Illinois Senator and US President-elect Barack Obama for personal gain, among other charges, offering to give the seat to the highest bidder.
Governor Mark Sanford Reveals Extramarital Affair with Argentinean Mistress	June 24, 2009	Following an ethics investigation into his handling of state travel funds, South Carolina Governor Mark Sanford admits to an extramarital affair with an Argentinean woman and resigns from his post as chairman of the Republican Governors Association.
Sarah Palin announces her resignation as Governor of Alaska	July 3, 2009	After the McCain-Palin ticket was defeated in the 2008 presidential elections, vice-presidential candidate and polarizing political figure Sarah Palin announces her resignation as governor of Alaska, citing the cost of fighting ethics investigations as one of several reasons.
Tiger Woods Announces an Indefinite Leave from Golf after Admitting to Infidelity	December, 2009	Tiger Woods announced that he would be taking an indefinite leave from golf after a series of scandalous affairs unravels the professional golfer's carefully cultivated image as devout family man, costing Woods his marriage and several lucrative endorsement deals.

■ Time Line

Additional dates on legislation, US Supreme Court cases, films, television shows, plays, literature, popular music, and sports can be found in other appendixes.

2000

International events: (Mar. 26) After serving as acting president of Russia following the resignation of President Boris Yeltsin in 1999, Vladimir Putin is elected president of Russia; he is reelected in 2004. (June 28) Elian Gonzalez, the subject of a public international child custody battle, returns to Cuba with his father and other family members. (Oct. 5) Serbian President Slobodan Milosevic leaves office. (Dec. 1) Vicente Fox of the National Action Party (PAN) is elected president of Mexico, ending seventy-one years of rule by the Institutional Revolutionary Party (PRI).

Government and politics: (July 1) HB847, a Vermont civil unions law, goes into effect, the first of its kind in the United States. (Nov. 7) Election of former Texas governor George W. Bush as president of the United States, an outcome that will not be made official for a month following a decision by Vice President Al Gore to contest Floridian ballots; Gore will eventually be declared winner of the popular vote (50.99 million versus 50.46 million). (Dec. 12) The Florida Supreme Court reaches a decision in *Bush v. Gore*, ending the rancorous contest over Floridian ballots in 2000 US Presidential election, with Bush deemed winner of the electoral vote (271 to 266).

Military and war: (Sept.29): Following a very public visit by Likud party leader Ariel Sharon of Israel to the Temple Mount in Jerusalem, large-scale rioting breaks out in the region, leading to the Al-Aqsa Intifada, the second Palestinian uprising since the late 1980s. (Oct. 12) Seventeen US crew members are killed and several more are injured during a suicide attack by al-Qaeda on the USS *Cole* in Aden, Yemen.

Society: (Apr. 12) Heavy metal band Metallica files a lawsuit in US District Court against peer-to-peer file-sharing software creator Napster, charging that the company enables digital piracy though copyright infringement. (Oct. 26) PlayStation 2 is released in North America; it will eventually become the best-selling video game console of all time.

Business and economics: (Jan. 10) Internet pioneer AOL purchases multinational media corporation Time Warner for $164 million. (Mar. 10) After reaching 5,132 the NASDAQ stock market index closes at 5,048, a closing value considered the peak of the so-called dot-com bubble.

Transportation: (Feb. 11) JetBlue Airways, considered a low-cost alternative to other airlines, begins operations out of John F. Kennedy International Airport in New York. (July 25) New York–bound Air France flight 4590 crashes in Gonesse, France, killing 109 passengers and crew members and four people on the ground.

Science and technology: (Jan. 6) The Pyrenean ibex subspecies becomes extinct after the death of its last remaining member; later efforts throughout the decade to clone the subspecies are unsuccessful. (Feb.) Imaging radar aboard the space shuttle *Endeavour* captures data to assemble the most comprehensive topographic map of Earth, covering 80 percent of its land surface. (Feb. 14) The Near Earth Asteroid Rendezvous (NEAR) spacecraft begins a yearlong orbit of the asteroid Eros, gathering data on its chemical composition, mineralogy, shape, and structure. (Mar.) By the end of March, thirty-four extrasolar planets have been discovered. By 2005, the number of known extrasolar planets exceeds 100. (June26) United States President Bill Clinton and British Prime Minister Tony Blair jointly announce that the Human Genome Project and Celera Genomics Corporation have completed a first survey of the human genome.

Environment and health: (Sept.28) The Food and Drug Administration approves medical abortions using mifepristone (RU-486) as an alternative to surgical abortion. (Oct. 11) A coal slurry spill in Martin County, Kentucky, in which more than 306 million gallons of slurry (containing hazardous arsenic and mercury) is released into the Tug Fork River results in one of the regions' largest environmental disasters.

Arts and literature: (June1) Marvel Studios releases *X-Men*, a film widely considered to be the first in a revitalization of superhero action films. (July 8)

Harry Potter and the Goblet of Fire, J. K. Rowling's fourth book in the Harry Potter series, is released simultaneously in the United States and Great Britain; the previous novels received earlier publications in Great Britain. (Sept. 13) The first Latin Grammy Awards ceremony is held in Los Angeles, California, with Luis Miguel winning album of the year honors for *Amarte Es Un Placer* and Cuban vocalist Ibrahim Ferrer winning the award for best new artist at the age of seventy-two.

Popular culture: (Jan. 15) Late-night television talk show host David Letterman undergoes quintuple heart bypass surgery; on February 21, he returns to *Late Night with David Letterman* after several weeks in postoperative recovery. (Feb. 13) In print for nearly fifty years, daily comic strip *Peanuts* ends following the death of creator Charles M. Schultz.

Sports: (May 17) Turkish football team Galatasary defeats Arsenal FC 4–1 on penalty kicks at the UEFA Cup Final in Copenhagen, Denmark, becoming the first Turkish team to win a European cup. (Mar. 26) The Kingdome, former home to Seattle, Washington, professional sports teams, is demolished. (Sept.15–Oct. 1) 2000 Summer Olympic Games are held in Sydney, Australia.

Crime: (Jan. 31) British general practitioner Harold Shipman is sentenced to fifteen life sentences for murdering his own patients; it is believed he killed 215 or more of his patients. (Mar. 9) Art dealer Ely Sakhai is arrested by FBI agents for peddling forgeries of impressionist and postimpressionist works by Marc Chagall and Paul Gauguin, among others.

2001

International events: (Mar. 2) Islamic fundamentalist leaders in Afghanistan, known as the Taliban, begin destroying statues of the Buddha in central Afghanistan as part of a wider effort to enforce strict Sharia law nationwide. (Sept. 9) Mahmoud Shah Massoud, a key commander in the Afghan National Alliance, a resistance group opposing the Taliban, is assassinated by suicide bomber in Afghanistan. (Dec. 13) The Indian Parliament building is attacked by terrorists, killing twelve, including police and security personnel; the incident leads to heightened tensions between the two nations, both of which have nuclear weapons and a history of international disputes.

Government and politics: (Feb. 18) FBI special agent Robert Hanssen is arrested after it is revealed he spied on the United States for Russia between 1979 and 2001. (Oct. 26) Having passed in the US House of Representatives by a vote of 357–66 and the Senate by 98–1, the USA PATRIOT Act is enacted, giving the US government broad antiterrorist powers.

Military and war: (Sept. 11) Nineteen al-Qaeda terrorists hijack passenger airplanes—American Airlines flights 11 and 77 and United Airlines flights 93 and 175—in suicide attacks on key US targets. In the aftermath, 2,996 people are killed at sites in New York City (the site of the World Trade Center), Washington, DC (the Pentagon), and Shanksville, Pennsylvania. (Oct. 7) Operation Enduring Freedom launches in Afghanistan in retaliation for the September 11 terrorist attacks. The military campaign consists of the US and allies Great Britain, France, Australia, and the Northern Alliance. The Taliban are ousted from the capitol Kabul in November, although key members of its leadership, as well as that of al-Qaeda, will remain on the run throughout the decade. The war will continue to be fought throughout the rest of the decade.

Society: (May 1) Washington, DC, intern Chandra Levy goes missing; it is later suspected her romantic involvement with married Congressman Gary Condit (D-CA) led to her disappearance, however it is later proven she was murdered by Ingmar Guandique, a Salvadoran immigrant. Throughout the summer, news coverage of the scandal and ensuing investigation increase, abating drastically on September 11.

Business and economics: (Sept. 6) The US Department of Justice announces it will seek a new, lesser settlement in *United States v. Microsoft,* ending speculation that it will force Microsoft to become two distinct companies. (Dec. 2) Energy company Enron files for Chapter 11 bankruptcy, the largest in history. It is later revealed that Enron executives, including CEO Kenneth Lay, sold their stock in Enron, even as the price plummeted from a high of $90 in 2000.

Transportation: (Dec. 3) After much public anticipation, inventor Dean Kamen announces the Segway PT, a battery-powered device that was designed to revolutionize personal transportation by utilizing a self-balancing system that keeps the vehicle upright and easily operated controls. (Dec. 22) So-called shoe-bomber Richard Reid, a British man with tenuous ties to al-Qaeda, attempts to blow up an American Airlines passenger flight from Paris, France, to Miami, Florida, but is stopped from doing so by several passengers and crew members.

Science and technology: (Jan. 15) The free online encyclopedia Wikipedia launches in English; by year's end, several international editions will be launched. By January 2002, the article count reaches nearly 20,000. (Feb.) The Agile Software Development Alliance is formed, leading to publication of a manifesto that revolutionizes software development methods. (Apr. 28) At a cost of $20 million, the first space tourist, Dennis Tito, arrives aboard the Soyuz TM-32 Russian space vehicle; Tito spends one week aboard the craft. (Nov. 2) United States Department of Justice and Microsoft agree to settle *United States v. Microsoft* antitrust lawsuit.

Environment and health: (Feb. 21) The European Commission bans imports of British livestock and livestock products such as meat and dairy after officials identify cases of foot-and-mouth disease in pigs leading to outbreak that results in mass slaughters of cattle, pigs, and sheep and over hundreds of millions of pounds in lost revenues and fears of international outbreaks.

Arts and literature: (Sept. 20) New Jersey poet laureate Amiri Baraka recites his poem "Somebody Blew Up America" at a public reading. The reading leads to public furor over Baraka's claims in the poem regarding alleged Israeli foreknowledge about the September 11 attacks. As a result, Governor James McGreevey attempts unsuccessfully to remove him from the poet laureate post. (Oct. 12) Novelist Jonathan Franzen, author of *The Corrections*, a September selection for the popular and lucrative Oprah's Book Club, expresses his disdain for the book club in an interview. When his comments are published, the book club selection and standard author appearance on Winfrey's television show are cancelled.

Popular culture: (Nov. 10) Apple launches the iPod, a digital music player that plays MP3 and other audio formats. After its launch, the iPod brand name will become synonymous with "MP3 player." (Nov.–Dec.) Two of the highest-grossing film adaptations of fantasy novels in history are released: *Harry Potter and the Sorcerer's Stone* (Nov. 16) and *The Lord of the Rings: Fellowship of the Ring* (Dec. 19).

Sports: (Feb. 18) NASCAR driver Dale Earnhardt Sr. dies in an accident during the final lap of the Daytona 500. (Apr. 8) Golfer Tiger Woods wins the 2001 Masters Tournament by two strokes over his closest competitor; this win means Woods holds all four major golf tournament titles simultaneously, the first ever to do so.

Crime: (June 11) Timothy McVeigh, who carried out the 1995 Oklahoma City bombings that killed 168 people, is executed by lethal injection at a federal prison in Indiana. (Oct. 6) Robert Stevens, a photo editor for the *Sun* tabloid newspaper, is the first person to die from a bioterrorist attack involving anthrax mailed to media outlets and the offices of two US senators. (Nov. 25) So-called American Taliban John Walker Lindh is captured in Northern Afghanistan by Northern Alliance troops; Lindh's collaboration with the Taliban began the previous May.

2002

International events: (Jan. 18) Sierra Leone civil war ends after nearly eleven years. (Apr. 4) Angolan civil war ends after twenty-seven years. (Apr. 11) A military coup d'état attempt against Venezuelan president Hugo Chavez fails following an outbreak of hostility toward Chavez's attempts to assert control over state-run oil company PDVSA; a popular uprising stops the coup attempt. (May 20) After being invaded shortly after independence from Portugal in 1975, East Timor achieves independence from Indonesia. (Oct. 12) Two hundred and two people, including Indonesians and Australian tourists, are killed in terrorist bombings at nightclubs in Bali, Indonesia; the attacks were allegedly carried out in retaliation for East Timorian independence. (Oct. 23) Russian authorities end a hostage crisis in a Moscow theater in which 116 of 763 hostages being held by Chechen rebels are killed.

Government and politics: (Jan. 29) US President George W. Bush uses the phrase "axis of evil" to describe Iraq, Iran, and North Korea and their threats to the US and its allies. (Apr. 11) The International Criminal Court is ratified by sixty member states of the United Nations, not including the United States. (Nov. 5) Drawing on post–September 11 support for the Bush administration, Republicans gain a 51–49 majority in the Senate while further cementing their majority in the

House of Representatives during midterm elections.

Military and war: (June 1) At a speech at the US Military Academy at West Point, Bush declares his pre-emptive warfare policy. (Mar. 2) Operation Anaconda is launched in an effort to rout al-Qaeda and Taliban forces in the Sha-i-Kot Valley, a mountainous region in eastern Afghanistan's Paktia province. (Sept.12) Echoing remarks made during a joint press conference with British Prime Minister Tony Blair on September 7, Bush calls for regime change in Iraq during a speech at the United Nations.

Society: (Mar. 24) Halle Berry becomes the first African American to win an Academy Award for best actress for her role in *Monster's Ball*; actor Denzel Washington wins best actor for his role in *Training Day*, marking the first time both top acting honors went to African Americans.

Business and economics: (Jan. 1) The euro is circulated in twelve European nations, including Germany, Spain, France, and Greece. (July 21) Telecommunications giant WorldCom files for Chapter 11 bankruptcy protection, beating Enron as the record-holder for the largest bankruptcy in US history; WorldCom, as MCI, will later be purchased by Verizon Communications.

Transportation (excluding communications for the 2000s): (May 24) Queen Elizabeth II of Great Britain is on hand for the opening of the Falkirk Wheel in Scotland. (Dec. 31) A ceremony is held in Shanghai, China, to inaugurate the Shanghai Maglev Train, the world's first magnetic levitation train line.

Science and technology: (Nov. 15) Microsoft launches its influential online video gaming service, Xbox Live, further adding to the growing online multiplayer format and helping to popularize its Xbox console, which had been launched the year before to compete with Sony's PlayStation 2 and Nintendo's GameCube consoles.

Environment and health: (Aug.) Flood waters ravage European nations Austria, Czech Republic, Germany, and others, killing one hundred people and causing more than 15 billion euros in damages.

Arts and literature: (Oct. 18) *Naqoyqatsi: Life as War*, a documentary film featuring music by American composer Phillip Glass, is released. The film is the third in a trilogy begun in 1983 with *Koyaanisqatsi: Life Out of Balance*.

Popular culture: (May 21) Television show *24*, starring Kiefer Sutherland as a counterterrorist operative, ends its first season. (Sept. 3) The Rolling Stones kick off a concert tour in Boston, Massachusetts, to celebrate their fortieth anniversary. (Dec. 13) Actor Sean Penn visits Baghdad, Iraq. An outspoken critic of the Bush administration, Penn will later travel to Cuba to interview President Raul Castro.

Sports: (Feb. 8–24) The 2002 Winter Olympics are held in Salt Lake City, Utah. These are the first games held in the United States since the 1996 Summer Olympics in Atlanta, Georgia. (Nov. 4) National League baseball team Arizona Diamondbacks defeat American League team New York Yankees in game 7 of the World Series, less than one month after the September 11 terrorist attacks in New York City.

Crime: (Feb. 1) *Wall Street Journal* bureau chief Daniel Pearl is executed by Pakistani militants in Karachi; a videotape of his death is circulated later that month. (Mar. 12) Andrea Yates, the mother of five children whom she murdered by drowning in June 2001, is sentenced to a life term; her sentence will later by overruled, in part because of conflicting testimony related to an episode of television show *Law & Order* which resembled the Yates case. She is later deemed not guilty by reason of insanity. (Oct. 24) Beltway sniper suspect John Allen Muhammad and his teenaged accomplice John Boyd Malvo are arrested in Maryland after a lengthy manhunt for the killer or killers of several people throughout the Maryland-DC-Virginia area; the pair are accused of killing and wounding more than a dozen people since the beginning of that month.

2003

International events: (Mar. 12) Serbian prime minister Zoran Dindic is assassinated by Zvezdan Jovanovic, allegedly a member of a Serbian organized crime syndicate. (Aug. 11) Liberian president Charles Taylor resigns following pressure from the administration of US president George W. Bush; Taylor is later tried for crimes against humanity and war crimes stemming from his actions during a civil war in neighboring Liberia.

Government and politics: (Feb. 5) US secretary of state Colin Powell delivers a speech before the United Nations to reveal irrefutable proof of Iraqi weapons of mass destruction, and thus proof that an invasion is justified; it is later revealed the proof was fabricated. (May 1) US president George W. Bush declares "mission accomplished" in Iraq during a speech aboard the USS *Abraham Lincoln* following the end of "major combat operations"; Bush will later be criticized for presumption of victory so soon after the fall of Baghdad.

Military and war: (Mar. 19) Operation Iraqi Freedom, the US-led invasion of Iraq, begins; while the first phase of operations lasts just three weeks ending April 9, and victory is declared by the US, the Iraq War will contain to be fought throughout the rest of the decade. (July 22) Qusay and Uday Hussein, sons of Iraqi president Saddam Hussein, are killed during a firefight with US soldiers in Mosul, Iraq. (Dec. 13) Saddam Hussein is captured in Adwar, Iraq, during Operation Red Dawn. He is held in US custody to await trial and sentencing and then hanged in 2006.

Society: (Fed 15) Antiwar demonstrations are held on five continents around the world in anticipation of US-led invasion of Iraq; estimates state that between 60 and 100 million people demonstrated worldwide, including in North America, throughout Europe, and even Antarctica. (Feb. 23) A nightclub fire in West Warwick, Rhode Island, kills one hundred people during a pyrotechnics display at a concert by the rock band Great White. (Aug. 14) A massive blackout affects approximately 55 million people in the Northeastern United States and Ontario, Canada. (Nov. 13) Alabama Supreme Court justice Roy Moore is removed from public office after refusing to obey an order to remove a monument to the Ten Commandments he installed on the grounds of the Alabama state judicial building in Montgomery.

Business and economics: (Apr. 28) Apple launches the iTunes Music Store, with sales of $1 million reached in five days. The application is launched for Windows in October. (Sept. 8) The Recording Industry Association of America announces 261 lawsuits have been filed against individual users of peer-to-peer file-sharing services.

Transportation: (Nov. 26) Following a devastating 2000 crash and a post–September 11 dip in the airline industry, the Concorde supersonic jet is retired.

Science and technology: (Feb. 1) NASA space shuttle *Columbia* breaks up upon reentry, killing all seven crew members; an investigation reveals that the causes of the accident were both physical (insulation foam striking the spacecraft's left wing at launch) as well as organizational. (Feb. 11) NASA releases images related to the Wilkinson Anisotropy Microwave Probe, which mapped the universe showing the cosmic background radiation, the "afterglow" of the big bang, and pinpoints the age of the universe at 13.7 billion years. (Apr. 14) The US National Human Genome Research Institute finishes the Human Genome Project; as a result of rapid computational and technological change throughout the project, the end is reached two years ahead of schedule. (June 7) *The Lancet* reports that the combination of conventional chemotherapy and new antiangiogenesis drugs—which starve cancer tumors of their blood supply by preventing them from growing blood vessels—proves effective with colon cancer patients. (Sept. 30) It is announced that biologists have discovered that mouse stem cells can develop into both sperm and egg cells in vitro, raising the question of whether the same is possible with human stem cells. (Oct. 13) The Public Library of Science launches its *PLoS Biology* journal, a pioneer in the open access scholarly publishing model. (Oct. 15) China becomes the third nation to launch a manned space mission with the twenty-one-hour Shenzhou 5 mission piloted by Yang Lewei. Its second manned space mission followed in 2005.

Environment and health: (Mar. 12) Following reports of outbreaks of SARS, or sudden acute respiratory syndrome, throughout Asian countries, the World Health Organization issues a global alert; by the time the outbreak is contained, 774 people have died and more than 8000 infected. (June–Aug.) A heat wave kills approximately tens of thousands of people across Western Europe, including nearly 15,000 in France; in 2008, it is reported that the death toll was 70,000 people.

Arts and literature: (Mar. 23) *Chicago* directed by Rob Marshall becomes the first movie musical to win best picture at the Academy Awards since *Oliver!* in 1968.

Popular culture: (Apr.) *Action Comics* #800 is released. The first issue of the Superman comic, published in 1938, will later sell at auction for a record $2.16 million. (Aug. 6) As a drive to recall California Governor Grey Davis (R) progresses, action movie star Arnold Schwarzenegger announces he will run for governor of California on *The Tonight Show with Jay Leno*; he is elected in October with 49 percent of the vote.

Sports: (June 17) Manchester United star David Beckham announces he is leaving the club to join Real Madrid. He leaves Real Madrid to play for the Los Angeles Galaxy in 2007. (July) A former United States Olympic Committee (USOC) drug control administrator accuses the USOC of failing to punish athletes who have failed tests for banned substances; this is later substantiated by Olympic runner Carl Lewis, who medaled in the 1988 Summer Olympics in Seoul, South Korea.

Crime: (Jan. 5) British police arrest several suspects in a planned ricin bioterrorist attack on the London Underground subway system. The incident sets off fears that Great Britain has become a major al-Qaeda target. (July 2) National Basketball Association star Kobe Bryant is accused of rape; the charges are dismissed in September 2004. (Nov. 20) Pop star Michael Jackson turns himself in to police in Santa Barbara, California, after allegations of child molestation surfaced, the second time such charges have been leveled against him since the 1990s. He is later deemed not guilty after a lengthy trial.

2004

International events: (Feb. 29) After a weeks-long effort to oust him, Haitian President Jean-Bertrand Aristide leaves office amid charges that the coup-d'état was aided by the US government. (May 1) Membership in the European Union increases after ten nations, including seven former Eastern Bloc nations, join; aside from the geographic change, the membership additions change the political makeup of the EU as well, effectively reestablishing several nations that had not fared well during the Cold War under Soviet rule, or after. (Sept. 18) United Nations Security Council resolution 1564 is adopted, threatening sanctions against Sudan if they do not agree to halt ethnic violence against Darfur; the attempted genocide in Sudan results in more than one million people fleeing to Western Sudan and neighboring Chad. (Dec. 26) A massive undersea earthquake in the Indian Ocean causes tsunamis which result in the deaths of over 280,000 people in Indonesia, Sri Lanka, Thailand, India, and elsewhere throughout the region.

Government and politics: (June 5) Former US president Ronald Reagan passes away at age ninety-three in California. Since the late 1980s, Reagan had been suffering from advancing stages of Alzheimer's disease since a diagnosis in the 1990s. (Nov. 2) President George W. Bush is reelected president of the United States over his opponent Senator John Kerry (D-MA). Bush carries the election with 286 electoral votes and 50.7 percent of the popular vote, while Kerry receives 251 electoral votes and 48.3 percent of the popular vote.

Military and war: (Mar. 11) A series of terrorist train bombings kills 191 people in Madrid, Spain; al-Qaeda claims that the attacks are in retaliation for Spanish support of the United States and its allies in the global War on Terrorism. (Oct. 9) Hamid Karzai becomes Afghan president after acting as interim president for the previous two years.

Society: (Feb. 1) Pop singer Janet Jackson's breast is partially exposed as a result of "wardrobe malfunction" during a live broadcast of the halftime show for Super Bowl XXXVIII. The incident raises questions about levels of indecency on network television. (May 17) Massachusetts becomes first state in the nation to allow same-sex marriage. Legal challenges will follow, as will other state laws allowing same-sex marriage.

Business and economics: (Feb. 4) Social media website Facebook launches for college students at Harvard University; after removing membership restrictions, the service will have over 300 million users by decade's end. (Aug. 19) Google's initial public offering (IPO) raises $1.6 billion after a second-quarter growth of 125 percent over the same period a year previously.

Transportation: (Dec. 22) The Transportation Safety Administration eases its policy on passenger body pat-downs at airports after several hundred women complain that the process is a personal violation.

Science and technology: (Jan. 4) The Mars exploration rovers, *Spirit* and *Opportunity*, land at different locations on the Martian surface and return unprecedented photographs of topographic features as well as geological data. (Jan. 26) The Mydoom e-mail worm, also known as Norvag and Mimail-R, is detected; despite concentrated efforts to destroy it by both government agencies and Internet security companies, the worm continues to spread for the rest of the decade. (June 21) *SpaceShipOne* embarks on the world's first privately funded manned space flight when it launches from a private facility in the Mohave Desert in California. Private space tourism pioneer Richard Branson later announces plans for *SpaceShipTwo*.

Environment and health: (Feb. 8) France bans sales of Red Bull energy drink after finding it contains excessive caffeine. (Feb. 21) British newspaper *The Guardian* reports that, in a secret report commissioned by a defense department advisor and allegedly suppressed by the Bush administration, climate change over the next two decades will result in anarchy, food shortages, and natural disasters.

Arts and literature: (Nov. 2) Dutch filmmaker Theo van Gogh is assassinated in retaliation for his film *Submission*, which his assassin perceived to be critical of Islam.

Popular culture: (June15) *Fahrenheit 9/11*, a controversial documentary directed by filmmaker Michael Moore is released; in the film, Moore criticized the Bush administration as illegitimate and acting in their own interests during the September 11 attacks and the ensuing War on Terrorism. (July 22–25) Nearing the 100,000 convention-goers mark, the San Diego Comic-Con expands to the entire exhibit area at the San Diego Convention Center.

Sports: (Apr. 22) Former Arizona Cardinals safety Pat Tillman is killed by friendly fire while serving as an Army Ranger in Afghanistan. Initial reports of his death state he was killed in an ambush but this is later determined to be untrue. (Sept. 17) During a game against the San Diego Padres, San Francisco Giants left-fielder Barry Bonds hits his 700th home run, the third player in major league baseball history to do so; he will break the career home run record in August 2007. (Oct. 27) The Boston Red Sox sweep the St. Louis Cardinals in the 2004 World Series; this is the first World Series title for the Red Sox since 1918, breaking the dreaded "Curse of the Bambino." They win again in 2007.

Crime: (Mar. 4) Media personality Martha Stewart is found guilty of obstruction of justice and lying to investigators in a case involving the sale of stocks of ImClone Systems. She will spend five months in prison between October 2004 and March 2005. (Aug. 22) *The Scream* (1893) and *Madonna* (1894) by Edvard Munch are stolen from Munch Museum in Oslo, Norway; the paintings are recovered

with some damage one year later. (Nov. 12) Scott Peterson is found guilty of murdering his wife, Laci Peterson, who disappeared in 2002. In 2005, Scott Peterson will be sentenced to death row at San Quentin State Prison in California.

2005

International events: (Feb. 8) North Korea claims to have manufactured nuclear weapons for purposes of self-defense against aggression under US president George W. Bush. In September, it will announce an end to its nuclear weapons program. (July 28) The army council of the Irish Republican Army announces it has ended its armed campaign in support of a peaceful strategy to end conflicts over British rule in Northern Ireland. (Aug. 15) Eviction of Israeli settlers from their homes in the Gaza Strip and the West Bank begins as part of a broader plan to remove forces from disputed territories. Riots and mass demonstrations by settlers ensue.

Government and politics: (May 31) Mark Felt, a former associate of the FBI, reveals he is Deep Throat, the informant who provided information to *Washington Post* reporters Bob Woodward and Carl Bernstein as they investigated the Watergate break-in and cover-up that led to the August 1974 resignation of President Richard M. Nixon. Before Felt's admission, the real identity of Deep Throat was a matter of political intrigue. (July 1) Supreme Court Justice Sandra Day O'Connor, appointed by President Ronald Reagan in 1981, announces that she will retire from the court. President Bush nominates John Roberts to replace her. During Roberts' confirmation period, on (Sept.5) Chief Justice William H. Rehnquist dies. Roberts is confirmed as Chief Justice later that month.

Military and war: (Apr. 9) Thousands of demonstrators in Baghdad, Iraq mark the second anniversary of US occupation of the country. Many protesters claim allegiance with Shiite leader Muqtada al-Sadr, one of several clerics claiming public support in the post-occupation political and religious landscape. (Apr. 30) *Newsweek* magazine reports on an alleged incident in which prison interrogators at the Guantanamo Bay detention facility in Cuba desecrated a Qur'an by flushing it down a toilet; public outcry over the charges leads to anti-US demonstrations across the Muslim world.

Society: (Mar. 31) Terri Schiavo, subject of a public right-to-life battle over the wish of her husband to terminate her life, dies in hospice. Like the assisted-suicide cases involving Dr. Jack Kevorkian in the 1990s, the Terri Schiavo case became a touchstone for issues related to medical ethics. (Apr. 2) Roman Catholic Pope John Paul II dies at age eighty-four; having held the position since 1978, he becomes the second-longest reigning pontiff in the history of the Church. At the time of his death, the Church is embroiled in a child sex abuse scandal that sees hundreds of millions of dollars in victim payouts throughout the rest of the decade. (Aug. 30) Pew Research Center for the People & the Press announces survey findings that 42 percent of Americans believe humans and animals have existed in "their present form since the beginning of time." (Oct. 25) A YouTube video appears featuring customers who, after waiting in line for an official product release at an Apple Store, purchase a video iPod then destroy it in front of sales staff and other customers. Throughout the decade, a trend in which customers wait in line for hours, days, and even weeks for new product releases continues to grow.

Business and economics: (July 3) In an effort to raise awareness about global poverty, a series of Live 8 rock concerts are held around the world, including in London, United Kingdom, and Philadelphia, Pennsylvania, attracting what is expected to be the largest television audience in history. Notable moments include a reunion by members of Pink Floyd.

Transportation: (Jan. 18) The world's largest civilian aircraft, the Airbus 380, is revealed at an exhibition in Toulouse, France. The A380 takes its maiden flight in April. (Dec. 20) New York City transit workers strike over contract disputes. The strike affects regular shopping for the winter holiday season, thus sending many commuters online to continue their gift shopping.

Science and technology: (Feb. 15) Internet video-sharing service YouTube is launched; as of January 2010, the website boasts as many as 2 billion views per day. (Feb. 17) Two human skulls discovered in Ethiopia by Richard Leakey in 1967 are redated to 195,000 years old, the oldest known remains of modern human beings. (July 4) The *Deep Impact* spacecraft reaches Comet Tempel 1 and launches a 372-kilogram copper projectile into the comet's icy surface to collect data. (July–Sept.) Xena, a body beyond Pluto that orbits the sun, is discovered by astronomers at the University of Hawaii's Keck Observatory in July and its moon Gabrielle is discovered in September. The question of Xena's planetary status—like those of several other trans-Neptunian objects discovered since 1995—is debated by astronomers. (Sept.) The US National Snow and Ice Data Center and the National Aeronautics and Space Administration report "a stunning reduction" in Arctic sea ice, 20 percent below the mean average during September from 1978 to 2001. (Nov. 27) Isabelle Dinoire becomes the world's first partial face transplant patient after a fifteen-hour surgery. Despite a series of setbacks and complications related to the surgery, the patient later reveals her satisfaction at the surgical outcome.

Environment and health: (Jan. 27) Oxford University's ClimatePrediction.net project announces evidence of a long-term increase in Earth's surface temperature in the range of 2 to 11 degrees Celsius as a result of global warming. (Feb. 16) The Kyoto Protocol, which seeks to curb greenhouse gas emissions, enters into force without being ratified by the US, China, India, or Australia. (Aug. 23-30) Hurricane Katrina kills more than 1,830 people and causes major destruction to parts of Louisiana, Mississippi and other southern states, with the majority of the deaths occurring in and around New Orleans, Louisiana. The disaster will become the most expensive in US history due to the extent of cleanup and recovery costs.

Arts and literature: (Dec. 7) British playwright Harold Pinter delivers pre-recorded speech upon receipt of the Nobel Prize in Literature; during his speech, Pinter excoriates US and British foreign policy rhetoric regarding the global War on Terrorism.

Popular culture: (May 1) Animated television show *Family Guy* returns to regular broadcast after a 2002 cancellation, followed by a viewer revival in syndication and high sales of recordings of previous season episodes.

Sports: (May 29) Racecar driver Danica Patrick becomes fourth woman in history to race in the Indianapolis 500 and the race's highest scoring female driver. (July 13) The National Hockey League lockout ends after an agreement is reached between players and league officials. This is the first year since 1919 that a Stanley Cup tournament is not played. (July 24) Professional cyclist Lance Armstrong wins a record seventh Tour de France with an average speed in the tour of 41.7 kilometers per hour; Armstrong retires following the race, and mounts a comeback in following years.

Crime: (Mar. 21) Jeffrey Weise, a teenaged resident of the Red Lake Indian reservation in Minnesota, shoots fourteen people, including twelve people at his high school; this is the worst mass shooting at a school since the Columbine High School shootings in April 1999. (Apr. 8) Fugitive Eric Rudolph agrees to plead guilty in connection with a series of bombings, including the 1996 bombings at the Summer Olympics in Atlanta, Georgia. Rudolph eluded law enforcement officials for five years between 1998 and 2003.

2006

International events: (Jan. 12) A stampede during a ritual ceremony kills 345 people during an annual hajj pilgrimage in Mecca, Saudi Arabia. (Jan. 25) Radical Islamist group Hamas wins majority in the Palestinian parliament, leading to internal conflicts that result in heightened hostilities with rival party Fatah. (Mar. 11) Former Serbian President Slobodan Milosevic, facing charges of genocide and crimes against humanity, dies of a heart attack in his jail cell at The Hague. (Apr. 14) Israeli Prime Minister Ariel Sharon, incapacitated after a January stroke, is replaced by fellow Kadima party member, former Jerusalem mayor Ehud Olmert; false reports of Sharon's death persist over the next few years.

Government and politics: (Nov. 7) Nancy Pelosi becomes the first female Speaker of the House of Representatives; Democrats pick up seats in both houses of Congress, as well as several governorships. (Dec. 11) Operation Michocoan, a joint initiative between Mexican law enforcement and the military, is launched in the state of Michocoan in response to the growing threat of organized crime throughout the country and in the United States, which purchases the vast majority of illicit drugs supplied by Mexican cartels.

Military and war: (Apr.) Over several days, Iran claims to have test-fired several secret missiles and torpedoes during war games held in the Arabian Sea. Among these is the Fajr-3, which has a radar-avoidance system and can strike multiple targets simul-

taneously. (Sept. 6) US president George W. Bush acknowledges publically that the United States maintains secret CIA-run prisons, also known as black site prisons, around the world; later investigations claim that the secret locations include Poland and Romania. Further claims arise that the United States used the black sites as a way of deflecting claims it tortures prisoners in the War on Terrorism. (Dec. 5) Former Iranian dictator Saddam Hussein is executed by hanging at a prison in Baghdad, Iraq. Official and unofficial video footage of the execution are released, including a controversial cell phone video that depicts the execution in graphic detail.

Society: (Mar. 25) In Los Angeles, California, half a million protesters march in demonstration against US immigration policies that would detrimentally affect illegal immigrants and their families. The demonstrations culminate in May with the so-called Great American Boycott, a one-day general strike designed to demonstrate the economic and political power of illegal immigrants throughout the United States.

Business and economics: (Nov. 19) Nintendo releases the Wii video game console featuring an innovative wireless controller. The console is notable for its popularity among nontraditional gamers who found other controllers difficult or cumbersome to use.

Transportation: (Jan. 13) After years of planning and construction, the last phase of Boston's Central Artery/Tunnel Project, known locally as the Big Dig, is completed.

Science and technology: (Apr.) Paleontologists announce the discovery in the Nunavut territory of Canada of a 375-million-year-old "fishapod" (*Tiktaalik roseae*), a new transitional species bridging the gap between fish and tetrapods (four-legged vertebrate). (Feb. 22) Developed as a program to service Apple's numerous personal devices, iTunes surpasses 1 billion downloads. The user with the billionth download receives $10,000 credit at iTunes. (Mar. 10) NASA reports that imagery from the *Cassini-Huygens* spacecraft reveals possible presence of water below the crust of Enceladus, one of Saturn's moons; this and later findings support the possibility that life could be sustained on Enceladus. (July 25) The microblogging service Twitter is launched. Within months the service sees 60,000 tweets per day; by the end of the decade it reaches nearly 50 million tweets per day, or 600 tweets per second. (Sept. 13) Pluto is reclassified as a minor planet by the International Astronomic Union.

Environment and health: (May) The World Health Organization issues guidelines on treatment and management of human cases of H5N1 virus, also known as avian or bird flu; by year's end, the human death toll from H5N1 in nine countries is seventy-nine in 2006 alone. The virus continues to spread, with fifty-nine reported deaths the following year. (Oct. 6) The US Centers for Disease Control and Prevention reports that three people have died and 199 people been infected during an outbreak of *E. coli* across the nation. The source of the outbreak is bagged spinach. In December, a similar outbreak is related to lettuce sold to fast food taco restaurants.

Arts and literature: (Nov. 2) Media mogul David Geffen completes the private sale of a painting by abstract expressionist Jackson Pollock, *No. 5, 1948*, for $140 million.

Popular culture: (Sept. 4) Popular television host and naturalist Steve Irwin, known as the Crocodile Hunter, dies on location of documentary film shoot after being stung in the chest by a stingray. (Nov. 14) *Casino Royale*, a reboot of the James Bond film series with new Bond Daniel Craig, opens to critical acclaim. Craig becomes the sixth actor to portray Bond in the film series.

Sports: (July 9) During the World Cup association football final match between Italy and France, French midfielder Zinedine Zidane ends his football career following a head butt to the chest of Italian center-back Marco Materazzi; the match is decided for Italy in a penalty shoot-out, 5–3.

Crime: (May 4) Zacarias Moussaoui, an acknowledged co-conspirator in the September 11 terrorist attacks, is sentenced to life in prison for his role. During his trial, Moussaoui claims he and so-called shoe-bomber Richard Reid were to have hijacked a fifth airliner in the attacks. (Aug. 3) In Phoenix, Arizona, serial shooters Dale Hausner and Samuel Dieteman are arrested and charged in connection with a string of shootings, shooting deaths, and animal shootings between May 2005 and July 2006; their spree roughly coincides with the crimes committed by Mark Goudeau, also known as the Baseline Shooter, who is arrested on September 4 and charged in connection with nine murders.

2007

International events: (June 27) Gordon Brown succeeds Tony Blair as British Prime Minister. A major influence within the British Labour Party before and during Blair's term, Brown will preside over the loss of political power to the Conservative party in the 2010 general elections which resulted in a hung parliament. (Nov. 3) Pakistani President Pervez Musharraf suspends the Pakistani constitution and declares a state of emergency in an effort to oust the nation's supreme court of political enemies, including the chief justice. He will leave Pakistan the following year to begin a period of political exile. (Dec. 27) Former Pakistani Prime Minister Benazir Bhutto is assassinated following a political campaign rally appearance in the city of Rawalpindi. During her career, Bhutto had weathered political executions of family members, assassination attempts on her own life, corruption charges, and exile.

Government and politics: (June 11) US Senator Larry Craig (R-ID) is arrested on charges of lewd conduct following an incident in the men's restroom at the Minneapolis–St. Paul International Airport. After the Senator's initial plea of guilt, he recants and expresses a desire to seek a fourth term in office. He does not seek reelection. (Dec. 26) Former US president Gerald R. Ford dies at age ninety-three at his home in California. Ford served from August 1974, following the resignation of President Richard Nixon, until January 1977.

Military and war: (Jan. 10) US president George W. Bush announces he intends to increase the number of soldiers serving in Iraq by 20,000. The policy change is designed to stabilize the region in response to enemy strength and persistence. (Sept. 3) British soldiers leave Basra bases following a siege by the Mahdi army. The previous month, Danish troops had left Basra, while the British would eventually leave Iraq in 2009. (Sept. 10) General David Petraeus, commander of coalition forces in Iraq, recommends in a report on military progress in Iraq to Congress that, as a result of the surge, military goals are being met in Iraq and requests a gradual withdrawal of troops.

Society: (Mar. 16) The US Food and Drug Administration issues a product recall announcement for pet food ingredients manufactured in China; it is discovered the pet food products contains melamine, which is linked to kidney failure in animals. The same ingredient is discovered in 2008 to have been included in baby food, resulting in the deaths of six infants, with tens of thousands more becoming ill.

Business and economics: (Aug.) After US stock markets continue to close downward, financial markets around the world begin to fear the US economic downturn will eventually become a global recession. (May 2) Australian media magnate Rupert Murdoch's News Corp. completes merger with Dow Jones & Company, giving Murdoch control of the *Wall Street Journal* daily newspaper; the newspaper promises to retain its editorial integrity.

Transportation: (Nov. 13) Unionized transportation workers in France go on strike following pension reform proposals by President Nicolas Sarkozy. The strikes cause massive delays in travel throughout the country.

Science and technology: (Apr. 13) John Asara and colleagues report their analysis of soft tissue found in the well-preserved leg bone of a *Tyrannosaurus rex* from Montana, concluding that it had proteins similar to those of chickens. (Nov.) A group led by Shinya Yamanaka of Kyoto University uses a virus to reprogram human skin cells to form stem cells for growing tumor-free muscle, fat, heart, and nerve tissues without having to destroy human embryos.

Environment and health: (Jan. 22) The Susan G. Komen Breast Cancer Foundation launches a campaign featuring a pink ribbon and a new logo. (Nov. 13) Pharmaceutical company Merck settles lawsuits related to its Vioxx arthritis drug, which researchers found doubled heart attack and stroke risk in patients. Merck agrees to pay out $4.85 billion.

Arts and literature: (Apr. 11) Novelist and cultural critic Kurt Vonnegut Jr. dies at age eighty-four. (July 21) *Harry Potter and the Deathly Hallows*, the final book in the famed series by author J. K. Rowling, is published. In July 2008, it is reported the series has sold 400 million copies worldwide since 1997. (Nov. 19) Amazon launches the Kindle e-book reader. Throughout the decade, e-book readers will continue to create more and more market space for the format.

Popular culture: (Jan. 16) Television talent show *American Idol* premieres its sixth season with an estimated viewership of 38.1 million people. (Feb. 9)

Former Playboy Playmate and reality television star Anna Nicole Smith dies of an accidental drug overdose at a hotel casino in North Hollywood, Florida. (June 10) The final episode of cable television series *The Sopranos* airs, causing consternation among some viewers regarding the ending, which does not clearly offer clues to the fate of the protagonist and his family. (Sept. 13) Oprah Winfrey gives a 2005 Pontiac G-6 to every audience member during a television taping of *The Oprah Winfrey Show.* (Nov. 5) A strike by the Writer's Guild of America begins; the striking film and television writers are concerned over issues related to residual payments from new media formats, including DVDs and Internet video services. The strike lasts one hundred days.

Sports: (Dec. 12) The International Olympic Committee rules that former Olympic gold- and bronze-medalist runner Marion Jones must return her medals as a result of her admission that she lied to investigators about taking performance-enhancing steroids. In 2008, she will serve a six-month sentence in federal prison. (Dec. 13) The Mitchell Report on the illegal use of performance-enhancing steroids in Major League Baseball is published, naming eighty-nine athletes alleged to have used steroids, including home-run king Barry Bonds, pitching legend Roger Clemens, and many others.

Crime: (Mar. 6) The federal trial of former vice-presidential aide Lewis "Scooter" Libby ends in his conviction for lying and obstruction of justice in an investigation involving the leak of the identity of CIA agent Valerie Plame. Critics of Libby's action believed the leak was orchestrated by Bush administration officials following the publication of an article by Plame's husband, Ambassador Joe Wilson, contradicting statements made by administration officials over weapons of mass destruction in Iraq. (Apr. 16) Virginia Tech student Seung-Hui Cho kills thirty-three people, including himself, during a shooting spree on campus in Blacksburg, Virginia; a video featuring Cho expressing his anger that led to the shootings is mailed to NBS television studios.

2008

International events: (Feb. 27) After an announcement by long-serving Cuban dictator Raul Castro that he will step down, his brother Raul Castro is unanimously elected to replace him. (Apr.) The International Monetary Fund forecasts a global recession stemming from the financial meltdown in the United States (May 12) An earthquake in Sichuan province, China, registers an 8.0 magnitude; nearly 70,000 people die in the disaster. (June 11) Canadian Prime Minister Stephen Harper offers official apologies to First Nations students who attended residential schools throughout Canada; many students were forcibly removed from their families and were victims of systematic neglect and mistreatment. (July 2) Ingrid Betancourt and several others are rescued from imprisonment by FARC rebels in Colombia; Betancourt had been kidnapped in 2002 while a presidential candidate and was the target of several unsuccessful rescue attempts. (Nov. 26–29) Islamic extremists kill more than 160 people during a series of staged attacks in Mumbai, India; it is later alleged the attacks took place with the coordination of Pakistani intelligence.

Government and politics: (June 7) Senator Hillary Clinton (D-NY) ends her campaign for the presidency. In January 2009, she will be selected by President Barack Obama as secretary of state. (Aug. 29) Republican presidential nominee Senator John McCain (R-AZ) announces Sarah Palin as his choice for vice president, introducing her to the world of national politics. (Sept. 8) In an effort to stop further financial institution failures, US treasury secretary Henry Paulson announces the US government will place failing lenders Fannie Mae and Freddie Mac in conservatorship. The action comes amid a growing financial crisis related to the swelling numbers of home foreclosures throughout the nation. By year's end, home foreclosures will reach over 3 million, an 81 percent increase over 2007, and 225 percent increase over 2006. (Sept.–Dec.) Financial institutions affected by growing global economic uncertainty include Lehman Brothers, American Insurance Group (AIG), Goldman Sachs, Morgan Stanley, Wachovia, and Citigroup. (Nov. 4) Senator Barack Obama (D-IL) is elected US president in a victory over John McCain; Obama receives 365 electoral votes and 52.9 percent of the popular vote, while McCain receives 173 electoral votes and 45.7 percent of the popular vote.

Military and war: (June 1) The US Department of Defense reports they have 182,060 troops on active duty in Iraq and 48,250 in Afghanistan. (June 16) British Prime Minister Gordon Brown increases the number of British troops in Afghanistan to over 8,000. As of June, the number of British troops who have died in Afghanistan since 2001, at 102, is higher than in Iraq. (Aug. 5) Prior to a ground invasion of South Ossetia, Georgia launches a series of cyber attacks designed to wipe out news and communications networks. Russian involvement is suspected, as it was in a 2007 attack on Estonian websites.

Society: (June 1) China bans plastic grocery bags in an effort to improve its public image leading up to the 2008 Summer Olympics. (Nov. 28) A Walmart employee at a store in Long Island, New York, dies after being crushed by overzealous holiday shoppers waiting in line for Black Friday sales. (Dec.) As reported by the US Bureau of Labor Statistics the following month, the unemployment rate stands at 10 percent, and the number of unemployed at 15.3 million. Both figures are roughly double from December 2007. (Dec. 23) Pew Research announces results of a survey that finds more people are claiming to get their news and information from the Internet than from newspapers. Another report in August reported that a slight majority of Americans have grown weary of mixing politics and religion.

Business and economics: (Mar. 14) The Federal Reserve Bank of New York agrees to aid failing securities firm Bear Stearns after investors make a run on their capital investments, driving stock prices for the firm down. Within days, a merger with JP Morgan Chase is announced, saving the company from insolvency. (July 4) The price of crude oil peaks at $145.29, dropping to $80 by December 31, 2009. (Oct. 3) The Emergency Economic Stabilization Act of 2008 is enacted in response to the continuing mortgage crisis. The legislation enables the US Treasury secretary to infuse the economy with $700 million dollar by purchasing distressed assets in an effort to strengthen the credit market.

Transportation (excluding communications for the 2000s): (Jan.) At the Ninth Annual Auto Expo in New Delhi, India, the Tata Nano is announced. The minicar is designed to offer a low-cost, low-carbon alternative to more expensive traditional vehicles. (May 15) Toyota announces that sales of its Prius gas-electric hybrid vehicle have surpassed

1 million units. (June 1) The International Air Transport Association stops issuing paper airline tickets to travel agencies.

Science and technology: (Jan. 14) NASA's *Messenger* spacecraft makes its first flyby of Mercury on its way to orbiting the planet, providing evidence for past volcanic activity on the surface, and a large amount of water in the outer atmosphere. (May–Nov.) NASA's *Phoenix* lander becomes the first to land on the north polar region of Mars, documenting water and finding small amounts of nutrients for life as well as perchlorate salts that are dangerous for life. (Sept. 10–19) The Large Hadron Collider (LHC) makes its first successful run before a superconducting magnet breakdown delays its probe of the most basic structure of matter. (Nov.) Penn State biochemist Stevan Schuster announces the reconstruction of 80 percent of the genome of an ancient wooly mammoth from clumps of hair in excavated remains

Environment and health: (Jan. 15) The US Food and Drug Administration announces that it has found food produced from cloned animals and their offspring is safe to eat. It also states food produced from cloned animals such as milk or meat will not need to be labeled as originating from clones. (June) A trachea implant patient at a hospital in Barcelona, Spain, receives a windpipe constructed in part from her own stem cells.

Arts and literature: (Sept.12) Novelist and essayist David Foster Wallace, considered one the most innovative novelists of his generation, commits suicide at age forty-six at his home in Claremont, California. (Nov. 4) Popular novelist Michael Crichton dies of throat cancer at age sixty-six.

Popular culture: (Jan. 22) Actor Heath Ledger dies from an accidental overdose of prescription drugs. He will later win a posthumous Academy Award for his performance as the Joker in the film *The Dark Knight*. (Oct. 18) Vice-presidential nominee Sarah Palin appears on *Saturday Night Live* to play herself after a series of parodies in which Palin was portrayed by comedian Tina Fey.

Sports: (Aug. 17) At the 2008 Summer Olympics held (Aug 8–24) in Beijing, China, US competitive swimmer Michael Phelps wins an eighth gold medal during the 400-meter medley relay, breaking the record for most gold medals won in a single Olympic competition held by swimmer Mark Spitz, who won seven at the 1972 Munich Summer Olympics in 1972. Afghanistan wins its first medal ever when Rohullah Nikpai wins bronze in tae kwon do. The US women's soccer team wins its fourth Olympic gold medal in a match against Brazil.

Crime: (July 29) Bruce Ivins, a suspect in the 2001 anthrax attacks that killed five people in the United States, commits suicide after learning he is a suspect in the FBI investigation into the attacks. (Sept. 4) Former lobbyist Jack Abramoff is sentenced to four years in prison for his role in a series of crimes including fraud, conspiracy to bribe public officials, and tax evasion. Abramoff's actions led to widespread concerns over corruption within the Republican Party.

2009

International events: (Jan. 18) A cease fire is reached in a three-week war in the Gaza Strip between Israel and Hamas. The engagement between the Palestinian Arabs and Israelis is part of a much longer struggle that continues into the next decade with signs of little progress in finding peace between the two peoples. (June 13) Protests break out across Iran in protest of the results of a presidential election in which President Mahmoud Ahmadinejad is reelected. Dubbed the Green Revolution, the protests presage similar revolts that will occur throughout the Arab world beginning in Tunisia in December 2010. During the 2010 uprisings, the political makeup of the Arab world will undergo massive transformation, with populist uprisings ousting autocratic dictators including Tunisian president Zine El Abidine Ben Ali, Egyptian president Hosni Mubarak, and Libyan leader Muammar Gaddafi. No such change in leadership occurs in Iran. (July 31) Americans Shane Bauer, Joshua Fattel, and Sarah Shourd are arrested by Iranian border police while hiking near the eastern Iranian border in Iraq and accused of being American spies. Shourd is released after more than a year in detention, while Bauer and Fettel are each sentenced to eight years imprisonment.

Government and politics: (Jan. 9) Illinois governor Rod Blagojevich is impeached by the Illinois House after he is accused of attempting to sell the seat vacated by former senator Barack Obama following the 2008 presidential election. Blagojevich is later sentenced to fourteen years in federal prison. (Jan. 30) Former lieutenant governor Michael Steele is elected chairman of the Republican National Committee, the first African American to be elected to the post in the party's history. (Aug. 4) American journalists Laura Ling and Euna Lee are released by North Korea after being held in detention and accused of being spies. Former president Bill Clinton flies to North Korea to successfully negotiate the pair's release. (Dec. 24) The US Senate passes the Patient Protection and Affordable Care for America Act (HR 3962). The legislation is designed to address needed reforms in the US health care system.

Military and war: (Feb. 27) US president Obama announces a draw-down in American troop strength in Iraq, with a goal of ending American combat operations by August 2010. (July 3) In a sign of eased tensions between the United States and Russia since the start of the Afghan war, Russia allows the United States to use its airspace to ferry troops and deliver supplies to war efforts in Afghanistan. (Aug. 6) Obama administration officials declare an end to the use of the phrase "war on terror" in its efforts to reduce global terror networks of al-Qaeda. (Dec. 1) President Obama announces an increased commitment of 30,000 soldiers to Afghanistan in an escalation of American efforts in the war.

Society: (Sept. 12) Tens of thousands of Tea Party demonstrators march on the White House in protest of the domestic policies of President Obama. The Tea Party, a movement partially characterized by antitaxation and "big government" sentiments, will assert influence in the 2010 midterm elections and beyond. (Dec.) By the end of the 2000s, the cost of tuition, room, and board for undergraduates at public institutions has risen 42 percent since the 2000–2001 school year. The same costs increased 31 percent at private, nonprofit institutions, and only 5 percent at private, for-profit institutions. (Dec. 21) According to Pew Research, half of Americans report their feelings about the decade 2000–2009 as negative when compared with the previous four decades; 59 percent report their hope that the 2010s will be better.

Business and economics: (Jan. 6) European nations report that their supplies of gas have been disrupted during a battle over prices between Russia and Ukraine. The disputes between Russia and Ukraine over controls and pricing have been waged in stages ever since the end of the Cold War. (Feb. 23) The Dow Jones Industrial Average closes at 7,114.8, as US shares reach their lowest point in over a decade amid a deepening economic recession.

Transportation: (Jan. 23) The journal *Science* reports that scientists at the Joint Quantum Institute at University of Maryland have successfully teleported information a distance of one meter. (June 1) Automotive company General Motors Corp. enters Chapter 11 bankruptcy protection, becoming the largest manufacturer to do so. As a result of this action and others involving auto manufacturers, and amid fears of an impending meltdown of the industry, the US government agrees to measures resulting in what will be termed a bailout of the automobile industry.

Science and technology: (Aug. 13) In a letter to the editors of the *New England Journal of Medicine*, a researcher announces the safe and effective treatment of a patient with impaired vision using gene therapy. Throughout the year, other scientists and researchers demonstrate first safe gene therapies applied to blindness, brain disorders, skin problems, and weak immune systems in a variety of approaches. (July 16) The journal *Nature* reports that the drug rapamycin extended the life of mice by the equivalent of thirteen extra years, the first drug-based extension of mammalian life. (Oct. 1) Paleontologists announce their discovery in Ethiopia of four-million year old *Ardipithecus ramidus*, called Ardi, an upright-walking primate a million years older than Lucy. (Nov. 12) NASA announces the discovery of water on the moon after it found at least 25 gallons of water vapor and ice in the plume formed by crashing the Lunar Crater Observation and Sensing Satellite (LCROSS) into a lunar crater.

Environment and health: (June 11) The World Health Organization announces that the spread of H1N1 flu virus has reached global pandemic stage, with 30,000 cases confirmed in seventy-four countries. The US Centers for Disease Control and Prevention reports between 151,700 and 575,450 deaths occurred during the pandemic. (Nov. 3) Drug maker GlaxoSmithKline announces that trials for a malaria vaccine are underway in Nairobi, Kenya. Overall, deaths from malaria fell 20 percent compared to the previous decade.

Arts and literature: (Apr. 19) British science fiction author J. G. Ballard, considered one of the most influential British authors of the modern age, dies at age seventy-eight from prostate cancer. (Aug. 4) Novelist Thomas Pynchon publishes *Inherent Vice*, his second novel in three years after 2006's *Against the Day*.

Popular culture: (June 25) Pop singer Michael Jackson dies at his Los Angeles, California home at age fifty. His death is attributed to a combination of pharmaceutical abuse, much of it stemming back several years, and patient mismanagement by his personal physician.

Sports: (July 5) The men's singles final match at Wimbledon between Roger Federer and Andy Roddick lasts seventy-seven games, the most games played in the history of Grand Slam tournaments. The match lasts more than four hours, with Federer eventually winning.

Crime: (Mar. 12) A judge in the case of Bernard Madoff remands him to federal custody. Madoff had been charged with operating a Ponzi scheme in which he bilked investors out of billions of dollars. In June, he is sentenced to 150 years in prison.

■ Bibliography

This annotated bibliography lists books, websites, and other sources containing substantial material about a wide variety of basic topics pertaining to the 2000s. Many additional works, and especially works on narrower subjects, can be found in the "Further Reading" notes at the end of each essay in *The 2000s in America*.

General Works

Batchelor, Bob. *The 2000s*. Westport: Greenwood, 2009. Print. American Popular Culture through History. Examines the popular culture of the decade as a result of historical forces, such as economic crises and political tenor of the decade, as well as the new media landscape that affected youth throughout the first decade of the twenty-first century. The author devotes chapters to specific discussions of advertising, architecture, fashion, food, leisure, literature, music, performing arts, travel, and visual arts. An appendix lists common product prices for the decade.

Corrigan, Jim. *The 2000s: Decade in Photos*. Berkeley Heights: Enslow, 2010. Print. Presents images of notable people, events, and things of the decade, including both color and black-and-white images. Themes include politics, the wars in Iraq and Afghanistan, terrorism, digital technology, and other representations of the 2000s.

Norris, Kathleen and Robert Atwan (series ed.), *The Best American Essays 2001*. New York: Houghton, 2001. Print. The Best American Essays series, published in each year of the decade, features notable essays from some of the decade's most important and innovative thinkers. Guest editors for the series include Stephen Jay Gould, David Foster Wallace, and Susan Orleans. Each collection offers a fair overview of the common concerns and talking points of the previous year, serving as a check-in on the post-millennium zeitgeist. Companion series include The Best Nonrequired Reading and The Best American Comics (since 2002 and 2006, respectively).

Steffen, Alex and Carissa Bluestone, *Worldchanging: A User's Guide for the 21st Century*. Rev. ed. New York: Abrams, 2011. Print. A companion to the Worldchanging.com website, this volume offers an expansive list of topics of concern to those interested in the myriad ways global sustainability can enact change at even the smallest of levels and be enacted by any citizen. Food, transportation, climate, cities, consumer issues, politics and governance, shelter, and much more receive attention, with each section offering a wealth of bibliographic resources for further research. Includes color illustrations throughout.

Sutherland, James. *The Ten-Year Century: Explaining the First Decade of the New Millennium*. New York: Viking, 2010. Print. This volume, aimed at the younger reader (ages twelve and up), summarizes the defining political and cultural changes across the decade, with emphasis on making sense of the political developments under the Bush administration and the wars in Afghanistan and Iraq, and how these things changed not only America but the geopolitics of the era.

Government, Politics, Economics, and Environment

Duncan, W. Raymond, Barbara Jancar-Webster and Bob Switky. *World Politics in the 21st Century*. Student Choice ed. Boston: Houghton, 2009. Print. The authors of this textbook on global politics examine a history of related topics, including human rights, nationalism, terrorism, and sustainable development, with a goal of providing students a better understanding of the world at the start of the twenty-first century. The authors of the text acknowledge in the introduction that the books was in part derived from the work of students and instructors who were key to the development of the text and learning materials throughout. Key terms, topical page references, study questions, outlines, illustrations, and links to online resources accompany chapters.

Epping, Randy Charles. *The 21st Century Economy: A Beginner's Guide*. New York: Vintage, 2008. Print. With reference to current events and economic developments, the authors present a primer on economic theory and application across the spectrum of macroeconomic topics. Maps, informational blurbs, and tables are provided throughout the book.

Friedman, Thomas L. *The World Is Flat 3.0: A Brief History of the Twenty-first Century*. New York: Picador,

2007. Print. Updated edition of Friedman's popular, award-winning book on globalization from 2005. The new edition contains new chapters and revisions to the original. The author's thesis is based around the ways that late-twentieth and early twenty-first century convergences of technology and new economic opportunities have enabled an equal global reach, or "flattened the playing field" for anyone willing to engage with the new tools available to them in the twenty-first century.

Levitt, Steven D. and Stephen J. Dubner. *Freakonomics: A Rogue Economist Explores the Hidden Side of Everything*. New York: Harper, 2009. Print. Levitt and Dubner employ levity and creative examples to demonstrate the serious effects of statistics in the modern world (e.g., chapter three is entitled "Why do drug dealers still live with their moms?"). Of particular interest to students is the relevance of the authors' work at a time when opportunities to use and be used for data mining are increasing exponentially. Notes and bibliography provide fodder for further research.

Priest, Dana and William M. Arkin. *Top Secret America: The Rise of the New American Security State*. New York: Little, 2011. Print. This book represents an effort to unravel the increasingly complex system of intelligence and security agencies, organizations, and companies that grew up in the wake of September 11. In examining these entities, the authors conclude that the system is dysfunctional and a potential risk to national security. Glossary, index, and reporting notes are included, but researchers should be aware that this is a work of investigative journalism, and therefore some sources are not identified.

Sirota, David. *Back to Our Future: How the 1980s Explain the World We Live in Now-Our Culture, Our Politics, Our Everything*. New York: Ballantine, 2011. Print. Sirota explains how certain characteristics of cultural and political life in the twenty-first century, such as militarism, vilification of hippies, and unrealistic aspirations (to be like Michael Jordan, for example) are tied to the culture and values of the conservative 1980s. A glossary of references will help readers make sense of some of the more obscure references to 1980s popular culture.

Skocpol, Theda and Vanessa Williamson. *The Tea Party and the Remaking of Republican Conservatism*. New York: Oxford UP, 2012. Print. The authors use an objective tone to describe the origins and impact of the at times volatile Tea Party movement—its serious ideological basis as well as its dramatic rhetoric—not only on the Republican Party and conservative ideology, but on the entire American political landscape. Contains survey data, bibliography, and index.

Wilentz, Sean. *The Age of Reagan: A History, 1974–2008*. New York: Harper, 2008. Print. In this examination of the American political scene following President Richard Nixon's 1974 resignation, The author chronicles the rise of conservatism during and after the rise of former California governor Ronald Reagan, who was to become the movement's leader, through his presidency, into the 1990s, and then the 2000s. While a small portion of the book deals explicitly with the Bush years—the era of "compassionate conservatism"—this work will connect the dots between the 1970s and the early twenty-first century, an era that is little known to today's students and misunderstood by many who lived through them. With black-and-white illustrations, notes and index, of particular interest is an extensive selection of sources and readings.

Sociology, Character, and Culture

Arnold, Jeanne E., et al. *Life at Home in the Twenty-first Century: 32 Families Open Their Doors*. Los Angeles: Cotsen Inst. of Archaeology P, 2012. Print. This book, filled with rich images of middle class homes in California, offers a portrait of life at the end of the decade. The images and text document contemporary American life by way of materialism, living spaces, the things we fill those spaces with, and the effect our things have on our relationships. Color illustrations throughout, with notes, photographic index, and bibliography.

Carr, Nicholas. *The Shallows: What the Internet Is Doing to Our Brains*. New York: Norton, 2010. Print. In a famous article that preceded this book, Carr asked the provocative question, "Is Google making us stupid?" In this work, Carr extends his inquiry into the ways the Internet and digital literacy are affecting our brains and processing abilities, as well as the struggle to manage the seemingly endless array of distractions that accompanies information in the digital age.

49 Up. Dir. Michael Apted. First Run Features, 2005. DVD. This documentary film is part of a long-running documentary series that has traced the lives of the same Britons through interviews every seven years since 1964, when the subjects were seven years old. In this feature, the subjects are forty-nine years old. Interviews feature comments from subjects on everyday issues like life milestones, marriage, family, and work.

Greenberg, Eric and Karl Weber. *Generation We: How Millennial Youth are Taking Over America and Changing Our World Forever.* Emeryville: Pachatusan, 2008. Print. This work presents the results of a demographic survey of people born between 1978 and 2000, otherwise known as the millennial generation, approximately 95 million strong at the time of writing, larger than the baby boom generation who came of age in the 1960s and 1970s. Survey results, including attitudes on issues and scenarios facing the millennials, as well as infographics and illustrations, accompany a call to action to make a positive impact on the global future.

Greenhouse, Steven. *The Big Squeeze: Tough Times for the American Worker.* New York: Anchor, 2009. Print. Drawing from his background as a labor correspondent, Greenhouse examines issues of concern for workers in the economic and management climate of the 2000s, including low wages, offshoring of jobs, rising health care costs, and attitudes towards labor in the twenty-first century. Index and notes are included.

Halliwell, Martin and Catherine Morley, eds. *American Thought and Culture in the 21st Century.* Edinburgh: Edinburgh UP, 2008. Print. The editors present an anthology of writings on American society, culture, and politics during the twenty-first century by a range of academic authors from the United States, United Kingdom, and beyond. While the articles are scholarly, the overall breadth of topics (religion, medicine, sociology, and digital media all find a place in the anthology) presents an overview of how historical forces converged in unique ways throughout the decade.

Hunter, Nick. *Popular Culture: 2000 and Beyond.* Eds. Adam Miller, Andrew Farrow, and Adrian Vigliano. Chicago: Heinemann Lib., 2013. Print. Written for younger readers, this volume in a series on popular culture since the 1990s knits together information on technological changes, celebrities, and other disparate themes through informational blurbs and color illustrations and

includes chronologies, best-of-decade lists, and resources to present an introduction to high points of pop culture in the 2000s.

Pew Research Center for the People & the Press. Pew Research Center, 2013. Web. 7 Jan. 2013. This website presents survey data, reports, and analysis related to Pew Research public opinion polls between 2000 and 2009. Reports are searchable by year, topic, or publication type.

Pollan, Michael. *The Omnivore's Dilemma: A Natural History of Four Meals.* New York: Penguin, 2009. Print. Also available in an edition for younger readers, Pollan's book considers the contemporary state of food production, both industrial and organic, and what he considers to be appropriate food preparation that represents an ethical consideration of what and how we eat.

Settersten, Richard and Barbara E. Ray. *Not Quite Adults: Why 20-Somethings Are Choosing a Slower Path to Adulthood, and Why It's Good for Everyone.* New York: Bantam, 2010. Print. The authors present conclusions about the millennial generation based on several years' worth of data and research on people in the eighteen-to-thirty-four age range and the choices and life milestones they face, such as marriage and moving away from parents. Includes chapter notes and index.

This American Life. Chicago Public Media and Ira Glass, 1995–2013. Web. 15 Oct. 2012. This website contains an archive of podcasts of episodes of *This American Life,* a weekly radio program produced by WBEZ, including those broadcast between 2000 and 2009. Episodes are searchable by date. Each program offers a glimpse into cultural trends and attitudes that help define the decade.

Science and Technology

Castronova, Edward. *Synthetic Worlds: The Business and Culture of Online Games.* Chicago: U of Chicago P, 2005. Print. This work presents an overview of the growth and dynamics of the economics of online gaming within virtual worlds like World of Warcraft and Second Life. In considering the economics of online gaming, Castronova details how lucrative and complex virtual economies had become by mid-decade. Provides extensive notes, bibliography, and index; an appendix explores the connection between virtual worlds and previous developments in virtual reality.

Clarke, Richard A. and Robert K. Knake. *Cyber War: The Next Threat to National Security and What to Do about It.* New York: Ecco, 2010. Print. Clarke, formerly a national security advisor to President George W. Bush, explores the history, conceptual vacuums, practical hurdles, and technical details that make cyberwarfare a threat to future generations. Includes an index.

Cohen, Jessie, ed. *The Best of the Best of American Science Writing.* New York: Ecco, 2000. Print. This anthology presents selections from annual best-of collections of science writing from leading science writers throughout the decade, including Freeman Dyson, David Quammen, Jack Hitt, and Margaret Talbot, as selected by the guest editors from previous volumes in the series. Topics considered include evolution, emergent trends in genomics, nutrition, and zoology. Provides an overview of the choices that went into the annual anthologies each article was culled from, as well as notes from contributors on the published articles.

Kaku, Michio. *Physics of the Impossible: A Scientific Exploration into the World of Phasers, Force Fields, Teleportation, and Time Travel.* New York: Doubleday, 2009. Print. Kaku, a self-described "popularizer of science," uses nontechnical language to address as-yet physically impossible technologies that may be made possible by emergent trends in computation and scientific research. Valuable for the author's insights and forecasts related to how exponential trends in technology and science development may radically alter perceptions of what is considered impossible. Includes bibliographic notes and index.

Keen, Andrew. *The Cult of the Amateur: How Blogs, MySpace, YouTube, and the Rest of Today's User-Generated Media Are Destroying Our Economy, Our Culture, and Our Values.* New York: Doubleday, 2008. Print. Keen's work criticizes the effects of user-generated content and social media on the role of (and corresponding respect for) expertise, professionalism, traditional media industries, copyright, and culture in general. While the tone is markedly pessimistic in outlook, it is not out of place next to other contemporaneous chronicles of the effects of the digital age on society.

Lessig, Lawrence. *Free Culture: How Big Media Uses Technology and the Law to Lock Down Culture.* New York: Penguin, 2004. Print. Lessig, a constitutional law professor, documents the core issues facing copyright and ownership in the twenty-first century, including dramatic extension of copyright length and the effects of twenty-first century copyright law on content users, creativity, and creative industries. Provides recommendations for "reclaiming a free culture," notes, and index.

Shirky, Clay. *Here Comes Everybody: The Power of Organizing Without Organizations.* New York: Penguin, 2008. Print. This book examines the assortment of ways social media and networks, software, and the Internet present opportunities for democratization, personal and political expression, and creative expansion of popular organizing in the twenty-first century. Shirky's work may be seen as a contrast to Andrew Keen's above. Includes chapter notes and index.

Singer, P.W. *Wired for War: The Robotics Revolution and Conflict in the 21st Century.* New York: Penguin, 2009. Print. This work examines the development of, along with cyberwarfare, the other major military technological advance of the twenty-first century, the roboticization of warfare. This work draws on historical research into robotics and automation of weapons, as well as interviews with civilians, contractors, roboticists, and military personnel to consider what the future holds for an increasingly roboticized battlefield. Also helpful is the author's exploration into the ethical questions related to using robotic weapons.

■ Glossary

This detailed list is a representative collection of words and phrases that gained prominence during the 2000s in the United States.

AMBER Alert: Missing child alert system used throughout the United States and internationally. Originally promoted and adopted at state levels in the 1990s, AMBER Alert systems received a federal coordinator (in the Department of Justice) with passage of the PROTECT Act of 2003.

app: Shorthand phrase for "application," or computer software. Common uses include "app store" and "mobile app."

axis of evil: Reference to Iraq, Iran, and North Korea, all of whom were alleged by US president George W. Bush to be state sponsors of terrorism against the United States and its allies. The first reference made to an axis of evil was in the 2002 State of the Union address, in which Bush declared, "States like these and their terrorist allies constitute an axis of evil, arming to threaten the peace of the world. By seeking weapons of mass destruction, these regimes pose a grave and growing danger."

baby-daddy/baby-mama: Phrases describing the roles of unmarried partners in a relationship in which a child is born. With roots in Jamaican slang, the phrase was popularized after its use in the song "Mrs. Jackson" by hip-hop artists OutKast in 2000. Although used pejoratively in some cases, not all uses are negative, suggesting that the social stigma attached to being a single parent lessened during the 2000s.

bailout: Term used to describe governmental or institutional assistance to financially troubled institutions or industries, such as companies within the financial services and automotive industries. Prominent recipients of bailouts during the 2000s include financial institutions Fannie Mae and Freddie Mac, AIG Inc., Goldman Sachs Group, and Bank of America, and automobile manufacturers General Motors and Chrysler.

birther: Pejorative phrase for a person who believes President Barack Obama was not born in Hawaii, as is officially claimed, but outside the United States, perhaps Kenya, thus making him constitutionally ineligible to be president.

blogosphere: Term used to describe the multitude of authors, commentators, citizen journalists, and trendsetters who publish work in the form of blogs on the Internet. References to the blogosphere during the decade were often tacit acknowledgement of the increasing influence of nontraditional media over traditional media.

boomerang generation: Nickname applied to people in their twenties and thirties who live with their parents or are otherwise financially dependent on them to various degrees as a result of economic conditions in the 2000s, particularly during and after the Great Recession of the late 2000s.

Brangelina: Combinatory nickname for the romantic partnership of celebrity actors Brad Pitt and Angelina Jolie. Combining names in this manner became common practice for so-called celeb-watcher media references to celebrities whose union appears more influential than each partner's individual influence. Such nicknames are also meta-references to the absurdity of newly created words.

carbon footprint: Reference to the "overall amount of carbon dioxide (CO_2) and other greenhouse gas (GHG) emissions (e.g. methane, laughing gas, etc.) associated with a product," according to the European Commission. During the decade, concerns about direct and indirect impacts on, or contributions to, global warming through consumer habits or energy usage, for example, were couched in terms of one's personal carbon footprint.

chick lit: Phrase used to describe popular fiction that deals explicitly with issues important to women. Popular chick lit authors of the decade include Sophie Kinsella (the Shopaholic series, 2000–), Jennifer Weiner (*In Her Shoes*, 2002), Jodi Picoult (*My Sister's Keeper*, 2004), and Lauren Weisberger (*The Devil Wears Prada*, 2006). If used in a pejorative sense, the genre tag diminishes the importance of women as authors and readers of serious literature; in many cases, however, it is used as an objective reference to women's issues and female authors as vital to mainstream culture.

climate change skepticism: Euphemism used to describe those who do not believe either a) that manmade climate change has a scientific basis, or b) that global warming is occurring to an extent that merits actions, either public or private, designed to mitigate it. Among climate science researchers and others who have studied the issues related to global warming and climate change, these positions are untenable, while many skeptics believe that climate change is an excuse to increase environmental regulations across various industries.

corporate personhood: Subject of legal consideration that questions whether or not corporations have or deserve civil rights, such as freedom of speech and the ability to sue or be sued. This was the central question in *Citizens United v. SEC* (argued 2009, decided 2010, by the US Supreme Court). Proponents argue corporate personhood offers necessary legal protections against illegal search-and-seizure and double jeopardy; opponents claim corporate personhood both denigrates the unique value of human beings and citizenship while offering a means for individual stakeholders to circumvent accountability and culpability for actions of corporations they are involved with.

crowdsourcing: Collective actions of disparate networked people and organizations on the Internet, often with the intention of knowledge-gathering or problem-solving. Crowdsourcing is identifiable in such entities as Wikipedia, which is written, edited, and maintained by "crowds" of people, all of whose efforts ensure accountability to truthfulness and a sense of collective enterprise for the common good, making this potentially better than encyclopedia entries written by individual experts. It is also evident in fundraising efforts through funding contribution websites and Internet forums for commercial and noncommercial product users.

cut and run: Phrase used by US president George W. Bush during the Iraq War to express his belief that the United States' departure from Iraq before the infrastructure there could survive without US military support would be premature and inadvisable. Statement: "We're not going to cut and run from the people who long for freedom."

cyberwarfare: Phrase coined to describe computer-based military engagement. According to former Bush administration national security advisor Richard Clarke, cyberwarfare involves "actions by a nation-state to penetrate another nation's computers or networks for the purposes of causing damage or disruption." Forms of cyber warfare include attacks on military systems and infrastruc-

tures, as well as attacks on public utilities and private computer networks.

death panel: Term arising from the mischaracterization of optional health care advisory assistance available to patients under section 1233 of HR 3200, or America's Affordable Health Choices Act of 2009. Former vice-presidential candidate Sarah Palin famously used the term to demonize what she and others interpreted as bureaucratized committees convened to determine the health-care worthiness of certain Medicare patients if the legislation was enacted.

dirty bomb: Conventional explosive that contains radioactive material, notable for its relatively small impact compared with large-scale nuclear weapons. The threat of use of dirty bombs played prominent roles in the arrest and detainment of José Padilla (US) and Dhiren Barot (UK), who were accused of plotting terrorist attacks in collaboration with Islamic fundamentalist terrorist organizations.

drone: Unmanned aerial vehicle, typically robotic. Military use of drones increased significantly during the wars in Iraq and Afghanistan, not only as a result of the incremental technological advances of that period but also as a result of their usefulness in performing a variety of functions (e.g., communications, reconnaissance, bombardment). Drones were used as far back as the hostilities in Lebanon during the 1980s, and continued to be developed during the Persian Gulf War, the intervention in Kosovo in 1999, and then in the wars of the 2000s. Under the Obama administration, drones came to represent an even greater force than under the Bush administration. Drones are used for nonmilitary purposes as well, such as political assassinations by intelligence agencies operating in the region. By end of decade, approximately fifty nations were developing drone programs.

embedded: Phrase related to the control of journalists by the US military during the invasion and subsequent occupation of Iraq beginning in 2003; used widely to describe the status of journalists reporting on both the Iraq and Afghanistan wars. Embedded journalists took direction from military controllers regarding their own safety as well as the operational safety of the campaigns.

emo: Subcultural group that came to prominence in the 1990s and early 2000s. Originally a reference to an underground genre of punk and pop-punk music, emo has come to signify a self-referential, angst-ridden, introverted worldview that is the decade's rough emotional equivalent of Goth during the 1980s and 1990s.

enemy combatant: Phrase used by the Bush administration after September 11 to refer to anyone suspected of being a member of the Taliban or al-Qaeda. Designation as "enemy combatant" meant suspects were not entitled to the same consideration as prisoners of war under the Third Geneva Convention. Civil liberties advocates opposed the use of the term under Bush, charging that its use was a way for the administration to circumvent internationally recognized standards of human and civil rights, while the administration claimed it eased their execution of the global War on Terrorism.

ethical hacker: Phrase used to delineate nonmalicious, or "white hat," hackers from malicious, or "black hat," hackers. Ethical hackers act always with a goal toward doing no harm, acting with full disclosure, respecting privacy of systems and users, maintaining the integrity of data, respecting information security, and generally acting in the best interests of the public at large. Throughout the decade, as more hackers came online than ever before, and as malicious hacking became more pervasive than ever before, the idea of the ethical hacker came to represent the broader hacking community who act with an eye toward using powerful technology tools for the betterment of mankind rather than for malice.

evacuee: Phrase used to describe people displaced by the deluge of Hurricane Katrina. After the disaster, the preferred use of *refugee* versus *evacuee* claimed a small part of the public discussion about the disaster and its aftermath. Many objected that *refugee* carried thinly veiled racism by conjuring the desperate flight of Third Worlders from terrible sociopolitical conditions, while *evacuee* suggested those rescued were simply fellow Americans in need of temporary help.

evildoers: Term used by US president George W. Bush to describe terrorists in numerous public statements made after the September11 attacks. His use of the arcane noun is indicative of a unique approach to rhetoric and linguistic style that came to be known (and sometimes parodied) as "Bushisms."

exergaming: Type of video-gaming that involves exercise. The combination of exercise or physical ac-

tivity and video gaming predates the 2000s, but the concept became more marketable—and more widely marketed—during the decade, with the introduction of more advanced body-motion tracking capabilities and games that offered incentives (through controllers or game play) for an interest in exergaming. For example, the Wii was heralded as a game system promoting physical activity in a media landscape that seemingly promoted more sedentary engagement.

fail: Interjection popularized throughout the decade to refer to anything that can be either subjectively derided as a failure, such as personal fashion choices and unfortunate body poses (as seen in photographs), or objectively derided as a failure, such as a skateboarding accident or mistranslation of, say, Chinese into English (as happened notably during the 2008 Summer Olympics in Beijing, China).

flash mob: Collective gathering of people for brief, seemingly random, acts, often organized via social media, text message, or e-mail. While flash mobbing efforts are by their nature self-consciously absurdist, the term has come to describe any similar effort used for explicitly meaningful purposes, such as social protests.

food desert: Phrase used to describe mostly urban areas in which fresh, nutritious food is seemingly absent, in short supply, or more expensive than fast food options. As the rates of obesity-related illnesses, such as diabetes, increased, food deserts remained a common cause for concern throughout the decade, with some ascribing them as primary causes of public health problems.

fracking: Abbreviated term for hydraulic fracturing, a technique for extracting natural gas using pressurized, chemically treated water. Although the natural gas industry claims the technique is safe, opponents of fracking claim it is a public health hazard because of, among other concerns, the wastewater and hydrocarbon pollution created during the process.

freedom fries: Euphemism for French fries proposed in March 2003 by members of the US Congress following French opposition to the United States' impending invasion of Iraq. The decision to change the name of food in the congressional cafeteria was derided by those who felt the decision was frivolous and a distraction from appropriate political discourse, while others supported the name change because they believed anti-French sentiment was an appropriate response to the lack of international support for the invasion.

freeganism: Activist movement that derides food waste to the extent that adherents are willing to reclaim and consume food that is thrown out, spoiled, or what is commonly considered disposable or inedible based on "sell by" dates or legal food-handling standards. Freegans advocate practices such as Dumpster diving and barter in an effort to undermine what they see as unhealthy or immoral materialism and rampant consumerism.

friending: Practice of inviting friends, acquaintances, peers, coworkers, and others to share personal pages and data on Facebook with the purpose of building a social media network. The term is generalized beyond just that medium since most social media have means for broadening one's network through invitations and sharing of personal page links. It is also one of the decade's most notable instances of the creation of new verbs based on online activity (similar to "googling" information).

Great Recession: Descriptive term for the global economic recession that began in 2008. The use of "great" to describe the recession equates the emotional weight Americans invested in the Great Depression of the 1930s and 1940s with the diminishing economic expectations of the latter half of the 2000s.

Ground Zero: Name given to the site where the World Trade Center buildings collapsed during the September 11 terrorist attacks. The name has previously been given to other locations where enormous losses of life and destruction occurred, including the atomic bombings of Hiroshima and Nagasaki, Japan in August 1945.

hacktivism: Use of hacking techniques in order to engage in acts of social or political activism. While some acts of hacktivism, such as distributed denial-of-service (DDoS) attacks or data theft, are illegal in some countries and therefore considered forms of malicious hacking, it is worth noting that these same actions targeting enemies of the free world could be construed as promoting democratic ideals. Because of this potential conceptual vacuum, there are fundamental questions about the morality of hacktivism.

hashtag: Metadata tag using the hash symbol (#) as a prefix to denote the topic of a tweet.

helicopter parent: Phrase used to describe the generalization that parents of millennials, or people born sometime between approximately 1980 and 2000, are overprotective, particularly in regard to the educational well-being of their offspring. The helicopter metaphor describes behavior in which a parent will hover, so to speak, as if in readiness to aid their child, and then return to hovering in wait for the next problem.

hipster: Subcultural group that came to cultural prominence in the late 1990s to early 2000s. Hipsters are noted (and often derided by others) for their popular cultural tastes, such as indie music and film, self-conscious fashion sense, commitment to irony, and generally aloof nature.

homeland security: Post–September 11 phrase used to describe the vast network of agencies, actions, and intentions that would keep the United States safe from further terrorist attacks. The Homeland Security Act of 2002 created a cabinet-level position to organize and manage homeland security efforts and agencies.

identity theft: Theft of personally identifiable data, often using electronic or digital sources. Identity theft may be committed in association with fraudulent activity, such as use of a Social Security number for purposes of misrepresentation or a personal identification number (PIN) to access personal finances. Identity theft became more lucrative than ever before in this decade due to the ubiquity of unsecured data, the increase in ownership of digital devices carrying personal data, and the vast growth in tools that enabled identity theft.

Internet hygiene: Euphemism for personal responsibility in maintaining Internet and computer security. As rates of data theft and other acts of malicious hacking grew during the decade, a social norm evolved related to taking personal responsibility for maintaining security of home networks, locking digital devices, using difficult-to-crack passwords, and other actions designed to keep the digital environment "clean."

keyboard courage: Phrase used to describe the rhetorical empowerment granted to anyone with a keyboard, a computer, and an Internet connection. Someone displaying keyboard courage might do it out of malice in order to provoke others or simply be taking advantage of online anonymity to engage in discourse with others in a way that is uncharacteristic of them in "real" life. The key to which is the nonexclusive freedom offered by online forums where a person can, if they choose, remain free of social conflict or getting found out. For example, they may state things online they would be hesitant to say aloud in front of others or experiment with attitudes or tones of voice in order to test social waters in a safe manner.

let's roll: Phrase used by United Airlines Flight 93 passenger Todd Beamer as he and other passengers attempted to counterattack terrorists aboard their hijacked aircraft. The phrase became a post–September 11 rallying cry for heroic acts in the face of terrorist threats.

locavore: Movement which promotes the purchase and consumption of locally grown food items. Locavores promote farmer's markets and home-based farming as a way to enrich public health and local economies.

lolcat: Internet meme combining pictures of felines with text for the sake of humor. Lolcats commonly reference topics related to geek culture but can be general enough that anyone can enjoy them. The humor stems in part from both the notion that cats cannot speak, much less speak correctly, nor are they self-aware enough to comment on human endeavors, lending lolcats a healthy appeal to absurdism.

mashup: Sound recording or live performance of a song created by combining elements of at least two other sound recordings. While mashup as an art form precedes the decade, the proliferation of digital tools for separating and mixing recordings is notable. Well-known mashup artists from the 2000s include Danger Mouse, whose *The Grey Album* (2004) combined vocal and instrumental tracks from The Beatles' self-titled album known as *The White Album* (1968) with Jay-Z's *The Black Album* (2003); Girl Talk (*Night Ripper*, 2006; *Feed the Animals*, 2006); and mashups created for the popular television show *Glee*.

metrosexual: Stereotype that came to prominence in the decade to describe heterosexual men who share sensibilities related to personal appearance and attire with gay men. In past centuries, similar cultural phenomenon has occurred, such as the "dandy," although the metrosexual can be delineated from predecessors by virtue of his consumer awareness and postmodern self-awareness.

millennials: Generation of children born approximately between 1980 and 2000; also known as generation Y.

multitasking: Behavior exhibited while seemingly performing simultaneous actions, or "doing several things at once." In common parlance, it often relates to rapid switching between multimedia interactions, such as watching a film while browsing the Internet, or reading an online comic while researching for a college essay. Critics claim that multitasking is merely performing simultaneous actions less adeptly than giving one of these actions one's full attention and that it can lead to negative outcomes, such as automobile accidents involving texting while driving.

New Atheism: Label associated with rising rates of people who, variously, admit they do not believe in traditional notions of God, are not affiliated with a religion, or believe that arguments against the existence of God can be arrived at through reason. The movement gained traction through a series of publications by authors Richard Dawkins, Daniel Dennett, Sam Harris, and Christopher Hitchens, who together became known as the "Four Horsemen of New Atheism" during a 2007 debate about religious criticism. Their beliefs are outlined in such titles as Dawkins' *The God Delusion* (2006) and Hitchens's *God Is Not Great* (2007).

no income, no asset (NINA) loans: Term applied to types of mortgage loans given to applicants whose income and assets cannot be verified by a lender. During the housing crisis, it was believed by many that some homeowners received mortgages despite having no job or assets to their name. NINA loans became symbolic of the corrupt practices that played a role in the mortgage crises that affected millions of homeowners throughout the nation and globally beginning circa 2007.

pay-per-click advertising: Internet advertising model that determines advertisement price by the number of user mouse-clicks on an advertisement. For example, clicking a banner ad on a website will result in the website operator receiving a payment from the advertiser. This model predominated throughout the decade as a lucrative revenue model for companies such as Google and Yahoo!, as well as increasing web traffic

peak oil: Name given to the theoretical notion that global oil production and supply will peak, after which production rates will decrease and supplies will begin to deplete. Forecasts for peak oil hover around the years 2015–20, with expectations sliding based on discoveries of energy reserves.

podcast: Derived from the words "iPod" and "broadcast, the term refers to a downloadable or steaming type of multimedia digital file that is often episodic in nature and which can be accessed through the Internet.

preemptive strike: Controversial key measure of the foreign policy of US president George W. Bush in which it was asserted that a preemptive strike of Iraq was justified for reasons related to their weapons of mass destruction capacity and supplies, as well as the general national security threat from the nation.

red state/blue state: Euphemism for states that, often historically, vote for Republican presidential candidates (red states) versus those which historically vote for Democrat presidential candidates (blue states). The distinction originated as a result of the color codes assigned to the electoral vote counts given to candidates by individual states during election-night broadcasts of the 2000 presidential election eventually won by George W. Bush. The distinction further serves to delineate general political will, presidential preferences notwithstanding—i.e., red states are considered bastions of socially and politically conservative views, while blue states are considered to be generally socially and politically liberal on the same issues.

regime change: Term used throughout the administration of US president George W. Bush to refer to the necessity, and vital US foreign policy goal, of replacing Saddam Hussein as the leader of Iraq. The term was often used as shorthand for the goal of the United States in Iraq.

same-sex marriage: Phrase that describes not only gay marriages, but also, in reference to the variety of sexual preferences among humans, marriages in which partners are bisexual, heterosexual, or even asexual. The use of the phrase grew during the decade, gradually overtaking the term "gay marriage" as the primary reference for what is considered conservatively to be any nontraditional marriage involving a heterosexual man and a heterosexual woman.

shock-and-awe: Military strategy employed by the United States in its bombing of Baghdad, Iraq, during the 2003 invasion. While the phrase existed prior to the bombings, it came into promi-

nence and common usage as a result of prewar statements made by Bush administration and US military spokespeople.

short sale: Type of real estate transaction in which a seller sells a home for less money than is owed to a mortgage lender. Short sales became increasingly common during the mortgage crisis, in part because the short sale offers the seller an alternative to simply walking away from a home and forcing a foreclosure. It also benefits homebuyers because short sales are commonly cheaper than full-priced homes.

staycation: Term for spending time off at home or nearby; viewed as a less expensive alternative to a vacation away from home and one's local environs. Staycations became associated not only with the economic instability of the 2000s, and the average consumer's need to spend less on luxuries and leisure, but also a sense that the benefits of vacations are fleeting when compared to the benefits of using one's home and local environment for meaningful relaxation.

strategic default: The practice of willfully stopping payments on a home mortgage with the intention of forcing a bank foreclosure; also known as "walking away" from a mortgage. During the housing crisis of the 2000s, such defaults became widely used by homeowners whose homes were worth less than their mortgages (see "underwater") and who felt no particular obligation, moral or otherwise, to honoring their mortgage contract, often because there were few penalties for strategic default beyond a credit score decrease.

subprime: Type of lending classification in which loans are made to people whose credit scores and history represent a risk, and therefore warrant high, or subprime, interest rates. Subprime mortgages, many of which had adjustable rates and therefore faced risk of rate increases, made up a significant number of home foreclosures during the housing crisis. Subprime rates became associated with lax financial practices that led to the economic crises of the 2000s.

surge: Term that became synonymous with increases to troop strength during the Iraq War following a January 2007 speech by US president George W. Bush. While controversial at the time, the surge was credited with making gains for the US over time, and helping to stabilize Iraq following a period of increased instability.

swiftboating: Phrase used to describe the practice of undermining the moral stature of a political candidate. The term originated after a group known as the Swift Vets and POWs for Truth sent presidential candidate Senator John Kerry (D-MA) a letter asking him to account for his actions following his return from active duty aboard a swift boat during the Vietnam War. In the early 1970s, Kerry became a prominent antiwar activist; the swift vets and former prisoners of war alleged his actions would make him an illegitimate commander in chief.

Teabaggers: Pejorative term for members of the Tea Party movement. Tea Party loyalists adhere to platforms that promote balancing the federal budget, maintaining a strong military and small government, an end to illegal immigration, and other issues that they feel strengthen the United States' core constitutional foundations.

toxic asset: An asset, held either by a financial entity (such as a bank or an investor), that cannot be sold to another financial entity once its risks are exposed. Commonly, a toxic asset refers to something like a mortgage loan that is in foreclosure and therefore losing money for its holder. Because many such assets are bundled and sold in quantities, during the economic crises fears of toxic assets ran rampant within financial industries, causing the markets to freeze and stocks of assets to stagnate on company books.

truthiness: A satirical word coined by comedian and actor Stephen Colbert, the parodic talk-show host of *The Colbert Report*. Colbert explained that truthiness refers to an attitude prevalent among government representatives and conservative members of the media. According to Colbert, "Truthiness is 'What I say is right, and [nothing] anyone else says could possibly be true.'" It was named word of the year in 2006 by Merriam-Webster.

tweet: Term used to describe a 140-character posting on the social media site Twitter. Similar to friending, the act of tweeting is also a notable instance of the creation of new verbs based on online activity.

underwater: Term used to describe the state of owing more money on a home than it is worth on the current market. Many homeowners found themselves underwater when the market values of their homes at the time of purchase were wiped away by the negative equity they assumed as the markets collapsed.

unfriend: Practice of delisting or removing a Facebook friend. Unfriending removes the ability for a person or group to access a Facebook page.

War on Christmas: Phrase used to describe an allegedly concerted effort to delegitimize Christmas, a Christian holiday, or to affirm the need for secularism in an increasingly multicultural nation. The phrase is often used in backlash against notions of political correctness or efforts to restrict Christian references, such as Christmas, in public schools, governmental institutions, or public spaces. A so-called weapon in the War on Christmas might be the use of the phrase "Happy holidays!" instead of "Merry Christmas." While some critics, like conservative talk show host Bill O'Reilly, have claimed to see alarming signs of the war, others believe it may be merely a sociopolitical phantasm of exuberant cultural critics.

wardriving: Practice of using a vehicle to search for unsecured wireless networks using a laptop or other device that can track the signal. Wardriving is not illegal, though it may be unethical if the exploit is malicious in nature or there is usage of the Wi-Fi signal but no disclosure to the person whose signal is being used by the wardriver. Ethical hackers see wardriving as an opportunity to expose the need for increased network security among private and commercial network users.

waterboarding: An "enhanced interrogation technique" which simulates the experience of drowning. The Central Intelligence Agency used the technique as a method of interrogation during the 2000s. Opponents decry the practice as torture.

weapons of mass destruction: Term used to describe those weapons that produce widespread and indiscriminate destruction and death. The US-led invasion of Iraq in 2003 was based in part on the suspicion that Iraq's leader, Saddam Hussein, had weapons of mass destruction, including biological weapons, and the intent to use them.

Wii elbow: Physical condition brought about by overuse or strenuous use of the Wii remote motion-sensitive video game controller, first noticed within days following the release of the Wii system. The Wii remote, also known as the Wiimote, is a wireless device and therefore can be swung about with impunity, causing some users to feel elbow pain. The phrase is similar to predecessors like *Nintendo thumb* (pain induced by using the Nintendo button controller) and *tennis elbow.*

Y2K: Abbreviation for "year 2000." At the turn of the millennium, the phrase became the standard shorthand for 2000 CE. The phrase grew in importance as it became associated with a looming computer bug which many felt would, if unchecked, devastate computer-controlled systems such as banks or public utilities as the date changed over from 1999 to 2000.

Yes, we can: Campaign slogan used by presidential candidate Barack Obama during the 2008 US presidential race. It is an approximate English translation of a Spanish slogan used prominently during civil rights demonstrations involving United Farm Workers leader Cesar Chavez in the early 1970s, "Sí, se puede!"

■ List of Entries by Category

Roper v. Simmons
Rowley, Coleen
Sarbanes–Oxley Act of 2002
School violence
Steroids in baseball
Stewart, Martha
Wikileaks.org
Worldcom scandal

Disasters
Alaska Airlines Flight 261
American Airlines flight 587
California electricity crisis
Cincinnati riots of 2001
Ehime Maru and USS *Greeneville*
　collision
H1N1 flu pandemic of 2009
Hurricane Ike
Hurricane Katrina
Hurricane Rita
Indian Ocean earthquake and
　tsunami
Large-scale Forest Death
Minneapolis I-35W bridge collapse
Northeastern blackout of 2003
Rhode Island nightclub fire
September 11, 2001, Terrorist
　Attacks
Space Shuttle *Columbia* disaster
2007 California wildfires
US Airways Flight 1549
Virginia Tech Massacre
West Virginia/Kentucky Coal Sludge
　Spill

Economics
Automotive industry crisis
Business and economy in Canada
Business and economy in the United
　States
California electricity crisis
Commodity Futures Moderniza-
　tion Act of 2000
Early 2000s recession
Economic Growth and Tax Relief
　Reconciliation Act of 2001
Emergency Economic Stabilization
　Act of 2008
Employment in Canada
Employment in the United States

Greenspan, Alan
Housing market in the United
　States
Income and wages in the United
　States
Job Creation and Worker Assistance
　Act of 2002
Jobs and Growth Tax Relief
　Reconciliation Act of 2003
Krugman, Paul
Late 2000s recession
Minimum wage increase
National debt
Oil crisis
Paulson, Henry
Retirement income system
Subprime mortgage crisis
Troubled Asset Relief Program

Education
ebooks
Education in Canada
Education in the United States
No Child Left Behind Act of 2001
Pausch, Randy
School violence
Virginia Tech Massacre
Wikipedia
Zelman v. Simmons-Harris

Environmental Issues
Biofuel
Domestic and Offshore oil drilling
Energy Policy Act of 2005
Energy Policy of the United States
Global warming debate
Green business (Sustainable
　business)
Green technology
Honeybee Colony Collapse
　Disorder
Hybrid automobiles
Kyoto Protocol
Large-scale Forest Death
Marianas Trench Marine National
　Monument
Oil crisis
Organic food industry
Pickens, T. Boone
Sustainable food movement

Film
Academy Awards
Anderson, Wes
Apatow, Judd
Avatar
Brokeback Mountain
Cameron, James
Clooney, George
Dark Knight, The
Depp, Johnny
DiCaprio, Leonardo
Fahrenheit 9/11
Fast Food Nation
Film in the United States
Galifianakis, Zach
Gibson, Mel
Gladiator
Hanks, Tom
Harry Potter films
Hoffman, Philip Seymour
Hurt Locker, The
IMAX
Inconvenient Truth, An
Ledger, Heath
Lord of the Rings Trilogy, The
Lost in Translation
Mortensen, Viggo
Passion of the Christ, The
Pirates of the Caribbean series
Pixar Animation Studios
Saw franchise
Shrek film series
Slumdog Millionaire
Smith, Will
Spielberg, Steven
Super Size Me
Superhero films
There Will Be Blood
Washington, Denzel
Writer's Guild of America strike

Health and Medicine
Autism
Cancer research
Decriminalization of marijuana
Electronic health records
Food allergies
Genetically modified foods
Gonzales v. Carhart
H1N1 flu pandemic of 2009

Beck, Glenn
Benoit, Chris
Bernanke, Ben
Biden, Joe
Blagojevich, Rod
Bonds, Barry
Brady, Tom
Brin, Sergey and Larry Page
Bush, George W.
Bush, Laura
Cameron, James
Chabon, Michael
Cheney, Dick
Chrétien, Jean
Clinton, Hillary Rodham
Clooney, George
Cooper, Anderson
Couric, Katie
DeGeneres, Ellen
Depp, Johnny
Díaz, Junot
Edwards, John
Eggers, Dave
Emanuel, Rahm
Eminem
Fairey, Shepard
Federer, Roger
Fey, Tina
Franks, Tommy
Franzen, Jonathan
Gaiman, Neil
Galifianakis, Zach
Gates, Bill and Melinda
Gates, Robert
Geithner, Timothy
Gibson, Mel
Giuliani, Rudolph
Gladwell, Malcom
Gonzales, Alberto
Gore, Al
Greenspan, Alan
Hanks, Tom
Harper, Stephen
Hilton, Paris
Hoffman, Philip Seymour
Hosseini, Khaled
Huffington, Ariana
Jackson, Michael
James, LeBron

Jay-Z
Jeffs, Warren
Jobs, Steve
Johnson, Denis
Johnson, Jimmie
Jones, Norah
Kennedy, Ted
Kerry, John
Keys, Alicia
Kilpatrick, Kwame
Knowles, Beyoncé
Koons, Jeff
Krugman, Paul
Kurzweil, Ray
Lady Gaga
Ledger, Heath
Lindh, John Walker
Maddow, Rachel
Martin, Paul
McCain, John
McCarthy, Cormac
Miller, Judith
Murdoch, Rupert
Newmark, Craig
Obama, Barack
Obama, Michelle
O'Reilly, Bill
Osteen, Joel
Oz, Mehmet
Palin, Sarah
Paul, Ron
Paulson, Henry
Pausch, Randy
Pelosi, Nancy
Phelps, Michael
Pickens, T. Boone
Plouffe, David
Powell, Colin
Ray, Rachael
Rice, Condoleezza
Roberts, John
Romney, Mitt
Rove, Karl
Rowley, Coleen
Rumsfeld, Donald
Schwarzenegger, Arnold
Smith, Will
Sotomayor, Sonia
Spears, Britney

Spielberg, Steven
Stewart, Jon
Stewart, Martha
Timberlake, Justin
Trump, Donald
Usher
Venter, Craig
Vick, Michael
Wales, Jimmy
Wallace, David Foster
Warren, Rick
Washington, Denzel
West, Kanye
White, Jack
Williams, Serena
Winfrey, Oprah
Wolfowitz, Paul
Woods, Tiger
Wright, Jeremiah
Zuckerberg, Mark

Politics and Government

Ashcroft, John
Bernanke, Ben
Biden, Joe
Bush Administration scandals
Bush v. Gore
Bush, George W.
Bush, Laura
Cheney, Dick
Chrétien, Jean
Clinton, Hillary Rodham
Department of Homeland Security
Edwards, John
Elections in Canada
Elections in the United States, 2000
Elections in the United States, 2004
Elections in the United States, 2008
Elections in the United States,
    midterm
Emanuel, Rahm
Energy Policy of the United States
Faith-based organizations
Foreign Policy of the United States
Gates, Robert
Geithner, Timothy
Giuliani, Rudolph
Gonzales, Alberto
Gore, Al

Politics and Government (continued)
Harper, Stephen
Kennedy, Ted
Kerry, John
Martin, Paul
McCain, John
National debt
Obama, Barack
Obama, Michelle
Palin, Sarah
Paul, Ron
Paulson, Henry
Pelosi, Nancy
Plame Scandal
Plouffe, David
Political talk radio
Powell, Colin
Rice, Condoleezza
Romney, Mitt
Rove, Karl
Rowley, Coleen
Rumsfeld, Donald
Schwarzenegger, Arnold
Tea Party Movement
Wolfowitz, Paul

Popular Culture
Digital reading
DIY culture
Energy drinks
Fads
Flash mobs
Food trends
Halo franchise
Internet memes
Low carb diets
Millennium celebrations
Online gambling
Reality television
Second Life
Sims, The
Slang and slogans
Social media
Super Bowl XXXVIII halftime show
    controversy
Superhero films
Texting
Twilight series
Video games
World of Warcraft

Religion and Spirituality
Faith-based organizations
Growth of megachurches
Intelligent design
Jeffs, Warren
Kitzmiller v. Dover Area School District
Osteen, Joel
Passion of the Christ, The
Religion and spirituality in the
    United States
Warren, Rick
Wright, Jeremiah

Science and Technology
Apple Inc.
Biofuel
Blackberrys
Blogging
Blu-ray discs
Brin, Sergey and Larry Page
Cloud computing
Computer worms and viruses
craigslist
Cybercrime
Dot-com bubble
eBay
ebooks
Ecommerce
Electronic health records
Facebook
Genetically modified foods
Google
GPS navigation systems and tracking
Green technology
Honeybee Colony Collapse
    Disorder
Hulu
Human Genome Project
Intelligent design
Inventions
iPhone
iPod
Jobs, Steve
Kurzweil, Ray
Mars Exploration Rover Mission
Mobile phones
MySpace
Newmark, Craig
Nobel Prizes
Online gambling

Online music services
Open source code
Photovoltaics
Satellite radio
Science and technology
Second Life
Social media
Space tourism
Stem cell research
Twitter
Venter, Craig
Wales, Jimmy
Wifi
Wikileaks.org
Wikipedia
YouTube
Zuckerberg, Mark

Sexuality
Hate crimes
Homosexuality and gay rights
Lady Gaga
Same-sex marriage

Social Issues
Abortion
Children on the Internet
Cincinnati riots of 2001
Concussions in sports
Cyberbullying
Demographics of Canada
Demographics of the United States
Grutter v. Bollinger
Hate crimes
Health care
Housing market in the United States
Immigration to the United States
Iraq and Afghanistan war veterans
Omnivore's Dilemma, The
Police brutality
Private militias
Retirement income system
Same-sex marriage
School violence
Women's rights

Sports
Armstrong, Lance
Benoit, Chris
Bonds, Barry

Brady, Tom
Concussions in sports
Federer, Roger
FIFA World Cup
James, LeBron
Johnson, Jimmie
Olympic Games
Phelps, Michael
Soccer
Steroids in baseball
Super Bowl XXXVIII halftime show
  controversy
Vick, Michael
Williams, Serena
Woods, Tiger

Television
American Idol
Arrested Development
Clarkson, Kelly
Colbert Report, The
Cooper, Anderson
Couric, Katie
CSI: Crime Scene Investigation
DeGeneres, Ellen
Desperate Housewives
Family Guy
Fey, Tina
Lost

Mad Men
Maddow, Rachel
Modern Family
Office, The
O'Reilly, Bill
Osbournes, The
Oz, Mehmet
Ray, Rachael
Reality television
Sopranos, The
Stewart, Jon
Super Bowl XXXVIII halftime show
  controversy
Survivor
Television (overview)
Trump, Donald
24
Winfrey, Oprah
Wire, The
Writer's Guild of America strike

Terrorism
al-Qaeda
Anthrax attacks
Border security
Department of Homeland Security
Extraordinary rendition
Guantanamo Bay detention camp
Hamdan v. Rumsfeld

Hostages in Iraq
Iraq Resolution (2002)
Iraq War
Lindh, John Walker
Private military companies
Saddam Hussein capture
September 11, 2001, Terrorist
  Attacks
Terrorist attacks
United States v. Zacarias Moussaoui
USA PATRIOT Act
USS *Cole* bombing
War in Afghanistan
War on Terrorism
Waterboarding

Transportation
Airline industry
Hybrid automobiles

Women's Issues
Abortion
Clinton, Hillary Rodham
Gonzales v. Carhart
March for Women's Lives
Partial-Birth Abortion Ban Act
Women's rights

Indexes

■ Photo Index

■ Subject Index